Social Work Practice with Families

Also available from Lyceum Books, Inc.

Advisory Editor: Thomas M. Meenaghan, *New York University*

CHILD AND FAMILY PRACTICE: A RELATIONAL PERSPECTIVE
by Shelley Cohen Konrad

CHILDREN AND LOSS: A PRACTICAL HANDBOOK FOR PROFESSIONALS
edited by Elizabeth C. Pomeroy and Renée Bradford Garcia

DIVERSITY IN FAMILY CONSTELLATIONS: IMPLICATIONS FOR PRACTICE
edited by Krishna L. Guadalupe and Debra L. Welkley

BEST PRACTICES IN COMMUNITY MENTAL HEALTH: A POCKET GUIDE
edited by Vikki L. Vandiver

UNDERSTANDING AND MANAGING THE THERAPEUTIC RELATIONSHIP
by Fred R. McKenzie

THE COSTS OF COURAGE: COMBAT STRESS, WARRIORS, AND FAMILY
SURVIVAL
by Josephine G. Price, Col. David H. Price, and Kimberly K. Shackleford

CHARACTER FORMATION AND IDENTITY IN ADOLESCENCE
by Randolph L. Lucente

THE RECOVERY PHILOSOPHY AND DIRECT SOCIAL WORK PRACTICE
by Joseph Walsh

CIVIC YOUTH WORK: COCREATING DEMOCRATIC YOUTH SPACES
edited by Ross VeLure Roholt, Michael Baizerman, and R. W. Hildreth

THE USE OF SELF: THE ESSENCE OF PROFESSIONAL EDUCATION
by Raymond Fox

HOW TO TEACH EFFECTIVELY: A BRIEF GUIDE, SECOND EDITION
by Bruce Friedman

Social Work Practice with Families

A Resiliency-Based Approach

SECOND EDITION

Mary Patricia Van Hook
University of Central Florida

LYCEUM
BOOKS, INC.

Chicago, Illinois

© 2014 by Lyceum Books, Inc.

Published by
  LYCEUM BOOKS, INC.
  5758 S. Blackstone Avenue
  Chicago, Illinois 60637
  773-643-1903 fax
  773-643-1902 phone
  lyceum@lyceumbooks.com
  www.lyceumbooks.com

6 5 4 3 2 1   14 15 16 17 18

ISBN 978-1-935871-30-9

Printed in the United States of America.

Library of Congress Cataloging-in-Publication Data

Van Hook, Mary.
  Social work practice with families : a resiliency-based approach / Mary Van Hook, University
of Central Florida.—Second Edition.
    pages cm
  Includes bibliographical references and index.
  ISBN 978-1-935871-30-9 (pbk. : alk. paper)
  1. Family social work. I. Title.
HV697.V36 2014
362.82'53—dc23
          2012046579

Contents

Acknowledgments

Many people have helped make this book possible. The families I have had the privilege to work with during my years of clinical practice have provided essential insights into the challenges facing families and the sources of resiliency. A draft version of this manuscript was used with social work graduate students at the University of Central Florida. The feedback provided by these students and their faculty members Michael Rothenberg and Mary Beth Harris was invaluable. My husband's editing skills and support were essential. I am also deeply indebted to my mentor Sallie Churchill, professor emeritus of the University of Michigan School of Social Work, whose clinical wisdom has encouraged me to think in terms of resiliency. I would also like to thank Bruce Friedman, Mary Helen Hayden, Shelley Cohen Konrad, Marian Mattison, Fred McKenzie, Tom Meenaghan, Renee Pogue, William Powell, Pat Sickinger, Wendy Smith, and Martha Wilson, whose reviews of earlier versions of the manuscript provided invaluable probing questions and insights. My thanks also to Olga Molina whose comments on the first edition led to improvements in this edition, and to Timothy Myland for his insights regarding the Canadian social services situation. I would like to thank David Follmer, whose ongoing encouragement and advice made this book a reality.

Preface

The term *resiliency* has received increased attention with widespread recognition that people have the ability to cope with a variety of difficult life events. The issue of *Newsweek* marking the ten-year anniversary of the tragic events of September 11 had RESILIENCE in bold letters on the cover. Communities seeking to restore life after deadly tornadoes or floods are described as resilient. The strengths and assets-based approaches to micro and macro practice rely on concepts associated with the literature on resiliency. For me personally, the path to thinking about resiliency began early in my social work career as part of an attempt to understand how people managed to not only overcome difficult early life experiences but to emerge as contributing individuals.

As a beginning social worker I was working at a major New York City teaching psychiatric hospital on the children's services unit. In the course of arranging with a local foster care agency to place one of the children, we met the prospective foster father, a compassionate and responsible family man and father of two children. He and his wife were willing to open their home to a five-year-old boy from our program. He told his own childhood story of going from foster home to foster home until he grew too old for the foster-care system. During these years he developed the goal of providing a stable foster home to protect other children from his own experience. The time had now come to fulfill this commitment and he and his wife agreed to accept this little boy into their home. After meeting with this prospective foster father, the staff of the children's services discussed our own limitations in understanding the emotional and interpersonal strength of this man. If he had been a patient in the hospital and we had been asked to explain why he was in the hospital and unable to function or relate effectively with other people, we would have had no difficulty explaining his illness. We would have talked about attachment problems, ego deficits, and other contributing factors. We recognized that our theoretical tools had limited answers for why he was the caring, responsible man that he currently was. We were humbled at the complex nature of human beings and the presence of strength despite great odds.

Several years ago a colleague and friend of mine received a major award for his contributions to the field of mental health. He had been responsible for creating some important changes in mental health services and had developed and administered several important mental health programs. In his acceptance speech, he described the source of his commitment to making a difference in the services offered. When he was a child, his father, a volunteer fireman, had died rushing to respond to a fire. He and his brothers were then raised by their mother, a fragile woman with many serious mental health problems. She was in and out of hospitals, and the boys experienced the stigma of family mental illness in their small community with very limited resources to help the family. As a result, he grew up dedicated to ensuring that other families would receive the help they needed—help that had not been available to him and his family. He became a committed and effective leader in the field of mental health, especially in providing care to those in underserved areas. When I described my friend's background to my students and asked for their description of his current situation, their stories were replete with pathology—inability to hold down a job, problems in relationships, perhaps substance abuse. They were surprised and rather skeptical when I described instead a caring husband and father, a respected leader in the mental health field, and a good friend to those around him. Perhaps if we had met his two older brothers, both of whom grew up to be dedicated public servants, and had learned more about the legacy left by his father we would have had some clue as to the source of his resiliency.

In the media we hear and read of children caught up in crime and drugs within their troubled neighborhoods. Many of these children join the case rolls of social workers and other counselors. Their stories reveal the trauma and ongoing dysfunction in the lives of the people involved. But receiving less attention are the children who somehow manage to forge productive and satisfying lives despite living in the same areas. We live in a world in which people must contend with the aftermath of accidents, violent actions, or severe illness that leaves families without a parent or partner. Other families face problems of poverty or political or social oppression. Families experience the loss of children through illness or accidents. No family is immune to at least some of these adverse life events, and many of the families that we see in social work have experienced several of them.

Social workers and related professionals realize that while discovering and identifying why people develop problems and disabilities are important, this information is inadequate for the assessment and treatment process. It is essential to find answers to how people manage to endure, cope, and even sometimes thrive under the troubles that can be part of the human condition. It is further important to identify the specific aspects of a person's life that make such coping possible (Blundo, 2002). The strengths perspective reminds us that such answers are critical in the design and implementation of prevention and treatment efforts and can promote the healing process (Saleebey, 2000). McQuaide (2000) in writing about women's resiliency at midlife goes even further. She describes assessment and treatment that is vulnerability- and pathology-based as participating "in the process of subjugation—the subjugation of the resilient selves" (p. 74).

Recognizing the importance of identifying sources of strength, vitality, and effective coping in our work with families, this book draws upon the concept of resiliency—*the ability to bounce back after difficult times.* Resiliency offers a theoretically and empirically grounded framework for assessing the strengths of families and enhancing their ability to cope with difficult life events. This book is organized to explain the concepts of resiliency and the process of engaging and assessing families in ways that promote resiliency. It further links assessment with the selection of appropriate treatment models and techniques and illustrates how these models are used with families.

Part I of the book introduces the reader to the concepts of resiliency, the process of engaging and assessing families using a resiliency perspective (chapter 1, "The Nature and Sources of Resiliency"; chapter 2, "Setting the Stage for Work with Families: Development of the Therapeutic Alliance"; and chapter 3, "Assessment of Families"). Chapter 4 expands the treatment of resiliency regarding risk and protective factors in terms of cultural and family structural issues.

Part II discusses important family counseling approaches from a resiliency-based perspective (social learning/cognitive, psychoeducational, structural, solution-focused, narrative, multisystems, family-systems-Bowenian, and object relations). Each chapter identifies the key tenets of the model, ways in which it can promote resiliency, the role of the therapist, key treatment strategies, and the application with specific families. Several chapters include information about adaptations of the approach for specific cultural groups or problems facing families. This section concludes with chapter 13, "Spirituality," an important aspect of life that can play a role in various models.

Part III includes chapter 14, "Families Coping with Difficult Life Circumstances," which discusses the literature in terms of risk and protective factors for families that are facing a variety of difficult life events. Chapter 15, "Conclusion," includes a brief summary of the elements of a resiliency-based approach to social work practice with families and a discussion of the important aspects of this approach in strengthening families.

Note: Some of the case illustrations in this book are drawn from the lives of real families. All names and identifying information have been changed to preserve confidentiality.

Competencies

This book is designed to address important competencies required by the Council on Social Work Education. The following identifies practice and human behavior competencies and ways in which they are addressed.

2.1.3 Apply critical thinking to inform and communicate professional knowledge.

A. *Distinguish, appraise, and integrate multiple sources of knowledge including research-based knowledge and practice wisdom.*

This approach is infused through the book. It incorporates information drawn from the world of research-derived knowledge and practice wisdom and defined as such. This information is presented to enable readers to integrate this information to draw informed decisions in the area of assessment and treatment.

B. *Analyze models of assessment, prevention, intervention, and evaluation.*

While the book is organized in terms of the basic theoretical framework of resiliency theory, the premise of the book is that resiliency theory can be a tool for selecting specific models of assessment, prevention, intervention, and evaluation. The book gives a basic model of assessment in the "Nature and Sources of Resiliency" chapter and the "Assessment of Families" chapter. It then moves beyond this to draw upon a number of specific theoretical frameworks that can be used for a specific type of assessment, model of prevention, intervention, and evaluation. This process occurs in all the chapters on treatment models (chapters 5–13) as well the chapter on "Families Coping with Difficult Life Circumstances."

1.2.4. Engage diversity and difference in practice.

A. *Recognize the extent to which a culture's structures and values may oppress, marginalize, alienate, or create or enhance privilege and power.*

This issue is addressed in several ways in the book. Chapter 1 describes some of the important contextual risk factors that include poverty, oppression, neighborhoods that lack good schools, and problems regarding economic opportunities. These contrast with protective factors that provide individuals with economic security, safe neighborhoods, good schools, and economic opportunities. Issues related to cultural structures that oppress and marginalize are further discussed in the chapter on culture, specifically a detailed discussion regarding ways in which members of cultural groups in the United States and Canada (including Latinos, African Americans, First Nations and other Indigenous peoples, and families of Asian origin) and family structure (gay and lesbian families) have been oppressed during their history as well as current marginalization. Case examples further illustrate these issues.

B. *Gain sufficient self-awareness to eliminate the influence of personal biases and values in working with diverse groups.*

In addition to information about diverse cultural groups that is designed to broaden one's understanding of diverse groups (especially chapter 4 plus case illustrations throughout the book), there is also a discussion about the issue of self-reflection in this book. It is especially addressed in terms of the barriers to the engagement process (chapter 2) and the need for self-reflection in dealing with spirituality and object relations.

C. *Recognize and communicate their understanding of the importance of differences in shaping life experiences.*

The chapters addressing assessments (chapter 3) and engagement (chapter 2) address frameworks to help the reader understand differences that shape the life experience (for example, culture, life cycle issues, unique family circumstances) and ways to incorporate these in the engagement and assessment process. The subsequent discussion of treatment models further points out how differences in family characteristics and life stories shape the nature of approaches to families.

D. *View themselves as learners and engage those with whom they work as informants.*

The treatment approach used in this book represents a partnership model between the counselor and the family members. In order to create an effective partnerships relationship, counselors must view themselves as learners from the family. Family members have the role of informing the counselor about the nature of the family, their goals, and their choices in terms of ways to address these goals. This crucial role of the family helps give a message of strength to the family members.

2.1.7. Apply knowledge of human behavior and the social environment.

A. *Utilize conceptual frameworks to guide the processes of assessment, intervention, and evaluation.*

This book is organized around conceptual frameworks to guide the process of assessment, intervention, and evaluation. In addition to an introduction to resilience (chapter 1), and chapter 3 ("Assessment"), the book contains a series of chapters (chapters 5–13) that describe specific conceptual frameworks and the process of assessment, intervention, and ongoing evaluation in the use of these intervention frameworks. The resiliency framework is used as a means of selecting appropriate types of interventions. In addition, chapter 14, "Coping with Difficult Life Circumstances," also describes a series of problems facing families from a resiliency framework and some of the interventions that would be appropriate.

B. *Critique and apply knowledge to understand person and environment.*

This book draws upon the resiliency framework to critique and apply knowledge about persons and the environment. It gives a framework in chapter 3, "Assessment," and expands on this in the further chapters 5–13 regarding intervention methods. It also draws upon resiliency theory to understand persons and their environment in chapter 4, "Cultural Issues, Family Structure, and Resiliency."

1.2.10 (a)–(d) Engage, assess, intervene and evaluate with individuals, families, groups, organizations, and communities.

A. *Substantially and effectively prepare for action with individuals, families, groups, organizations, and communities.*

The entire book is designed to give social workers the tools to prepare them to take action with families and family members (individuals). While the focus is on families, there is also discussion regarding interventions that are community-based (for example, response to First Nations and Inuit youth, multisystems model of treatment). Although the emphasis in this book is on families, there is also a discussion of the role of community risk and protective factors in chapters 2 through 14.

B. *Use empathy and interpersonal skills.*

The focus of this book is to enable the reader to use empathy and interpersonal skills informed by understanding of the family and its members. Chapter 2 especially addresses the skills involved in joining with a family. The subsequent chapters, especially chapters 5–14, identify skills in the assessment and intervention process.

C. *Develop a mutually agreed-upon focus of work and desired outcomes.*

The resiliency perspective discussed in this book is predicated upon a partnership between the family members and the counselor. Such partnerships need to have mutually agreed-upon focus and outcomes. Chapter 2, "Setting the Stage for Work with Families," discusses this issue in depth. The issue is discussed further in the chapters regarding specific models of treatment (5–13).

D. *Collect, organize, and interpret client data.*

Chapter 3, "Assessment of Families," is organized around the process of collecting, organizing, and interpreting client data. It uses the resiliency risk and protective factors model for organizing the data regarding individuals, families, extended family, and wider community as it pertains to the family system. Chapters 5–13 further this process by discussing the process of collecting, organizing, and interpreting client data in terms of specific treatment approaches.

E. *Assess client strengths and limitations.*

Assessment of client strengths (protective factors) and limitations (risk factors) plays a key role in this book. Chapter 1 describes some of the risk and protective factors that have been identified in the research and practice literature. Chapter 3, "Assessment of Families," describes the process of assessing family strengths and limitations (at the level of individuals, family, and community). Chapters 5–13 discuss assessment of these issues through the lens of specific treatment approaches.

F. *Develop mutually agreed-on intervention goals and objectives.*

This book is based on a premise that a partnership between the family members and the counselor is the appropriate approach. As a result, goals and objectives must be mutually agreed upon. Chapter 2, "Setting the Stage for Work with Families: Development of the Therapeutic Alliance," describes the process of developing these mutually agreed-upon goals and objectives. The process is further discussed in chapters 5–15 in terms of specific treatment models.

G. *Select appropriate intervention strategies.*

The premise of this book is that the counselor must select an appropriate intervention strategy based on the assessment process. Chapter 3, "Assessment," begins the process of linking assessment to treatment models. Chapters 5–13 further provide clinical and theoretical information to identify the nature of an appropriate treatment approach for this particular family at this point in time.

I. *Implement prevention interventions that enhance client capacities.*

A resiliency approach views life as a circular process. As a result, as family members are able to cope with life events more effectively by changing the ways they appraise them, by learning new skills, and by experiencing themselves as capable people, they are able to cope with future life difficulties in a more effective manner. From this perspective, treatment and prevention are part of this circle. The book describes treatment approaches that are designed to enhance the capacities of clients to cope. The introduction to resiliency chapter gives the theoretical basis for understanding how these life changes have a long-term prevention effect. Chapters 5–13 describe specific approaches. In addition, in the discussion regarding culture (for example, military families, Inuit youth), and problems (for example, substance abuse), issues related to prevention are included. The psychoeducational model has a strong prevention component.

J. *Help clients resolve problems.*

The entire book is organized around theoretical and treatment approaches that are designed to help clients resolve problems. The chapter on "Cultural Issues, Family Structure, and Resiliency" includes information about coping with problems, especially in terms of military families. While introduced earlier, information about coping with problems especially occurs during the chapters addressing the specific treatment approaches: chapters 5–13. Chapter 14, "Coping with Difficult Life Circumstances," describes the risk and protective factors created by problems and some of the treatment approaches that can be useful in helping families cope with these problems.

K. *Negotiate, mediate, and advocate for clients.*

While the primary focus in this book is on work with clients, chapter 2 includes a discussion of potential reasons why clients might be reluctant to engage as a result of issues related to the referring agency or other services and the importance of advocating for clients and interpreting the client's situation to the referring organization. The chapter "Multisystems Family Therapy" includes an extensive discussion about the importance of working with communities to develop new services to meet community needs, of advocating on behalf of clients, and the importance of mediating between families and community services to help families receive appropriate help.

L. *Facilitate transitions and ending.*

The treatment approaches in this book are designed to help families develop the skills and resources to address the problems that they are facing as well as gain strengths for future life issues. The discussion in chapter 10, "Multisystems Family Therapy," specifically addresses the issues involved in helping families access other services and the transition process required. Helping families gain a sense of themselves as capable of addressing their life struggles (self-efficacy) and identifying the nature of these strengths (their coping strategies) is an essential part of the ending process. Part of the ending process is the consolidation of gains, and this topic is part of the treatment discussions.

M. Critically analyze, monitor, and evaluate intervention.

The partnership model supported by this book suggests that the process of evaluating an intervention is part of the partnership process. Counselors and family members together identify if and how the intervention approach is being helpful and modify it accordingly. Chapters on treatment approaches also contain information regarding evaluation studies of treatment approaches as they relate to specific problems and family types.

Part I

Introduction to Resiliency-Based Practice

1

The Nature and Sources of Resiliency

WHAT IS RESILIENCY?

The term *resiliency* has been used to describe the process by which people manage not only to endure hardships but also to create and sustain lives that have meaning and contribute to those around them. The phrase *success against odds* is often used to capture the essence of resiliency. Resiliency thus involves the process of becoming successful in life despite exposure to high risks. It also includes the ability to recover successfully from trauma (Fraser, Kirby, & Smokowski, 2004; Greene & Conrad, 2002; Walsh, 2006). Masten, Best, and Garmezy describe resiliency as "the process, capacity for, or outcomes of successful adaptation despite challenging or threatening circumstances" (1991, p. 426). Rutter defines resiliency as "reduced vulnerability to environmental risk experiences, the overcoming of a stress or adversity, a relatively good outcome despite risk experiences" (2012, p. 336). Resilient individuals are able to draw on their own internal resources, their family, and potential ones in their extended environment to cope with challenges. McCubbin, Thompson, Thompson, and Fromer (1998) define resiliency in terms of behavior: "The positive behavioral patterns and functional competence individuals and families demonstrate under stressful or adverse circumstances" (p. xvi). Resiliency moves beyond the absence of pathology to the ability to cope, to find meaning, and continuity in the presence of adversity (Greene & Conrad, 2002). Walsh stresses that resiliency represents more than surviving from trauma; rather it represents the qualities "that enable people to heal from painful wounds, to take charge of their lives, and to go on to live fully and love well (2006, p. 5). At the same time, Rutter reminds us that resiliency does not require superior functioning, rather "relatively better functioning compared with that shown by others experiencing the same level of stress or adversity" (2012, p. 336).

The purpose of this book is to identify characteristics that contribute to or hinder the process of resiliency in families and their members and ways

3

to promote resiliency in families. The characteristics that contribute to the process of resiliency are multifaceted and interact in important ways throughout the life cycle of individuals and the family unit as the challenges facing individuals and their potential resources vary during this time. Although having to cope with difficult life events can create a burden, the process of coping successfully leads to increased confidence and self-efficacy and enhances resiliency (Gutheil & Congress, 2000; Masten, Best, & Garmezy, 1990; Masten & Garmezy, 1983; Rutter, 2012). Rather than emerging despite adversity, resiliency is "forged *through* adversity" (Walsh, 2006, p. 7). Walsh (2006) goes further to state that "resiliency is promoted when hardship, tragedy, failure, or disappointment can also be instructive and serve as an impetus for change and growth" (p. 79). Rutter points out that adversity can have either a steeling effect (reducing adversity to vulnerabilities) or increase vunerabilities through a sensitization effect. The question thus is why does adversity have different effects and what are the mechanisms at work (Rutter, 2012). Resiliency is thus described as a process "woven in a web of relationships and experiences over the course of a life lived from birth through death" (Walsh, 1998, p. 12).

TYPES OF RESILIENCY

Fraser, Kirby, and Smokowski (2004) describe three types of resiliency: overcoming the odds, sustained competence under stress, and recovery from trauma (p. 23). Overcoming the odds is defined as the attainment of positive outcomes despite high-risk status, for example a preterm baby who does not experience negative outcomes or a child who grows up in a very high-risk neighborhood to become a contributing adult. Sustained competence under stress refers to the ability to cope despite ongoing difficult circumstances. People who either struggle with serious chronic illnesses or who care for such individuals can demonstrate this type of resiliency. Recovery from trauma is reflected in individuals who function well after a highly stressful event (e.g., war, violence, accidents).

RISK, VULNERABILITY, AND PROTECTIVE FACTORS

Several related concepts help in understanding resiliency: risk factors, vulnerability factors, and protective factors. These factors interact in the process of stress and resiliency and vary over the life course as well as from individual to individual.

Risk factors include those aspects of life that increase the likelihood of a negative outcome. Risk factors can be characterized in terms of specific events (e.g., loss of a job, death of a parent, problems in reading) or cumulative/additive risk factors by which a cluster of individual events (for example, illness followed by loss of a job) contributes to the likelihood of this outcome (Fraser & Galinsky, 2004; Fraser, Kirby, & Smokowski, 2004; Greene & Conrad, 2002; Norman, 2000). The concept of cumulative/additive risk factors has received increased attention with recognition that "there is no single path to many social problems" (Fraser, Richman, & Galinsky, 1999, p. 132). For many family members, their story is one of several risk factors that are impinging upon the family. A study of African American children living in single-mother households revealed the increased stress as the risk factors increased from three to four factors (Jones, Forehand, Brody, & Armistead, 2002). In an earlier study conducted with rural families who had suffered from the economic problems associated with the farm crisis, it was the number and extent of such problems rather than the nature of specific problems that emerged as the best predictor of the presence of symptoms (Van Hook, 1990b). Many of the families social workers work with are experiencing a combination of factors both currently and in their life span, for example, loss of a job, followed by illness of a child and then marital strain.

Risk factors can also be characterized in terms of their relative closeness to the individual's immediate environment. Proximal risk factors are closer to the individual (e.g., homelessness) than are distal risk factors (e.g., the economy in the community) (Greene & Conrad, 2002). Distal risk factors frequently increase stress by influencing proximal risk factors; for example, community poverty that negatively affects the child by diminishing the parent-child relationship or making it more likely that a family will be homeless, or a war in Iraq that leads to a family member's being called up to active duty with subsequent stress on all the family members. Therefore, it is important to understand the nature of the distal risk factors facing a family and the ways in which these factors influence the family members in more direct ways.

The process by which risk factors influence people needs to be viewed as a dynamic one depending on the individual, the developmental stage of the individual, and the life context (Greene & Conrad, 2002). While the emphasis in this discussion is on ways to promote resiliency, a careful assessment of risk factors is also necessary to identify the needs of individuals and to select appropriate intervention strategies.

Vulnerability factors refers to the concept that some people with risk factors are more likely than others to develop a negative outcome. A vulnerability factor is a characteristic of an individual that makes that person more susceptible to a particular threat during the life course. Vulnerability can take many forms involving the biological, psychological, developmental, and social aspects of the person. For example, a child born premature would be more vulnerable to the stresses faced by an infant. A young woman who was raped could be more vulnerable to being anxious when moving away from home to live in a college world. Although one can talk about resiliency, it is a myth that anyone is invulnerable to all life stresses (Walsh, 2006).

Protective factors are the aspects of life that buffer the negative impact of risk factors. Protective factors can be internal to the person (e.g., intelligence, sense of self-efficacy), part of the supportive family context (e.g., loving parents), or the larger social context that is supportive (e.g., an interested youth leader, good schools, job opportunities) (Greene & Conrad, 2002; Norman, 2000; Walsh, 2006).

Protective factors can be characterized in terms of playing one of three roles. They can buffer risk factors so that they cushion the negative impact of aversive life experiences. In the moving book *Tuesdays with Morrie*, Morrie describes the important role played by a warm and loving stepmother in the lives of two boys left bereft by the death of their mother and an emotionally detached father (Albom, 1997). Protection can also occur through interrupting the risk chain, so that the protective factors eliminate the link between the aversive circumstances and the negative result (e.g., parents can receive help from a counselor dealing with the stress associated with economic strain). This service can potentially interrupt the risk chain because family conflict generated by these economic problems can be reduced and thus the chain of risk between economic problems and the negative impact on the children is reduced. Protection can also prevent the initial occurrence of a risk factor by changing the situation (e.g., a caring grandparent can give a child a sustaining relationship during the illness of a parent who is unable to care for the child). The presence of this grandparent thus changes the situation for the child (Fraser, Kirby, & Smokowski, 2004, pp. 32–33).

Resiliency thus represents a dynamic process during the life cycle of the individual and the family during which the multiple stresses of life are balanced by the ability to cope. Context influences the nature of the risk factors as well as potential means of coping. The family's resiliency is tested especially in times of transition (for example, a new stage in the family life cycle, moves to new locations or responsibilities). The experience of being successful in coping with difficult life events increases an individual's or a family's sense of competence (Walsh, 2006).

Resiliency can be viewed as a continuum that varies by degree depending not only on individuals but also on their developmental stage of life and the life event facing them. As a result, individuals can differ in their ability to cope effectively depending on the developmental issues involved and the nature of the problem (Greene & Conrad, 2002). For example, Glen Elder's (1974) study of young people who experienced the Great Depression of the 1920s and 1930s revealed such a life cycle issue in terms of how age played a critical role in terms of impact. Adolescents were sometimes strengthened by this adversity because they had to take on adult roles and did so successfully—finding that they could succeed made them more resilient. In contrast, younger children became sensitized (increased vulnerability) by this stress.

LIFE EVENTS AND RESILIENCY

Life events can demand very different coping and adaptive capacities. Greene and Conrad (2002) describe several ways to categorize life events. Events can be categorized in terms of either non-normative events that are idiosyncratic to the individual or a small number of people (e.g., the birth of a child with serious developmental disabilities), or normative events that are influenced by social definitions of the stage of life (e.g., loss of a spouse, retirement), or cohort events that are common to people who are part of a cohort of individuals (e.g., the Great Depression, Vietnam War, political shifts within a country such as war in Iraq, the fall of Communism in Eastern Europe, the split of Korea into North and South Korea). Events can also represent major traumatic life events that can readily overwhelm an individual's coping capacity. Examples include natural events such as tornadoes or hurricanes, human-induced events such as the terrorist attack on the World Trade Center, and accidents such as a plane crash or a major earthquake (Greene & Conrad, 2002).

The dynamic nature of resiliency presented in both the preceding and following discussion highlights the roles that social workers and other helping professionals can play in enhancing and supporting resiliency within families. While genetic characteristics and certain background factors of individuals may be givens in the situations, resiliency is a dynamic process influenced by the ongoing interplay between life events and individuals and families. Social workers and other helping professionals can enhance the ability of families to cope, to overcome adversity, and to move toward a more fulfilling future. Counselors' efforts to address contextual issues and the social support system (for example, improved school services) in the design of prevention and treatment approaches can also enhance resiliency. Given the developmental nature of resiliency, such efforts not only help families cope with the present situation but can also enable them to gain a sense of self-efficacy and skills that can then enable them to cope more effectively with future life demands. Walsh (2006) refers to these efforts in terms of immunizing people with resiliency skills to address future adversities.

HISTORICAL BACKGROUND

Early studies in the 1970s to 1980s regarding resiliency in individuals recognized that despite difficult circumstances, some children were able to develop into relatively well-adjusted people who coped effectively with life. Families were also able to weather major problems, find a sense of meaning in these events, and forge ahead. These findings indicated that mechanistic views of life based on deterministic models that assume a certain set of problems (risk factors) inevitably create an accompanying list of maladaptive responses were inaccurate and unduly pessimistic. They pointed out the need to examine not only the factors that contribute to maladjustment (risk factors) but also the characteristics that contribute to this resiliency (protective factors). The emphasis on risk factors was balanced with a focus on the protective factors that enable people to adapt and cope effectively (protective factors). While appreciating the pain and possible damage to individuals and families created by difficult life events, there is also a respect for the potential strength and resiliency present within individuals and families. Resiliency from this perspective is a strength-affirming perspective that believes it is worthwhile to look for the competencies and abilities within families.

The following chapter is organized in three sections: traits that influence individual resiliency, elements associated with family resiliency, and models describing the process by which families cope with stressors. The discussion regarding factors that increase risk and protection must be understood within the context that while these are valuable general statements, a careful assessment must be made in terms of individuals regarding the specific elements at work for this individual at this point in time.

INDIVIDUAL RESILIENCY

Studies regarding resiliency of youth have identified basic themes that promote resiliency: personality characteristics such as self-esteem, easygoing personality, or intelligence; nurturing family environments; and support systems external to the family system that offer opportunities for personal growth and mentoring (Conger & Elder, 1994; Elder & Conger, 2000; Fraser, Kirby, & Smokowski, 2004; Masten & Tellegen, 2012; Rutter, 2012).

A landmark longitudinal study conducted by Werner and colleagues in Hawaii with children who grew up in high-risk environments revealed the importance of these individual traits as well as family and interpersonal relationships. The results were also encouraging because even the majority of youth who had juvenile criminal backgrounds became productive adults, especially those who were able to gain important educational and vocational skills, to create constructive social connections, and to develop a sense of spirituality (Werner & Smith, 1992). Similar patterns emerged in a small qualitative study conducted with African Americans who had made it against the odds. Factors promoting resiliency included individuals' traits (efforts related to pro-social goals, a sense of autonomy [locus of control], spiritual connections), sustaining interpersonal relationships in the course of their development, and positive meanings of life events (Gordon & Song, 1994, cited in Greene, 2002).

The University of Minnesota conducted another study to examine children at risk for mental health and behavior disorders. The Project Competence Longitudinal Study (PCLS) was designed to study resiliency over a period of twenty years. The first set of findings at year ten revealed important patterns related to individual and family characteristics. Children who had good cognitive skills and received good parenting were able to cope with adversity and demonstrate adequate competence in developmental tasks in childhood, adolescence, and early adulthood. In contrast, children who had to cope with the same level of adversity without good cognitive skills and good parenting demonstrated maladaptive patterns of adjustment (Masten & Tellegen, 2012).

As children matured, their paths tended to diverge further. Young people "characterized by competence and resiliency shared a pattern of positive traits: average or better socioeconomic status, cognitive skills, openness to experience, drive for mastery, conscientiousness, close relationships with parents, adult support outside the family, and feelings of self worth" (p. 357).

In contrast, children who did not evidence competence in the face of adversity, demonstrated higher rates of negative emotionality, lower IQ scores, and high levels of negative behavior experienced by late adolescence (e.g., being arrested, conflict in relationships). As they grew older, they began making decisions that created further negative consequences.

Yet, just as in the Kwai, Hawaii, study by Werner, some young people in the University of Minnesota study were able to turn their lives around. Several characteristics seemed to make the difference: planfulness, autonomy, and adult support outside the family. They moved away from negative peers and created healthier relationships through marriage or employment. They also appeared to have been more conscientious as children.

The final ten-year profile in the University of Minnesota study revealed a similar pattern of competence and resiliency demonstrating that in general adult competence has its roots in childhood competence. "Adaptive children generally became adaptive adults" (Masten & Tellegen, 2012, p. 357). The role of adversity played a role particularly in the absence of protection from protective factors (Masten & Tellegen, 2012; Shiner & Masten, 2012). A similar pattern of continuity from childhood to adulthood emerged in other longitudinal studies (Burt & Paysnick, 2012).

These studies indicate the need to understand resiliency and individuals from a broader ecological perspective rather than traits limited to the individual. The preceding discussion regarding resiliency illustrates the nature of the individual existing within the family as a living system occurring over time within an ecological framework. As a living system, the family has ongoing information and energy exchanges with its individual members, the family as a unit, and its larger context. The family is composed of individual members with their unique developmental history and individual characteristics that are both shaped by the family and its larger context and in turn influence the family and its context. The family as a unit also has a developmental history and organizational structures that in turn are influenced by individual members, life cycle issues, and the larger context. The family operates within and is shaped by a larger cultural and community context (e.g., neighborhood, employment and educational organizations, faith-based or other voluntary organizations) that in turn is influenced by family units. As a result, it is important to understand risk and resiliency factors from the perspective of individuals, family units, and the larger community context. These systems in turn interact in ongoing ways.

As an example of this ongoing systematic interaction, the serious chronic illness of a child within a family not only affects the child but has an important impact on all the members of the family as well as the nature of the demands on the family unit. The illness of the child potentially creates emotional strain for all the family members, makes demands on parental time and attention, forces the family to make potentially difficult decisions regarding parental employment and viable day care arrangements, and requires additional funds to pay for the treatment of the child. The child and her illness in turn are influenced by the interpersonal and economic resources of the nuclear and extended family—the ability of family members to provide adequate physical and emotional care, the nature of the marital/parental relationship and what effect this strain has on the relationship, extended family members who can provide respite care, adequacy of the family's medical insurance or governmental policies in terms of medical services, other economic resources, and parental belief systems regarding the nature of appropriate care and the meaning of the child's illness. The nature of the community health-care system and social policies regarding payment of health care are critical for this family life. These policies in turn are potentially shaped by parent organizations that advocate for the needs of children with this illness, the nature of available community resources, and larger societal views regarding the role of health care. Canadian health care policies that extend medical care to virtually all residents compared to the current debate in the United States regarding health care policies represent ways in which the contextual factors influence the nature of health care resources available to families. Our granddaughter, for example, recently developed a life-threatening form of malaria. The statistics regarding survival and adverse consequences were frightening. Fortunately, she was living in Boston where she was able to receive highly sophisticated medical care and emerged unscathed from the illness. In addition her parents had access to good medical insurance. Sadly for many children who are stricken with this illness in African communities with limited medical services, their outcomes are more likely to match these alarming statistics. Parental devotion and commitment need the support of a medical system of care that family members can access.

These findings give support to a living system model in which individuals, the family unit, and the larger context interact on an ongoing basis. Fraser, Kirby, and Smokowski (2004) and Benzies and Mychasiuk (2009) use an ecological approach to organize risk and protective factors in terms of these three system levels: (1) broad environmental conditions, including neighborhood and school, (2) family conditions, and (3) individual (psychosocial and biological). The following risk and protective factors have emerged as important in these reviews of the research on resiliency as well as findings from longitudinal and other studies (Burt & Paysnick, 2012; Masten & Tellegen, 2012; Rutter, 2012).

ENVIRONMENTAL LEVEL

Risk factors include few opportunities for education and employment, racial discrimination and injustice, and poverty (often associated with poor housing, unsafe neighborhoods, and lack of access to health care).

Protective factors include many opportunities for education, housing in safe neighborhoods, employment, adequate income, growth, and achievement; collective efficacy, and presence of caring adults (e.g., caring teachers, youth leaders, social workers, and other supportive community members), sources of social support, health care services.

FAMILY LEVEL

Risk factors include child maltreatment, parental conflict, parental neglect, parental psychopathology that impedes parenting, and harsh parenting.

Protective factors include positive parent-child and family relationships and effective parenting.

INDIVIDUAL LEVEL

Risk factors include biomedical problems (including genetic liability) and changes in brain functioning as a result of extreme adverse conditions.

Protective factors include easy temperament as an infant, self-esteem and hardiness, competence in normative roles, self-efficacy, self regulation, and high intelligence.

Environmental Level

The nature of educational opportunities plays a critical role in enabling children to gain the necessary academic skills required to cope with an increasingly complex and demanding world. Employment opportunities shape the family's economic resources as well as family members' sense of self-worth and competence. Discrimination in various forms reduces opportunities and expectations that efforts will be worthwhile. Injustice further limits opportunities for individuals and families. Poverty plays an important role regarding economic resources and furthermore is frequently associated with poorer educational options, greater danger in living arrangements, and problems in health care. It also places a burden on family members who are attempting to provide adequate care for their family. Communities that provide members with opportunities for growth (for example, recreation, athletics, the arts) give youth a broader array of coping strategies and opportunities for developing a sense of self-efficacy and worth. Communities that have confidence (collective self-efficacy) that they are able to meet the needs of the community members rather than those that are demoralized because of an ongoing sense of powerlessness represent a supportive context for members. Communities and their members are further supported by the presence of caring and competent adults who take an interest in the development of their youth and families.

Interpersonal Level

Positive and caring relationships within the family or other intimate environments support resiliency (Benzies & Mychasiuk, 2009; Masten, Best, & Garmezy, 1990; Masten & Coatsworth, 1998; Rutter, 2012; Masten & Tellegen, 2012; Walsh, 2006). Drawing from theoretical perspectives regarding development, these relationships foster development in several ways. In terms of object relations theory, Winnicott described the importance of "good enough mothering" or a "holding environment" that provides what the child needs at various developmental stages and in turn enables the child to develop an integrated sense of the self who can have genuine relationships with others (Goldstein, 1995; Kilpatrick, Kilpatrick, & Callaway, 2000). Attachment theory stresses the importance of someone that a young child can feel connected to and is able to trust his or her accessibility and responsiveness. Attachment theory studies have identified the following patterns as supportive of personal maturity: "mutual trust and approval between the child and his parents" (including acceptance, trust, open communication, encouragement of wider social relationships, and congenial parental relationships) and "consistency of family life" (including regular routines, consistency of parenting, participation of members in family activities) (Bowlby, 1973, p. 335).

The interaction between interpersonal relationships and individual personal qualities is further supported by research related to the brain. Nurturing relationships help build healthy brain architecture in young children, buffer the impact of stress of the development process (Shonkoff, 2005; Shonkoff & Phillips, 2000), and increase the ability to regulate affect (Shapiro, 2000).

When such positive relationships are not found within the immediate family, individuals have been able to find someone within the extended family, teachers, neighbors, church members, and others within the community to establish these connections (Walsh, 2006). Similar to the language of attachment theory, Norman (2000) describes these persons as offering "a safe harbor promoting autonomy and competence" (p. 9). While such relationships are important, recent research with economically troubled farm families points out the limitations of such relationships for teenagers when, for example, economic distress engenders harsh parenting by parents (Elder & Conger, 2000) Resiliency is also promoted when the child has relationships with others who hold positive and realistic expectations of the child (Norman, 2000, p. 10).

A sobering study was conducted by Kaiser Permanente with a large (over 17,000) number of primarily middle-class individuals who were being seen for routine physical care. Individuals were asked to self-report about childhood experiences related to physical, emotional, and sexual abuse; neglect; family dysfunctions (alcohol or drug use by parents, loss of parents, depression/mental health problems of parents, mother treated violently, family member imprisoned). As the number of categories of these negative life experiences increased (not merely number of times within a category), individuals in later life reported substantially higher levels of mental health problems, addictions, violence, rates of heart disease and other illnesses, and lower life expectancies. This study thus demonstrates that the risk factors associated with some of these early life interpersonal experiences cast a long shadow (Anda, Felitti, Bremner, Walker, Whitfield, Perry, Dube, & Giles, 2005; Felitti, 2012).

Individual Level

Key personality and related individual characteristics that support resiliency in individuals include self-efficacy, a realistic appraisal of the environment, an ability to make plans, social problem-solving skills, a sense of direction or mission, empathy, humor, androgynous sex role behavior that provides for flexibility of behavior in different circumstances, and adaptive distancing—the ability to avoid being enmeshed by the problems and dysfunctional patterns of the family while at the same time remaining connected to the persons involved (Norman, 2000).

Self-efficacy includes both "a sense of self-worth or self-esteem, and a sense of mastery of one's self and the external environment (sometimes called an internal locus of control)" (Norman, 2000, p. 5). Self-efficacy as a protective factor is enhanced by successfully overcoming adversity (Walsh, 2006). Self-efficacy is specific to context. Self-efficacy can take several different forms that contribute to resiliency in different contexts; for example, academic efficacy (confidence in ability to learn), social efficacy (confidence regarding social relationships), and self-regulatory efficacy (ability to resist pressure from peers and others) (Fraser, Kirby, & Smokowski, 2004).

Self-efficacy is enhanced by the ability to appraise one's environment in a realistic manner. This includes a realistic understanding of the nature of the situation and what one can do to change it. The ability to draw upon appropriate problem-solving skills also enhances self-efficacy. Individuals need a range of problem-solving skills to address the variety of situations they will face over time (Walsh, 1998, 2006). Self-efficacy with the accompanying actions to take control of one's life emerged as an important factor in supporting resiliency in studies including the Hawaiian cohort of Werner and Smith (1992), high-risk children (Rutter, 1984), the offspring of mentally ill parents (Garmezy, 1985), and the street children of Colombia (Felsman, 1989).

Sense of direction or mission has been identified in groups ranging from concentration camp survivors (Moskowitz, 1983) to civil rights workers (Beardslee, 1989), and the young people from Hawaii (Norman, 2000; Werner & Smith, 1992). Ruby Bridges, the young girl who integrated her New Orleans elementary school, was able to walk the gauntlet of threats while praying for those who threatened her, and survived this experience as a strong and happy person (Coles, 1964).

Self-regulation is important in developing competence in a variety of spheres associated with effective development. It is supported by means of loving but firm parenting efforts (Benzies & Mychasiuk, 2009; Masten & Coatsworth, 1998). Such self- regulation enables individuals to draw upon effective coping strategies in a planned manner rather than acting in an impulsive manner. A child with effective self-regulation is able to complete an essential assignment for school rather than be tempted by a video game or to resist getting into a fight with a teammate during a basketball game and thus risk being thrown out of the game.

Hardiness refers to several related contents that draw upon previously described concepts. Fraser, Kirby, and Smokowski (2004, p. 48) identify three components: (1) control—the ability to assess a situation and select and carry out the appropriate strategies, (2) commitment to a set of values that impart a sense of purpose, and (3) a response to the stressors or challenges that creates a sense of motivation and capability to solve the problem.

Intelligence contributes in several ways. It helps young people gain academic success that in turn builds self-efficacy and also helps them develop effective problem solving skills (Fraser, Kirby, & Smokowski, 2004, pp. 48–49).

Easy going temperament permits a young child to respond in a less intense way to stressful event and to be more adaptable. Children with more easy going temperaments are able to elicit more positive responses from their parents and others that further support development (Fraser, Kirby, & Smokowski, 2004).

Without spelling out the many potential risk and protective factors, one can appreciate the interaction between personal and contextual factors that take place in both negative and positive ways. For one child a negative interaction pattern takes place when this child with a very reactive temperament is being reared by parents who worry where they will be living next week and what they will do to protect their children from the violence that is being played out around them. In contrast, a second child with an easy temperament being raised by parents with a secure economic base and supported by a loving extended family and effective programs for families experiences a benign interaction.

FAMILY RESILIENCY

Walsh (2006) describes family resilience as "the coping and adaptational processes in the family as a functional unit. . . . How a family confronts and manages a disruptive experience, buffers stress, effectively reorganizes and moves forward with life" will influence how the family and its members adapt and survive in the immediate and long term (p. 15). Resiliency does not refer to a family that is problem-free, but rather a family that is able to absorb the shock of problems and discover strategies to solve them while finding ways to meet the needs of family members and the family unit. The challenge of social workers is to find ways to empower families to cope in this manner with the myriad of problems that are part of the ongoing life experience of families, for example, illness, loss of jobs, or death of members. Efforts to empower families in this manner help strengthen resiliency within families and in turn enable them to cope in more effective ways when facing future life difficulties.

The family plays a critical role in terms of risk and protective factors for individual members. It is thus important for members to support elements that reduce risk and promote resiliency within the family unit. Caring and stable relationships within the family are identified as protective while conflictual family relationships emerge as risk factors in various studies and theoretical frameworks. The presence of caring adults emerges as the "most important and consistent protective factor" in terms of dealing with multiple types of stress (Masten, Best, & Garmezy, 1990, p. 431). The development of competence that supports resiliency is nourished within an interpersonal context. Family members also respond in ways that encourage the sociability and sense of competence of the child—"the child and parent dance." Relationships set the stage for how events and potential resources are perceived. For example, depending on culture and individual family circumstances, families can value quite different traits for their children. For one family, academic excellence might be highly valued while in another family athletic prowess is honored. Within the family, children can also be valued for different reasons—one child might be valued for academic achievement while another for artistic or athletic ability.

Because families play crucial roles in the lives of their members and in supporting the ability of children to become resilient, it is important to understand the aspects within the family and the broader community that support families and promote family resiliency. Knowledge of these elements can help in the design of prevention and healing approaches that support resiliency both within families and individuals. While the specific forms of family units may change and vary over time and between cultures (e.g., extended families in some cultures compared to nuclear families in others, larger numbers of single parents, divorced and blended families, and gay and lesbian couples raising children), the family unit remains the key institution for providing children with the essential physical and emotional nourishment needed. The family unit gives its members a key sense of identity. Family members can turn to each other for companionship and ongoing social support in good and trying times. Families develop meaning systems that help members interpret the world around them and life events. These interpretations help in coping or contribute to ongoing struggles.

An emphasis on family resiliency also influences the basic nature of the relationship between the family and the helping professional. Using a collaborative relationship between the counselor and the family members is most effective when it identifies sources of resiliency and encourages the family's efforts in recovery and growth. Such an approach empowers people and enables them to cope with the current problem and prepares them to address the challenges of the future. Walsh emphasizes the importance of a collaborative relationship (2006) and asserts that the resiliency-based approach "affirms the family's potential for self-repair and growth out of crisis and challenge" (1998, p. 16). Research in the area of resiliency provides empirical grounding for assessment and treatment intervention strategies. While the specific focus of this book is on counseling approaches in working with families, evidence regarding resiliency points out the additional need for interventions in the areas of social and economic policies that address aspects of life that have a profound impact on families.

Research regarding family resiliency has grown out of two basic streams of research and thought: the nature of healthy family processes and family response to stressors and related family crisis theory. There is considerable overlap in the family and contextual characteristics that influence resiliency identified within these traditions. The following discussion is organized first in terms of the factors that have been identified that enhance resiliency within families, and second the process that occurs when families attempt to cope in terms of ways that can promote resiliency or lead to further distress.

Principles of Family Resiliency

In her excellent discussions of healthy family processes and resiliency, Walsh (1998, 2006) uses a family system approach to describe the interaction between individuals, families, and the wider context. The health of the family and the hardiness of individuals are influenced by the interaction between individuals, families, and their context. Crisis events affect the family as a whole as well as individual family members. While maladaptive responses increase vulnerability and distress, protective processes that buffer stress promote resiliency. The outcome of potential crisis events is influenced by family processes, for example, the ability of the organization of the family to cope with required changes, to communicate as needed, and to give members adequate support. Walsh offers a strength-affirming stance: "All families have the potential for resiliency, and we can maximize that potential by encouraging their best efforts and strengthening key processes" (1998, p. 24).

Key Factors of Family Resiliency

The keys to family resiliency can be understood in terms of three important family elements: belief systems, organizational patterns, and coping process (Benzies & Mychasiuk, 2009; Lietz, 2007; Walsh, 1998, p. 24). These elements are further influenced by the social support system of the family, the community, and cultural context and the reactivation of past issues that heighten positive or negative aspects of family members. The presence of several risk factors increases the vulnerability of families. A recent qualitative study of families in which children were successfully reunified gives further support to the protective factors identified in these studies (Lietz & Strength, 2011). Table 1 summarizes risk and protective factors identified in the family crisis and strengths traditions. The following section discusses ways in which these factors contribute to either vulnerability or resiliency within families.

Belief Systems

Family belief systems are the product of the historical and cultural context of families as well as the unique experiences of the extended and immediate family members. Families develop paradigms (organized belief systems about the world and individuals' relationship to it) that influence how they view the world and appropriate survival responses (Reiss, 1981). These belief systems provide a sense of coherence to family life events. Adversity in one form or another is part of the life journey for members of all families. Even if family members should be fortunate enough to escape economic and major interpersonal problems, loss is an inevitable part of the family story (for example, death of parents or grandparents). How family members interpret these events is critical in influencing how families are able to cope. Walsh (1998, 2006) asserts the importance of families creating meaning out of adversity and the value of sharing a sense of meaning by family members. Interpretations of mastery contribute to self-efficacy on the part of the family

TABLE 1. Family Risk and Protective Factors

Risk Factors	*Protective Factors*
Belief Systems	
Lack of sense of "we" in terms of the family	Relational perspective
Lack of trust	Trust of family, loyalty, affection
Lack of self-efficacy	Self-efficacy, mastery
Negative cultural beliefs	Appropriate cultural beliefs
Lack of developmental perspective	Developmental perspective
Demoralization	Sense of coherence
Fatalist views	Hope, courage, perseverance
Blaming and scapegoating	Recognition of complex patterns
All or nothing thinking	Recognition of what is possible
Negative aspects of spirituality	Transcendent beliefs that promote meaning
Role Models	
Ineffective role models	Role models of strength
Organizational Patterns	
Lack of cohesion, rigidity	Cohesion, flexibility
Lack of effective leadership, chaotic or abusive power	Effective leadership
Ineffective communication	Clear, open communication
Conflict	Positive interactions, trust
Ineffective problem-solving/coping strategies	Effective problem-solving and coping strategies
Lack of sense of humor	Humor
Social Support System	
Lack of social support	Social support
Economic Resources	
Poverty	Adequate resources
Community Context	
Poverty, lack of economic and educational opportunities	Economic and educational opportunities
Reactivation of Past Events	
Evidence of weakness and unresolved conflict	Evidence of strength and family support

that emerges as an important protective factor. Belief systems also influence important aspects of family organization and process.

The family's definition of the nature of life events influences the strategies that family members employ to address problems and the preferred solutions (Benzies and Mychasiuk, 2009; Hill, 1949; McCubbin, Thompson,

Thompson, & Fromer, 1998; Reiss, 1981; Robinson, 2000; Walsh, 1998, 2006). These definitions influence, for example, whether or not the family can deal with it through its own internal resources, if it is appropriate to seek help from others outside of the family, and what type of help to seek. When problems or issues are identified as something that the family is ashamed of, family members may be reluctant to seek help from those outside the family circle. A potential resource within the community is not a resource to the family unless defined so by the family and the family is able to access this resource.

Cultural messages shape perceptions of the meaning of life events, for example, the relative value of possessions, family ties, family honor, and history. They influence how people view what contributes to success or difficulties in life and how to address problems (Delgado, 2007; Falicov, 1999; Magana & Ybarra, 2010; McCubbin, McCubbin, Thompson, & Thompson, 1999; McGoldrick & Giordano, 1986; Smith, Bakir, & Montilla, 2006; Walsh, 2006; Yeh, Borrero, & Kwong, 2011). As an example, when my daughter was serving as a Peace Corps volunteer in a small village in the African country of Chad, a land stricken by poverty and decimated by a recent war and other problems, she was surprised to see how happy the people were despite having nothing in terms of the usual sense of belongings from a middle-class American standard of living. While from our perspective these people were extremely poor, they had close family and relational ties that made life meaningful. When it was time for her assignment to end after two years, some people were surprised that she would actually leave "the best place on earth to live." When my other daughter (also in her early twenties) joined the Peace Corps, she lived with a family during her training period in the Cameroons. The wife in this family was a lovely young woman who did not leave the family compound (the buildings that composed the home) without her husband's permission. The family was economically quite well off and she was able to send others to the market to get the daily needs of the family. This woman felt fortunate to be cared for in this way and worried about my daughter, who had no one to take care of her. The life circumstances and cultures of each of these young women had led them to value quite different aspects of life—security/adventure.

Relevant cultural messages influence how family members view events and the appropriate types of help. Members of some cultures turn to folk healers while others might see solutions in terms of medical doctors or financial advisors. HIV/AIDS represents a critical global health problem with painful social and family definitions that have impeded people from seeking or receiving help because of the stigma involved. Advocates in the field of mental health have fought and are continuing to fight a battle against the stigma that has prevented people from receiving help and definitions of mental health that have long supported decreased insurance funding.

Relational Perspective. The belief that we face problems together, that the situation represents a shared challenge, provides relational resilience (Walsh, 1998, 2006). Families are strengthened by a sense of closeness as they tackle problems together (Beavers & Hampson, 1990; Walsh, 1998, 2006). This sense of relational resilience is illustrated by a junior high boy who said when asked why his family that was experiencing major financial problems and related interpersonal ones had come for counseling, "Our family is having some hard times and *we* are here to find out ways that *we* can make things better in our family." The emphasis on the "we" made it clear that he viewed the job of solving the family problem as belonging to the entire family unit.

Trust. A sense of trust encourages this relational perspective and further strengthens families. This sense of trust enables family members to turn to others within the family for help and collaboration (Beavers & Hampson, 1990; Walsh, 1998, 2006). Krasner (1986) describes trustworthiness as the primal family resource.

Family trustworthiness occurs within the realistic complexity of family relationships with the inevitability of unfair expectations, doubts, and misunderstandings along with the possibilities of attachment, caring, and support. Family members are able to look beyond the negative aspects to the enduring elements of trust within relationships. Supporting family trustworthiness are valuable relational rules of respect that communicate that others are valued, reciprocity that entails fairness and give and take among members, reliability that enables people to count on and trust each other, and repair that involves efforts to make up for damage done in relationships (Karpel, 1986, p. 186).

Self-Efficacy and Competence. Meanings are influenced by past life events within the extended family circle. These events create fundamental views about the nature of the world and the family's place in it (Reiss, 1981). Families who view themselves as having overcome difficult events in the past are most likely to have confidence in their ability to cope with the current event (McCubbin, Thompson, Thompson, Elver, McCubbin, 1998; Robinson, 2000; Walsh, 2006). As White and Epston (1990) stress in narrative family therapy, individuals and families have a variety of stories (narrative interpretations of life events) available to them that influence how life events are experienced. While some stories promote a sense of competence and strength and facilitate healing, other stories disqualify and are demeaning to the persons involved. The nature of these stories is important in promoting resiliency. As some family members said in a study with financially troubled farm families, "We got through tough times in the past and will do so again" (Van Hook, 1990b). Such an interpretation contributes to self-efficacy and an important sense of competence.

Developmental Perspective. The ability to take a life cycle, a developmental perspective, so that issues that arise are viewed as part of the rhythms of life further strengthens families. This perspective permits families to view change as developmental challenges rather than threats to the family (Walsh, 1998, 2006). Such families are able to recognize the growing pains of adolescents without viewing them as a threat to the family. A developmental perspective can be especially helpful since threats to resiliency are especially likely to occur during times of family transition.

The family life cycle presents family members and the family unit with a number of transitions and accompanying tasks. McGoldrick and Carter identify stages in the family life cycle that begins with the single young adult (McGoldrick & Carter, 1982, p. 176). The following describes some of the tasks related to this stage.

1. The unattached young adult who must establish a new relationship with the family of origin and social and work relationships and responsibilities.

2. The newly married couple who must commit to a new family system while realigning their relationships to other family and friends.

3. Family with young children who must now take on parental roles and make room in the family system for a child. Their parents have now moved into grandparent roles.

4. Family with adolescents who need to alter family roles to accommodate growing adolescent independence and relationships with peers, new challenges in the world of careers, and concerns for the older generation.

5. Family with children who are launching out of the family require a family with flexible boundaries, adult-to-adult relationships between parents and offspring, and the grandparents' challenge of dealing with growing older.

6. Family in later years that must adapt to new roles and possible loss of family members.

The family transitions described above require new coping skills and can potentially reduce prior sources of support (while potentially offering a new set of ones). Demands for change can reduce the important sense of self-efficacy in addition to the sadness evoked by some of these changes. In terms of the meaning of life events, as family members grow up and marry, the resilient family is able to incorporate new members rather than to focus on the loss of connection.

While the preceding represents one prototype of a family life cycle, the reality of family life can represent major differences that bring with them new sets of meanings and life tasks. Many people never marry. Many couples remain childless or lose young children. Parents and spouses can die at any age, leaving family members with the challenge of coping with this new family arrangement. High rates of divorce at different stages in the relationship mean that many family members are addressing ways to negotiate this change. When parents remarry, family members have to negotiate ways to establish new sets of relationships and redefine already existing ones. Young people can become parents while still needing the care of their parents who have now become grandparents as well as parents of teenagers. The case examples in this book illustrate a number of these variations within the family life cycle.

In the insightful 1960 musical *The Fantasticks* by Harvey Schmidt and Tom Jones, the fathers seek to protect and script a happy life for their children. As both the parents and the young people discover, however, depth of character and a genuine relationship between the two young people are forged through pain and adversity, not through the father's protective activities.

Coherence. A sense of coherence—that life is comprehensible and meaningful—also supports resiliency (Antonovsky, 1998; McCubbin, Thompson, Thompson, & Fromer, 1998; Walsh, 1998, 2006). Such an orientation to life promotes confidence in the ability to clarify the nature of problems so that they are understandable and predictable. This orientation is related to the self-efficacy identified earlier in terms of resiliency in individuals but goes beyond it to include issues of meaning and purpose of life. Family members are able to view life events as having a sense of purpose and ways in which the family can respond accordingly. Family members are able to view problems, for example, as ways that the family will be strengthened in the long term or as opportunities for growth for family members.

Traumatic events can create problems for family members in terms of this sense of coherence. The news is replete with fatal accidents, murders, warfare, and other traumatic events experienced by family members. Walsh describes a potential way that "resilient persons—and communities—often draw something positive out of a tragic situation by finding something to salvage and seeing new possibilities in the midst of the wreckage" (2006, p. 77). One set of parents, for example, funded a center to serve young people from a community where youth had murdered their daughter in South Africa. It was their way of honoring their daughter and furthering her work.

Recognition of Complex Patterns. Effective families are able to recognize that events are products of complex patterns and to explain life events accordingly rather than to blame individual family members. Poorly functioning families, on the other hand, tend to lock onto one explanation for a problem and to be organized in terms of blaming and scapegoating (Beavers & Hampson, 1990). These are the families whose members are either so busy trying to point the finger of blame or defending against blame that they have little energy left to work together to solve their problems.

Views of the Future. The belief that family members can have a positive impact on what happens to them strengthens them and gives them the impetus to continue to try. Families suffer when family members hold fatalist views that nothing can be done or expect that one person should be able to control everything (Walsh, 1998, 2006). Several important elements that contribute to a positive outlook include perseverance, courage and encouragement, hope and optimism, and mastery of the art of the possible (Walsh, 1998, 2006).

Perseverance—"the ability to struggle well and persist in the face of overwhelming adversity—is a key element in resilience. It enables family members to continue to struggle despite odds" (Walsh, 2006, p. 69). In the many accounts of ways in which families have coped with the difficult life events created by the tragedy of September 11, 2001, a key theme has been the family's determination and ability to continue to move forward as a family despite terrible losses and pain. Families who struggled to find new lives for their families following the Katrina disaster in New Orleans and other Gulf Coast communities also demonstrated such persistence.

The courage of family members to cope, especially combined with the support of others, further supports resiliency (Walsh, 1998, 2006, p. 70). Courage can be manifested in facing dramatic life events as well as the daily efforts to move ahead despite difficulties. An individual who runs into a burning building to save a child demonstrates courage—so does the daily act of holding down two difficult jobs while also meeting the many needs of family members or caring for family members despite ongoing severe health problems. The latter type of courage is frequently not identified as such by the parties involved but is manifested in many of the families seen by social workers and other counselors.

Hope promotes resiliency by enabling people to look to a brighter future despite the bleak past and present and thus to persevere. Resilient families have an "optimistic orientation in dealing with stress and crisis" (Walsh, 1998, p. 63, 2006). These views enable family members to think about ways that they can contribute to the solution. As counselors recognize, one of the key elements in any effective counseling endeavor is the ability to engender hope for the future that enables individuals and families to mobilize their efforts to meet their goals.

Hopefulness is supported by beliefs and mind-sets. The family's belief that they have the ability to match the current challenge promotes hope (Friedman, 1986; Walsh, 2006). There is an ongoing interaction between belief systems and life experiences. This positive mind-set needs to be reinforced by experiences that give evidence of success and a context that is supportive. Such experience encourages the sense of self-efficacy described earlier. Positive illusions contribute by enabling people to hold to the possibility of optimistic outcomes (Walsh, 2006, p. 69). Such hopeful mind-sets encourage families and individuals to maintain the efforts to cope and address difficult life events in contrast to a sense of helplessness that discourages efforts to try.

Interpretations about success and failure also influence resiliency. Resilient families are more likely to view mistakes or failure as experiences from which to learn rather than occasions of defeat. They view difficult life events as possibilities for growth and strengthening of the family. Such life events are viewed as opportunities to reassess life and even "to be seen as a gift that opens a new phase of life or new opportunities" (Walsh, 1998, p. 76).

Mastery of the Art of the Possible. Resilient families are able to assess what is possible to accomplish in a situation and to organize their efforts accordingly rather than being governed by all-or-nothing thinking (Walsh, 2006). Families can thus direct their attention to these steps. Such successful efforts provide confidence about future success or opportunities for learning for future actions (Walsh, 1998, p. 124, 2006). Mastering the possible is reflected in families whose members can identify the specific steps that are needed and possible in the current context or ones that the family can influence. Family members can then direct their efforts accordingly.

Culture influences what success means in this context. Walsh (1998, 2006), for example, contrasts the orientation of control and of mastery of people from Western backgrounds to that of living in harmony of families from Eastern and Native American traditions. Regardless of the tradition, families need to be able to identify what are the steps that enable the family to work toward these cultural goals. Related to this is the ability of family members to use their creative imagination to envision new possibilities for the family (Walsh, 1998).

Transcendent Beliefs and Spirituality. For some family members, these beliefs can potentially enable them to cope with difficult life experiences by providing a link to the transcendent and providing a sense of meaning. This transcendent value system enables people to define their lives as meaningful and significant (Benzies & Mychasiuk, 2009; Walsh, 1998, 1999, 2006). Families can especially need such a sense of meaning when tragedy and hardship strikes (Wright, 1999). Studies drawn from a variety of traditions suggest ways in which religion can potentially provide a sense of meaning and support for families as well as some of the risk factors that religion can pose (Falicov, 1999; Van Hook, Hugen, & Aguilar, 2002; Walsh, 1999, 2006). Spirituality and religion can offer a sense of purpose, the comfort of being cared for, meaningful rituals, and the support of common community. On the other hand, beliefs centered around punishment can create additional distress.

Role Models. Role models can be viewed in terms of the organization of the family as well as the belief systems that are created. Members of the family can model ways to cope with life in ways that contribute to effective solutions (for example, going to work on a regular basis rather than skipping work to drink, parents dealing with conflict in ways that promote effective solutions and convey mutual respect). These role models give children lessons on effective ways to behave that can be used both within the family and in larger social contexts. They also contribute to empowering belief systems by giving images of strength and new possibilities. These images can be drawn from role models of strength within the family or the larger context (for example, teachers, youth leaders). Such strength can be identified in response to the big challenges of life as well as to ongoing efforts to address the challenges of daily life. Social workers regularly encounter family members who demonstrate such strength as they care for family members with disabilities, raise children in dangerous neighborhoods, and work in difficult and dangerous conditions to support their families. These role models within the family can be the source of powerful messages that create beliefs systems of hope and strength that support resiliency.

Organizational Patterns

Organizational patterns refer to the ongoing interpersonal arrangements within the family unit. Research from the traditions of normal family processes, family resources, and family crisis identify specific organizational patterns that contribute to family resiliency.

Flexibility and Connectedness (Cohesion). Flexibility refers to the ability of family members to assume new roles or to change the nature of family roles and responsibilities as needs arise. Connectedness (cohesion) refers to the sense of closeness, of togetherness of family members. These two concepts are important because they enable families to respond to the changes and vicissitudes of life while maintaining an essential sense of relatedness and support within the family. Walsh (2006, p. 83) describes these characteristics as family shock absorbers. Optimally families require a balance of these characteristics so that flexibility is within the context of some stability and connection permits individual family members their own individuality (Beavers & Hampson, 1990; Olson, 1993).

Families need to be flexible to respond to a variety of positive and negative changes. When one parent can no longer carry out her or his accustomed family role due to illness, death, or change in the economic situation, or military deployment, other family members must be able to rise to the challenge and take over these responsibilities in some form or another (Beavers & Hampson, 1990; McCubbin & Patterson, 1983; Robinson, 2000; Walsh, 1998, 2006). When young people from rural families struggling with the farm crisis were asked how their families survived, many described changes in family roles—mothers who went to work outside the home, fathers and sons who took over home responsibilities (Van Hook, 1990a). At the same time, families also need a degree of stability and consistency that helps give life a sense of predictability (Olson, 1993). Family rituals and routines can help create this sense of stability. The challenge is to balance change with stability. Too many demands for change on the family can result in a state of crisis.

Cohesion or connectedness supports family resiliency by enabling families to experience the strength of drawing together to deal with difficult life circumstances (Benzies & Mychasiuk, 2009; McCubbin & Patterson, 1983; Van Hook, 1990a, 1990b; Walsh, 1998, 2006). This experience further strengthens the mutual respect and sense of trustworthiness within families. Cultural messages help shape the nature of the family circle (often including people who are not related by blood) and the degree of connectedness that is viewed as appropriate.

Leadership. Families need leadership within the family to mobilize its resources appropriately (Friedman, 1986, Walsh, 2006). Friedman (1986) describes effective family leadership as occurring "when a family member has the capacity to maintain enough distance from the surrounding emotional whirlwinds so as to be able to keep his or her own life's goals (maintain his or her own horizons and integrity) and can articulate them and follow them despite the family's crisis, and can as a result of this capacity maintain a nonanxious presence in the system" (p. 77).

Families need leadership to provide for nurturing, protecting, and guiding of children and care of older adults and other vulnerable family members. Collaborative efforts among family leaders that involve individuals working together as partners are important (Walsh, 2006). Parents who can work together and provide a united front give stability to children. The style of the leadership varies depending on circumstances and the life stages of the family. While warmth remains an important element of family leadership, the relative firmness required depends on the context and the developmental life stage of family members (Walsh, 1998). Parents with very young children, for example, need to exercise leadership in a different manner than those with adolescents and young adults. Parents of families living in potentially dangerous settings may need to exercise greater firmness than those living in more safe environments. Family leaders within the immediate and extended families provide mentoring opportunities.

Identifying and strengthening such potential for leadership within the family is a key element in successful therapy with families. Such efforts require sensitivity to cultural nuances in terms of gender roles and other messages in terms of appropriate family leadership. Cultural gender issues can become especially sensitive in working with families dealing with cultural change between generations or differences in cultural expectations from their own backgrounds and current community expectations (McGoldrick & Giordano, 1986; Walsh, 1998, 2006).

Coping Process

Communication. Three aspects of communication contribute to effective communication: clarity, open emotional expression, and collaborative problem solving (Walsh, 1998, 2006). Clarity enables family members to communicate accurately in terms of the nature of relationships, family rules, and information. Clear communication during times of crisis is important in enabling families to manage life events in an honest manner.

Emotional sharing involves the ability of families to express, encourage, and accept a range of emotions, to demonstrate an empathic understanding of the feelings of other family members, to accept differences within the family, and to take ownership for their own emotions (Robinson, 2000; Walsh, 1998, pp. 109–110; 2006, pp. 110–115). Cultural patterns strongly shape the specific form that emotional expression takes within families. While some cultures encourage dramatic emotional expressiveness, others support more understated verbal expression for the same degree of emotion. Direct expression is supported in some cultures while indirection regarding sensitive issues is the norm in others. Members within this culture typically understand the cultural norms that might seem puzzling to those from outside the cultural group. The critical issue is one of understanding by family members.

Communication that facilitates collaborative problem solving is critical in identifying effective strategies and mobilizing the appropriate family resources. Effective collaborative efforts rest within the context of mutual respect and trust identified earlier to enable family members to feel safe in their efforts to seek to work together to solve problems.

While family members may be secretive with the goal of protecting other family members, such efforts sometimes lead to additional stress within the family. A seven-year-old boy was referred to me for nightmares, fears of monsters, and excessive worry when his mother became ill. I learned from the mother that the father had been married before and his first wife and mother of several now-grown children had died. When the father remarried and two children were born of the second marriage, the entire family colluded to protect the children from fear of losing their mother. They created a fictitious story about the person whose grave they visited and led the children to believe that all of the children were from the current mother and father. The boy told me his view of what had happened within the family. It was a much more frightening version than the actual family events. When the parents were encouraged and helped to tell the children what had really happened, the boy became markedly less anxious as evidenced by the absence of nightmares and his relaxed response to his mother.

The Rogers family case example at the end of this chapter further illustrates family problems in communication that can create tension. In this family, the parents assumed that they had explained the nature of their complex financial problems, but the children interpreted these events in terms of their own sense of blame because they did not understand the complexity of the situation.

Positive Interactions. As family members struggle to cope, finding ways in which family members can enjoy each other, can express positive feelings toward each other, and find pleasure in their company and activities are important in enabling families to be successful (Karpel, 1986). These positive interactions buffer stress and help provide an important foundation for the family (Benzies & Mychasiuk, 2009). These interactions support family connectedness. When interviewing youth about ways in which their families coped and survived the difficult economic times of the farm crisis, one thirteen-year-old answered immediately that he knew how they had coped and what was important to him—they had gone out and done enjoyable things as a family. His mother reported that they did so to avoid the bill collectors and was surprised at the meaning these events had for their son—but now intended to do so intentionally to help strengthen the family.

Collaborative Problem Solving. As described earlier in terms of communication, when families face inevitable difficult life events, the ability of family members to work together to problem solve supports resiliency (Orthner, Jones-Sanpei, & Williamson, 2004; Robinson, 2000; Walsh, 1998, 2006). Collaborative problem solving is enhanced by the ability of family members to communicate in assessing the problem, identifying and implementing appropriate coping strategies, and drawing on the resources available to the family to address the problem. Effective negotiation strategies enable family members to recognize their differences and find ways to work together toward the mutual goals of the family. Such efforts transcend win-and-lose mind-sets to look at what the family unit needs. Gender differences in styles of communication can complicate such a process in the family (Walsh, 1998, 2006).

Effective conflict resolution skills in addressing issues further support family resiliency. Both conflict avoidance and uncontrollable conflict undermine the family unit (Walsh, 1998, 2006).

Humor. Humor is an important family asset that enables family members to accept the limitations of family members and their efforts. During periods of stress, humor can offer a welcome respite. It can also communicate acceptance and enables interactions to go more smoothly (Beavers & Hampson, 1990; Karpel, 1986; Walsh, 1998, 2006).

Social Support Systems

Resiliency is supported by adequate social support in the form of instrumental assistance (for example, money for rent, child care help) as well as emotional support and a sense of meaning (Fraser, Kirby, & Smokowski, 2004; Greene, 2002; Orthner, Jones-Sanpei, & Williamson, 2004; Walsh, 1998, 2006; Werner & Smith 1992). Social resources are only effective if family members feel comfortable in accessing them. Families thus need to be able to trust their social support network and to feel comfortable in seeking this help. In the process of interviewing rural families who had suffered great losses during the farm crisis of the 1980s, for example, it became very clear that while family, church, and community social support systems were viewed as potential sources of help by some family members, they were viewed as sources of blame and criticism by others (Van Hook, 1990b). As discussed earlier, views regarding HIV/AIDS have reduced the ability of people to turn to the external world for help. Families who were able to regain their children from the child welfare system also described how important it was for them to help others, as they had received help from others (Lietz & Strength, 2011).

Cultural traditions regarding the nature of available and acceptable social support strongly influence the resources available for people. Cultural prescriptions influence, for example, the roles of folk healers, clergy, extended family members, and mental health professionals (McGoldrick & Giordano, 1986; Shobe & Coffman, 2010; Tsai & Yeh, 2011). Issues regarding social support for some racial/cultural groups are discussed in greater length in chapter 4.

Economic Resources

Adequate family resources are important in promoting family resiliency. Families that are on the edge financially or must struggle from day to day to meet the basic needs of the family face additional odds in coping with a variety of life problems. (Benzies & Mychasiuk, 2009; Walsh, 2006). Poverty creates a situation of multiple stressors and inadequate resources to meet family needs (Fraser, Kirby, & Smokowski, 2004). Many of the families seen by social workers are struggling with major financial pressures due to low wages, unemployment, or financial pressures due to illness or other catastrophic expenses. Such financial problems contribute to the pileup of stressors identified as very stressful for families. Conger and Elder (1994), in their extensive study of rural families experiencing financial crisis, document the negative impact of such economic problems on marital and parent-child relationships.

The cushion of a safe place to live, money to hire a babysitter when the pressure gets too intense, and resources for adequate food and medical care can make a profound difference in the ability of families to cope with the ongoing challenges of life. I volunteer at a program for homeless families and watch these parents (usually mothers) try to raise their children in a setting where they must pack up and move to a different place every week. This is such a contrast to the world of my grandchildren with the security and sense of place of their own beds and toys and mementoes. I admire the strength and organizational skills required of these women who are able to maintain effective family life with such challenges.

Community Context

Family poverty also typically occurs within the context of neighborhoods that are disadvantaged in terms of employment opportunities, crime, violence, residential mobility, cultural conflict, broken families, and limited access to resources. Fraser, Kirby, and Smokowski (2004) assert the importance of looking at how poverty impacts the individual, the family, the school, and the neighborhood risk factors that disadvantage children. As a result, families face a compounding of family and community economic risk factors.

Reactivation of Past Events

Current life events can bring back associations of past life events that are viewed as connected in some way to current life circumstances. Activation of these past events can give meaning to current life circumstances. Posttraumatic stress is one extreme and adverse example of such a reactivation. As illustrated in greater detail in the case illustrations in chapter 3, reactivation of past events can influence the family's ability to handle the current situation. Past events can represent evidence of the family's ability to handle difficult times and thus increase current self-efficacy. They can also bring back memories that erode confidence by reminding people of their inability to cope in the past as well as potentially eroding the family members' trust in other family members. The meanings attributed to these past events are also crucial—do they represent learning opportunities or evidence of failure and blame?

Implications for Family Assessment and Interventions

Based on the preceding discussion, approaches that enable families to cope with the demands of life are likely to include the following: addressing the meaning systems created by families that enhance a sense of hopefulness and purpose; supporting organizational structures that provide effective leadership and a balance of flexibility and stability; promoting clear, empathic, and supportive communication patterns; enhancing the positive relationships between family members; promoting the problem-solving ability of family members; improving the social support system accessible to the family; and enhancing the community and economic resources available to the family. Such efforts draw upon a multisystems and multilevel approach to families. The assessment process requires an understanding of the demands placed on the family, the specific elements that are important at this particular time in the life of the family, developmental issues, the nature of the particular family, and the context in identifying both stressors and resources to support the resiliency of the family.

FAMILY CRISIS AND RESILIENCY MODELS

Family crisis theory and related models of resiliency describe the process by which family appraisals, family coping strategies, and resources within the larger community impact the family's ability to cope with potentially stressful life events. Many of the family and community protective factors identified within this tradition echo those previously described within the family strengths tradition and were thus incorporated into the preceding discussion. The emphasis in these family crisis models is on the process that influences how families respond to events, how families become overwhelmed by difficult events, or manage to forge effective ways to respond to them. As described in the following models, this process is frequently cyclical in nature and is influenced by the balance of demands and available resources.

The family crisis model for coping and resiliency grew out of the early work by Rubin Hill and colleagues who examined how families coped with potentially stressful life events in terms of what created disabling crises or enabled families to cope. Hill's model (Family ABCX model) identified the role that A (stressor events), B (family resources), C (family definition of the stressor), and X (crisis) factors played in mediating how families respond to difficult life events (Hill, 1949).

The subsequent double ABCX family crisis model was built on this foundation and highlighted the need to look at how the family's response to the first set of stressor events can in turn affect the family by creating a second round of stressors, resources, and definitions (McCubbin & Patterson, 1983). The family that deals with high medical bills due to the illness of a family member by having one of the parents assume extra work hours can experience stress as the parents find themselves stretched to meet the other needs of family members.

More recently McCubbin and McCubbin (1996) developed the Resiliency Model. It emphasizes the family's relational processes of adaptation and the family's appraisal processes that involve ethnicity and culture and that facilitate the ability to institute new patterns of functioning and achieve harmony while promoting the well-being and development of its members. The Resiliency Model focuses on family change and adaptation over time to understand how the family adapts after the period of potential crisis is completed. While McCubbin, McCubbin, Thompson, and Thompson (1999) describe this model in terms of ethnic families, all families develop a culture that influences how they experience the world. As a result, although the meaning of these elements for specific families will vary, the framework is useful as a basic outline of the processes and elements involved.

The Resiliency Model has two discernible phases: adjustment (minor changes) and adaptation (more major changes). The following information is drawn from the work of McCubbin, McCubbin, Thompson, and Thompson (1999) in their introduction to research on the resiliency of Native American and other immigrant families. Figure 1 represents this model in terms of Round One—the adjustment phase—and Round Two—the adaptation phase.

Adjustment Phase

The adjustment phase involves *minor* changes that the family institutes to address stressful life events and the series of interacting components involved (McCubbin, Thompson, Thompson, Elver, & McCubbin, 1998). The actions of the family can result in outcomes that vary along a continuum from positive (bonoadjustment), in which established patterns of functioning are maintained, to the extreme of maladjustment, a family crisis that demands changes in the established pattern of functioning (McCubbin, Thompson, Thompson, Elver, & McCubbin, 1998). The nature of the outcome depends on the nature of the event, family circumstances that influence vulnerability, the organizational pattern of families, the belief systems of family members, and the coping strategies of families. The following outlines these elements that influence the adjustment phase. While the model assumes that the first set of responses represent more minor changes, some families either choose to or are forced by circumstances to respond with major changes.

First, the *stressor (A)* places demands on the family. The negative impact of this stressor depends on several aspects: the extent to which it threatens the family unit's stability (for example, potential divorce), disrupts the ways in which the family unit functions (for example, severe illness of the mother of young children), or places major demands on and depletes the family resources (for example, unemployment) (McCubbin, Thompson, Thompson, Elver, & McCubbin, 1998).

Second, *family vulnerability (V) pileup of stressors and family life cycle changes.* Vulnerability is the fragile interpersonal and organizational condition of the family system. A pileup of stressor events (e.g., loss of a job, unwanted move) or difficulty associated with life cycle changes can increase the family's vulnerability (McCubbin, Thompson, Thompson, Elver, & McCubbin, 1998). A family might be experiencing the challenge of the loss of a job while needing to assume greater financial responsibility and care for an older parent with serious health problems or a heart attack by the husband while the wife is dealing with the health problems of her parents. This concept is similar to additive stressors described earlier.

Third, *family typology of established patterns of functioning (T)* represents the predictable pattern by which the family copes. Families whose patterns include a balance of flexibility and cohesion (family bonding) are best able to handle difficult life events (McCubbin, Thompson, Thompson, Elver, & McCubbin, 1998).

FIGURE 1. Adjustment and Adaptation Processes

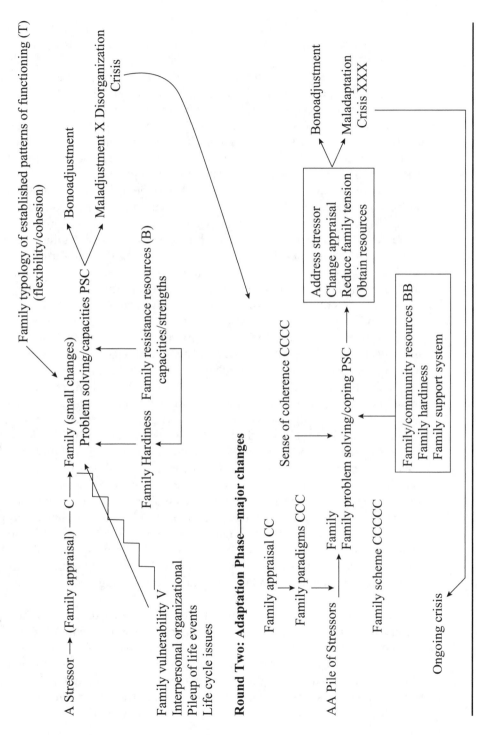

Fourth, *family resistance resources (B) include capabilities and strengths.* These resources enable the family to manage the stressor without creating major changes in the patterns of functioning. Important family resources were described in the preceding discussion and are included in table 1 (McCubbin, McCubbin, Thompson, & Thompson, 1999, p. 8).

Fifth, *family appraisal of the stressor* includes the family's definition of the stressors in terms of the seriousness of the stressor for the family. The family's schemas of life strongly influence how they perceive specific events. As a result, the meaning to the individuals involved can be quite different from what an outsider might imagine the stress would be.

When interviewing farm families who had gone through difficult times during the farm crisis of the 1980s in Iowa, one question related to how much change they had experienced. One farmer who was still living on the same family farm and raising hogs, but now under contract rather than independently, described his situation as representing the highest change possible. Another man who had given up his farm, moved to another state, and was now managing the mechanical equipment of the science building at a college described the change he had experienced at a very low level. The second man described his work in both settings as that of a manager. As would not be surprising, the level of current stress reported by both men also reflected the change that they had experienced, with the symptoms of stress for the first man much higher than for the second man.

Sixth, *family problem solving and coping (PSC).* Problem solving is a critical step. Some important abilities that can help families include organizing a stressor into manageable components, identifying alternative courses of action to deal with each of these components, initiating steps to resolve the issues involved, and developing and cultivating the patterns of problem-solving communication needed to solve the family problems. Coping refers to a wide range of behaviors that the family uses to cope. Some of the tasks include "maintaining and strengthening the family as a whole, maintaining the emotional stability and well-being of members, obtaining or using family and community resources to manage the situation, and initiating efforts to resolve family hardships created by the stressor" (McCubbin, McCubbin, Thompson, & Thompson, 1999, p. 9). Given the many different threats potentially facing families, families benefit from developing a rich repertoire of coping strategies (Friedman, 1986).

Family hardiness helps to mitigate the impact of stress on families because it influences how the life event is appraised and the family's ability to cope with it. Hardiness is "characterized by a sense of control over the outcome of life events and hardships, a view of change as beneficial and growth producing, and an active rather than passive orientation in adjusting to and managing stressful situations" (McCubbin, Thompson, Thompson, Elver, & McCubbin, 1998, p. 54). Family problem solving, communication, and available community social support contribute to family hardiness (McCubbin, Thompson, Thompson, Elver, & McCubbin, 1998).

A family can respond to these series of stressors, family patterns, resources, appraisals, and problem-solving efforts in ways that promote effective coping (bonoadjustment) or that create potential tension, stress, and distress (maladjustment). When a family experiences an imbalance in the demands placed on the family compared with the available resources, a family experiences stress, eventually reaching the point of *disorganization and a crisis for the family (X)*. Families experience a crisis when they are unable to restore their stability and experience a state of disorganization within the family system. Families initially seek to cope by making small adjustments; however, when these are not adequate to address the situation, major changes in the family patterns can be required at this stage in the process (McCubbin, Thompson, Thompson, Elver, & McCubbin, 1998). Efforts to begin to make these changes mark the beginning of the adaptation phase (Round Two).

Family Adaptation Phase

Family adaptation refers to the *major* changes that a family may need to make to cope with the demands facing it. The family adaptation phase of the Resiliency Model examines how the family seeks to cope following the crisis (McCubbin, Thompson, Thompson, Elver, & McCubbin, 1998). Similar to the double ABCX family crisis model, these processes include a second round of life events, appraisals, family and community resources, and coping behaviors. The family's response to the crisis is influenced by the interaction among a series of components: the pileup (AA) of demands on the family system created by the situation, the family life cycle, or unresolved strains in interaction with the family's new way of functioning. These interact with the family resources (BB) that can include support from the extended family and community and the family's appraisal and coping strategies.

Family Appraisal Process

Several layers influence how family members interpret an event. The family begins by appraising the situation (CC) in terms of the available resources and demands (e.g., does the family have adequate medical insurance to cover the cost of a needed surgery for the parent). Such appraisal interacts with the family's more general paradigms (CCC)—basic beliefs pertaining to a specific area of life (e.g., health is all important and the families do everything that they can do to help). These paradigms are shaped by the family's sense of coherence (CCCC), a worldview that gives a sense of order to life (e.g., there is a purpose for everything that happens in life) (McCubbin,

Thompson, Thompson, Elver, & McCubbin, 1998). The family also appraises the situation in terms of the family's schema (CCCCC)—the shared values, beliefs, and expectations of the family. These beliefs legitimate family coping efforts and are very difficult to change (e.g., the entire extended family bands together when one person in the family has a need). These appraisals interact with "the family's problem-solving and coping repertoire (PSC)" to influence how the family adapts to the crisis situation (McCubbin, Thompson, Thompson, Elver, & McCubbin, 1998) (e.g., asking for help from members of the extended family to help pay for this surgery). The cultural heritage of families profoundly influences this appraisal process by shaping the meaning of life events, the legitimate ways to cope, and the nature of the coping repertoire of families (for example, calling on extended family to help is appropriate, relying on spiritual healers can be valuable). It can also give a sense of meaning to life events.

Demands

Pileup of demands (AA) recognizes that families are frequently facing more than one stressful event—the additive events described earlier. These events can relate to the current situation, issues of life transitions (for example, divorce, death in the family, job loss), earlier life experiences, long-standing family strains, family efforts to cope, and lack of clarity regarding how to cope (McCubbin, Thompson, Thompson, Elver, & McCubbin, 1998). Such a pileup of stressful life events is certainly common in the families seeking help from social workers. These families might be struggling simultaneously with economic loss, difficulties in housing, and the school adjustment problems of a child, or persons in caregiver roles might themselves be contending with health problems of their own.

Family resources (BB) can belong to the family unit, individual family members, and the community. Some personal resources of individual family members include traits identified earlier: intelligence, appropriate knowledge and skills, personality characteristics (e.g., sense of humor), physical, spiritual, and emotional health of members, sense of mastery, self-esteem, and ethnicity and cultural identity (McCubbin, McCubbin, Thompson, & Thompson, 1999). In contrast, weakening of self-esteem can be a source of vulnerability of family members facing a pileup of stress that threatens mastery (p. 19), and the challenges of this situation can also erode the self-esteem of family members.

Family system resources are listed in table 1 and in the discussion regarding family protective factors. Family hardiness here refers to the internal strengths and durability of the family unit. As discussed earlier, it refers to the family's sense that they have some control over the outcome. Family hardiness serves as a buffer by mediating the effects of stresses and demands.

Social support (BBB) can include several dimensions: (1) emotional support that leads family members to believe they are cared for, (2) esteem support that conveys to family members that they are respected and valued, and (3) network support that leads family members to believe they belong to a network that can offer mutual support and understanding. Social support can be emotional as well as instrumental (specific forms of help). Cultural context influences the social support process.

Family problem solving and coping (PSC) strategies can help by addressing the specific stressor, obtaining additional resources, managing the reduction of the family tension, and/or changing the meaning of the life event. Coping can further be identified in terms of specific coping behaviors (e.g., talk about ways to reduce family expenses and reduce eating out when facing a salary reduction) and general family patterns (e.g., communicate in a problem-solving manner about family problems and take actions based on the family discussion). These behaviors and patterns can be contrasted with another family in which the patterns are to hide problems and take risks to address them (do not discuss the cut in salary with others and purchase a number of lottery tickets in hopes of a big payoff to solve the problem). As part of the ongoing coping process, families need to find ways by which these new patterns become a natural part of the family lifestyle.

In the adaptation process, new family patterns may need to be established in one or more critical areas of family functioning: rules, routines and traditions, coalitions in the family unit; patterns of communication; and relationships to the broader community (McCubbin, McCubbin, Thompson, & Thompson, 1999, p. 18). As a result, a family whose original rules established gender patterns by which the mother stayed home with the children while the father worked outside of the home may need to adjust these rules when the plant in which the father worked moves away from the area while employment possibilities for the mother exist in the community. Families in which the typical communication was through the mother will have to change these patterns when the mother has a stroke and can no longer serve as the "family switchboard," thus requiring the father to assume an important role of family communicator. Families who were able to cope without asking for help from the community might need to reassess the situation so that they can turn for the appropriate type of community support.

Family adaptation process, bonadaptation, and maladaptation, and crisis (XX) family adaptation can thus include changing the appraisal of the situation in ways that promote coping and support needed changes, addressing the specific stressor, and making needed changes within the family functioning. If families do not adapt satisfactorily (maladaptation) they return to a crisis situation and must find other ways to adapt (McCubbin, McCubbin, Thompson, & Thompson, 1999, p. 33).

Case Examples

The following is a very sad story of desperate attempts to cope and save a family that demand a high price from family members. It illustrates ways in which coping strategies that are designed to save some family members, and thereby the family, create additional problems for others and in turn for the family as a unit. It also illustrates the role of cultural and community context throughout time as well as the current life span of the family in shaping people's view of life events and thus the choices that they make. Unlike the next case example, it does not come with a happy ending despite the love of parents for their child.

> The Stern family story began in northern Europe prior to World War II. In the context of facing the stressors of the persecution of Jewish families, members of the mother's and the father's families left Europe for Israel—the place of refuge for Jewish families—the place "flowing with milk and honey." This was a fortunate decision because those who did not leave were murdered in the Holocaust of World War II. Mr. and Mrs. Stern met in Israel and married in their early twenties. They grieved the family members they had lost but were determined to create a "good life" in Israel. The family was Conservative Jewish and observed the rituals of the religious tradition.
>
> The first years were good for the couple and two boys were born. They then rejoiced in the birth of a daughter. Tragically, the family soon experienced their first major stressor—the death of their daughter of an illness (A). The family banded together to cope (PSC) with this tragic event. It was particularly difficult to cope with because they shared the view of Israel as a place of refuge from pain and suffering (C) but it was still something that they could cope with (family hardiness) resulting in a bonoadjustment. The family then rejoiced in the birth of two more girls.
>
> When the youngest child was four years old, tragedy struck again. The older daughter died suddenly of yet another illness—bringing back the sadness of the loss of the first child as well of this daughter (AA). This second death was too much for this family's coping capacities to match. Again the context of the tragedy in the land of refuge from death (CC) shared by this family and other refugees caused further pain. As indicated, the death of the first child contributed to the family's vulnerability (V). The mother was especially devastated and unable to attend the funeral of the daughter or to function. The father and the sons feared for her sanity and life (CC) and took desperate measures to protect her and the family (paradigm CCC regarding the value of the mother and the family). All mention of the daughter was taboo and all pictures that were taken during her lifetime were destroyed (PSC). The family coped by trying to act as if the death (and also the life) had never occurred (addressing the stressors—trying to bury its existence). The family did not reach out to other members of the community (BB) because this would mean acknowledging the existence and death of

the child. While this method of coping was feasible for the parents and sons, it created a great hardship for the youngest daughter who later revealed that she thought that she was to blame (CC) for her sister's death. Developmentally she was at the magical thinking age and viewed her sometimes angry feelings toward her sister as the cause of death. She kept these thoughts to herself because no one was allowed to talk about the deceased child (PSC).

The younger child then began to develop emotional problems (AA) and the mother found living in Israel carried too many reminders of tragedy (AA) (maladjustment—crisis). As a result, the family made a major adaptation— they left Israel for New York City where they moved to a Jewish community in the city. They continued their coping through the taboo of talking about the daughter who had died. While the move helped relieve some of the family members' pain, the family problems and the adjustment to a new setting created further (AA) problems for the younger daughter. Her emotional problems reached the point that she had to be hospitalized (yet another source of stress for the family [AA]). It was during this time that the child revealed to her counselor her interpretation of the death of her sister.

The mental health staff then presented to the parents the importance of talking to their daughter about the sister to help free her from her sense of guilt. The family (father and sons) appraised this suggested way of coping with great fear because they worried that it would destroy the mother (CCC). Gradually they began to believe that this was something that they should do and the mother was able to reassure them that she had the strength to do so (change the appraisal—a glimpse of hardiness). The family gathered their courage to begin this conversation with their daughter (PSC). Despite the family's fears about the mother's fragility, she did not fall apart with these conversations. Sadly, the next real burden this family faced (AAA) was the youngest daughter's ongoing serious illness.

Despite the family's efforts to address the stressor experienced by their daughter and to use the resources of the mental health system (BB), the young girl did not respond and continued to be quite ill. Given the great burden facing this family and wishing not to compound their burden, the mental health staff stressed with the family members how much they had tried to do for their daughter, despite the high emotional cost involved for everyone. Despite their fears, they had done everything the mental health staff had asked of them and had shown their love for their daughter.

A second family story illustrates ways in which although family members move away from the family, they remain connected by strong emotional ties, and life events of members continue to impact others. Family members sometimes make major changes as a first line of response to a stressful event. In contrast to the Stern family, in this situation, only a small intervention on the part of the counselor enabled the family members to access their resources after many years of hurt and alienation.

The Martin family lived in a small town with close ties among community members. The culture of the town was very socially conservative (with consequent high expectations for families holding leadership positions). The father was the school principal, his wife worked as a secretary. Their son and daughters were in high school and middle school. As a high school student, Mike "made his girlfriend pregnant" (his words) (stressor A). He felt that he had let his father down (appraisal C) and left town without marrying his girlfriend (coping—crisis X). Following the family culture, the issue was addressed by silence on the part of all parties.

In an attempt to redeem himself, he joined the military (PSC). His father had previously served in the military and the family had been proud of his contribution. At this time, the family experienced another blow that further distanced Mike from his family—his father died suddenly of a heart attack (AA). Mike appraised this event further as another reason for guilt that he had created such stress for his father and the death of a hope that he could ever make amends and a connection with his father (CC). In his guilt, he did not feel that he could come home for the funeral and face his family and the community (PSC). He also coped with his second stressor (AA) and his appraisal of this life event (CC) by beginning to drink heavily (PSC—negative coping strategy). His mother in turn appraised (CC) his absence as not caring enough about his father to come to the funeral.

As a result of his heavy drinking, he was dismissed from the military (a further stressor accompanied by additional appraisals of failure). He returned to civilian life and married but this marriage ended in failure as a result of his drinking (further stressors AA)—only digging him further into the pit of guilt and sense of failure (CC).

After a few years, Mike took an important step to go to substance abuse rehabilitation and was successful in breaking his cycle of addiction (PSC—finally successful coping). This gave him hope (appraisal CC) that he might be able to make amends with his family. He returned to the small town where his mother and sisters were still living (PSC coping) and contacted the local mental health center for help (PSC).

Mike and his family now had the opportunity to alter the many appraisals that had contributed to vulnerability (V) in this family and furthered the cycle of crises. At his request, the counselor facilitated a meeting between the mother and Mike so that Mike could finally explain his great love and admiration for his father—it was this love that made him leave town, that made him try to make amends by going into the military, that made him feel so guilty that he could not bring himself to come to the funeral. This new way of coping (PSC) made a profound impact on the mother's appraisal of the situation (and subsequently on the sisters'). The family was finally able to cope by speaking openly and honestly about their hurts and their love (PSC). Together the family visited the grave site of the father (PSC) as a step in this healing process. In this process, the family drew upon the family resources (BB) of abiding love of the mother for her son and the son's genuine love for his family, as well as the services of the mental health program. In so doing, the family was able to change their previous ways (silence, distant hurt) of relating. As a result, the family was able to build on this to end the ongoing cycle of crises (XXX) and create new and healing relationships (bonoadjustment). Mike was able to continue living in the community where he established himself as a respected member. When his younger sister became very ill, he was able to be a strong source of support for her and his mother. He also volunteered to serve as a mentor for other young people who were struggling. Instead of running from the issue of faith that had represented guilt to him earlier, he became active in his family's church, which became another source of support for him. As a reflection of the respect that he had earned in the community, he was subsequently elected to a leadership role within the church.

FAMILY ILLUSTRATIONS

The following three family situations represent ways in which families respond to crisis events in ways that reflect their appraisals of the event and their coping strategies. Their appraisals and coping strategies are influenced by culture, context, family patterns, and life cycle issues. While these families come from different cultural backgrounds and are facing different problems, all illustrate the sense of "we" that can influence the nature of the stressors as well as the resources available. This motif also helps guide appropriate responses to the family in ways that support resiliency.

The following family also indicates the complex role that family appraisals (in terms of the family as a whole and individual members) can play because valuing family and family members created both distress and the resources that led to healing.

This family illustrates ways in which relatively small changes (adjustment) can make profound changes in the family's ability to cope.

> Mrs. Rogers called a neighboring mental health clinic because their fifteen-year-old daughter, Joan, was suffering from bulimia. She also added that her husband was suffering from severe depression and perhaps suicidal thoughts but that he would not seek help for himself. She also indicated that the family was experiencing serious financial difficulties that were contributing to his depression. The Rogers family is the family mentioned previously in terms of the junior high boy explaining why they have come for help. As indicated previously, when the young people were asked why they had come the boy said that they were having problems as a family and had come to find ways they could work on them. The parents described the financial problems they were having with the family farm and said that they thought that these problems were bothering their teenage daughter but not

their son. At this the son chimed in that they were bothering him because he felt that he was to blame for them. This comment astonished his parents, who thought that they had explained things to the children. The boy said that the parents had bought him a used moped that had cost $250 and this money had helped cause their problems. With this comment, the daughter interrupted to say that she was the one who was really to blame because in addition to her moped, her parents had also paid for her and her friend to go to the movies. Although the parents thought that they had communicated the nature of the problem to their children, clearly the children did not understand the complexities of a situation involving devaluation of land and changes in prices due to market conditions. The first step thus was to help the parents explain the situation in ways that were understandable to the children and reduce their sense of guilt.

When the social worker met separately with the parents, both expressed the burdens that they were experiencing. The father described his sense of despair and failure because he was putting his family through such a difficult time. The mother told of her sense of failure because she had not been able to help all the family members be happy. When the social worker met individually with the daughter, Joan, she forcefully expressed her anger that her father was being treated so unfairly by life. She described her father as a person who worked long hours for his family and was a wonderful man and father. Joan said she wanted to tell her father what a wonderful father he was and how much she loved him and how proud she was of him but did not know how to do so. After the social worker said she would help her, they returned to the family as a whole. With little prompting, Joan began to tell her father how much he meant to her, what a good father he was, and how much she loved him. Father and daughter then spoke of their love for each other.

When the family was seen the next week, the mood within the family had improved remarkably. The father indicated that although their family's financial situation had not changed at all, he felt like a ton had been lifted off his shoulders now that he knew that the children did not feel that he was a failure. He was no longer feeling depressed. The children in turn also felt relieved of a great burden. Family members' love toward each other and sense of cohesion as a family were no longer burdens but had become resources that enabled the family to mobilize to cope with an external problem. The family members felt energized to address the problems without the burdens of guilt that had created such distress.

The family had a strong sense of the value of the family and was characterized as having a relational perspective. While a potential strength and protective factor for this family, family members were so burdened down by their sense of guilt that they had let the family down, that this relational perspective initially represented a burden (risk) for family members. The situation was further compounded by another series of risk factors. The complexity of the economic situation had taxed the family's communication patterns (misunderstanding by the children of the nature of the problem). The wider social and economic context was creating economic hardships for the family. The father's appraisal that he had failed the family had diminished his ability to exercise effective leadership (his current depression and sense of failure). The social context facing many farmers was also an important external risk factor.

The family also had a set of important protective resources that were unleashed when the family members were helped to communicate more effectively. A clearer style of communication between parents and children regarding the nature of their problem helped reduce the burden of guilt experienced by the children. The daughter's statement to her father that he had not failed the family and instead was a good father reached his core value of being a good father and relieved him of his sense of guilt. With these changes, family members were able to enlist their loyalty to their family, their hope for change, their family communication patterns, and to gain a sense of self-efficacy in terms of their family's ability to handle their current situation.

The following situation illustrates the impact of family life cycle transitions (childhood to adolescence, refugees in a new country), family appraisals, family connectedness, and culture in both the family story as well as specific risk and protective factors. These life events required the family to make more substantial changes.

The Lo family came to the United States as refugees from the Communist government in Vietnam. They had lived previously in a small community in South Vietnam before fleeing the country and living in a refugee camp in Thailand for some time. They were currently living in a small community in rural Iowa where they were one of several such families in the area. The traditional authority role of the father in the family had been substantially jeopardized because he had hurt his back and was unable to find work that did not require heavy lifting. His poor English-language skills limited his employment possibilities to manual labor. Several of the older children were now grown and had moved to neighboring communities but remained in close contact with the family. Two teenagers (a boy and girl) were currently living at home.

The social worker from the local mental health center was called by the hospital staff and the church sponsor of the family because their high school daughter Song became severely ill at school caused by an overdose of pills. Song then had to be hospitalized. Such an event would represent a crisis in any family but the situation was even more layered with meaning for the Lo family. The parents knew that Song had taken the pills but had panicked because they were afraid that the whole family would be deported back to the refugee camp and, even worse, perhaps back to Vietnam where they would be imprisoned by the Communist government for their cooperation with the United States government. As they appraised the situation, the action of the daughter placed the entire family in grave danger. Feeling desperate and not knowing what else to do, they tried to cover up the event by insisting that the older brother bring her to school and that neither of the young people reveal what had happened. The parents' fear also prevented them from seeking help from the church sponsor who had been an important resource in many other areas of life.

Fortunately, when the social worker met with the entire family (including the grown children), she was able to learn about the family's frightening interpretation of the situation and to correct their misunderstanding of the risk involved. She assured the family that the daughter's action would not cause them to be deported and that the important thing was to make sure that Song received the help that she needed. Song's attempt at suicide was defined in the context of teenage suicide being a serious problem in the United States and that Song's action would be understood in this way by the school and the church sponsor.

Song had previously told the worker how her action had been in response to feeling caught between two contradictory alternatives that related to her obligations to a friend and her family. These alternatives and the situation reflected the influence of the two diverse cultures on her and the family as well as developmental issues. Song was a close friend with another teenager from a Vietnamese family living in a neighboring community. During their previous life in Vietnam, the family and community ties were very close and the behavior of the young people was closely regulated by shared family and community codes. In the United States these families were scattered throughout the area and were isolated both from their previous communities in Vietnam and the support of their fellow families. The families were struggling with a new problem—an increasing number of young girls becoming pregnant as young teenagers. Song felt torn because her parents had told her that she should tell them if her friend was going to do something that could cause the friend to become pregnant. Her friend had made her promise that she would not tell her parents. Caught between these sets of contradictory demands created by parents and her friend, Song did not know what to do when she learned that her friend was going to run away with her boyfriend. In the context of this dilemma she overdosed on the pills. Given the cultural context of the family, she had betrayed her family in several ways. In addition to creating the fear of deportation, she had also violated cultural codes of family honor and name because both the important institutions of the school and the sponsoring church became involved in the situation and the family felt a great sense of shame. These organizations represented the support system for the family and the family feared loss of support from them. The social worker thus helped Song apologize to her family for bringing shame to the family as well as communicate to her family the stress that she was experiencing due to this situation and some other circumstances reflective of the cultural transition of the family from Vietnam to rural Iowa. The family members were able to listen to Song in an empathic manner and to enlist the social worker as a cultural interpreter and ongoing counselor for their daughter and sister. The older siblings endorsed this step in their ongoing role of support system for their parents and Song. The family crisis was thus redefined both in terms of the consequences and potential resources in a way that enabled Song and her family members to problem solve and cope in a more effective manner.

The Lo family has important protective and risk factors within the family unit and the wider community. The family illustrates important issues related to transition—coming to the United States as refugees and children moving into the teenage years. Along with protection from potential destruction in their home of origin, the transition as refugees from their life in Vietnam to the United States came with a set of risk and protective factors.

Lack of facility in English and problems in finding appropriate employment have diminished parental authority. The cultural codes that supported parental authority in their home community were also weakened. The combination of parental misunderstanding of their current context and consequent appraisal that their daughter's behavior would lead to the family's deportation represented a major risk factor that led to the parents' decision to send her to school. As a teenager, Song's commitment both to her family and her friend along with the inability to communicate this with others within the family created painful turmoil that pushed her beyond her coping skills. The situation escalated to the point that the parents experienced that their family honor and ability to access help had been damaged in terms of the community support system.

In the face of these risk factors, there were also important protective features. There is a strong commitment to the family as a unit by the wider family circle, as evidenced by the willingness of the grown children to attend a family session and offer their support. While lacking the coping skills to negotiate the situation effectively, Song takes very seriously her commitment to her friends and her family. When the family was able to understand that they need not fear deportation, they were able to be understanding and supportive of Song. In addition to several other Vietnamese families in the area, the family had a network of community members who were concerned about the family (the school, the church members, the health care system, the mental health program) and willing to provide the needed help.

The following family situation illustrates the impact of life cycles changes in terms of family transitions and the complex role of the extended family and the community as well as the cultural context.

The Rodriguez family owns and operates a successful neighborhood restaurant that features Caribbean food. The restaurant has become a favorite family eating spot in the community for people from a variety of backgrounds. People appreciate the delicious food at reasonable prices and the welcome they receive from family members, especially the host Mr. R. The R family members who make this business possible include the mother (Mrs. R, age 70) and father (Mr. R, age 73), who moved to Florida from Puerto Rico some time ago, along with their adult sons and their wives, their adult daughter and her husband, and their teenage and college-age grandchildren. While all the family members have been involved, the primary force behind the business has been the parents, who have continued to make the major decisions. Their ongoing presence in the restaurant as host and hostess has helped create and maintain their clientele.

The R family is a tight-knit family group. The parents came to Florida with experience in the restaurant business in Puerto Rico. Several years after coming to Florida they were able to begin their own business. Mr. R tended to be the decision maker in the business while Mrs. R was the center of organizing the family. Together they created a context that facilitated a family business. As the children became older, they started helping in the family business. All of their children have graduated from high school and had some advanced course work at the area community college. The grandchildren contributed as they grew older and as their school responsibilities permitted. While all family businesses have their share of family conflict, under the direction of Mr. R the family unit has been able to work together to help the family grow with minimal tensions. Although all adults felt free to express their concerns and make suggestions in a respectful manner toward other members of the family, when issues arose that needed a final decision within the business, Mr. R always had the last word.

The R family is also part of a larger Puerto Rican community in terms of friends and joint efforts to help promote the community. Mr. R earned a place of respect and leadership within their community and is turned to when issues arise within the community. The family has also been active within their local religious community as their business responsibilities permitted.

The R family and the business are now facing a crisis because Mr. R experienced a major stroke that has severely affected his speech and has paralyzed one side. This health event has had a demoralizing effect on Mr. R, who is struggling with his current disabilities. Mrs. R has been by his side throughout the entire ordeal. She has also been able to turn to the extended family, who have been taking turns spending time with their father and mother. Other members of the Puerto Rican community have also come to the aid of the family. The family now has to face the reality that even with extensive rehabilitation services, it is very unlikely that Mr. R will be able to regain full use of his speech and his physical abilities. In the meantime, Mrs. R will not be able to provide the necessary care for her husband when he leaves the hospital and the rehabilitation program. In the context of a strong commitment to family responsibility, family members are wrestling with the issue of how to make sure that Mr. R receives the care he needs and that Mrs. R is not overwhelmed with these responsibilities. At the same time, the family members are beginning to recognize how much Mr. R was responsible for the success of the business through his wise decision making and his congenial hosting. Mr. R had assumed that he would be able to occupy this role for years to come and had not prepared his sons and daughter to take over these responsibilities. The sons and daughter are struggling with their commitment to the family and the family business as well as the new roles that they are having to assume without either their father or mother as arbitrators or facilitators in this process.

The Rodriguez family is facing a very serious transition in terms of the life cycle of the family. Mr. R has been the leader of the family and its associated business and the wider community. His role has been important both to the family and to Mr. R. In facing this difficult transition, the family has some important risk and protective factors.

The Rodriguez family has a strong sense of commitment to the family unit and the parents. Family members evidenced loyalty and affection to family members. The mother is committed to her husband. Their grown children are invested in helping both their father and their mother. They have demonstrated this by being there to help their parents. In terms of social support, they also have a community that is committed to helping this family and cultural codes that support helping older family members. Family members have been able to use respectful forms of communication to discuss issues related to the family and the business. The family had developed a set of coping skills that had served them well in terms of the family and the business. The family has created an adequate economic basis for the family. Family members have been involved in the religious community (yet to be explored is the meaning and potential support offered here). The family has a history of strength that can potentially be a source of hope and support.

The significant transition event (Mr. R's stroke) has also created an important set of risk factors. Mr. R had been the key leader of the family, especially related to the family business. He had assumed that he would be able to continue this role and had not prepared others to assume part of this responsibility. As a result, family members have discovered that they have not developed the coping skills to handle difficult situations without the leadership of their father. Mrs. R will not be able to provide care for Mr. R without extensive help from others. Mr. R has become demoralized as a result of his stroke and change in life circumstances.

The preceding examples illustrated ways in which cultural and social contexts influence how families perceive the meaning of situations and legitimate coping strategies. Chapter 4 discusses issues related to culture in specific cultural groups as well as family organizational structures. Families also experience problems (e.g., illness, economic hardship, trauma) as illustrated in subsequent case illustrations and chapter 14. Sometimes these challenges are reflected in the problems experienced by children in the family.

SUMMARY

Based on the literature on the resiliency of individuals and families, themes emerge in terms of what promotes resiliency. These themes include family appraisals of life events and their own capacity for coping, organizational and process qualities of the family, and the support system available to the family. These themes provide guidelines for assessing families and developing prevention and intervention strategies. Combining an assessment of risk and vulnerability with strengths and areas in which resiliency can be promoted can help family members address the variety of issues that they are currently facing as well as future life challenges.

Self-appraisals that encourage family members to view themselves as capable of dealing with a problem and the family unit as a resource for change promote resiliency. Paradigms and schemas that contain messages that permit family members to draw upon appropriate problem-solving skills are important. Also needed are family organizational patterns that incorporate effective leadership, are adaptable, and provide members with a sense of belonging and stability through cohesion and dependable routines. Clear family communication enables people to support each other and problem solve effectively. Climates of trust and mutual respect support family members. Families need the skills that enable them to solve a wide variety of life problems. Social networks within the community that can offer appropriate types of social support are also invaluable. The presence of educational and economic opportunities within the community promotes resiliency, and the absence of this represents a risk factor. Cultural issues help shape how events are experienced and the coping strategies that are appropriate.

Understanding what contributes to resiliency offers a guide in assessing families and in developing prevention and intervention strategies that support the resiliency of families. Such an approach recognizes the reality of the risk factors and the stressors facing families while it searches for protective factors and ways to enhance resiliency. In view of the many interactive features that contribute to resiliency within families, it is useful to be able to draw upon a variety of models of assessing and working with families to strengthen families facing a variety of vulnerabilities and situations. Some important models include those that address ways in which family members interpret and create their stories of life events, that promote linkages between family members and the social network and community resources, that help family members learn and practice new problem-solving skills, that promote effective communication patterns within family members, that support family efforts to have effective leadership patterns within the family, that promote trust and mutual respect within family members, and that increase self-understanding among family members in such a way that promotes genuine family relationships. While the emphasis has been upon the processes that promote resiliency within the family, clearly families do not live in isolation. The community plays a role in terms of vulnerability factors and support systems. Since community plays a role in family vulnerability and support, interventions that address the community context, for example, the promotion of safe neighborhoods, the provision of adequate and affordable housing, and the implementation of wage scales that can realistically support families, are also crucial.

DISCUSSION QUESTIONS

Discuss the pathways from poverty to decreased resiliency.

In what ways can adversity contribute to increased resiliency?

How does age serve as both a protective or a risk factor depending on the circumstances?

How do beliefs influence the impact of a potential stressor and contribute to either risk or protective factors?

How does the phrase "the last straw" fit in with discussions regarding resiliency?

How does the reactivation of past events serve as a risk or a protective factor depending on the circumstances?

2

Setting the Stage for Work with Families

Development of the Therapeutic Alliance

The family counselor serves as a catalyst for change. The role of the social worker or other family counselor is to help create change within the family system and its relationship with the wider context. The terms *social worker, family therapist,* and *counselor* will be used interchangeably in the following discussion when referring to the role of the social worker as a family counselor or family therapist. The social worker works through a therapeutic alliance to become a collaborative partner with the family in order to meet their goals. Defining the counselor in this way recognizes that the role of the family therapist is always quite limited and the family occupies center stage no matter how long the counseling effort. Pressure for brief treatment in the current world of managed care makes this limitation an even more present reality. Given the context of the life of the family, the few hours spent with the counselor pale in comparison to the time family members spend with each other and with other important people in their lives. As a result, taking a resiliency-based approach to engaging with family members serves as a way of enhancing the strengths that family members bring to the counseling effort as well as recognizing the risk factors that they face. The family and its support system take center stage while the counselor plays a supporting role.

Prior to beginning with the family, the counselor needs to prepare by looking at the available information about the family, for example, the nature of the presenting problem, gender, ages, and cultural background, because these can potentially shape the process of joining as well as subsequent treatment. At the same time, the counselor must be open to recognizing the unique nature of this family.

There are two crucial steps in creating an effective working relationship with families. First, it is important to develop a *therapeutic alliance*— engaging or joining with family members and the family as a whole. The process of joining refers to actions of the therapist to create an alliance by which two systems join forces in family counseling—the family and its extended members and the social worker within the agency setting—*to work together toward a mutual goal.* If family members are going to entrust their family's pain, hopes, fears, troubles, and dreams to the counseling endeavor represented by this social worker/agency system, they need to trust the counselor's competence, ability to understand, and concern for the welfare of their family. The situation is further complicated for many families who are referred to social workers because they have been sent by others who view the family as having a problem.

The second step is *to create the climate and structure* for the counseling process. Family members frequently come to counseling with limited understanding of what is to take place or perhaps with misunderstandings based on the media, comments from others, the referral source, and previous experiences with other organizations. In order for an alliance to be effective, there needs to be clarity and understanding regarding the respective roles and guidelines for how these roles are to be carried out by the parties involved. Adequate structure in these sessions is important in the success of this process.

DEVELOPING THE THERAPEUTIC ALLIANCE

The term *joining* as used in family therapy refers to the actions taken by the counselor in the engagement process. The concept of joining recognizes that creating a therapeutic alliance requires actions on the part of the counselor and that building trust is a process. Joining requires sensitivity to the nature of the family. "To join a family system, the therapist must accept the family's organization and style and blend with them. He must experience the family's transactional patterns and the strength of these patterns. That is, he should feel a family member's pain at being excluded, or scapegoated, and his pleasure at being loved, depended on, or otherwise confirmed within the family" (Minuchin, 1974, p. 123).

In joining, it is crucial to remember that the interview process is a two-way one. While social workers are assessing the family and its members, the members are also interviewing and assessing the counselor. When dealing with families, there are multiple interviews occurring because every member of the family is conducting his or her own interview of the counselor. Kantor and Kupferman (1985) describe key questions that clients ask in their interview of the counselor to determine if they can entrust their family concerns to the counselor:

A. Is the therapist strong enough, gentle enough, honest enough for me to risk investing my fuller, deeper self?
B. What is her experience with families? (Married? Children? Divorced?)
C. Does his experience prepare him for knowing what it is like to be a (man, woman, child) in this family?
D. Is his caring and interest purely professional or will I become known on my own terms?
E. Will she respect our differences?
F. Will I be able to influence him or is it all one-directional?
G. Does she know how to listen?
H. Does he understand the unique culture of my experience (class, ethnicity, gender)?
I. How does she know how to approach us? Me? How quickly to pace her moves, how close to get?
J. Is his idea of a family (what marriage is, how to raise kids, how to make decisions, how to die) at odds with mine, others?
K. What is the fit between the counselor and us as members of the family (p. 231)

Several themes emerge from these questions—what is the fit between our family and the social worker; is the counselor competent enough as a person and a professional to be entrusted with our family; and how much will the counselor truly understand what it is to be us? The answers to these questions will help determine whether or not the family views the social worker as an appropriate person to partner with in order to address their family's concerns.

Both the family and the social worker bring to the encounter uniqueness in terms of gender, age, sexual orientation, and racial and ethnic background, as well as personal experiences that will influence the joining process. While the family members and the social worker do not have to be similar in these aspects, the social worker must be able to appreciate and understand the family's paradigms and how these fit with those of the counselor and be able to communicate this to the family. Understanding what these characteristics might mean to the client system is important and must be part of the ongoing assessment process. Unique life experiences of the family and cultural codes play important roles in how these characteristics will influence the joining process. Cultural codes regarding gender, age, and ethnicity all play a role here. As a result, the nature of this engagement will inevitably be unique to the specific family and counselor (Minuchin & Fishman, 1981).

Worden (2003) describes three important operations to joining.

1. *Maintenance.* "The therapist confirms or supports a family's position" (p. 42). The counselor can support a family dealing with major

change by indicating the stress that such an event might create within a family. Walsh (2006) described the importance of normalizing these reactions on the part of families to reduce the sense of failure and blame.

2. *Tracking.* "The therapist uses a series of clarifying questions to track or follow a sequence of events in the family and the interactions of family members" (Worden, 2003, p. 42).

3. *Mimesis.* "The therapist adopts the family's style and tempo of communication" (ibid.). If the family describes events through understatement, the counselor follows suit in the initial process.

While all effective counseling requires a therapeutic alliance, joining with families represents an additional challenge from that of individual counseling because one needs to join both with the family as a whole and with the individual members of the family. Unlike individual counseling where there is typically only one agenda represented by the client, many family members have their own agendas and these may be competing or in conflict. When the family counselor is seeking to engage the family around the typical issue of the purpose of the family's coming for counseling and what the family hopes to accomplish, the counselor quickly discovers multiple and conflicting goals. Parents might be trying to enlist the social worker to make their teenager behave while their teenager wants the worker to get the parents to back off. Some family members want the tension in the family to be reduced, which frequently translates into someone else in the family changing. Families can also be motivated to get the school or the Department of Social Services to leave them alone. While this goal unites the family, members' views of how this is to be done and who has to change vary. The family counselor faces the important task of working with the family to identify a goal that can be shared by the family and thereby help unify the family's efforts rather than having the family members work at cross-purposes.

Part of joining the family entails joining as a partner in the family dance. Family members have reoccurring behavior patterns similar to a dance step. Because of these patterns, everyone in the family knows what other people are likely to do in a situation. Everyone in the family is expert in knowing the buttons to push to create reactions in other family members. Children know the exact tone of voice used by their parents that signals the parents are about to become very angry or to cave in to their whining. When the parent says, "I mean it" in a certain tone of voice, children know they have pushed one of these buttons. It is these patterns that help make family life predictable to family members. Counselors quickly feel that they have been drawn into the extended family system as individual family members seek to enlist the counselor as their partner in the family dance. It is important for counselors to be aware of this process in order to do so freely rather than to have their behavior dictated in ways that perpetuate problems in the family patterns. Counselors can subsequently realize that they have been inducted into the family dance by ignoring the family isolate, by speaking primarily to the family spokesperson, by becoming annoyed with the family scapegoat, or by helping the helpless family member (Minuchin & Fishman, 1981).

Joining with the family requires that the counselor pass the family's test of fitness, work with the family to identify a purpose for the counseling that is meaningful for the family members, and be purposeful in the way in which the counselor joins in the family's typical ways of interacting—the family dance. The unique nature of the alliance will vary depending on the nature of the family and the counselor and the selected goals.

Greeting

The first stage in joining is to make family members feel at ease in what is inevitably a situation with a degree of anxiety and uncertainty. Hospitality is the theme as family members are ushered into the family interview room and encouraged to choose their seats. The counselor then tries to help family members feel at ease through brief conversation that serves as a hospitable bridge, for example, How was traffic? Was it hard to find our office?

Engagement with Members

The second stage in joining is to engage with each of the family members. This process can begin by asking members of the leadership structure (typically the parents or grandparents depending on the family situation) to introduce the members of the family. The counselor engages in a conversation with each of the family members through questions and interaction designed to get to know the individuals. Depending on the nature of the presenting problem, children, for example, can be asked about their school, what they like to do after school, their special interests (e.g., favorite teams, music groups). Such conversations also set the stage for recognizing that people in the family are more than the problems that brought them into counseling. These conversations also provide opportunities to identify some appropriate commonalties between the counselor and family members—for example, a shared interest in a hobby—that can help in the alliance process.

Carl Whitaker (1989) described in a workshop how he engaged effectively with a family who brought a baby to the session. He played with the baby and in other ways showed the family his admiration for its baby. By this time, he was thoroughly trusted and accepted by the parents and grandparents of the child.

STRUCTURE OF THE COUNSELING PROCESS

One of the structuring tasks of the first session is to set the stage for the counseling process. Families need information regarding how the family counselor and the family will be working together. Part of this involves setting the ground rules for the session. This is a task that requires both tact and clarity because the goal is to create a collaborative partnerships arrangement. Family members can be helped to understand that all of the family members will be asked for their input regarding what they hope to accomplish and their views on what is happening within the family. Family members will be asked to speak one at a time so the counselor can hear each person because the perspective of everyone in the family is important in identifying the goals and the way to reach these goals. Family members will be asked about their concerns for the family and their ideas on how to solve these problems because they are the experts on the family.

The counselor also needs to clarify what the confidentiality ground rules will be. The issue of confidentiality may relate to your role as a mandatory reporter, information that needs to be shared with the insurance company or other referrals sources. It also refers to information that will be shared with other family members if the counselor should meet with family members on an individual basis.

Setting the stage also involves explaining the counselor's model of working together. While all counseling models encourage family input regarding ways to solve family problems, counseling using a resiliency model is explicitly a partnership arrangement. This means that the professional competence of the counselor is paired with the expertise of the family members regarding their life experiences and potential ways to address the problems they are facing. Family members need to be informed that their input will be solicited and valued. The family will make the important decisions in terms of identifying its goals, how to reach them, and how to evaluate the progress that is being made. Because the first session represents a sample of the way in which the counseling process will occur, it is especially important to demonstrate this manner of working during the engagement process.

The family counselor also discusses timetable issues—the nature of insurance, and the expectations of family members. Counselors can explain the process in terms of a time of learning about the family and its situation, developing with the family a plan for addressing it, working out a timetable for the counseling activities with the family, and mutually evaluating how helpful the counseling efforts are in reaching the family goals.

Identification of Goals

The next step is to identify what the family hopes to accomplish and to link the counseling effort with goals that are meaningful for the family.

1. "What prompted you to come?"
2. "What does the family hope to accomplish?"

These two questions are paired. One seeks to identify the nature of the problems and the context of the process of seeking help and the other the goals of the family. The question of what one hopes to accomplish also sets in motion the process of solving issues. It is future-oriented.

This set of questions quickly elicits the agendas of family members. As indicated, family members frequently identify different reasons for coming for counseling: parents—make my teenager behave; teenager—get my parents off my back.

Families can also come to counseling because they have been forced to do so by a community agency with power over the family. Understanding what this referring organization expects you to accomplish, and the family's understanding of this process, as well as the family's own agenda, is important here.

At this stage, it is important to ask all of the family members why they came. There are several ways to go about doing this. The counselor can throw out the question to the family in general and wait to see who answers it. Typically this is the family spokesperson (not necessarily the family leader) and frequently the person who made the contact. It is important to recognize when cultural codes or family situations dictate who should be shown the respect of being asked first. Asian American and Latino cultural codes have hierarchical patterns in the family that indicate the value of supporting such by soliciting information from the parents initially. A quick assessment of the situation, perhaps based on the early telephone call, referral source, or initial appraisal can also clue the counselor into recognizing that the leadership structure of the family (parents or parent surrogates) is under siege and needs support. As a result, it is important for the counselor to demonstrate support through the respect of asking the parents' view first. When in doubt, the safest approach is to begin with adults who are responsible for the family.

The counselor uses a respectful questioning style described in greater detail in chapter 3. These questions are designed to elicit a family view on both the problems and risk factors and the protective factors for families. The process of careful tracking frequently reveals complex and circular patterns. Families tend to view family events in linear fashion—Bob's (aged fifteen years) behavior is causing the parents to become distrustful of him and to place greater restrictions on him. During the engagement and assessment process, the family counselor also seeks to create a more realistic circular and systemic view of the family dance. Careful tracking of the sequence of events might reveal that the more the parents voice their distrust of Bob and place severe restrictions on him, the more he loses hope that he can ever gain his parents' trust, gives up even trying, and shows his anger by rebelling. The vicious circle winds tighter and tighter. A related circle is the praise that the parents give the older sister (aged seventeen years). Words meant to motivate Bob ("You could be like your sister if you tried.") to improve his behavior might only fuel his anger, hopelessness, and acting-out behavior. The relationship between Bob and his sister that might be a source of support for Bob becomes even more strained and distant. The counselor thus seeks to expand the family vision of the situation to reflect a more comprehensive and circular picture of the problem and the type of solutions that reflect this expanded view.

An important task in identification of goals is to help the family move beyond the agenda of specific individuals to a goal that involves the family and one that members can agree on. Family members frequently come with a specific issue and attempt to enlist the counselor to side with one of the coalitions within the family. Rather than being caught up in the ongoing family arguments, the family counselor can help the family move up to another level that represents process, for example, helping the family members discuss issues in such a way that they can resolve them. In this way, the issue is not "getting Bob to behave" or "getting Mom and Dad to stop nagging me" but "How the parents and Bob can work together more effectively to resolve the issue at hand."

In working with families toward change, it is important to recognize that families have two pressures placed on them. The first relates to stability needs—morphostasis, the pressure for people to stay in their old roles. It is this pressure that causes old family roles and patterns to play out during family gatherings. The second is the need for change—morphogenesis, the pressure for change to meet new situations. People and families must adapt as life cycle and external events create new circumstances. The challenge of the family is thus to respond adequately to change imposed by life cycle and external events while maintaining adequate stability (Worden, 2003). Stability supports a family's sense of coherence. Yet families also need flexibility in terms of roles and the capacity to learn and implement coping strategies that contribute to a positive adaptation process. As a result, the role of the social worker in terms of the family dance is to promote new patterns that enable families to be flexible while at the same time retaining a sense of stability.

Recent brief therapy models raise the important question whether we have a problem focus or a solution focus in our working relationship with families. The problem focus is organized in terms of what is the nature of the problem, what has caused it, and how do we address it. While strengths are required to address it, sometimes there is a danger of emphasizing the problems and who is contributing to these problems. The solution focus directs the attention to what are the potential solutions and what inputs and individuals can be used in the solution process.

Selection of Participants

In the engagement process, the decision to use problem focus or solution focus can influence the answer to the question, Whom do we need to engage in order to promote change? From a problem focus, the question becomes, Who is contributing to the problem? The solution focus raises the question, Who can contribute to the solution? This in turn raises the question, Who can contribute to healing in this family? The last question is particularly relevant to resiliency-based treatment given the role of support systems and positive organizational patterns within the family.

The decision to use a problem focus or solution focus also influences the basis on which people are asked to be part of the process. Are parents enlisted because there is an implicit blame for having created the problem or are they enlisted as resources—the people who know their children best and can be of help? Are there other family members who are invested in the family situation and are willing to help in this process? Family members naturally make these decisions, but the counselor frequently needs to set the context and raise these issues by asking a question such as "Are there other people in your family or circle who are concerned about your family and could be of help?" Family members can identify other members of the extended family as well as pastors, or others who have been a source of support during this difficult time.

Additional family members can be enlisted early in the engagement process or later as issues arise. Reflecting cultural as well as individual family patterns, when the Lo family was seen following the overdose of pills by the their high-school-age daughter, all of the grown children from neighboring states came to be part of the first family interview. Their presence was very supportive to the frightened parents and their endorsement of the ongoing counseling situation was very helpful.

Seeking for Strengths

As discussed in chapter 3, the social worker needs to take seriously the problems that brought the family for help while also seeking evidence of what the family is doing right and the protective factors within the life space of the family. As family members describe the pain and tension within the family, maintenance operations can include giving credit for recognizing the problem and seeking help for it, for being willing to face and trying to address these difficulties. One can explore times in which the family members managed to handle the situation in a less painful way. By engaging family members in terms of both the problems and favorable outcomes, one can also help inject the important elements of self-efficacy and hope into the counseling relationship and process.

BARRIERS IN THE ENGAGEMENT PROCESS

During the engagement process, many issues can contribute to the family members' reluctance to create a partnership and to participate in the ongoing process of change with the counselor. The source of these barriers can come from both the family and the counselor as well other organizations within the community. As a result, counselors need to examine how their own behaviors can be contributing to this process. Reluctance can be protective and must be assessed accordingly.

Ambivalence About Change

Families and individuals are sometimes ambivalent about change. Although they are seeking something different, there are many reasons for being uncomfortable about change. Family members are accustomed to their long-standing dance and are frequently uncertain and sometimes even fearful about what will replace it. While the current situation brings pain to family members, it also represents stability within the family, and the unknown can be a source of fear and anxiety.

Family members might fear what could be the alternatives. Parents might be distressed by the defiant behavior of their teenager but are also afraid about what a change in their behavior might produce—will taking a stronger stance create an irrevocable breach or cause the teenager to act in a way that would be dangerous to himself or others? Earlier life experiences within the family or others that they know might contribute to these fears. Perhaps a nephew felt pushed from his home because of his behavior and ended up in a serious accident. While problems bring stress, they can also be viewed in other ways as helpful to the family. The problem in this situation has become a solution to yet another issue. The difficult teenager can represent a project that helps keep parents together rather than having to address the tensions in their relationship. The young adult who continually rebels against his parents might really be afraid to grow up. Rather than deal with employers and landlords, he continues to bait his parents in a familiar family dance. Parents in turn might doubt the competence of their son or daughter and continue the circle. While family members might want to change, they can doubt their ability to do so because they have lacked role models and have not developed the needed skills.

Contribution of the Counselor

Family counselors can contribute to these barriers by not being sensitive to the individual family and related social cultural issues as well as the characteristics of the parties involved. As Minuchin (1974) asserts, family members need to sense that the counselor can truly understand what it is to be a member of this family. In this context the family's reluctance to engage serves as a protective function. Counselors need to be aware of their own biases, ways of presenting themselves, and their own personal issues that might be affected by the situation that can create barriers. Counselors can hold inappropriate expectations of family members. Based on their own view of healthy family behavior, counselors can encourage children to speak up about their concerns regarding the family without recognizing that such behavior in this family with their cultural background means bringing unacceptable shame to the family in the presence of outsiders. For example, asking children from an Asian American or Hispanic family to do so would be especially problematic. Counselors can hold different views regarding family gender roles than are supported by the culture of the family. Counselors can move too quickly before family members trust the counselor or are ready to discuss certain issues. Family counselors can also allow themselves to be pulled into the family dance in ways that are viewed as problematic to other family members.

Barriers can also occur because of perceived or real disjunctures between the counselor and the family members that create barriers to trust. I remember being especially aware of this while working with poor rural families in Appalachia where the fact that I had teeth and the women my age did not symbolized a potential barrier that I had to work to overcome. Gender, race, and other characteristics can pose initial barriers, perhaps as a result of past experiences, that can require additional effort on the part of the worker to develop trust.

The important role of the counselor requires counselors to be self-reflective in terms of their own biases and life experiences. Bias is always a potential danger—whether the counselor is similar to or different from the family in question. Even the best-intentioned counselor can discover that specific family circumstances evoke thoughts and feelings that are problematic. Sometimes this is triggered by cultural differences or the unique life experiences of the parties involved. Problematic responses can take the form of being judgmental or distant from the families or overly identifying with the family and thus losing objectivity. Although this is an important issue in the initial engagement process, it continues to be an important issue through the counseling process that requires ongoing self-reflection.

Previous Negative Experiences

Family members might have had previous negative experiences that make them reluctant to engage with their current counselor. They might have met earlier with counselors who did not show respect or violated cultural patterns. This can be particularly true of families with multiple problems, families from cultural groups that are different from the counselors, and members of groups that face potential stigma. As a result, these families protect themselves by being wary and testing the counselor in a variety of ways. It can take time before the family realizes that this counselor will respect them and their cultural values and can be trusted. What becomes labeled as resistance can be realistic caution.

Other Organizations or Community Members

Family members can also bring to the counseling situation negative experiences with other organizations that make them distrust the current counselor. Referral sources can be imposing changes that are viewed as unwelcome and anxiety-producing to family members. It is thus important to identify how the family views these interactions and expectations. It may also be necessary to interpret to the referring source what are appropriate expectations. A family was once referred to the author by a pastor to "make" their child forgive the grandfather who sexually abused her. It was thus important to explain to the referring source the unrealistic nature of this expectation and to clarify this with the family.

Families are sometimes forced to attend through court orders or other mandatory arrangements. Not only might the expected changes be unwelcome by family members, but the arrangement also contributes to resentment and a sense of disempowerment. The challenge for the counselor in this setting is to recognize with the family the circumstances of the referral and what it means to the family to be placed in such a situation. One can acknowledge their feelings of being forced into counseling. Listening is an essential part of the engagement process—what have people experienced, what do they want, what do they think might work and what will not work (National Family Preservation Network, 2012). It is also important to be clear what the role of the counselor is in this arrangement—especially the role of the family as a genuine partner. If one is to go further than having families merely attend physically but not really be participants, it is important to work with the family members to identify some goals that are genuinely meaningful to them. It might be, for example, getting one's children back and thus exploring with the family the necessary steps that might be addressed in the counseling process (finding a home, seeking treatment for substance abuse, learning new parenting skills, finding appropriate child care).

STAGES IN THE CHANGE PROCESS

Studies of the change process in therapy and individuals struggling with various addictions have identified some important steps in the change process that can be useful in engaging with the family to work toward its goals in a variety of areas. Prochaska, DiClemente, and Norcross (1992) have identified the following stages: precontemplation, contemplation, preparation, action, and maintenance.

Precontemplation. Individuals do not recognize that they have a problem and are not interested in changing. While others (staff of the school, judicial or child welfare system) view the family as having problems, the family does not share this view. As soon as the external pressure is off, the family or members of the family return to their former ways. Solution-focused therapists view such families as visitors. Unless such families can come to recognize that they have problems and that it is to their advantage to address them, these families are not truly invested in the change process. The task of the social worker is to try to find some way to help family members realize that addressing this problem represents a step that is in the interest of the family.

Contemplation. Individuals recognize that they have a problem and are considering changing but have not yet made a commitment to actually take this action. Individuals in this stage are continuing to weigh the pros and cons of change. As indicated in the previous discussion, recognizing and addressing ambivalence toward change is important in creating an effective working alliance. The therapist can help family members identify some of the potential advantages of making the changes—ways that they would help meet the family's stated goals. The counselor can also help promote the self-efficacy of family members in terms of their ability to take these steps. Family members can be helped to identify other situations in which they were able to take such steps or the positive effects for the family when they made similar changes in the past.

Preparation. People are seriously thinking about change but have not made the actual step. They are beginning to identify the cognitive and behavior steps that will be needed for this to occur. The counselor can help the family identify some of the barriers to making the change and specific steps that the family can take to address these. The family and the counselor can also identify some of the external support systems that would make this change possible and begin to create these changes. Parents who want to make changes in their parenting but are still not certain about how to make this change can be given material about a parenting class that has been designed for parents similar to themselves. In addition to going over the course material with them, the counselor can arrange a meeting with the family and the leader of the group to permit the family to ask questions and feel more comfortable with this arrangement.

Action. Individuals are in the action stage if they have actually modified their behavior to address their goals. This stage represents considerable time and energy to create such change. Parents who had relied on physical force with their children can be actively taking the steps to use alternative strategies such as time-outs and natural consequences. Couples who had turned discussions into shouting matches that left everyone hurt and angry can be practicing their new skills of problem solving and conflict resolution. The family counselor needs to recognize with the family the big step that they have taken and the effort involved in doing so.

Maintenance. Individuals are seeking to maintain and stabilize the change that they have made. Such a stage recognizes that the process of change requires ongoing commitment and effort in order not to slip back into old patterns. Parents that have developed more effective parenting skills can find themselves slipping back under the pressure of other demands on the family (e.g., loss of a job, illness of family member) or transition to a new developmental stage in the family (e.g., child becomes a teenager). Families can thus seek help because they fear relapsing into their old patterns and are looking for help in maintaining positive changes. The social worker validates the difficult challenge of maintaining change and works with families to identify what the challenges are to their maintaining the positive changes and what offers them needed support.

SUMMARY

The engagement process is in important ways a sample of the way in which the counselor and the family will work together. Family counseling from a resiliency perspective involves a partnership between the counselor and the family. The family-counselor alliance is a collaboration. How the counselor engages the family represents whether or not the family is viewed as a contributing partner to this endeavor. Recognizing possible signs of reluctance and identifying the issues involved in the change process can aid in the engagement. Families can also be in different stages in the change process with accompanying implications regarding the response to the social worker.

DISCUSSION QUESTIONS

Discuss ways in which the nature of the engagement process can increase resiliency. What does it mean to be part of the family dance?

What are the implications of describing the therapeutic relationship as a partnership?

Discuss ways in which the counselor might be contributing to barriers in the engagement process.

How might you try to engage a family who has been *sent* to counseling rather than one who is seeking it out to address a concern the family has identified?

What are the implications for engagement depending on what stage family members are in the change process?

3

Assessment of Families

Assessment of risk and protective factors and their interaction is a key step in using a resiliency-based approach to counseling families. The counselor and the family are partners on a collaborative venture to understand the life space of the family, the distress experienced by family members, the potential resources and sources of resiliency for the family, and the barriers that might prevent the family from accessing these resources. The assessment process also sets the tone for the working partnership between the family and the counselor. As Walsh (1998) indicates, "a common approach regarding family resiliency is the conviction that there are strong advantages to working with family members in a collaborative manner and finding solutions to shared problems. Family therapy is most effective when it identifies key processes for resiliency and encourages a family's own best efforts for recovery and growth. Such an approach is empowering and enables families not only to address the current problem but helps to prepare them to address the challenges of the future" (p. 16). The assessment process is a critical step in guiding decisions regarding the appropriate intervention strategies.

RESILIENCY-BASED APPROACH TO ASSESSMENT

Families are often discouraged and demoralized when they come for help. Before seeking help from a social worker or other professional counselor they have typically tried their usual coping strategies and turned to their informal support systems within their extended family, friends, and other sources of help without success. In terms of the family coping models, their efforts to cope have led them to a state of maladaptation or crisis. Sometimes their efforts have in turn created yet another set of demands on the family requiring further coping strategies and changes that have proved insufficient to meet these demands. They might have been sent for counseling by organizations with authority in the community with a message that they need help because they were unable to handle the problem. These are clearly not the descriptions of families who feel empowered. This potential demoralization of families is important. It is not only painful for the individuals involved but also depletes the sense of coherence and self-efficacy that support resiliency. Rather than being strengthened by viewing themselves as successful in and capable of addressing life situations, families can become even less able to handle already difficult situations. Their family stories risk becoming problem-saturated.

Assessment from a resiliency-based perspective thus seeks to support the resiliency of families by explicitly identifying sources of resiliency within the family in ways that can engender hope to family members. The social worker searches for signs of strength within the family and protective factors within the life space of the family. Evidences of strength and tools for resiliency are not merely noted in charts but acknowledged as such with family members throughout the process. In so doing, the family's sense of self-efficacy and mastery is enhanced and the family becomes a more effective partner.

Assessment also identifies areas of family functioning that need to be strengthened or addressed as well as stressors within the environment. Problematic communication patterns, unresolved family conflicts, lack of effective parenting skills, and isolation from potential sources of community support represent several areas that can need strengthening. Community violence, lack of educational opportunities, and high levels of unemployment represent community stressors.

While a theoretical framework guides assessment and treatment decisions set within the resiliency framework, use of this framework does not limit the family counselor to a single treatment theoretical model. Based on the results of the assessment of the risk and protective factors at the individual, family, and contextual levels, a variety of treatment approaches might be appropriate depending on the areas of risk factors and sources of strength identified. The following brief vignettes illustrate how very different patterns of risk and protective factors can be present.

> The Bowen family has recently moved to the community and has not had the opportunity to develop any support network within the community. Their youngest child has developed a serious illness. The family members are able to communicate with each other about the situation, ways to address it, and their response to it. At the same time, they are feeling very alone because they lack any source of support within their new community.

> The Anderson family is concerned about one of their children who is demonstrating misbehavior in school. The school has contacted them and asked them to be partners in creating a reinforcement system that will discourage such behavior. The parents love their children deeply. At the same time, they are reluctant to set limits on their son. Both of them grew up in very abusive family situations and they promised themselves that they would be loving parents to their children. They are both reluctant to punish their child and also have not developed a repertoire of parenting skills in this area.

The Cutler family is struggling with severe financial problems. The father developed cancer that has limited his ability to work and has caused the family severe financial hardship. Fortunately, they have potential resources from their extended family if they can ask for help.

The Dodge family is worried about their teenage son who has begun to skip school and engage in substance abuse. The parents love their son and are desperate to try to find a way to stop his behavior. They have begun to threaten him but their son in turn just says that he will run away.

The Eduardo family had lived in their home for many years. It had been the center of their family and they were very proud of what they had been able to accomplish. Unfortunately, their home was destroyed in a recent hurricane. Not only are they uncertain if their insurance will be adequate to purchase a new home, but they are also grieving the loss of a home that had so many good memories attached to it. In the meantime, they are able to live temporarily with the father's brother and his family.

These abbreviated vignettes illustrate some different family patterns and circumstances that would require different intervention strategies. Based on the assessment, the counselor in partnership with the family identifies the appropriate and effective ways to help the family members cope with the current sources of distress and strengthen protective factors for the present and, hopefully, ones that will also serve them for the future. Use of a resiliency approach in this manner can facilitate clinical judgment regarding the selection of appropriate intervention strategies. Assessment is always an ongoing process and subject to revision based on new information and developments within the life space of the family.

Chapter 1 describes family and contextual characteristics that support resiliency (see table 1). Family characteristics include belief systems that engender hope; a sense of mastery and self-efficacy; a sense of purpose and meaning; family organizational patterns that promote effective communication, a balance of flexibility and cohesion, and adequate leadership; positive interactions and trust; humor; problem-solving and coping skills to address the problem at hand; and appropriate support systems in the wider community. Risk factors can be contextual: poverty, community disorganization and violence, and lack of economic and educational opportunities. They can also reflect family patterns that lead to conflict, lack of leadership, poor coping skills, rigidity, or chaotic family patterns. Families can also be isolated from potential support systems or appropriate resources can be absent from the community.

ASSESSMENT PROCESS

The assessment process can use a variety of strategies, including formal assessment tools, visual devices, an interview format, observation, information obtained from others (for example, referral source), and the social worker's general knowledge of the community context. Regardless of the tools used, assessment from a resiliency-based framework is organized around the following questions that reflect a risk and protective factors perspective as appraised by the family members.

What are the sources of distress in the lives of family members? (risk factors)

How do family members view these issues? (appraisal)

What aspects within the family and their extended world contribute to these sources of distress? (risk factors)

Are there additional factors that contribute to this distress? (additive factors)

What are the resources for coping and support possessed by family members, the family as an organization, and their external world? (protective factors)

How can family members use these resources? (access to resources)

How can these resources be enhanced? (strengthening of resources)

What barriers are preventing family members from using these resources? (barriers to resources)

How can these barriers be reduced? (strengthening access to resources)

Assessment occurs at the beginning of work with families as well as throughout the entire process. New information can emerge as the social worker gains the trust of the family members. Life circumstances of families change due to circumstances within the family extended circle as well as the larger community context. As a result, social workers need to be responsive to these changes and reflect these changes in their selection of the appropriate intervention strategies.

Based on the recommendation of Fraser and Galinsky (2004) and Chazin, Kaplin, and Terio (2000), the following skills and principles are important in using a resiliency model in the assessment process.

1. Assess the risk and protective factors present within the family, the community, and the larger social context.

2. Demonstrate respect for the clients as possessing strengths and potential resources—listen for their survival strategies.

3. Help clients recognize their strengths.

4. Engage the family members as partners in the assessment process.

5. Identify the risk and protective factors that can be changed.

6. Engage the family in the selection of the interventions.

7. Be knowledgeable about practice interventions that can address the risk factors and support their protective factors.

Fraser and Galinsky (2004) stress the importance of practitioners identifying keystone risk factors—the family and social conditions that are important causal factors and can be changed through an intervention. Identifying the factors that are both causal and subject to change enables the social worker and the family to address the problem in an effective manner. Families bring to counseling sessions a variety of problems. One important task is to help family members identify where we can begin. What are the areas that are amenable to change and if changed would have an important impact on the family (and frequently on some of the other problems as well)? The concept of keystone risk factors can be helpful in answering this question. Efforts directed toward these factors can help create additional positive change because positive changes reverberate throughout the family system and thus encourage families to believe that they can make a difference. As Walsh stresses (2006), it is important to think in terms of mastering the possible, not only because it can create change but also because such effectiveness enhances self-efficacy and hope for the future.

ASSESSMENT TOOLS

Assessment tools have been developed to help understand the current functioning of the family unit. Several of these are relatively narrow in focus, like the behavior of the children or the nature of conflict within the family, while others provide a wider picture of the functioning within the family.

Measurement Instruments

Some of these measures look at the wide range of family functioning and others target more specific aspects of the family. The following list of instruments designed to look at a wide range of family functioning is followed by those that target more specific areas.

The following three measures evaluate a wide range of family functioning.

The Self-Report Family Inventory (SFI) developed by Beavers and Hampson (1990) measures family functioning. It has been used with families from a wide range of socioeconomic groups (Thomlison, 2004).

The Multi-Problem Screening Inventory (MPSI) (Hudson & McMurtry, 1997) assesses family relationship problems, marital satisfaction, partner abuse, personal stress, and partner or child problems.

The McMaster Family Assessment Device (FAD) (Epstein, Baldwin, & Bishop, 1983) measures six areas of family functioning including problem solving, communication (verbal communication in terms of instrumental, affective, clear or masked, direct or indirect), roles, affective responsiveness, affective involvement, and behavior control. These dimensions are relevant to a resiliency perspective. The information obtained from this instrument can be used to identify transactional patterns within the family. Whether or not specific patterns are dysfunctional or adaptive is determined by the larger context of what emerges as helpful for the individual family in this setting (Miller, Kabacoff, Bishop, Epstein, & Keitner, 1994; Miller, Ryan, Keitner, Bishop, & Epstein, 1999).

The following two measures evaluate specific dimensions. McCubbin and colleagues have developed instruments designed to assess dimensions of families based on their theoretical work on family coping.

The Family Crisis Oriented Personal Evaluation Scale, developed by Hamilton McCubbin, David Olson, and Andrea Larsen, looks at family problem-solving strategies. It includes thirty items of different problem-solving strategies. There are also French and Hebrew versions of the scale (McCubbin, Thompson, & McCubbin, 1996).

The Family Coping Index, developed by Hamilton McCubbin, Ann Thompson, and Kelly Elver, examines how families cope with difficult life circumstances. It includes twenty-four possible coping strategies (McCubbin, Thompson, & McCubbin, 1996).

Visual Devices

The ecogram and genogram are two visual tools used widely in assessment with families. They are useful in identifying patterns within the family and the family's relationships to the larger environment. These tools provide mechanisms by which the family counselor and the family can collaborate to identify sources of strain and distress and important resources for the family.

Eco Map

The eco map is a visual representation of the family's transactions with the wider environment. These transactions include those of individual family members as well as the family as a unit. Families can be asked to map out their relationships with important aspects of their external world. Some of the important dimensions that are typically included are schools (for families with school-age children), extended family members, employment, health systems, and other social services that are part of the family life. Families can be encouraged to identify other entities that are relevant to their family life, for example, the church and the local recreation program. Arrows and lines are then used to describe the flow of energy from family members to aspects of the environment. Arrows describe direction and the width of the line indicates the degree of energy involved. Conflictual transactions can be delineated by cross-hatching. This set of lines thus conveys to the family sources of support as well as possible exhaustion and tensions.

The eco map has the advantage of making visible the sources of support (external resources) and strains within the family in terms of its transaction with the wider world. While people often experience distress or feel nourished by other interactions, seeing such patterns on paper can be quite powerful in identifying the nature of them in their lives. Creation of the eco map sets the stage for discussion about what might possibly be done to reduce the stresses and to enhance the resources in ways that can promote the resiliency of the family.

The Kastor family consists of Mr. and Mrs. Kastor, their seven-year-old son Jack, and five-year-old son Chad. The family receives support from a grandparent who helps take care of the children when they are ill and cannot attend day care. One of the children has been having difficulty in school and the parents dread calls from the teacher. The parents have been pillars of their church for many years. They feel valued in this setting and experience their relationships with fellow church members as their main support system. Mr. Kastor is concerned about the stability of his job because there have been layoffs and people are worried about who will be next. As a result, there is pressure on everyone to work extra hours to prove their worth to the company so that they can escape the next round of layoffs. Mrs. Kastor is feeling satisfied with her employment situation. One of the children has some serious health problems and the parents have had problems in getting clear answers regarding the nature of these problems and possible effective remedies. The family's current health insurance is linked to the threatened employment situation of Mr. Kastor (see figure 2).

Genogram

The genogram is a visual map of the family over time (McGoldrick & Gerson, 1985). Families can use the genogram to describe the family story as it emerges across several generations. Use of the genogram is based on the recognition that family messages, loyalties, expectations, or tensions are communicated from one generation to the next. As one student said after doing a genogram of her family, "I realized I either had to marry a Lutheran pastor or become one." The genogram includes available information about the parties involved—names, brief personal descriptions, employment, health, and other relevant information. A history of substance abuse can represent a multigenerational risk factor. Several generations of substance abuse followed by lack of such problems in the current generation can be used to identify sources of strength and resiliency within the family. The genogram can reveal a history of physical problems, for example, early death caused by heart problems, which represent a legitimate health concern within the family or prompt unrealistic worry. The genogram can represent

FIGURE 2. Kastor Family Eco Map

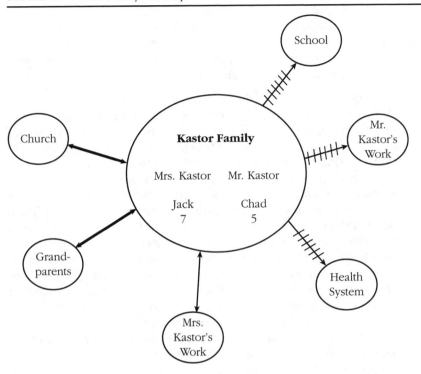

expectations in terms of education, religion, employment, and other areas. Names from one generation to the next can convey important messages.

The genogram can also describe relationships among people. Circles are used to describe close ties among groups of people, broad lines to indicate strong relationships, and jagged lines to describe conflict between people. Lines can also be drawn to identify cutoffs that have occurred within the family.

The genogram enables family members to place family events within a cultural or historical context. The family might have emigrated to another country or lost contact with family members due to war (for example, the split between North and South Korea). Historical events also help explain why families made the choices that they did. People may discover the limited options that family members had due to war, political oppression, and community poverty when they made decisions that might appear puzzling or hurtful without this context. A social work student had felt abandoned by her parents who had placed her as a young child with relatives. Although she came from a Mexican family in which such relative placements are acceptable, she always felt hurt by the parents' actions. When she created her family genogram and placed the historical context in the background, she realized the terrible economic hardship to the point of the danger of starvation that was facing her family during these times. The visual image of the genogram helped her understand for the first time the social context of her parents' decision and to recognize that it was made to protect her rather than because her parents did not care enough for her.

> The Loden family came to the session because Ted Loden feels that Sue Loden is too overprotective of their twelve-year-old son, Mark. Mark is resentful of his mother's overprotective ways, and the father and son have created a close alliance from which the mother feels excluded. As the family creates a genogram, a family pattern emerges that helps put some of her anxiety into perspective and enables the family to problem solve alternative solutions. The Lodens have one child because Sue had several miscarriages both prior to and following Mark's birth. Mark has been a healthy child but has seen more than his share of doctors' offices due to Sue's anxiety about his health. A genogram revealed a history of health problems on the maternal side of the family. Although the family was aware of some of this history, they had not fully recognized the extent and impact. Sue has a sister, Carol, who has been healthy, but her brother, Jim, died when he was eighteen. He had been playing basketball with a friend when he died suddenly of a previously undetected heart problem. Her father, Mark Matthews, died of a heart attack when he was in his forties leaving her mother, who has always been very healthy, to financially support and in other ways raise the family. Her uncle Peter had successful heart surgery for a birth defect when he was a child and has been able to live a relatively normal life. Another uncle, John, died in his fifties from heart disease. The genogram of the paternal side revealed no pattern of significant health problems for the Lodens, and the men in this family were described as very physically active.

Although the Loden family members were aware of health problems within the family, the genogram gave a vivid reality to the health problems facing the male members of Sue's family and the fear that had been deeply embedded into her. While it helped other family members appreciate her worry, it also helped her begin to recognize the need to distinguish her son from other family members and to recognize their son's potential strengths from his father. Creation of the genogram contributed to a better understanding within the family of the situation facing the family currently and enabled family members to dialogue more effectively about ways to address it (see figure 3).

Creation of the genogram is a process that involves members of the family and the family counselor. Relationships among family members and between the family and the counselor can be critical in this process. As a result, one should not expect that a final genogram is accomplished during the first visit with a family or that it is always advisable to begin the process

FIGURE 3. Loden Family Genogram

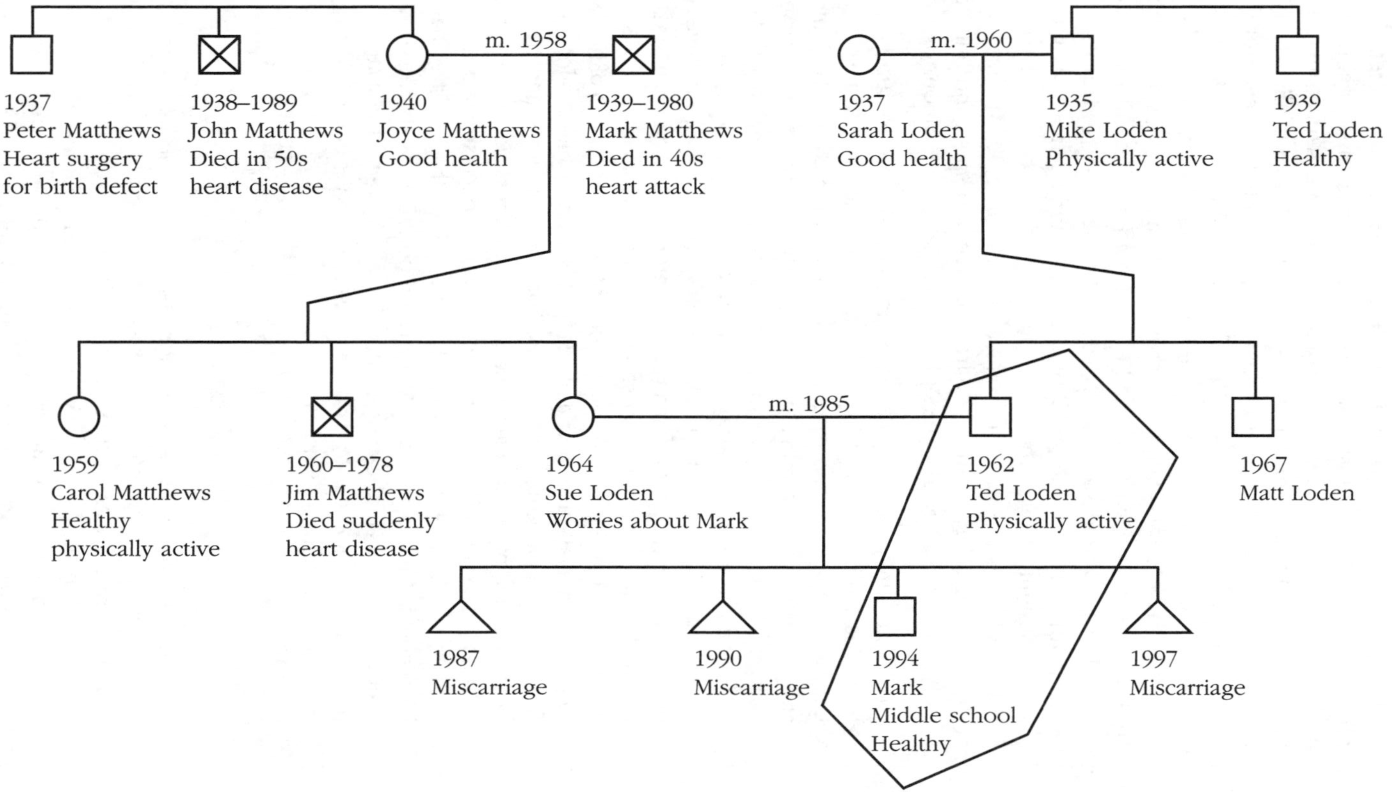

of a genogram during the first visit. Families frequently have secrets that they are protecting due to codes of family loyalty or a sense of shame. As families learn to trust, they may be more willing to include these aspects in the genogram and to incorporate them in ways that can promote healing within the family. Sometimes family members have kept secrets from each other and are reluctant to reveal them. An adult friend of mine who was involved in family genealogy was excited because he discovered some colorful characters in what had otherwise been a rather staid family background. When he shared his excitement with his mother, she was horrified at his discovery and responded that this was a family secret that he wasn't to learn about. As the genogram is created, the social worker and family members can explore themes that illumine the current situation.

Family legacies take many forms within families. Some of these legacies support people's ability to survive hardships while others contribute to vulnerability, sometimes because they place unrealistic expectations on people.

> The White family has a legacy that supports them in their current difficult time. The family members are facing a new challenge as their son Isaac returned home from Iraq with a severe injury from an IED. He joined the armed services after completing his AA at the local community college. In doing so he was following a strong family tradition of military service. His father had served in the army and his uncle in the navy. Isaac's wife and young son were living with his parents while he was in Iraq and have continued doing so. Isaac's father had recently returned to working in one of the automobile-related plants after several years of unemployment. His mother is employed as a dental assistant. His parents were very proud of his decision to join the military although anxious for his safety while serving in battle. They are committed to helping their son and his family and have some understanding of his experience because his father served in the earlier war with Iraq, Operation Desert Freedom. They have been strong advocates for Isaac in terms of receiving needed services from the VA. They have also been able to turn to their local African Methodist Episcopal congregation for support. Members of the congregation have volunteered to watch the children while Isaac's wife Latoya goes with Isaac to his various medical appointments and works with him on his rehab.

INTERVIEW

The interview is an essential assessment strategy for the family counselor. The assessment interview within the resiliency-based framework is guided by a search for risk and protective factors that provide the context for understanding the distress of the family and potential sources of healing. This search is carried out by asking key questions, requesting family members to enact family events, and by observing the family members in action. The interview process thus includes both a directed conversation and observations of nonverbal behavior. The moving drama of the family is played out during the family interview and reveals much about the life of the family. Figure 4 summarizes the areas addressed in the assessment discussion.

Verbal and Nonverbal

The interaction of family members as well as their words in response to the counselor's questions and comments offer a wealth of information. Everyone who has ever lived in a family knows the power of the verbal and nonverbal gestures of other family members during a conversation. When a family

FIGURE 4.   Family Assessment Interview

1. Verbal and nonverbal messages
2. Thematic dimensions
    Verbal and nonverbal communication
    Communication content and process
    Linear and circular perspective
3. Information from various family members
    Different scripts created by
    A. Family and individual life cycle
    B. Family communication patterns
    C. Family alliances
4. Use of self and response to family members
5. Current stressor
    A. Onset/context
    B. Impact on the family
    C. Additive factors
6. Family appraisal of the situation
    A. Attributions of responsibility
    B. View of the impact on the family
    C. Appropriate ways to address situation

7. Potential resources available to family
    A. Repertoire of coping strategies
    B. Belief systems—self-efficacy, mastery, hope
    C. Family trust and loyalty
    D. Spirituality/faith
8. Family organizational patterns
    A. Family cohesion
    B. Leadership
    C. Communication
    D. Flexibility of family roles
    E. Humor
9. Community context
    A. Resources
    B. Definitions re situation and coping
10. Levels of family functioning
    A. Basic needs
    B. Family structure and organization
    C. Family boundaries
    D. Riches of intimacy and meaning

member rolls his or her eyes to the ceiling or leans forward attentively when another family member is expressing a concern, these gestures convey powerful messages. Silence can communicate volumes of multifaceted meanings within families. It is important for social workers and family counselors to inquire whether or not their interpretations of these silences fit with the meaning intended and experienced by the family members. For example, when one member of a family brings up an issue and there is marked and tense silence by the other members, the family counselor can ask "I am getting the impression that this is a topic that people find difficult to talk about—am I reading this situation right?" On the other hand, if people feel comfortable with the silence, the counselor could comment, "I am getting the impression that the rest of you feel comfortable with the way that (dad, mom) has described this issue—am I reading you right?" Comments such as these not only help the counselor understand the family accurately but also convey the message that the assessment process is a partnership endeavor. Observation of the family patterns gives access to the meta-messages of communication within the family. Family members understand the subtext of comments made. Their verbal and nonverbal reactions in turn provide additional information to the social worker in the assessment process. Family members interact during the interview by adding their comments to statements made by other members or by becoming obviously silent.

Thematic Dimensions

In assessing the family verbal and nonverbal messages, it is useful to think in terms of two major thematic dimensions. These relate to content and process and linear and circular understanding of family interactions. They are not specific topics, but instead ways in which family members communicate and understand what takes place within the family story.

Content and Process. Content refers to the specific topic or events being discussed. Family members can be talking about a curfew for their adolescent daughter, financial struggles, decisions regarding employment, and a host of other specific topics. Process refers to the ways in which the family interacts in terms of communication, family roles, and issues related to family organization. While family members typically talk in terms of content, understanding process is critical in identifying the repetitive patterns that occur within families. Family members might be arguing about curfew, but this topic reveals the ways in which parents attempt to exert control over their growing children, how parents deal with their own relationship, and how parents and children communicate their differences. These process themes are likely to transcend specific topics in the family situation and reflect family system characteristics. Patterns can take various forms. Family members can have codes of silence that make certain topics taboo. Specific family members can dominate the conversation and thus exert control. Family members can use indirection or understatement to communicate. Silence, tears, shouts, and so on can be used to control the conversation.

The family dance of process takes place as the family members deal with a variety of content issues. If the assessment and subsequent interventions are limited to content, important family patterns that maintain problematic interactions can remain unidentified, untouched, and unchallenged. The struggle for growing independence by an adolescent family member, for example, can occur in the context of curfew, participation in family activities, use of money, and appearance. When the focus is on content, the family counselor can quickly become overwhelmed with the multitude of issues and begin to lose a focus with the family.

Linear and Circular Questioning. Families frequently come to the session with a linear mind-set that A causes B. They do not consider that various circular loops are occurring. During the family assessment process, the counselor can not only assess the extent to which the family is locked into this mind-set but also has the potential opportunity to ask questions in such a way to introduce a more complex interaction loop. The following example illustrates the nature of such circular questions introduced into the assessment process.

The Brown family can view the tension in the family as due solely to thirteen-year-old Jim's problem behavior and, therefore, that this is the only change needed. Of course, from Jim's perspective the problem is that his parents are being too strict with him. Each party in this family is hoping that the social worker will accept his or her linear perspective of which of these themes is responsible for the family tension and the circle of blaming within the family that serves to increase the tension. A careful tracking of the sequence through *circular* questions such as, Who steps in first when there is tension? What has been happening with other family members? How have the parents changed in their reactions? How do other siblings react to what is going on? might reveal a more complex and circular pattern within the family. It might uncover tension between the parents regarding how to discipline Jim or increased worry within the family. Jim's older brother has developed a substance-abuse problem, and the frightened parents have created a very strict code for Jim because they are frightened that he will get in the same trouble. It might also reveal a boy who has not found ways to earn the praise of his parents for his academic or sports performance and has discovered a way to get his worried parents involved in his life. It might reveal a boy who is worried because he has overheard his parents talking about possible layoffs at his father's job. These concerns on the part of the parents have made them less attentive to the children and more impatient of the behavior of the children, who in turn have reacted by adopting more difficult behavior. Such circular patterns of behavior frequently are a more realistic reflection of events within the family. Inclusion of these circular patterns in the assessment process also offers additional opportunities for addressing problems within families.

Information from Other Family Members

Eliciting information from various family members gives a broader and more systemic picture of the family story and relationship issues. Recognizing that individuals always come to situations with their own agendas and perceptual frameworks, differences in the family story that emerge can subsequently be explored as appropriate. Aside from personal differences within family members, there are several factors that contribute to these differing scripts.

Life cycle issues can be important contributors to these differences. Children and adults typically view life events from very different developmental perspectives. Teenagers and their parents, for example, frequently disagree on many issues. Young children can be limited in their understanding of complex situations and create a sense of meanings based on life as they see it. The Rogers family described earlier illustrated problems in the children understanding a complex situation. The following example illustrates how developmental issues influence perceptions as they relate to the counseling process.

> Five-year-old Anne was referred for counseling because she had become very frightened of bugs. She had also become very good, but this change had not prompted the referral. Her family included her mother who had been recently widowed, leaving her with the responsibility of the two teenage boys from her husband's previous marriage. Anne revealed that she felt that she had to be very good or her mother would kill herself. Apparently when her mother was feeling upset, she would say, "You boys will be the death of me yet." From the literal perspective of a five-year-old, Anne interpreted these words to mean that her mother would kill herself if she did not help by being good. Naturally the mother was astonished as her daughter explained what these words meant to her. Anne's mother quickly clarified that she was not going to kill herself and that these words were just an expression of her frustration. Anne's fear of bugs and her excessively good behavior went away almost immediately.

> Sarah, another five-year-old, was referred for counseling because of her serious behavior problems in school combined with excessive fears. She had been adopted at birth and had had no contact with her birth mother. When she was two her adoptive mother developed bone cancer and died within six months. Because of her mother's severe health problems, Sarah's aunt cared for her during the illness until the father was ready to remarry. In order to help the child bond with her stepmother and because her own health

was problematic, the aunt then dropped out of the picture. During the counseling process, the child revealed that she believed two of her mothers had already died and she was thus afraid that her third mother would also die. From her perspective, the odds were against her stepmother living. Although her parents had never told her that her birth mother had died, the young child assumed that if she had been adopted, her mother must have died. While giving her the correct information did not effect the immediate change evident in the earlier situation, it represented a crucial step toward reducing her fears.

Generational differences can also emerge in other contexts.

Mrs. Green (age 86) had been experiencing declining physical health. She had broken her hip and was having difficulty going up the stairs in her home. Her grown children were worried that she might injure herself. They recently expressed concern that she might fall and wondered if something should be done. Mrs. Green became very defensive because she interpreted these comments to mean that her children wanted her to sell her home and move into an assisted living facility. Her home was very precious to her and she treasured her independence. She told them that she knew what she was doing and they should "mind their own business." As a result, her children have been reluctant to bring up their concerns and the two generations were at a standstill of silence: resentment and anxiety on one side and worry on the other. Fortunately a favorite grandchild was able to be the family mediator. In reality, Mrs. Green's children were not really thinking in terms of having her move out of her house—rather their plan was to turn the downstairs den into a bedroom and use one of the alert necklaces that would permit her to ask for help if needed. Mrs. Green was willing to consider this plan when she realized that she would not be pushed out of her home and her children were willing to treat her as an intelligent partner.

Communication patterns within the family can contribute to differences in perspectives because information might be shared selectively within the family. Generational boundaries are frequently marked by the information that is shared. My husband was motivated to learn some Dutch because information that the children were not supposed to understand was spoken in Dutch when he was a child. When I interviewed youth in rural families that were experiencing financial problems, many described a pattern of generational boundaries that contributed to their anxiety. The parents would talk about the family's financial problems between themselves but would not discuss them openly with the children. The children of the family would join forces to elicit or overhear whatever information they could in order to piece together what was happening in their family. As one can imagine, such a situation is ripe for multiple interpretations and misunderstandings of a situation.

Problems in clear communication in the family can contribute to differences in perspective. People can communicate in oblique, ambivalent, or contradictory patterns. Sometimes situations are complex, and parents assume that children understand this complexity or do not think that it is important to give detailed information. Even when parents believe that they have communicated with their children, the example of the Rogers family in which the children believed that their mopeds had caused the family's financial problems demonstrates that people can still not understand the larger picture.

> Jim, a teenage boy, was referred to me because he had been stealing gas from the neighbors. He was frightened that the family would need to live on his mother's Avon earnings because the family was going into bankruptcy. What he did not understand was that the father was declaring Chapter 11 bankruptcy for the family business. His parents had not realized the importance of explaining to Jim the different types of bankruptcies and the implications of Chapter 11 for the family.

Family alliances based on gender, generations, or unique family circumstances can also influence communication patterns within families. Family members who are part of a specific family alliance are likely to communicate more with each other and perhaps exclude others. They can also share a similar perspective on family issues. Eliciting information about the situation and potential resources from different family members can help identify some of these issues. The patterns reflected in these differences can potentially reveal problematic communication patterns, family alliances, or other issues that might need to be addressed in the counseling situation.

Social Worker's Reaction

The social worker can also use her or his own reaction to the family as part of the assessment process. Since families enlist their counselor into the family dance, the social worker also begins to experience the family patterns. One can begin to experience the pressure to blame or ignore a specific family member or to avoid certain topics because family members dodge around them. I have caught myself turning toward family members who engage me and in the process ignoring others until I realized that I was mirroring long-standing family patterns that tended to marginalize certain family members. Without intending to do so, I was reinforcing patterns that isolated family members. The family dance can be a very powerful one.

Coping Process

In assessing the ability of family members to cope, it is important to recognize that coping does not occur within a vacuum. It is influenced by the nature of the challenge facing the family. Community and cultural expectations also create varying scripts regarding appropriate ways to cope. These scripts help family members learn coping skills as well as offer support or censure for differing behaviors. The use of coping strategies that are effective in addressing a situation contributes to the process of resiliency within families. Effective coping in this context refers to actions that represent a positive adaptation to circumstances.

The following represent key areas identified in the resiliency literature that influence how families are able to cope. As is evident from the discussion regarding family coping, these items form a circle as events are appraised and addressed. As described in chapter 1, the Family Resiliency model developed by McCubbin et al., 1998, identifies a process by which family members can seek to address stressors through changing their appraisal of the situation, by addressing the stressor, by managing or reducing family tension, and by obtaining additional resources. As a result, it is important to include an understanding of the nature of the stressor and how it is appraised by the family, the family's resources to address the problem, the family's ability to reduce tension within the family, and the potential resources within the wider context in the assessment process. Appraisals influence the nature of the coping strategies employed, and the results of these coping strategies in turn influence appraisals. For example, use of a coping strategy that has a favorable outcome changes the definition of a situation from overwhelming to manageable and in turn increases the self-efficacy of family members. This circle sets in play yet a second circle in response and interacts with other ongoing patterns within the family and the community.

The Current Stressor

This stressor is frequently the presenting problem. Questions such as "What brought you here?" "Why did you contact our agency?" "What type of help are you looking for?" "How can we help you?" and "What changes do you wish to occur?" can be useful in eliciting this information. Given the complexities of family life, such stressors can represent one of a wide variety of life circumstances. The current stressor may be a referral from the school because the thirteen-year-old son or daughter is skipping school or a major conflict between the parents on how to spend their limited money. It can be the discovery by parents that one of their teenagers has been abusing alcohol or other drugs, the sudden illness of the grandmother who had been the emotional mainstay of the family, the family's eviction from their apartment, or pressure from the court due to neglect of a child. While this list contains only single items, families frequently seek help because several related problems are creating distress. This issue will be discussed subsequently in terms of additive sources of stress. The nature of this stressor can begin to shape the picture of the needs to be addressed in the counseling process.

Onset of Stressor

It is valuable to identify the issues related to the onset of the current stressor. Is the problem at hand a recent one with a sudden onset (an acute problem), or is it a long-term problem that has in some way become more serious or intolerable due to other life circumstances that make it difficult for the family to cope with it, or has now caused community members to insist that the family seek help? The exploration of these differences can help identify the context of the current stressor, the presence of additive stressful events, the meaning of this event in the life of the family (appraisal), and potential resources.

The following families are seeking help for housing with quite a different combination of onsets and accompanying situations.

> The Andrews family comes for help with housing because they were recently evicted from their apartment for nonpayment of rent. They have a long history of being evicted from apartments for failure to pay their rent. The employment pattern of both parents is sporadic.

> The Bowen family is also seeking housing help in response to eviction, but their situation is quite different. One parent recently lost a steady job that had been held for several years due to downsizing at the plant. Loss of income combined with family health problems by the other parent resulted in the family being unable to pay their rent.

> The Conner family is also seeking housing because a major tornado devastated their home. They returned from the shelter to discover that the storm had blown off their roof and a large tree had fallen on it and made the house unsafe for habitation. They had lived in this home for the last ten years following a move to the community after they retired. Their home was part of a neighborhood that had been devastated by the storm. While they had insurance, it was not adequate to cover their costs and they needed additional financial aid.

Based on this information, the Andrews family reveals a risk pattern of long-term financial instability and poor management coping strategies with possible problematic employment skills. While further information is needed before making a final assessment, it is likely that the situation will not be solved merely by referrals for a new low-rent housing option or job placement. On the protective side, family members have stayed together as a family despite all of these problems that might have driven them apart. This suggests a level of cohesion and sense of identity as a family. They have not become demoralized from their ongoing problem. The Bowen family demonstrates the coping strategies needed for long-term employment and generally adequate financial management coping abilities. Their family members also have retained a sense of family despite their current crisis. The Conner family was caught in the vortex of a natural disaster. The family's ability to turn to neighbors is limited because they too were caught up in the storm, but they have been together as a couple for some time. Fortunately, the Conner family will be eligible for federal assistance because their community was declared a disaster area. Further exploration might reveal that the Andrews family appraises their current situation as part of their usual pattern of life, while for the Bowen family it represents a major disruption in their pattern and family identity. The Conner family members are feeling the shock of their long-term home and mementoes being destroyed and the destruction of their neighborhood, but they are grateful that they survived it together because others were killed in the storm.

Impact on Family

What has been the impact on the family of this stressor? Typically people do not seek help unless some event has either created distress for members of the family or on the part of people who have some power or influence over the family. The impact of the stressor on the family is a reflection of the potential disruption, the family appraisals of the problem and resources, and the family coping strategies and resources. The impact of life events of family members can vary widely depending on the appraisal of the situation and potential individual, family, and contextual resources. Assessment must include positive as well as negative changes. Some useful questions that elicit information regarding the impact of the event on the family include:

How has this affected you as a family (as well as individual family members)?

How has this been difficult for you?

What was there about this event that led you to contact our agency?

What have been your concerns?

How has this changed your family and your way of thinking?

What do you think might help?

In what ways has this affected your relationships with people outside of your family?

The nature of this impact is influenced by various risk and resiliency factors. Exploration regarding the impact often opens the door to these issues. The impact of events on families is affected by additive factors, appraisals, and coping strategies, as well as the risk and protective factors identified earlier and discussed in greater detail in this chapter.

Additive Factors

Resiliency research indicates that a series of difficult events is more stressful for families than even the summation of the individual situations. The question here relates to what are some of the other issues in the life of the family that are increasing the distress the family experiences. Such additive factors may be related to the following issues.

Life cycle issues within the family. Families go through a variety of changes during the ongoing life cycle, and people enter and leave the family circle and change their roles within the family and the wider context. A child who had been the intermediary between the parents goes off to college. A parent or grandparent dies. A much-awaited new baby creates time and energy demands on the couple who are now parents. A marriage brings together two very different families. Retirement changes roles within the family and the family's relationship within the wider community. A child moves into adolescence. Chapter 1 contains a description of one prototype of a family life cycle as well as variations regarding the family life cycle.

Additional circumstances. Families are frequently experiencing several difficult life circumstances at the same time. Family members can lose jobs, experience legal problems, or have substance abuse issues or other health problems. Problems within the school setting can challenge families. Domestic violence can be a major threat to the family life. Extended family members can make demands on the family as a result of illness and other issues. Families can live in violent neighborhoods that impact in various ways on the members. Families might have moved from other cultures and face acculturation challenges. These circumstances can interact in complex ways that increase the stress experienced by families.

Unresolved issues activated by current stressors. Family members can reexperience difficult times in their lives that are activated by current stressors. Divorce can reactivate the feelings of being rejected by parents. Absence of a partner who has been called to active duty can evoke feelings of being vulnerable due to an earlier experience with rape or fears of abandonment. Loss of a job can reactivate feelings of worthlessness. A child's difficulties in school can activate parental feelings of failure due to the parent's own educational problems in school.

Contextual issues. Community poverty with the attendant lack of opportunities can increase the pain of job loss. Discrimination can be experienced as oppressive and reducing hope for new opportunities. Violence and crime within the community can create realistic fears of safety or worries about the role models available to youth.

Additive factors can be explored in many ways. The following are useful questions or prompts for eliciting the family's perspective on additive factors that can increase the stress.

Have you had your hands full with any other problems or difficulties?

Has anything happened in your family that has made this more difficult to cope with?

Are you having to contend with any other problems/or changes?

Has anything been happening in your own family life or your community that has made this worse?

Has this problem prompted any other difficulty in your life?

Are there other worries you have that are making this problem worse?

Has anything else been happening in your family that has influenced how you have been able to handle this?

Mr. Warren illustrates the power of several of these additive factors, including a reactivation of past life events, as well as the resiliency present within the family system.

Mr. Warren (a man in his late fifties) contacted the local mental health center at the urging of his wife due to his deepening depression. He was experiencing serious financial problems with his farm and was depressed and discouraged about the future. He was also feeling that he had failed his family. Mr. Warren described his experience as a boy growing up in the Netherlands during World War II. As the older brother, he felt that it was his responsibility to take care of and protect his younger brother. But a ten-year-old boy was no match for the bombs, devastation, and near starvation experienced by the people in the community. Appraising this situation within the cognitive framework of a child, he believed that he was a failure. He grew up determined to protect his family in the future. As an adult, Mr. Warren was true to his word. He worked hard, supported his family well, and provided his children with college educations. Now caught up in the major economic depression of the agriculture sector, his careful arrangement of care for his family was falling down around him. The depressed economic situation in his community had decreased other employment opportunities. He was worried that his age would also jeopardize these opportunities.

As a result, additive factors due to life cycle, previously unresolved life issues, and contextual issues all interacted with the initial stressor to set in motion and intensify his depression. Fortunately for Mr. Warren, powerful resources were also present. His wife was a caring person who loved him deeply. When she learned of his feelings of guilt and sense of failure, she took steps to alter them with other sources of information. She contacted the adult children who in turn were quick to reach out to their father with words of thanks and appreciation for all that he had given them. The family mounted a campaign to change his view of himself from that of a failure to a hero who had created a viable business out of very little and had launched his children into successful adulthood through his efforts. They also indicated that they were now at a stage of life where they could and should help out their parents if the need should arise.

While the message of additive life events relates to the presence of increased risk factors, this part of the assessment process can also be used to highlight family resources. As family members describe the presence of multiple stressors that the family is experiencing, the social worker can highlight some of the signs of resources that have also emerged in this context. That the family has somehow or other managed to stay together as a family, or ensured that children continue to go to school, that no serious abuse has occurred, or that family members have not succumbed to the temptation of substance abuse or have been able to stop abusing drugs to escape the tension, are all signs of strength within the family. The counselor can comment that other families might have long ago given up and thrown in the towel, while they are still staying together trying as a family. This information provides the opportunity later to explore with the family what have been some of their sources of resiliency—how did they manage to cope, what gave them the strength to go on, what kept them from giving up, what enabled them to pick themselves up during these difficult times.

Family Appraisals of the Situation

As described in the family strengths and family crisis literature, how family members interpret life events shapes how they will experience and respond to stressors. These appraisals are influenced by the family's own unique paradigms as well as the schemas that are part of the cultural framework. The family therapy technique reframing in which events are placed within a new meaning system is based on recognition of the importance of the meaning that is attributed to an event. Mr. Warren interpreted his business financial problems as evidence that he had failed his family members yet again. His wife and children fortunately did not share his interpretation and instead pointed out that he had cared for his family. The Lo family feared that their daughter's attempted suicide would cause the family to be deported. In the Rogers family, both the young people in the family felt guilty because they felt responsible for the family's problems. The family resiliency literature indicates that resilient families are able to recognize complex causes of situations instead of blaming and scapegoating family members. Understanding events within a developmental perspective can also be helpful because it permits family members to recognize the role that development plays and that change is possible.

Appraisals can include attributions of responsibility, views on what is the likely impact of the event, and ways to address it. As family members describe their current and past stressors, questions that evoke attributions of responsibility and meanings of events can be useful. This information can be elicited as part of the ongoing conversation with the family about the event. Patterns of blaming and scapegoating within the family can emerge.

Attributions can be powerfully influenced by cultural views of what is important or appropriate behavior. Families can also be influenced by the way in which community members view issues. HIV/AIDS is associated with stigma in many societies. This community definition can be a powerful influence on the nature of resources available to the family. Community appraisals that have been internalized by the family members will be reflected in the appraisals given by family members. The process of exploring other resources within the community often reveals other community perspectives on the issue. Questions such as the following can help prompt information in the areas of attribution and impact.

What did you make of . . . ?

What do you think helped make this happen?

What have you told yourself about this event in your family?

What has been your interpretation of this event?

Have you ever asked why this happened?

Appraisals of how to address the problem are important in understanding the family's choice of coping strategies and view of the nature of appropriate resources and ways to access them. Questions related to this issue are helpful in identifying information regarding several critical areas including the family's expectation of the counseling situation, the family's paradigms regarding how to address problems of this nature, the nature of the family's support system within the larger community, and the family's previous attempts to address this problem. Some useful questions and probes in this realm include

What have been your thoughts on ways to help this situation?

Has anything been useful so far that would be valuable in trying to address this problem?

What do you think would be helpful?

What do you hope to get out of coming here?

Identifying Appropriate Resources

Coping Efforts

A repertoire of coping efforts is an important source of resiliency because life requires many different approaches to life events. While the nature of effective coping efforts varies depending on the situation, the ability of the family to pull together to address family issues is a consistently important family resource. Eliciting information about what the family has already done to try to solve this problem and the results can be valuable in assessing family coping strategies as well as the nature of the resources available to family members.

How have you tried to solve this problem and with what results?

What have you already done to try to make this situation better (and with what results)?

Have there been people in your family or community that you have turned to address this problem (with what results)?

If not, what has kept you from seeking help from others about this problem?

These questions can be effective in identifying possible resources within the extended family and community as well as barriers in this process and the views of the community regarding the stressor. One can elicit feelings of support as well as those of shame, alienation, and isolation. As described earlier, coping can address how people interpret life events, change the nature of the stressful event, reduce family tension, and obtain resources.

Belief Systems

Self-Efficacy, Mastery, Hope

In terms of beliefs of self-efficacy, mastery, and hope, families quickly reveal either their sense of feeling defeated in their coping efforts or their feeling that they can address the problem given a little extra help. These families seem hopeful that their problem can be solved. When families are demoralized about their coping efforts, it is common for them to use words to convey that they are discouraged because they have tried everything and feel that nothing has helped. They project a sense of hopelessness about their situation.

The family's definition of appropriate and available resources and ways to access these resources are important. Cultural background, community definitions, the nature of the problem, and unique family circumstances all help shape these definitions. Questions that relate to whom they can turn for help and in what way are useful in eliciting this information. As discussed earlier, while one family in a community might view a resource as available and acceptable, this same potential resource can be viewed as unavailable and unacceptable by others.

From a resiliency perspective, the social worker needs to be constantly surveying the situation for possible sources of resiliency. As a result, it can be valuable to extend the focus of the conversation beyond the immediate problem and situation. What evidence is there in the family history or current context that might have some parallels to the current situation that can be used to enhance the family's sense of self-efficacy and hopefulness regarding their ability to address this problem or to identify supports within their family or community?

> Have you ever experienced a situation at all similar to the one that you are going through now? If so, how did you handle this?
>
> What did you do as a family to try to make it better? (identification of coping strategies)
>
> Were you able to turn to others to try to make it better (with what effect)?

A family can become so overwhelmed by its current situation that it loses sight of possible strengths within its family or support system. Information regarding effective coping with similar current or past events can be used to highlight the ability of the family to cope. Such information can also influence how both the family and stressors are appraised. Similarly, information about help received from others can be used to highlight possible resources.

Family Trust, Loyalty, and Affection

Family trust, loyalty, and affection are important sources of family resiliency. The counselor needs to be attentive to verbal and nonverbal signs of such traits within the family as they play out the family drama in the session. Beyond specific comments by family members that reveal concern and unity versus anger and mistrust, gestures such as posture and seating positions can be revealing. Tones of voice that express caring or protection in contrast to anger or disdain are important clues. Sometimes hurt can be an indirect sign that people in the family are important to each other—the people who are important to us have the power to hurt us. If family members are embroiled in a current situation and are unable to access feelings of affection and caring, the social worker can probe for evidence that such feelings were present during the past. Visible signs of anger can mislead counselors into following up and concentrating on negative traits within the family that could be triggering this anger and as a result miss important resources of love.

> The Dodge family consists of Sharon, a college student who was adopted as a baby by her parents. Both were professionals. The father had experienced very difficult and dangerous times in Europe during World War II and was currently recovering from a very serious and life-threatening health condition. Sharon had a brother who was also adopted and did not attend the

sessions. Unlike his sister, who was an excellent student and very active in school activities, he was not invested in school and created many problems for the family because of his behavior problems. Sharon was referred for counseling because of a sudden onset of periods of dissociation. Her behavior during these periods was potentially dangerous for herself (going out in the frigid cold without a coat) and for others in the family (making threats to harm one of her parents). As a result, the counselor's focus was upon what was triggering her anger toward her parents or explorations perhaps even of how she might be acting out anger by one of her parents toward the other parent. Following a crisis during which she had to be hospitalized to protect her from a potential suicide attempt and her subsequent realization that she did not really want to kill herself, Sharon and her parents participated in a very meaningful and revealing family session. With tears Sharon explained to her parents that she was trying to be perfect because she felt that she had to make up for her brother to protect her father with his health problems. She was frightened that he might have another heart attack and die if she did not do so. It was her sense of family loyalty and affection that was the bottom line here. With her parents' assurance that they loved her, that she did not need to be perfect to make up for her brother, and that her parents did not need her help in this way, her serious symptoms quickly resolved themselves and did not reoccur.

Explorations regarding potential sources of help within the extended family can elicit information about possible sources of affection and caring within this wider circle. Once the family counselor has identified important supports within the family circle, the question arises as to how one can most effectively tap these sources of resiliency. On the principle that one wants to bring together the people who can help solve the problem, the assessment process will influence the nature of the cast of the family members invited to future sessions. Perhaps there are members of the extended family or other support systems within the circle of friends, pastors, and so on that would be appropriate to include in the sessions, and it can be useful to discuss this possibility with the family members.

Patterns of Spirituality or Faith

Because spirituality and faith can emerge as resources in several ways for some family members (Walsh, 1999, 2006), it can be valuable to explore whether or not this aspect is meaningful to the family in the assessment process. Some of this information will occur as family members describe the meaning that events have had in terms of their growth, in a sense of meaning or purpose, or perhaps their deepening of faith in others or their religious life. Spirituality and faith can also emerge as risk factors as people express bitterness or alienation. Counselors can ask if family members have any spiritual or faith concerns or possible sources of help or support in dealing with this issue. By including both concerns and sources of support, it opens the door to potential positives as well as problems. Depending on the answers, further exploration can occur. Chapter 13 discusses this process in further depth. On the negative side, family members might state how they have become alienated from their faith, how they feel burdened with guilt, how members of their faith community have turned their backs on them. In terms of support, family members could also describe helpful coping efforts that involve turning to members of their spiritual community for emotional or instrumental health. Life events can also have different meanings for family members depending on their spiritual tradition, for example, what happens after death, and the meaning of suffering. In this sense spiritual issues carry with them cultural implications just as ethnicity and race can. Exploring whether or not spiritual or faith issues are important for family members as they are going through this problem situation opens the door to learning how family members view these issues as potential sources of help or perhaps as burdens. Such an exploration can be especially useful because family members might not view the counselor as interested in these aspects of their life and thus not reveal them. As described in other areas, addressing this issue requires self-reflection on the part of the counselor so that one's own religious/spiritual biases do not cloud the assessment process.

Relationships with the divine (as viewed by the family and their spiritual tradition) can be important sources of support. Spiritual rituals can be sources of comfort and healing. While these represent positive responses that support resiliency, families can also feel alienated from their traditional faith or from members of their religious community. People can experience difficult life events as punishment from God and feel abandoned. Early life experiences can make concepts such as "God as my father" into reminders of failure, abandonment, or abuse. Individuals within the family can vary widely in terms of their experiences in the area of spirituality and religion, and thus the assessment must incorporate these differences and the impact on the family's resources for coping.

Organizational Patterns

Family Cohesion

An important source of family resiliency is cohesion, the family's ability to band together as a group to address the problems of life. As described in chapter 4 on "Cultural Issues," cultures vary in terms of what this means regarding codes of relatedness compared to individualism within families. Regardless of the continuum involved here, the ability of the family to view itself as a unit (we), for members to care about what happens to other family members and the family unit, and to band together to address the problems facing the family is an essential aspect of family resiliency. Family patterns of cohesion can be identified by the family's descriptions of how they appraise the nature of the problem (especially, their concern for its impact on the family as a whole) and views of potential ways to address the problem or their history of coping efforts. On the other side, family members can also describe problems in relying on family members, fear of turning to others out of risk of rejection, prior abandonment, or distancing. As one teenage girl said to me, "It hurts when I walk down the street and my father doesn't even say 'Hi' to me when he passes me."

Family Leadership

Resilient families have an effective leadership structure that can direct family efforts and ensure that family member needs are met within the resource constraints of the family. Ineffective leadership patterns can range from those in which leaders abuse their power in a dominating manner or where there is no sense of order within the family.

Leadership patterns can be identified as family members describe how they have responded previously to the presenting situation or other events within the family. Communication patterns within the session can also reveal leadership patterns within the family. Do children evidence appropriate respect for the parents who are speaking or are there constant interruptions or disparaging comments made? On the other hand, is leadership by one or more of the parents so overbearing that other family members are reluctant to speak?

As described earlier, it can be useful to expand the discussion beyond the problem at hand to other situations currently or in the past to identify leadership patterns. There may be evidence that effective leadership was present in the past but some event or circumstances, for example, the demoralization of loss of a job, or the onset of depression or illness, has diminished the ability of the parents to exercise leadership. Such circumstances suggest that the skills for leadership are potentially present and can be reactivated with appropriate help. Perhaps one of the parents had assumed the leadership role within the family and now this parent is no longer able to carry out this role due to separation or death. Families might have had leadership styles that were effective when the children were young but are no longer effective now that the children are adolescents and are challenging the previous leadership style. Cultural disjuncture can also play a role. Family members who have emigrated to other countries can sometimes have difficulties in establishing leadership styles that fit with the new culture and the change in roles in terms of the new community.

If gaps are identified, what are the possibilities for skill development or support for currently dormant leadership abilities? Identifying these aspects helps guide the treatment process.

Family Communication

Family communication patterns are important in terms of resiliency because effective communication is essential for problem solving and can contribute to the sense of trust within the family. Some of the issues of communication were identified in the earlier discussion regarding different perspectives of family issues.

The counselor can observe family communication patterns within the family interview. The following observations can be useful.

Are family members able to talk about difficult things?

When sensitive topics arise, do they veer off, change the subject, and become overly angry at one another?

Who are the people who appear to influence what is talked about and by whom in the family?

Can family members listen to each other?

Are the comments of some family members valued while others are discounted?

What patterns emerge as family members discuss the situation?

Social workers can also ask family members to enact in the family session some typical communication interaction patterns. When family members describe an ongoing disagreement or successful resolution, the family counselor can ask them to demonstrate in the session what occurs at home. This enactment permits the counselor to check with the family if the communication pattern present in the session reflects what occurs at home.

The social worker can use this information to identify effective and ineffective communication patterns to problems that need to be addressed in the counseling process. Assessment of family communication must, of course, consider cultural differences in communication. A social work student who had grown up in an urban community described her confusion in working with rural families who used terms such as "small problem" to refer to major events such as an impending eviction or serious health problems. A counselor accustomed to direct communication can be puzzled while working with a family from cultural groups that value indirection or understatement. What is critical here, of course, is how these family communication patterns work for the family members involved and their support systems.

Flexibility of Family Roles

Family resiliency is enhanced by the ability of family members to assume different responsibilities and roles within the family. As family members are called up to military duty, become ill, or lose jobs, other family members must be able and willing to carry out the roles of family members who are missing or are no longer able to meet the needs of the family in the previous manner.

Family flexibility can be assessed by using the information provided by family members regarding how they have attempted to cope with the current stressor and other issues within the family. Families can give evidence of parents who return to work, adolescent children who help out more with household tasks, or grandparents who become more active in helping with the care of the children.

On the other hand, they can reveal patterns that indicate that family members are locked into rigid family roles. A variety of these factors can contribute to this rigidity. Understanding the nature of these factors can be useful to identifying ways to increase flexibility within the family. Family members may be reluctant to take on new responsibilities because they lack these alternative coping skills or the needed self-confidence in their ability to take on new home or employment roles. Family and related community appraisal issues (strong family, community, or cultural prescriptions regarding family roles) may also deter flexibility.

Family transitions in terms of life cycle, moves, or changes to family employment or roles within the family or the external world can potentially be particularly stressful for family members (as well as open doors to new opportunities). The counselor can explore the presence of such transitions experienced by the family and the impact of this change. The combination of these factors, as for example in the Lo family, represents the impact of additive factors associated with life cycle and new cultural adaptation. The following discussion highlights transition issues related to family life cycle and geographic moves.

Family Life Cycle

One type of transition relates to changes within the family life cycle that requires new life challenges, tasks, and ways of behaving in terms of family members and those external to the family. Such life transitions require flexibility of family roles and organizational structures as well as individual coping strategies. The nature of this life cycle varies depending on social and cultural contexts; for example, the substantial decrease in the number of individuals who are marrying, cultural contexts in which the young married couple is absorbed into the parental subsystem, societal changes in terms of improved health and a wider range of interests among the older generation (i.e., no longer home to babysit the grandchildren), growing numbers of single parents, and the increased divorce rate among older adults.

As described in chapter 1, McGoldrick and Carter identified a set of life cycle issues and the accompanying tasks involved. This set of life cycle issues represents only one prototype of a family life cycle. The case examples in this book illustrate a number of variables within the family life cycle.

The assessment process can help identify issues related to family life cycle in terms of risks and challenges. For example, a family might be struggling with the recent death of the mother/grandmother who had been the glue that held the family together over the years. A parent who was the mainstay of the family business might become severely disabled and no longer able to assume this role in the same manner (the Rodriguez family). Another family might be delighted to finally have a grandchild as part of the family and eager to provide babysitting services to a struggling young couple with their first child. Another family might be challenged to deal with a child born with developmental disabilities while extended family members are also dealing with illness on the part of the grandparents. The current economic crisis has meant that many couples that were living independently now have young adult children living at home again. Adults who had counted on working until their full retirement age have had to scramble as companies have laid off older and more expensive employees.

Family location changes can also be an issue. Families move for a variety of reasons, including employment, retirement, the goal of being closer to other family members, or to seek a better life. While all moves bring with them new challenges and potential opportunities, some families experience moves that represent major cultural changes. Some families are escaping harsh conditions in their home country and come either as refugees or immigrants to countries that they hope will offer a safer and more benign setting. Understanding the context of this move can be essential in the assessment process. What shadows are this family experiencing from their past life? What expectations did they have in coming to their new land? What changes in family roles, in community expectations have they faced? What has been the change in their economic status or opportunities? What supports have they found in their new world? Have they felt welcomed in their new community? Have any of these issues played a role in the situation that has prompted their need for services?

Humor

Humor can be an essential family resource in dealing with some of the very tough circumstances of life. Humor might not emerge initially as family members are absorbed in their situation and pain. As family members become more relaxed with the family counselor and have had the opportunity to share their pain, the family's gift of humor may begin to emerge. Identifying these instances can provide the opportunity to explore with the family times of laughter (now or in the past) and their role in the family's life.

COMMUNITY CONTEXT

Cultural and community codes provide for a context for learning and reinforcing specific coping efforts. Families in transition can face a disjuncture between the coping strategies that they have learned and the current context in terms of the coping strategies that are viewed as appropriate. Thinking of what it meant for my grandparents to leave their homes in the Netherlands and move to a new country has increased my respect for them and the many others who have made this journey. The following illustration highlights how cultural codes influence the appropriate ways to access potential resources and the anxiety that it can create when the disjuncture is great and the stakes are high.

Our family faced such a cultural juncture several years ago when we visited our daughter in her village while she was serving in the Peace Corps in Chad. This experience has helped me appreciate the stress created by these situations and the need to recognize the influence of context. When we arrived in her community, our daughter informed us that while she had managed to get a ride for us into the town (a distance of a few hours), she had not yet found a ride out to catch our plane a week later (and planes only left twice a week). This was in a context in which there was absolutely no public transportation available. As Americans used to asking people in relatively direct ways we were operating in a cultural context in which it was viewed as inappropriate to do so and all conversations began with an hour asking about the health of immediate and extended family members. Culture mandated that one could tell others of one's situation but could not ask people if they could help you. Furthermore, these conversations were taking place in French (a language of which we possessed only limited understanding). Our skills to cope with this situation were woefully ill-matched to our needs. As a result, we would visit the handful of families who owned a vehicle and after an hour my husband anxiously asked our daughter if she had obtained a ride yet. She would whisper that she was still asking about the health of the uncle. After another hour, we would leave without an offer for a ride. Finally, someone was going to the city where the airport was located and came to our rescue.

The community context plays a vital role in terms of the nature of the risk and protective factors. Information regarding this context emerges in the interview as well as the eco map. Individuals can feel stressed as they must handle two jobs as well as a family in order to make ends meet or can have friends and family in the community to whom they can turn for help. The social worker also draws upon her or his knowledge of the community to identify potential risk and resiliency factors. Understanding if the family lives in an area of the community noted for high crime and violence or is protected from these problems is valuable information. Some schools have strong financial and other types of volunteer support from educated parents, while others seek to educate children whose parents are frequently too overwhelmed by their own struggles in life to contribute to their children's education. Some families live in areas of the community noted for their youth orchestras while others are on the news for the latest in gang violence.

Based on the resiliency perspective that there are potential resources within each environment, the social worker goes beyond these general descriptions to try to identify whatever resources might be available in the community. It might be a dedicated teacher; a youth leader at the church, mosque, temple, or synagogue; a concerned neighbor; or a community program for youth or adults.

The social worker collaborates with the family to use the information obtained through these various means to identify key aspects related to the nature of the distress experienced by the family, the relevant risk factors, and the strengths, protective factors, and sources of resiliency that are either part of the family system or that can be accessed as resources. Such a complex picture helps the worker identify appropriate strategies for helping the family to address problems in ways that contribute to healing and empower them to cope in more effective ways.

LEVELS OF FAMILY FUNCTIONING

Kilpatrick (2003) organizes the risk and protective factors of families in terms of levels. These levels indicate the risk and protective factors that are in place in this context of family needs and strengths. She uses the metaphor of a house in which the different levels represent aspects of the building.

Level I represents the foundation (basic survival needs of the family in terms of food, shelter, protection, medical care, minimal nurturance). These families tend to move from crisis to crisis and become overwhelmed with the number of risk factors and problematic events facing them. There are typically a number of contextual risk factors in the areas of housing, safe neighborhoods, access to health care, interpersonal support systems, and steady employment, along with problematic coping skills to address family needs. Family leadership is ineffective in meeting family needs (Kilpatrick, 2003).

Level II families represent the framing and the roof (structure and organization). These families have the protective factors that enable the family to meet the basic needs of members. There are risk factors in the area of effective family leadership along with difficulties in communication and coping skills needed to provide adequate family leadership (Kilpatrick, 2003).

Level III families represent the placement of the walls and doors (space and boundaries). They have the protective factors to enable them to meet the basic needs of the family and to offer leadership within the family that can ensure the safety and basic organization within the family. Risk factors here relate to family organizational patterns that prevent families from being appropriately flexible, creating appropriate boundaries within the family, and family members from developing close and supportive relationships that also permit family members to create their own sense of identity (Kilpatrick, 2003).

Level IV families represent the furnishings and the decorations (elements of richness and quality). They have the protective factors that enable them to meet the basic needs of survival as well as adequate leadership and organizational patterns that permit flexibility and appropriate family boundaries. Families have the communication and coping skills to meet these important family needs. At this level, families are looking for a greater sense of intimacy and meaning within the family. Issues of meaning in current relationships and those over time assume greater importance (Kilpatrick, 2003).

The combination of risk and protective factors within this context offers guidelines for selection of the appropriate intervention strategies. The more families are contending with a number of basic risk factors, the greater their need for an explicitly strengths-based focus (Kilpatrick, 2003).

ASSESSMENT AND TREATMENT PLANNING

The concept of key factors discussed earlier is valuable at this point in identifying a sense of direction for the counseling process. What is amenable to change and can make a difference? What are the relevant risk factors that can be addressed in this regard? What supports do family members need? Do the family members lack specific coping skills (perhaps parenting or other family relationships, adjustment to a new culture)? How do the appraisals of the family influence how they are experiencing the problem and potential solutions? Is the problem one of a weak support system or problematic interpretations (that a teenage suicide attempt would cause a family to be deported)? Does the family lack crucial resources (homes damaged by a storm, lack of income, major health problems without access to care) or some combination of these factors? What are the protective factors that can be supported or need to be enhanced? The answer to these questions can help formulate the goals and intervention strategies.

In this process, the counselor must never forget what Worden (2003) describes as the key rule of thumb with families: "Do not get ahead of the family. Address the members' chief concerns first" (p. 129). The assessment process within this framework permits the counselor and the family to develop the appropriate intervention plans through a collaborative process. The social worker can also maintain a focus on patterns and look at possible circularity in the process. The family counselor brings to this partnership knowledge of different interventions along with an understanding of the evidence of their effectiveness in addressing the present situation. The social worker also has information about potential community resources and ways to access them or at least ways to find out about such resources. The social worker's information is shared with the family in a collaborative manner so that important decisions can be made in terms of the selection of intervention strategies.

From the perspective of resiliency theory, if families can be helped to address some of the issues facing them more effectively, they will also strengthen their sense of self-efficacy to address problems in the future. Coping and appraisals have a reciprocal interaction. This process will strengthen their protective factors that can serve as tools for future concerns.

The following family vignettes illustrate several patterns of risk and resiliency factors and implications for treatment approaches. Some of these examples relate to the levels of family functioning and others refer to specific organizational and family process issues or major stressors. These illustrations are selective and do not do justice to the entire range of risk and resiliency patterns and potential intervention strategies. They do suggest ways in which the assessment process can influence the professional judgment process in terms of the nature of the interventions that are appropriate for specific families addressing their current life circumstances. Subsequent chapters will describe specific treatment approaches and their applications with families.

Basic Needs Risks

Mr. Matt Cole seeks help for his family. He has been raising his two children, aged seven and ten years, since the death of his ex-wife in an accident three years ago. Prior to that time Mr. Cole had visited the children but had not been the caretaker because they were divorced and Mr. Cole had been hospitalized several times for severe depression. Mr. Cole is on disability but would like to begin working to provide a better living for his family. He has been receiving his medication through his family doctor but has not been taking his medication recently and has been feeling increasingly depressed. His seven-year-old daughter is doing reasonably well in school but his ten-year-old son has recently been having difficulty both academically and behaviorally. Mr. Cole has been reluctant to talk with staff members of the school because his own experiences with school as a child were difficult ones. He dropped out of school at the age of sixteen and has bad memories of the school experience. He had difficulties academically and took a job with a company (since disbanded). Mr. Cole is alienated from one of his siblings but does see another one on a regular basis. His parents are dead.

He does not live near his ex-wife's parents, who are still alive and interested in their grandchildren. The Cole family lives in a part of the community where many of the homes need major repairs and their home is no exception. At the same time, he is worried that the family might be evicted because his ongoing financial problems have made it difficult to pay their rent. He has received one warning letter and dreads looking at the mail. Choices between paying for rent or his medicine have placed Mr. Cole in an impossible bind. Mr. Cole is feeling overwhelmed with his responsibilities as a father. He fears that he might become depressed again and will not be able to take care of the children. While he wants to help his son in terms of the school he feels intimidated by the school situation.

The Cole family is on the edge of being evicted and Mr. Cole is feeling the bind of potentially having to choose between his medication and rent for the house. He is struggling with an increasing problem with his depression that makes it difficult for him to carry out his life responsibilities. He is overwhelmed with his new role as a father. His employment job skills, especially in the current troubled economy, are problematic. The son is having difficulties in school. Mr. C. is intimated by the school situation because it reactivates his own problems as a student. He is alienated from one important sibling.

Despite these serious problems, there are also protective factors. Mr. C. has a sibling with whom he has a good relationship. The maternal grandparents are also invested in the children and the family. Although he is finding his role as parent difficult, Mr. C. appears to be motivated to take care of his children. His daughter is doing well in school. He has a relationship with a physician who has been treating him for his depression.

The multisystemic approach is appropriate for this family with its combination of risk and protective factors. Such an approach can help Mr. C. in terms of finding potential resources for his medication and work with him regarding employment issues. The counselor can also help Mr. C. create linkages with the school social worker or help Mr. C. feel more effective as a parent in dealing with the school system. The counselor can also help Mr. C. in gaining more effective parenting skills.

Structure and Rewards System

Mr. and Mrs. King have been married for two years. Both were married before. Mrs. King has three children, aged eight, eleven, and fourteen, from her first marriage. She and her first husband were divorced five years ago. Mrs. King's first husband left the family for another woman. She was hesitant to become involved again, but once Mr. King helped her overcome her doubts, she became committed to making this relationship work. She does not want to put the children or herself through yet another painful divorce. Mr. King has two children, aged seven and ten, from his first marriage that ended when his wife died four years ago. The couple met through their church group for single parents. Fortunately the family has adequate financial resources because Mr. King earns a good salary and there was life insurance money from his first wife. Mrs. King's first husband also helps pay some of the bills for the children. The maternal and paternal grandparents are supportive of this new family but do not live in the same geographic area. Mrs. King stays at home and has primary responsibility for the house. Mr. and Mrs. King have, however, been unable to work out an agreement regarding how to discipline the children. Mrs. King is relatively firm in her standards for the children and believes that children need structure and discipline. Mr. King believes that his children were traumatized by the death of their mother from cancer and is hesitant to exercise discipline. Prior to his marriage to Mrs. King the household was organized around the wishes of the children and the word "no" was seldom heard in the family. When Mrs. King seeks to discipline Mr. King's children they are quick to complain to their father about how unfairly they are being treated. Mr. King then caves in to their pleas. Mrs. King becomes angry because the children do not listen to her and she fears that her own children will also stop doing so. In fact, they are beginning to also turn to Mr. King as an ally during these times. Mr. and Mrs. King love each other and want a good family life for everyone, but tension is rising between them as well as between Mrs. King and the children.

From a risk and resiliency perspective, the King family has a number of resources. Unlike the Cole family, they have adequate financial resources that provide important stability in their lives. They are committed to each other (family cohesion) and to making their marriage work. They have a strong support base through their church. The grandparents are supportive of this family. Aside from the problem at hand, both parents are able to function effectively in their lives and have a sense of mastery in other areas.

The risk factors here relate to conflict between the parents regarding how to raise the children and problems in communication regarding this issue. This is a situation in which both parties brought to their marriage their own paradigms of child rearing shaped by a variety of factors. As a result, the children are being given mixed messages from the parents in terms of appropriate behavior and the parental substructure is being weakened and pulled apart by this issue. The children are becoming quite adept at the "divide and conquer" strategy for getting their way.

Drawing upon a resiliency framework, the social worker can readily point out the strengths of this family in terms of sense of commitment to the family unit and concern for the welfare of the children. The counselor can recognize the good organizational skills of the parents as evidenced in the work setting and other aspects of the family.

Several counseling approaches can be used to help this family. From a social learning perspective, parents can be helped to understand how the children are receiving mixed messages from the two parents and the impact of this on the children. They can be helped to understand that the mixed messages create a different set of reinforcements from the two parents so that parental leadership has become compromised. They can be helped to recognize how their differing paradigms influence how they are parenting the children. Recognizing the important role of belief systems in terms of behavior, parents can begin to examine their respective belief systems in terms of their appropriateness for the current situation. Parents can be helped to gain the needed communication skills required in blending their two different paradigms regarding parenting and in understanding how each party's approach was shaped by life experiences. Structural interventions can also be used to create more effective boundaries around the parental subsystem so that the parents can be united in their parenting efforts.

Major Health Issues

The Patel family moved to the multicultural city of Toronto about a year ago to live closer to their extended family members who had been in the community for many years. The Patels joined the family business—selling medical equipment. Mr. Patel was able to use his background in the medical technical field to work with area medical professionals. Mrs. Patel began working in the office part-time as an accountant. The family have three children: a son (Sanjay) age thirteen, a daughter (Niki) age seven, and another son (Sima) age five. During their many years in the community, the extended Patel family had established good relationships with community members as well as other members of the Hindu temple. The members of the temple were very close and concerned about each other's welfare.

While the family members were close, the oldest son occupied a special place in the hearts of the parents because he had struggled for years with a seizure disorder. While it was usually under control, there were occasional times when the seizures would reoccur. Sanjay was an excellent student and his parents had high hopes that he might become a scientist. The family enrolled him in a seizure disorder clinic after the family had lived in Canada for the mandatory three-months waiting period and he seemed to be doing well. They paid for this and his other family medical care out of their own and extended family resources prior to that time.

As Sanjay was walking to school one day, he began crossing the street at a corner without a traffic light. Unfortunately, he suffered a severe seizure and fell down. A car driven by a person distracted by talking on the cell phone was entering the intersection and did not see the boy in time before hitting him. People in the area immediately called 911 and others called his parents. He was transported to the local hospital where he was evaluated and received in patient care. While he survived the accident and the immediate injury, subsequent evaluation revealed that the fall followed by being hit by the car had created a severe closed head injury. Fortunately, he lives in a community with a major inpatient rehab center with an excellent rehabilitation program for children with traumatic brain injuries. The center is able to provide an inpatient multidisciplinary program for an extended period of time depending on his therapy needs. Other family members are also supported through this program. A social worker and a multidisciplinary team were assigned to the boy and his family to address the medical, therapy, educational, psychosocial, and family issues.

The trauma experienced by the boy represents a major blow to this close family unit. Fortunately, the family does not have to worry about how to finance the medical care and rehabilitation because he is covered by their provincial health plan. Because he sustained a brain injury as a result of a motor vehicle trauma, he is also eligible for private services funded through No Fault Insurance. Family members who are involved in the business fill in so parents can spend time with their son while others try to make sure that the younger children have their needs met. Despite the considerable support and services, the parents grieve as they gradually have come to realize that their dreams for their son might not be realized because of the impact of his injuries. Ongoing cognitive problems are making it difficult for him to do the schoolwork that had been easy before, his problem-solving skills are limited, and he is emotionally labile. Although the extended family tries to meet the needs of the younger children, they too feel the family tension and grief and they struggle to cope. The daughter's grades in school have begun to drop as she finds herself worrying about her brother and family rather than concentrating in school. She has heard her parents talking about her brother at night when she and her younger brother were supposed to be sleeping, and the little that she understood was the source of great concern. At the same time, since her parents have not given her this information directly, she does not feel comfortable asking them about what they had said. She tries to be protective of her younger brother.

The Patel family represents an important set of risk and protective factors. Their son's accident and consequent traumatic brain injury represent important risk factors not only for the boy but also for the family as a whole. The parents are consumed by worry about their son in terms of both the present and the future. This worry and the time commitment toward their son have compromised their ability to carry out their parental roles and manage other responsibilities. They are struggling to set realistic goals for Sanjay's future while trying to remain hopeful for a complete recovery.

They are trying to protect their younger children by not talking to them about it—which in turn is only creating further fears and isolation on the part of their daughter. The younger children are feeling the tension in the family. Their daughter has been having increased problems in school because of her worries. The school has assigned a social worker to the siblings, but the social worker's effectiveness is limited, so private counseling has been arranged through insurance and the rehab center.

The Patel family also has some very important protective factors that can support the resiliency of this family during this difficult time and the years ahead. The family members have a strong sense of commitment to the family and other members. Family loyalty is strong. Parents have a history of being able to provide effective leadership in the family prior to this most recent life event. The Patel family has the emotional and instrumental support of their extended family members who provide an economic basis, time away from work to spend time with their children, and care for the children. They also have the support of members of the embracing Hindu community. The family has access to excellent medical and rehabilitation services for their son and the family as a whole that are covered under their medical insurance program. The parents have an understanding of the medical field that can help them understand their son's situation, although at times it also frustrates them knowing how imperfect or dysfunctional the "system" can be at times. Although the Patel family has not lived in the city for a long period of time, the extended family ties with the community and the Hindu temple have provided considerable emotional and spiritual support for the family in this difficult time. This support circle is also part of Sanjay's rehab, as they visit regularly to encourage him and cheer him on.

The Patel family represents the value of a psychoeducational approach with families who are experiencing a major health problem by a family member. Such an approach can be especially valuable in a situation in which the health problem is not clearly understood and has considerable stigma attached to it. The psychoeducational approach combines education and emotional support for family members that address the risk and protective factors present in the Patel family. The psychoeducational approach is designed to enhance the ability of the family members to meet the needs of the individual with a brain injury as well as the family as a whole. Sanjay's family members need ongoing information about the nature of their son's needs, his rehabilitation therapy, possible future implications, and effective interpersonal and educational approaches. At the same time, they also need help in understanding the impact of this problem on the family as a whole and support in trying to address this issue. Parents can be given permission to experience their grief and express their worries. Parents can be helped to find ways to communicate to the younger children in ways that are meaningful to them and open the doors for the children to ask questions. Parents have demonstrated the ability to be effective leaders in the family and their approach can help support their leadership abilities. Given the important role played by the extended family, this approach can include grandparents, uncles and aunts, and so on as viewed appropriate by the parents. A group format consisting of other families experiencing such a health issue can also be a valuable resource.

Communication Patterns

The Rogers family was discussed in chapter 1. In this family, the teenaged daughter was struggling with bulimia and the father was feeling very depressed. The setting for this family was the severe financial problems facing the family. Everyone in the family was experiencing the burden of these financial problems in their own way. In this situation, communication was a key to helping family members understand the situation and in supporting each other. Communication required the ability to explain complex factual phenomena as well as emotional affirmation. Communication was especially effective because information created new meaning systems within the family. The parents helped the children understand that they were not to blame for the family's plight. The children helped the father understand that his children loved him and were proud of him. Family members realized that they could contribute to the healing process within the family even if their financial situation could not be readily resolved.

Interpersonal Relationship Issues

Mr. and Mrs. Norris have been married for twenty-three years. Currently they are spending more and more time arguing. They argue about their teenage son who is not doing as well in school as they expect him to. They also argue about the maternal grandfather who needs more support from Mrs. Norris. His wife died a few months ago and he is having difficulty coping by himself. While there are services for seniors in the Vancouver area that are potentially helpful for the maternal grandfather, Mrs. Norris still feels the burden of responsibility as a daughter. They have begun to view their relationship as marked by conflicts rather than appreciation for each other. They are committed to their marriage but are becoming discouraged about what their future will be like. They both work full time and have an adequate financial basis. Mrs. Norris has been under pressure at work because she has had to take time off to help her father. Mr. Norris thinks that she should be more willing to ask her siblings for help.

This family has important resources that support resiliency. They have a commitment to each other (cohesion) and their family. They demonstrate responsibility at work and in their family and have an adequate financial base. There are services in their community for elderly persons.

At the same time, they are struggling with increased tension due to problems regarding their son and Mrs. Norris's father. These tensions have created discouragement within the couple that has diminished any previous sense of mastery regarding their family and relationship. Humor has long since died in this home.

Several approaches might be appropriate for this set of risks and resiliency factors. Solution-focused treatment might address some of the risk factors and mobilize their strengths. The discouragement of Mr. and Mrs. Norris who have begun to view their family relationships as marked by tension and disagreements could suggest the value of a solution-focused approach. The couple has some realistic problems to address but have become discouraged by their disagreements. Their view of the situation has hindered their ability to problem solve effectively. Helping them to recognize the presence of exceptions and enabling them to identify the small steps they can make to improve their situation can reduce their discouragement and encourage them to enlist their resources to begin to make a positive difference.

Meaning Systems

Mrs. James sought counseling for her two children because they had been previously abused by their stepfather. She had been frightened when she learned from the children what was happening and confronted her husband with this information. She then decided to leave her husband. She had been supportive of the children during this time, although it presented some major financial hardship when she had to leave the family and lose her employment. She worked cooperatively with the local child protection team. Currently the daughter is in high school and the son is in junior high. Mrs. James continues to worry that the scars of the past will make it difficult for her children to become healthy individuals and feels guilty that she brought Mr. James into the family life. Both of the children are doing reasonably well in school but their personalities in other areas are quite different. The daughter, Marie (aged sixteen) is an outgoing, sociable girl who is engaged in a variety of school activities. This pattern matches the mother's view of a well-adjusted child. The son, John (aged thirteen) is quiet and likes to spend time in his room listening to his music or playing computer games. While he will go out when friends call, he typically does not take the initiative. The teacher does not report any concerns about his behavior in school. Mrs. James worries that his behavior is a sign of the scars of the past because it does not fit with her view of how a well-adjusted child behaves. Mrs. James continues to pressure John to lead a more active social life. It has reached the point that John is beginning to feel that he is letting his mother down and that she does not accept him as he is. The family dance is a circular one. The more Mrs. James pressures him the more insecure he feels, which in turn diminishes his confidence in the social realm. To make matters worse, his mother will ask him why he can't be more like his sister. Marie is usually too busy with her own life to say anything but will occasionally try to reassure her mother that John is going through a difficult time and her mother should stop worrying so much. Her mother does not really hear these words and continues to pressure John.

This family also has some key risk and resiliency elements. The family unit has successfully coped with a very difficult time. While the larger family unit separated, Mrs. James and her two children remained together and have developed into a very close unit. Mrs. James clearly loves her children dearly and wishes to protect them. There is evident family cohesion in the relationship between the mother and her two children. The two children are doing well in school. Marie demonstrates considerable social competence and has tried to reassure her mother about John. John will join his friends socially. Both of the children have received the support of counseling to help them deal with the abuse.

In terms of risk factors, both Marie and John were abused by their stepfather when they were younger. Mrs. James experienced the pain of having to deal with this difficult life event. Mrs. James is feeling guilty because she did not protect her children from being abused and is frightened that they might still be bearing scars as a result. As a result, she is pressuring John to act in a certain manner that will reassure her that he does not carry deep scars. Her actions only make John more insecure and he too feels that he is letting his mother down. The communication between the mother and John has become a circle by which the more the mother pressures John to be sociable, the more he retreats from her into his room which in turn only makes his mother more anxious and thus pressures him more. At thirteen, John is developmentally at a difficult age between childhood and adolescence.

From a resiliency perspective, addressing the meanings of these events can help this family. The mother has become so overwhelmed by her own sense of fear and guilt that she can only see signs of pathology in John (and thus in herself as a parent) rather than the abundant evidence that John has coped quite well. This in turn creates the vicious circle described earlier. Family counseling approaches that enable the mother to reduce her fear and to see signs of appropriate coping by John can be valuable. These signs can represent evidence of her own adequate care of the children and enable her to reduce the pressure that in turn is increasing behavior that intensifies her anxiety.

Solution-focused and narrative family interventions represent approaches that could help this family identify signs of coping and strength within the family. Both approaches help family members identify exceptions to the stated problem and ways in which family members can increase these positive outcomes. Narrative approaches stress reframing life events in terms of strengths. In helping to alter their family story from a problem-saturated one to a more positive one, the James family can be helped to claim their identity in terms of survivors.

Summary

Families bring to the counseling endeavor a variety of risk and protective factors that influence how they are able to cope with their current life circumstances. Using a collaborative partnership approach, the counselor helps the family identify their current sources of distress as well as the other factors that are contributing to the risk facing the family. The counselor also searches for protective factors in such a way as to identify potential healing resources. Along with structured instruments and visual tools, the interview with the family provides a wealth of information regarding the family. The assessment process is also used to help the family members claim their resources in order to increase the sense of self-efficacy and hope experienced by family members. Based on the assessment process, the counselor identifies intervention models and specific intervention strategies that are appropriate to the family goals and the risk and protective factors facing the family. The assessment process is an ongoing one as new information about the family and their situation emerges or changes occur. The social worker and family members use this new information in the ongoing process of designing and implementing intervention strategies.

DISCUSSION QUESTIONS

Discuss the implications of the fact that many families come to counseling feeling very demoralized about their ability to solve their family situation.

Discuss how the assessment process can be used to enhance the resiliency of family members.

Discuss how the assessment process influences the selection of the treatment approach.

Discuss the nature and value of key identifying risk factors.

Discuss how the eco map can contribute to the understanding of families.

Discuss the potential role of a genogram in family assessment.

Why is it important to be attuned to meta-messages in the assessment process?

Discuss the different roles of content and process in family communication and their contribution to understanding families.

Discuss some of the ways in which life cycle issues influence the account family members give of the family situation.

What are some of the issues that influence how different family members tell very different stories about what is happening within the family?

What can the potential role of additive factors be on current stress?

Why can it be important to expand the inquiry beyond the current problem situation?

Discuss the role of family enactments in assessing families.

Discuss how family life cycle issues play a role in the family's response to situations.

Discuss the role of information about the community in the family assessment process.

4

Cultural Issues, Family Structure, and Resiliency

CULTURAL ISSUES

Understanding the role that culture can play in the lives of families is an important part of the assessment process. Cultural issues profoundly shape many critical aspects of family resiliency by influencing the nature of the risk factors facing families, the protective factors available to families, and the interaction between these factors in terms of the family's path toward resiliency. Cultural messages shape the meaning systems (the paradigms and schemas) that affect how family members perceive life events and potential solutions, the organizational patterns of families, the ways in which family members communicate, the characteristics of the support system (the nature of the extended family and other external resources that are available), the nature of appropriate problem-solving strategies, and the type of situations facing families. Furthermore, membership in certain cultural groups can place some families at greater risk for vulnerability caused by poverty or discrimination and injustice that represent important risk factors (Conger et al., 2002; Fraser, Kirby, & Smokowski, 2004).

This chapter highlights risk and protective factors that have been identified as associated with various groups rather than giving a comprehensive picture of the cultural patterns of different cultural groups that are described in depth by other authors. Because of the great variation within specific members of groups, the following information should be viewed only as suggesting potential issues for consideration in the assessment and planning process. For example, while understanding that the wider family circle is always valuable in a family assessment, it might be especially important to explore issues related to the extended family when meeting with families who come from cultural groups in which the extended family frequently plays a critical role. Recognizing cultural patterns of the role of family honor, family communication styles, and family patterns of respect and affection can help guide the assessment process. Communication patterns can direct social workers in how they conduct themselves and how they interpret the verbal and nonverbal information that they receive from family members. Cultural patterns regarding help-seeking can provide some understanding about how potential resources might be viewed and what it meant for this family to seek help from your organization. Issues related to spirituality emerge for some groups that can serve as potential resources.

At the same time, one must always be open to seek further clarification rather than making assumptions based on general statements. The author was meeting with a woman referred for symptoms related to post-traumatic stress disorder that were triggered by a variety of recent events. One of these included a recent nosebleed. Her community sponsor stated that blood had special meaning within the culture. Mrs. L was a refugee from Laos and I was not aware of the details of her culture in this regard. When I asked her about the meaning of blood in her culture, she told me her story prior to coming to the United States: her imprisonment by the Communists, her fear of being raped while in prison, her subsequent mental breakdown, her later escape with her family by means of the boats ("the boat people") that entailed having to leave behind one of their friends who had been shot by soldiers and then bled to death because they were unable to bring both him and their children, and her ongoing guilt that she had been unable to save him. In this case, blood had deep symbolic meaning for her not because of a general cultural issue but because of the unique trauma and horror she and her family had experienced and were still struggling with. I was thankful that I had asked her about this meaning rather than just accepting the statement of her sponsor.

We recognize that it is impossible to include all possible groups and have selected a number that represent racial/ethnic, vocational, and regional patterns. For the most part the following discussion follows the general pattern of risk and protective factors described earlier in chapters 1, 2, and 3; however, it is organized from the macro community context to the individual: community and social factors, extended family, family organization and patterns, individuals. This arrangement is used because past and current conditions within the macro realm (distal factors) can have a powerful influence on families and individuals in terms of both protective and risk factors. These pathways are important in assessing families and designing potential interventions. While individuals can in turn influence their wider context, the power of the external world is typically stronger for most people and there is more research in this area related to resiliency.

Relational Perspective

Before discussing specific groups, it is useful to include McCubbin, Futrell, Thompson, and Thompson's (1998) discussion of a relational perspective on family resilience alluded to in chapter 1 because this perspective characterizes many of the groups encountered by social workers and other counselors. A relational perspective is characterized by an emphasis on harmony and the interdependence of the relationships that include mind, body, and spirit in the process of appraisal and adaptation. "The family's dimensions of interpersonal relationships, community relationships and relationships with nature, the family's development, well-being and spirituality, as well as the family's structure and functioning, are taken into account, guided by the goals of harmony and balance" (McCubbin, McCubbin, Thompson, & Thompson, 1999, p. 37). The relationship processes influence the appraisal of life events and the nature of family relationships and problem solving. Drawing on a relational perspective, strong family bonds including extended family members have been identified as moderators of risk for minority youth. Recognizing the strengths derived from cultural aspects of appraisal and coping, ethnic and racial socialization has emerged as an important resource. It helps to promote pride in one's group that can facilitate biculturalism, to enable youth to cope with racism and other forms of discrimination, and to help promote their internalization of culturally prescribed values (Gonzales & Kim, 1997).

Risk and Protective Factors for Specific Groups

The following discussion identifies the potential risk and protective factors of members of specific racial and cultural groups. While this discussion is organized in terms of specific groups, many of the themes that emerge echo those described in the resiliency literature in general.

Latino Families

The Latino population includes a wide range of ethnic/racial groups, for example, twenty-nine subgroups in the United States (Delgado, 2007). In the United States, Latinos comprise 16 percent of the population and constitute the largest "minority" group (Taylor, Lopez, Valasco, & Motel, 2012). In Canada, the number of individuals from the Caribbean and Mexico, Central, and South America is much smaller (878,000 out of a population of approximately 31,241,000) and reflects the Commonwealth ties to the English-speaking countries in the Caribbean. When only those categorized as Latin America are included, the number is 304,245 and mixed heritage is common. The largest groups in Canada are Jamaican (231,000), Haitian (102,000), and Mexican (61,000) (Statistics Canada, 2006). The following discussion describes the social context of Latinos in the United States with an emphasis on cultural issues that are frequently shared by many groups within the Latino tradition generally. There is also a description of the situation of the Jamaicans in Canada.

Forty-eight percent of Latinos in the United States are born in their current country and 52 percent are immigrants (Taylor, Lopez, Velasco, & Motel, 2012). As of the 2002 census, major Latino groups include Mexican (66.9%), Central and South American—many subgroups (14.3%), Puerto Rican (8.6%), and Cuban (3.7%) (Delgado, 2007, p. 25). With the exception of the Cuban population, Latino groups tend to be much younger than the population as a whole (Delgado, 2007). Because of important differences among Latino/ Hispanic groups, it is valuable to understand the historical context of the groups as well as of individual families. At the same time, intermarriage between groups can blur these distinctions in families (Delgado, 2007). While Latino groups are concentrated in certain areas of the country, they are now represented throughout the United States. Even the almost entirely white and English-speaking rural Iowa county where the author once lived now has a Spanish-speaking church as Latinos have been recruited to work in the meatpacking companies.

Recognizing the diversity within the Latino population, the following discussion identifies some themes that these groups share as well as studies that examine patterns within specific groups. In assessing individual families, it is important to understand the degree of acculturation in terms of traditional cultural patterns. The following discussion points out ways in which certain characteristics can be both protective and risk factors, depending on the fit with the current situation.

External Social and Economic Factors

The history of three major groups within the Latino community reflects the great diversity present within this group in terms of their entry and welcome into the United States. Mexican Americans were first created with the Treaty of Guadalupe Hidalgo in 1848 marking the end of the Mexican-American War in which Mexico had to cede almost half of its territory to the United States and the residents of that territory became U.S. residents and citizens. Beginning in the first half of the twentieth century and continuing until today, Mexicans have been migrating north to work. They have received an ambivalent reception depending upon labor needs and have had difficulty receiving social benefits. The island of Puerto Rico came under U.S. control in 1899 at the end of the Spanish-American War and residents were granted citizenship rights in 1917. Their movement into the mainland in large numbers began in the 1950s, primarily at this time to the larger cities to fill labor needs. The major group of the Cuban community came following the rise of Castro as Cubans fled his government and anticipated persecution. As a group, they were typically white and relatively wealthy. These individuals were welcomed and received extensive assistance. Members of other groups have their own unique context of immigration (Sanchez & Jones, 2010).

Poverty and discrimination represent risk factors for many Latino families with accompanying stress on families (Delgado, 2007; Ortiz, 2010). Poverty rates depend upon the specific group involved; for example, Cubans
have the lowest poverty rates and are comparable to whites, while Mexican
Americans and Puerto Ricans have poverty rates much higher than the
national averages (Sanchez & Jones, 2010). Many Latino families have struggled financially for many years—frequently working in low paying occupa-
tions (Southern, 2006). The recent economic problems in the United States
compounded economic vulnerability for Latino families. The 2012 report of
the Pew Hispanic Center (Taylor, Lopez, Velasco, & Motel, 2012) gives key
indicators of this impact and the Latino perspective on these developments.
Poverty rates increased to 26.6 percent. Many Latino families live in areas
where home values experienced a major increase followed by a drastic
decline. As relatively recent home buyers, many have found the values of
their homes drastically reduced and neighborhoods impacted by foreclosed
homes. Average household wealth fell by 66 percent. Unemployment rates
increased. Fifty-nine percent of Latino families reported that someone in
their household is out of work and looking for a job. Unemployment rates
are especially high among young adults of 18–29 years—70 percent. This is
particularly a problem for young adults with limited education. Given these
developments, 54 percent of Latinos believe that the economic downturn
affected their group the most. Immigrants are especially likely to view their
current situation as negative.

Some Latino families have experienced trauma in their home countries
prior to immigration. Family members fled war and conflict before immigrating.

Recent demands for increased protection of borders and United States
jobs for "legitimate" residents have increased the stress on Latino communities whose members have begun to live under a cloud of fear and uncertainty. There has been concern about potential racial profiling. Families are
worried about possible deportation of members. Governmental policies are
reducing access to community services. Lack of legal status is a major barrier
to health care services (Shobe & Coffman, 2010).

Lack of health care systems that are culturally appropriate and low levels of health insurance within the Latino community represent community-
based risk factors. The Latino population is the ethnic minority group with
the highest levels without health insurance (Delgado, 2007; Shobe & Coffman, 2010). Diabetes type 2 has become a major health problem within the
Latino community, with culture and diet playing roles (Delgado, 2007). HIV/
AIDS has also become a risk factor within the Latino community as rates of
new cases (19 percent) exceed the proportion within the community in general (13 percent in 2000) (Centers for Disease Control and Prevention,
2012a). Stigma and lack of awareness of the problem within the community
represent important problems in addressing the issue. Substance abuse has

also emerged as a health issue within the Latino community, associated with increased acculturation levels (Delgado, 2007). Folk healers play important roles in the Latino community (Delgado, 2007; Shobe & Coffman, 2010).

Supportive mentors and neighborhood support for education serve as protective factors regarding school engagement and educational achievement (Ceballo, 2004; Delgado, 2007). Educational programs that seek to draw upon the strengths within the community and the family, to foster caring relationships and pride in one's culture and coping in a more socially adaptive manner have shown promise with Mexican immigrant youth (Chavez & Gonzalez, 2000) and other Latino youth (Delgado, 2007).

The religious community is a source of support for Latino families. While the Catholic Church remains the major source of religious affiliation, Latino families currently are affiliated with a variety of religious groups, especially evangelical and Pentecostal groups (Shorkey, Garcia, & Windsor, 2010). Although individuals might not attend religious services on a regular basis, religious rites and festivals continue to be very important (Aguilar, 2002; Delgado, 2007; Shorkey, Garcia, & Windsor, 2010). Traditional spiritual healers (*santeria* and *curanderismo*) can be resources for healing (Aaredondo, 2006; Shorkey, Garcia, & Windsor, 2010).

Communities containing other members of the respective ethnic group provide a context that offers important support to all ages (Delgado, 2007). Services that are culturally sensitive serve as a second line of defense that the family cannot provide and support resiliency (Delgado, 2007; San Miguel, Morrison, & Weissglass, 1998). Unfortunately, these services are not always available (Bushy, 2002; Delgado, 2007).

Extended Family

The concept of family relatedness described earlier is very applicable to the traditional culture of Latino families. The family is central to life within the Latino community (Delgado, 2007; Falicov, 2006; Magana & Ybarra, 2010; Zuniga, 2001). The extended family and the related concept of *familismo* represent important protective factors for Latino families. These extended family groups can include members of several generations who interact with each other in an ongoing basis. Family members can turn to others for ongoing support to deal with the challenges of life and to share the joys. Family members are expected to be there to help others who are struggling with difficult problems. Family support continues as family members become more acculturated. The emphasis within these families is on the collective rather than the individual and on relationships and cooperation. Godparents broaden the extended family and represent further sources of support for young people (Falicov, 2006; Magana & Ybarra, 2010; Zuniga, 2001).

Family rituals represent important ways to support the extended family circle. The nature of these can vary depending on resources and tradition, but some form of regular family rituals continue to be important and supportive of the family (Falicov, 2006).

Personalismo, which represents the high level of personal involvement, further helps support family life and its members (Bernal & Shapiro, 1996; Falicov, 2006; Garcia-Preto, 1996a, 1996b; Perez-Koenig, 2000). Family honor further protects the family unit as people are expected to behave in such a way to protect the honor of the family (Falicov, 2006).

Extended families and the church circle serve as the first line of help. When this source of help is not available, formal support systems such as mental health and social service programs emerge as more important (San Miguel, Morrison, & Weinglass, 1998).

Family Organizational Patterns

The family as a unit plays a central role in Latino culture *(familismo)* (Delgado, 2007; Falicov, 2006; Magana & Ybarra, 2010). Acculturation influences the extent to which Latino families reflect traditional values. Latino families tend to be hierarchical in nature. Parents in Latino families are to be respected by their children even as they become adults. This respect comes with obligations to be dutiful and attend to the authority of the parents (Falicov, 2006). Mothers play very central and respected roles within the Latino family. The term *marianismo* captures the importance of motherhood, the spirituality of women, and the role of sexuality in terms of procreation (Delgado, 2007). While the all-encompassing and absorbing role of motherhood can be a source of affirmation, it also carries with it the risk of anxiety about her children and the burden of responsibility (Falicov, 2006). The bond between mothers and sons is especially close. While this arrangement can support both mother and son, such bonds can be so excessive and rigid that they impede the marital relationship and create problems for the son in terms of other relationships (Falicov, 2006). Fathers in some Latino families have a more authoritarian role (*machismo*), although this pattern varies depending on individual family circumstances, degree of acculturation, and patterns of immigration (Falicov, 2006; Zuniga, 2001)

Sibling ties within Latino families are strong, providing a valuable support network for family members (Falicov, 2006). Older siblings are granted authority within the family and are expected to assume responsibilities in terms of younger siblings. As a result, the oldest child tends to be "parentified." Such a pattern can be helpful for the family organization but can also potentially create difficulties for future life circumstances. Falicov gives a moving example of an oldest daughter who was needed by her family to help care for younger siblings. She was ambivalent about this role—she felt affirmed by her important role within the family and yet resented the constraints that these requirements placed on her. The situation came to a head when she was diagnosed with advanced cancer (Falicov, 2006, pp. 55–56).

Family verbal communication patterns are organized to maintain harmony within the family that provides for emotional nurturing of family members and family closeness. Family members are encouraged to be verbally affectionate to others. Affection and closeness are also demonstrated through physical affirmations (hugs, kisses) and closeness (Falicov, 2006). Public communication is organized around politeness and agreement. Cooperation within the family and with others outside the family circle is valued. Positive affirmations are important. Indirectness is used to deal with feelings of anger. Humor helps deal with tension. *Personalismo* seeks to create warm personal relationships with others who are also outside the family circle (Delgado, 2007).

Parental support for education promotes educational achievement for Latino youth (Delgado, 2007). This support may not translate into a parent's active involvement in the school and academic life of their children because of the parent's sense of inadequacy in this area. Consequently, school personnel might interpret their behavior as showing lack of interest (Ceballo, 2004).

Individuals

A balance between the familial self and the private self permits individuals to maintain a sense of emotional closeness and connectedness over a lifetime and yet create a personal self and individuate from the family (Falicov, 2006, p. 43).

Spirituality is important for Latino family members from a variety of specific religious traditions (Delgado, 2007; Shorkey, Garcia, & Windsor, 2010; Smith, Bakir, & Montilla, 2006). Young people who are actively involved in their religious community or view faith as important in their lives are more likely to achieve higher grades, to have higher educational expectations, and are less likely to engage in problematic behavior (Delgado, 2007, p. 151).

Lower levels of education increase the risk for poverty while higher levels serve as protective factors. Many Latino youth are disadvantaged in this area because high school dropout rates for Latino youth are higher than the population at large (Delgado, 2007). Graduation rates for Mexican Americans and Puerto Ricans are much lower than the national average (Sanchez & Jones, 2010). Self-efficacy translated into confidence regarding one's abilities and a commitment to success are associated with academic accomplishment for Latino youth (Ceballo, 2004; Gordon, 1996).

Older Latinos are especially at risk for poverty because they have typically been employed at low-wage jobs with limited retirement benefits. This risk is especially high for elderly Latinas, especially if they are unmarried. Latinos are also more likely to be employed in jobs with high accident rates. As a result, they are 40 percent more likely to experience job-related injuries and become disabled (Delgado, 2007; Ramos & Wright, 2010). They are also at increased risk for poor health compared with white elders, a situation compounded by underutilization of formal health services (Ramos & Wright, 2010). On the positive side, many are accorded respect by family members and their community, although some view their own situation as inferior to the respect accorded their own parents. Older adults are usually cared for by extended family members, although some families lack the resources to do so without stress or provide this care entirely (Ramos & Wright, 2010).

Latinos who immigrated to the United States were generally healthier in many dimensions than individuals who were born here or had lived in this country for some time (Delgado, 2007). Subgroup differences emerge in terms of acculturation. Mexican Americans who come to the United States are typically healthier than those who have lived here for some time; however, Puerto Ricans and to a lesser degree Cubans and Dominicans become healthier with time spent in the Unites States (Delgado, 2007). Higher obesity among Latinos is associated with acculturation (Delgado, 2007).

Hope for the future represents an important protective factor. While Latinos in general described the impact of the recent economic crisis in negative terms, they were more likely than other groups to be optimistic regarding the future. Immigrants were even more optimistic than those born in the United States (Taylor, Lopez, Velasco, & Motel, 2012).

Facility with the English language represents a protective factor in terms of education and employment. This is especially relevant for those living in areas where English is the dominant language of business. Many Latinos are bilingual, which gives them an advantage both culturally and economically.

Young people's affiliation with their Latino culture and sense of pride in their culture can contribute to self-esteem and are protective factors by buffering against negative community views (Ceballo, 2004; Delgado, 2007); however, some studies question this connection (Delgado, 2007). Issues relating to acculturation show a mixed picture of risk and protective factors for Latino youth. Biculturalism can serve as a protective factor as it helps youth navigate the world of their parents and their new community. Delgado (2007) describes it as a "survival skill" (p. 108). At the same time acculturation can also be associated with increased problematic behavior, especially substance abuse (Delgado, 2007; Prado, Pantin, & Tapia, 2010). Prado et al. (2010) discuss the potential risk and protective factors for Latino youth who have higher rates of substance abuse as young teenagers. This is especially true for those who were born in the United States. This increase in substance abuse related to acculturation may be influenced by acculturative stress and a decrease in traditional values of family and an erosion in collectivist values (Prado, Pantin, & Tapia, 2010). As Latino youth associate with peers who become their guides to the American culture, association with peers who are using substances increases substance abuse among Latino youth. Lack of investment in education and dropping out of school also enhance the risk of substance abuse. The situation is further compounded for many immigrant Latino youth who live in poor, socially disconnected neighborhoods with high crime rates and substance abuse. Because the family can play an important protective role, programs that enhance the effectiveness of parental communication and involvement and family functioning have been able to reduce youth substance abuse, for example, the Familias Unidas intervention (Prado, Pantin, & Tapia, 2010, pp. 223–224).

Cesar Chavez, the farm worker who successfully organized other farm workers to advocate for their rights, illustrates the role of protective factors in the context of a high-risk situation: growing up in an impoverished Mexican American family, being homeless at times, living in impoverished and dilapidated neighborhoods, working as a migrant farm worker. Countering these negatives were the protective factors of supportive relationships with his mother and grandmother, his connection to the church, and his overall positive self-concept (Gonzales, 2003).

The ability to identify their own personal risk factors and develop appropriate strategies emerged as important with a group of Dominican youth who were succeeding academically (a group traditionally with low levels of academic and economic success). The road to resiliency was a process and was individualized to the young person. After identifying their risk factors, they sought out protective factors that would mitigate the risk factors. The cycle then proceeded with the youth and the protective factors working in concert. While one protective factor might have been more important than others at the beginning of the process for specific individuals, all of the youth required a combination of protective factors. The combination of internal processes (the recognition and awareness by the youth) combined with the presence of potential protective factors in their life space was critical (Morales, 2000).

Jamaican Families

Jamaicans are the largest Caribbean group in Canada (1 percent) and are part of the English-speaking countries of the United Kingdom Commonwealth. They are especially likely to be living in Ontario, particularly in Toronto (3 percent of the population). The majority (53 percent) are foreign-born, and others typically came in the last several decades. About 657,000 Jamaicans are living in the United States, especially in Florida and New York. Residence in these areas in the United States and Canada provides a supportive Jamaican community. Jamaicans who come to these countries have an important English-language advantage (Glennie & Chappel, 2010). The

Jamaican community in Canada tends to be young; for example, in 2001, children under the age of 15 represented 29 percent of the Jamaican community, compared with 19 percent of the overall population, and only 6 percent were over the age of 65 compared with 12 percent of all Canadians (The Jamaican Community in Canada, 2007, Number 12).

Jamaicans have typically moved to Canada and the United States for reasons of economic advantage. Many continue to send remittances back to family in Jamaica (Glennie & Chappel, 2010) Adult Jamaicans in Canada are somewhat more likely to be working (68 percent in 2001) than the population as a whole (62 percent). Their incomes, however, are somewhat lower than the population as a whole. Employment is especially concentrated in the areas of health care, education, and social services. Women tend to be more highly educated than men: college graduates (women 26% compared with men 15%) and high school dropouts (women 26% compared with men 33%). Jamaican young people are making an investment in education as reflected in the fact that 60 percent of youth ages 15–24 are attending school full time, a rate slightly higher than the community at large (57%) in Canada (The Jamaican Community in Canada, 2007). Women are frequently the leaders in the immigration process. This situation has become even more common in the current economic and employment context because of the demand for professionals in the health care industry and the presence of more restrictive immigration policies (Glennie & Chappel, 2010). Jamaicans have been socialized to expect that they and their children will be able to achieve in their society. This has contributed to a hopeful outlook that has enhanced achievement (Brice-Baker, 1996).

The role of the family, including the extended family circle, is very important in the Jamaican community (Brice-Baker, 1996). Many people return to Jamaica to be closer to their family (Glennie & Chappel, 2010). As a result of family background, individual families can consist of members of a large range of hues (Brice-Baker, 1996). In terms of family structure, Jamaicans in Canada were more likely to be single parents (16%) than the population of adults as a whole (6%). In 2001, 25 percent of all adult women of Jamaican origin were single parents, compared with 10 percent of the adults in the overall population. Given economic conditions, this can have implications for family incomes. Jamaican older adults were more likely to be living with other relatives (15% of those aged 65 and older have lived with family compared with only 5% of all seniors in Canada) (The Jamaican Community in Canada, 2012).

African American Families

African Americans constitute 13.6 percent of the population in the United States, and are especially concentrated in the states of Mississippi (37%),

Louisiana (32%), and Georgia (30%) (Black Demographics, 2011). In Canada, the percentage of individuals describing themselves as black is much lower (approximately 2%, with about 60% indicating African origins) (Statistics Canada, 2006).

A number of scholars have explored the source of resiliency among African American families because these families as a people have been challenged by a long history of oppression. Several excellent resources for understanding resiliency in African American families include the Resiliency in Families Series edited by McCubbin and colleagues who have studied a wide range of families, and the Center for Family Research Institute that has focused on rural African American families. Again, it is important to remember that individual families can vary widely on the following dimensions and a careful assessment of individual families is necessary for an effective intervention effort.

External Social and Economic Factors

An adequate economic situation represents a protective factor for African American two-parent and single-parent families (Brody, Murray, Kim, & Brown, 2002; Conger, Wallace, Sun, Simons, McLoyd, & Brody, 2002). In contrast, poverty has been identified in general as a risk factor for serious childhood social problems (Fraser, Kirby, & Smokowski, 2004). While some African American families are very wealthy, many others struggle with poverty, unstable employment, or unemployment. The recent economic crisis has been particularly difficult for many African American families whose members have lost jobs and found the value of their most valuable asset, their home, plummeting. Families with a toehold in the middle class experienced themselves losing ground and falling back into poverty. African American families in the United States had the highest poverty rate (27.4%) and the lowest incomes of all racial/ethnic groups in 2010 ($32,000) compared with whites ($52,000), Asians ($64,000), and Hispanic families ($37,000) (Walt, Proctor, & Smith, 2011). Economic stress in turn has a potentially profound negative influence on family stability, marital relationships, and parenting (Brody, Murry, Kim, & Brown, 2002; Conger et al., 2002; Hill, 1999).

Given the struggles facing many African American families, Genero (1998) suggests that the concept of resiliency takes on new meaning. It is important to recognize that the ability to be ordinary under these circumstances represents an extraordinary achievement (p. 32).

The risk represented by poverty is accentuated by living in neighborhoods characterized by violence, crime, drugs, and other social problems that further family stress (Conger et al., 2002; Hill, 1999). Living in these neighborhoods contributes to the proximal risk factors of family stress and conflict and maternal depression (Conger et al., 2002; Murry, Bynum, Brody, Willert, & Stephens, 2001).

In contrast, a study set in both rural Iowa and Georgia supported the value of collective socialization—a community in which its members "take responsibility for monitoring and correcting the children living in the area"—for deterring conduct problems among young adolescents (Simons, Simons, Conger, & Brody, 2004, p. 287). Such communities reflect the often-quoted phrase, "It takes a village to raise a child."

Racism and discrimination represent interrelated risk factors that contribute to poverty. They have also been identified as risk factors for lack of educational achievement and decreased investment in education. Perceptions of discrimination and oppression are combined with employment limitations and are accompanied by a youth culture that discourages African American youth from succeeding in school. While parents might be committed to education, when they communicate verbally and through the reality of their lives that in spite of their education black youth will probably not do as well economically as white youth, young people may become less invested in their own education (Sirin & Rogers-Sirin, 2004). Perceived discrimination (of either the youth or their parents) produced distress that can make adolescents more susceptible to use of alcohol and related substances and to engage in thoughts that were supportive of risk behaviors (Gibbons, Gerrard, Cleveland, Wills, & Brody, 2004).

HIV/AIDS is a health problem that has had a major impact on the African American community because of high rates within the community in both the United States and Canada (Canada AIDS Statistics for Year and Age, 2012) . The high rate within the black male population has put black women at increased risk for contracting HIV. At the same time, stigma has prevented people from seeking medical care. In response, the United States Centers for Disease Control and Prevention (CDC) has created several new programs to address this issue (Centers for Disease Control, 2005b). The illness has been a source of great stress and grief for families. Accentuating the problem of HIV/AIDS in the African American community is the context of poverty, lack of access to quality health care, and higher rates of sexually transmitted diseses (STDs) that increase vulnerability to HIV (Centers for Disease Control and Prevention, 2011, 2012b).

Community Social Support Systems

Religious groups have long represented important protective factors within the African American community. The history of the church and religion within the African American community serves as a source of affirmation of worth and dignity, spiritual strength, and mutual aid with this community.

These groups sponsor a variety of programs that serve as healing forces within the community and contribute to community cohesion (Bagley & Carroll, 1998; Bell-Tolliver & Wilkerson, 2011; Boyd-Franklin, 2003; Grant, 2002; Hill, 1999). Participation in religion is associated in turn with protective factors within the family unit (more family cohesion, reduced interpersonal conflict, fewer problems of adolescents) (Brody & Flor, 1998; Brody, Stoneman, Flor, & McCrory, 1994). Frequent church attendance by parents and youth was associated with lower levels of substance abuse (Gibbons, Gerrard, Cleveland, Wills, & Brody, 2004).

Schools and classrooms that children and families view as positive and support the child's competence represent important resources (Brody, Dorsey, Forehand, & Armistead, 2002). As described earlier, schools that make children feel devalued represent risk factors.

Extended Family and Friends

Social support of extended family and friends represents an important protective factor for African American families. The tradition of the extended family as a source of support and aid within the African American community offers useful resources and buffers stress (Bell-Tolliver & Wilkerson, 2011; Fraser, Kirby, & Smokowski, 2004; Hill, 1999; McAdoo, 1998; Murry, Owens, Brody, Black, Willert, & Brown, 2003). The extended family, especially grandparents, in single-parent families offers potential emotional and instrumental support as well as mentoring for the mother and the presence of an effective caretaker for the children (Hess, Dapus, & Black, 2002; Murry, Bynum, Brody, Willert, & Stephens, 2001). The tradition within the African American community of adopting fictive kin who become "as if" family widens this supportive circle (Fraser, Kirby, & Smokowski, 2004; Hill, 1999).

At the same time, this support network can be a source of distress if individuals become overly burdened down by obligations (Boyd-Franklin, 2003). African American women are socialized to be caregivers with the cultural expectation that they will engage in self-sacrificing behaviors for the sake of the family. The expectation that one will be the strong matriarch can come with a price (Murry, Owens, Brody, Black, Willert, & Brown, 2003).

Extended family can also be sources of conflict and confusion regarding family roles. Grandparents can potentially lower the self-efficacy of parents (Murry, Bynum, Brody, Willert, & Stephens, 2001). Confrontational relationships between grandparents and teenage parents can reduce parental skills (Hess, Dapus, & Black, 2002).

Family Organization and Relationships

Genero (1998) describes the critical role that the family plays for African Americans in a context of "negative realities and social inequalities" (p. 37).

Families must find ways to judge when it is safe and appropriate to trust others and to engage in mutual relationships. Given the risk of external devaluation, the family serves as a critical source of validation. Family communication, trust, and friendship promote successful marriages within African American couples (Conner, 1998).

Family role flexibility represents a protective form of family organization. This permits family members to assume roles as the situation requires (McAdoo, 1998).

The Center for Family Research identifies important parenting patterns that represent protective factors. A pattern of "firm control exercised within affectively positive parent-child relationships predicts positive outcomes such as self-regulation, social competence, good emotional health, and school success among African American children" (Murry, Bynum, Brody, Willert, & Stephens, 2001, p. 139). Parenting styles that include vigilant parenting (monitoring the activities of youth), effective communication (the ability to discuss important issues in a collaborative manner), and warmth are protective factors associated with resiliency among African American youth (Brody, Kim, Murry, & Brown, 2004; Gibbons, Gerrard, Cleveland, Wills, & Brody, 2004; Murry, Bynum, Brody, Willert, & Stephens, 2001). These patterns are also associated with lower levels of substance abuse by youth (Murry et al., 2001).

Community context influences the nature of effective parenting. High levels of monitoring are especially important for children living in high-risk areas in order to protect them from involvement in problematic behavior. More moderate levels of control can be effective in community contexts in which peers are less likely to engage in problematic behavior (Murry, Bynum, Brody, Willert, & Stephens, 2001).

Parental conflict represents a risk factor that reduces positive parenting. This risk factor is exacerbated by economic stress (Conger et al., 2002).

A study of rural single-parent African American families identified the following parenting patterns that supported resiliency: structure, routinized home environments, positive mother-child relationships, high levels of control, and maternal school involvement (Murry, Bynum, Brody, Willert, & Stephens, 2001, p. 142). These behaviors furthered high academic performance, good social skills, and fewer behavioral and emotional problems among youth (Murry et al., 2001).

Positive family relationships in both impoverished and middle-class families are also key protective factors in terms of youth's engagement in their education. This engagement serves in turn as an important protective factor because it provides opportunities for positive social relationships and increases the likelihood that youth will gain needed coping skills and develop self-esteem. Lack of such commitment to education is associated with increased risk for behavioral problems (Caspi, Elder, & Berm, 1987;

Simons, Simons, Conger, & Brody, 2004). A strong work ethic and commitment to education are important protective factors (Hill, 1999).

High rates of female-headed households (29%) represent a poverty risk for family members and the community. More than 40 percent of female-headed households with children are living in poverty (Walt, Proctor, & Smith, 2011).

Individual Family Members

Several parental characteristics are protective in terms of substance for youth. These include low parental substance abuse (Murry et al., 2001), positive role modeling, negative parental attitudes toward deviance, and parental insistence upon school attendance (Gibbons et al., 2004). Positive racial identity and socialization can be important sources of resiliency for African American youth (Brown, 2008; Miller & Macintosh, 1999).

Self-esteem promotes effective parenting. This in turn helps young people develop self-regulation that is important in developing cognitive and social competencies (Brody, Flor, & Gibson, 1999; Brody, Murry, Kim, & Brown, 2002). Self-efficacy, effective parenting styles, and competence on the part of children represent a protective self-reinforcing cycle that also promotes the social and emotional competence of younger siblings (Brody, Kim, Murry, & Brown, 2004).

Religious beliefs and involvement are protective. They can help promote hope, reduce stress, provide support, and improve parenting and family cohesion and interpersonal relationships. (Bell-Tolliver & Wilkerson, 2011; Brody, Stoneman, Flor, & McCrory, 1994).

Higher levels of education are protective in several ways. They are associated with improved economic status, higher levels of self-esteem, and parenting that improves the self-regulation of children and their social and cognitive competence (Brody, Murry, Kim, & Brown, 2002).

Families of Asian Origin

Families of Asian origin represent a wide variety of individual national and cultural groups with different histories and religions. Counselors working with members of different cultural groups need to understand and acknowledge these differences, especially in view of historical events that have caused tensions among different groups. In 2008 there were an estimated 14 million individuals identified as Asian, along with additional individuals who identified themselves as Asian and other groups in the United States. Included among Asian Americans were Chinese (24%), Filipino (20%), Asian Indian (18%), Vietnamese (15%), Korean (11%), and Japanese (8%) (Leon,

Oka, & Lannert, 2011). Between 2000 and 2008, the Asian American population grew rapidly primarily as a result of increased immigration from Southeast Asia, especially individuals who have fled areas of military conflict and political turmoil. Increases were particularly high among Hmong and Vietnamese (increased by more than 82%) and Asian Indians (doubled). As a result of this immigration pattern, 64 percent of Asian Americans are first generation (Leon, Oka, & Lannert, 2011). In Canada, Asians from many different countries represent 11 percent of the population. The largest groups are Chinese (44%), East Indian (25%), and Filipino (10%) (Statistics Canada, 2006). While contextual issues can differ between the United States and Canada due to policy and historical circumstances, many of the broad cultural trends related to family transcend national boundaries.

Assessing and working with families requires an understanding of the process of immigration in terms of the generation involved, the reason for the immigration, and their experiences in their home countries and their current country of residence. Some family members have experienced major trauma due to war. Families also vary in terms of the degree of acculturation. Family situations can be complicated, and sometime tensions arise as family members vary widely in terms of adherence to traditional values and ways of life. The community context also influences the process of acculturation. Recognizing the many differences present, the relational perspective described earlier is relevant to understanding families of Asian origin and influences the way in which individuals appraise situations and their coping strategies.

External Social and Economic Factors

Some families have experienced major trauma due to war and conflict prior to immigrating. These early contextual issues can have long shadows on the individual involved; for example, in the family described earlier in which the teenage daughter was sent to school despite taking an overdose of pills because the parents feared that her behavior would mean that they would be deported back to the refugee camps and not allowed to return to the United States.

Despite popular images of families of Asian origin as the model minority with relatively high mean income levels ($64,300 in 2010 census [Walt, Proctor, & Smith, 2011]), the economic picture of this heterogeneous group represents great extremes—from those with high incomes and educational levels to those with very limited incomes and educational levels and major problems as indicated by a variety of indices.

Community contexts that include racial and ethnic discrimination create stress for family members. Leon, Oka, and Lannert (2011) describe racial stereotypes and discrimination as major risks that Asian American youth face.

Asian Americans continue to be regarded as foreigners even though they have been in the United States for several generations. Positive stereotypes can contribute to negative evaluations such as "overachievers" and resentment as well as justifying not looking at the difficulties facing Asian Americans and their need for services (Choi, 2011). Violent behavior by Asian American youth has been attributed to a strategy to survive in poor communities where they have been marginalized as well as for youth from more affluent families in response to their racial position in society (Choi, 2011).

Choi (2011) describes the stress experienced by Asian youth in the school setting. Asian youth describe being verbally and physically harassed more than members of other groups. Youth may in turn join antisocial peers as a way to be accepted and be protected.

Community contexts that support families by affirming important cultural rituals, food, and religious ties serve as protective factors. Language issues can be a source of stress for recent immigrants who lack the English skills needed to negotiate the new society.

Extended Family

The extended family is important and extends back in time to include ancestors as well as current family members. Family members are expected to contribute to the family as a whole and younger members have important obligations toward the previous generation. As a result, the family circle provides an important source of support for all ages and especially for the older generation (Fung, Ho, Louie, Martinez, & Lau, 2011). Studies examining how families deal with elderly members reveal the circular pattern of obligations and rewards within the extended Asian American families as well as how these patterns change depending on contextual factors.

The first study involved older adults and caretakers of refugee families from Cambodia and Vietnam. These families typically had fled their home countries, experienced major hardship and suffering in their journey, and had virtually no hope for return. "Suddenly and traumatically, family and friends, personal identity, possessions and a family world were lost" (Strumpf, Glicksman, Goldberg-Glen, Fox, & Logue, 2001, p. 234). Given the trauma that these individuals had experienced, they fit the prototype of "resilience despite major losses and stressors." Families revealed a powerful sense of obligation to care for elders along with limited knowledge of or use of community services. Both Cambodian and Vietnamese caregivers indicated a strong sense of love and obligation to care for their elderly parents.

Cultural ties with the previous world and life were also very important for the older adults. In turn it was important for the older members of the family to see themselves in the role of preserving and transmitting their culture to the younger generation (Strumpf et al., 2001).

As families remain in America, however, such strong filial expectations in terms of caring for older members can shift as illustrated in a small study involving older Chinese individuals. Respondents indicated the increasing role of friends alongside of children and grandchildren. Although older adults were willing to ask for help from their children, they also recognized that their children were busy with their own responsibilities and many reported asking them for help only when necessary (Pang, Jordan-Marsh, Silverstein, & Cody, 2003).

While social economic stress in general is described as problematic for families, this stress appears less for immigrant Asian families. They have been able to enlist broad family resources to cope (Kwak, 2003).

Family Organization and Patterns

Family plays a central role and individuals are expected to contribute to the family unit, even at the expense of personal needs and wishes. Families tend to be hierarchical, with parents granted honor and authority. Children are expected to fulfill their obligations to their parents in return for their parents' sacrificial caregiving (Fung et al., 2011; Yeh, Borrero, & Kwong, 2011).

Family loyalty and respect for the family are very important, and members are expected to uphold the honor of the family and to avoid bringing shame to the family. Individuals can bring honor to their family through good school performances or other behaviors that reflect favorably on their family (Bushy, 2002; Fung et al., 2011; Goldenberg & Goldenberg, 1998; Lee, 1996).

Family Members

A strong sense of ethnic identity and maintenance of cultural ties strengthens resilience among youth (Choi, 2011). The process of acculturation with the challenge of navigating two cultures facing Asian American youth represents both a potential risk as well as a protective factor. Youth in immigrant families who are able to both acculturate toward the American culture and maintain their ties to their heritage are better adjusted and higher achieving, while those who feel marginalized by these two cultures have the highest levels of stress (Fung et al., 2011). While academic distress, disrupted family relations, and discrimination and stereotypes increase vulnerability, values such as family cohesion and family obligation buffer youth against misconduct (Choi, 2011; Fung et al., 2011).

Immigrant status appears to be protective for Asian youth, with first-generation youth in general demonstrating more positive academic and social behaviors (Choi, 2011, p. 34). Such a pattern also has emerged with other racial and ethnic groups (Choi, 2011). Family members and the family unit can experience stress as a response to differing levels of acculturation of family members (especially between the generations [Fung et al., 2011]). Cultural codes that grant parents greater authority over their child can collide with an American culture that does not support this level of parental authority and create family conflict (Choi, 2011).

Fung et al. (2001) describe both the protective and risk factors for individuals related to the importance of bringing honor to the family. The ability to bring honor to the family by academic and other types of achievement can potentially bring a sense of satisfaction and self-worth. Individuals, however, can also experience great stress when they face family expectations that are unrealistic for them. Family tensions can then ensue when young people are not able to meet the standards set by parents. Young people who also have other time-consuming obligations to the family can especially feel this sense of stress to also achieve high academic accomplishments with the time obligations involved (Fung et al., 2011).

Spirituality and religion play important roles for many Asian families. The specific nature of the religious tradition and accompanying beliefs and practices varies widely (for example, Buddhism, Hinduism, Christianity, Islam, Taoism) depending primarily on the country of origin. Participation in rituals and the religious community represents an important protective factor for families. Related to some of the spiritual traditions (especially Buddhism and Taoism) is a sense of fatalism that can help people be more accepting of difficult life events as fate and thus use this belief to cope with their life circumstances (Yeh, Borrero, & Kwong, 2011).

Young people are helped by the ability to seek support from their peers. The nature of this support typically does not include talking about family problems because young people are concerned to protect the honor of their family (Yeh, Borrero, & Kwong, 2011).

First Nations People/Aboriginal People

First Nations people include a wide range of nations with diverse histories, cultures, and languages. In the United States, members of the First Nations represent 1.2 percent of the population. The percentage in Canada (approximately 3%) is higher and increasing, with about 60 percent belonging to North American Indian groups and the rest the Metis (descended from children of unions of Europeans and First Nations) and Inuits who have traditionally lived in the northern areas of Canada and who have recently been allocated their own territory (Nunavut; Statistics Canada, 2006). This population in Canada includes eleven major language groups, although only one in four are able to speak an Aboriginal language.

While many First Nations people live on land allocated to First Nations, the majority live in other rural and urban communities ranging from Alaska, through Canada, to southern areas of the United States. As with previous groups, it is important to learn from the family the nature of their national affiliation and how its culture currently influences the family because there is great diversity between groups.

The relational perspective described earlier in this chapter is applicable to the many cultures of First Nations. The relational perspective in this context emphasizes balance so that interventions are organized in terms of restoring balance. Cross (1999) describes a model that includes the four domains of mind, body, spirit, and context (family culture, work, community, history, environment). Families can thus draw upon resources within these four domains to support resilience and protect family members from the risk associated with oppression.

External and Social Issues

Despite their differences, First Nations people share a heritage of oppression at the hands of the Europeans and Americans who colonized the United States and Canada. Their land and wealth were appropriated through various ways. Their culture was systematically devalued to the extent that many young children were removed from their parents and placed in boarding schools where they were forced to abandon their traditional language and culture. Contemporary cultural messages can continue to devalue the cultures and people of the First Nations (Kirmayer, Brass, Holton, Paul, Simpson, & Tait, 2006; Winkelman, 2001; Yellow Horse Brave Heart, 2001, 2002). The past is still part of the present. Yellow Horse Brave Heart (2001, 2002) describes the long shadows of historical trauma that have affected First Nations people due to the many years of suffering and cultural degradation that were imposed on the people. Such trauma contributes to ongoing problems in the lives of family members. In a recent study perceived discrimination emerged as the most important risk factor for First Nation adolescents living in the American Midwest (LaFramboise, Hoyt, Oliver, & Whitbeck, 2006).

Kirmayer and colleagues (2006) identify the risk and protective factors regarding suicide in the history and culture of the various Aboriginal groups in Canada. The history of cultural discrimination is one of the important risk factors that contributes to the dramatically higher risk of suicide among members of Aboriginal groups. Although there is great variation among communities, bands, and nations, the suicide rate as a group is higher than the Canadian population in general—especially among the Inuit, where it is 6–11 times higher than the total population. Suicide in the Aboriginal people is especially a problem among the young. For teens and young adults, Aboriginal youth on the reserves are 5 to 6 times more likely to die of suicide than their peers in the total population. In the United States, suicide rates of

First Nations youth are 1.5 to 3 times as high as other young people, and seven times for those who are living in non-First Nations homes (Adams, 2012). Higher suicide rates in this population have also been associated with the context of forced dislocation. Given the small and close nature of many Aboriginal communities, with many people related and sharing the same histories of adversity, the impact of such a suicide can be especially painful and widespread (Kirmayer et al., 2006). A study of suicide rates comparing First Nations communities in British Columbia, Canada, with few or no completed suicides to those with high rates revealed important community protective factors that reflect community empowerment issues. These included children attending nation-controlled schools, nation-controlled police, fire, and health systems, cultural facilities, history of land claims, and a degree of self-government. A subsequent study added three factors: advanced land claims, women members of the local government, and local protective services (Kirmayer et al., 2006). Protective resources can include educational opportunities for children to learn about survival skills to deal with oppression and appreciation of the richness of the history of the people (Cross, 1999; Kirmayer et al., 2006). A suicide prevention program designed to fit with the Zuni culture was helpful with young people (LaFranbroise & Howard-Pitney, 1995)

In both the United States and Canada many groups and individuals who are members of the First Nations struggle with severe poverty (Kirmayer et al., 2006; Yellow Bird, 2001; Yellow Horse Brave Heart, 2001, 2002). In Canada, members of the Aboriginal people in general report higher unemployment rates and are more likely to be homeless or living in inadequate housing. Poverty among Aboriginal people in Canada is especially problematic in the Western areas (Kirmayer et al., 2006). Lakota elders describe risk factors in terms of poverty, lack of culturally appropriate health and other services, unemployment, and poor housing (Bowen, 1995) that are experienced by many members of First Nations (Yellow Bird, 2001; Yellow Horse Brave Heart, 2001, 2002).

Higher rates of incarceration represent another risk factor for members of the Aboriginal groups in Canada. These pose stress for the individuals involved as well as their families (Kirmayer et al., 2006).

Health problems represent challenges. High levels of substance abuse are present in many First Nations communities (Kirmayer et al., 2006; Winkelman, 2001). Chronic health problems, for example, diabetes, represent significant health problems within some nations. Traditional healing practices continue to play important roles, especially in addressing what are viewed as the ultimate causes of illness (Winkelman, 2001). HIV/AIDS has been a serious problem within the Aboriginal people in Canada (3% of the population yet 20.4% of the AIDS cases in 2009; note—the majority of people did not report their ethnic status in this report) (Avert, 2012).

Members of First Nations can also feel connected to the wider environment that helps give them a sense of meaning. The term *mitakuye oya'in* refers to this broader relationship view. According to the Lakota concept *mitakuye oya'in*, "everything that has ever been, or ever will be created— every person, every animal, every plant, every stone, all the waters, Father Sky, Mother Earth herself—are related" (Bowen, 1995, p. 129). Strength within this concept refers not just to physical strength but also strength of character, self-sufficiency, and the bond of relationships.

The nature of national/tribal identity can be very important for members of some groups. Yellow Bird describes the critical nature of one's tribal identity because it links people to the principal cultural group that can give "structure, meaning, direction, and purpose to one's life as its relates to specific tribal customs" (2001, p. 65). This identity prescribes behavior and a sense of belonging. Traditional cultural rituals further affirm this sense of identity (Yellow Bird, 2001).

The role of elders is important within the First Nations community and serves as an important resource within the relationship model (Cross, 1999). Community based programs involving respected elders to help transmit cultural values and coping strategies to youth can be important resources (Kirmayer, et al., 2006). Churches and social groups as well as natural helpers in the community are additional resources within the relational model (Cross, 1999). Church attendance by Inuit youth emerged as a protective factor in terms of suicide (Kirmayer et al., 2006).

The presence or absence of culturally grounded social and health services that not only serve individuals but also promote community health is an important issue. The study regarding suicide risk in the Aboriginal people in Canada suggests the value of approaches that support community continuity and empowerment. It is particularly important where communities as a whole have lost hope. An approach that supports community development and political empowerment enables young people to "move with their parents, elders and communities from a position of marginalization, powerlessness, and pessimism to one of agency, creativity, self-confidence, and hope" (Kirmeyer et al., 2006, p. xvii).

The following two programs set within Alaskan communities illustrate ways in which targeting community issues can be used to strengthen families and individuals. These programs reflect the holistic, relational, and contextual nature of resiliency identified in the earlier discussion.

Simmons, Franks, Peters, and Burham (2003) describe a community-based approach for enhancing resiliency in a small community in northern Alaska. Major signs of family and individual dysfunction (especially substance abuse and child abuse) were present among the Native Alaskan families in the community. Based on the assessment that the community as a whole was depressed and demoralized, it was important to find ways to promote a sense of self-worth and morale within the community. With this assessment and an understanding of the culture, the mental health program worked to re-create a sense of community and cultural reawakening among the people. Mental health staff members developed a holistic approach that drew upon traditional strengths within the community. They encouraged community members to carry out traditional activities and ceremonies and to celebrate life cycle events (for example, birthdays). These efforts at the community level had a profound positive impact on individual families and their members (Simmons, Franks, Peters, & Burham, 2003).

The Village Service Program established in Alaska to address substance abuse problems also reflects the importance of recognizing the community context and supporting traditional cultural practices. Community efforts acknowledged the elders as having knowledge of the cultural traditions and playing important roles in the healing process. Counselors made help accessible by participating with clients in traditional activities. The act of providing services in the context of traditional activities has helped to build the clients' confidence in themselves and their community. The program allows community members to "be exposed to the strength and healing of their traditional culture" (Capers, 2003, p. 10).

Social Support and Extended Family

Family life, family ties, including extended family and clans, represent an important sense of identity and resources for people of the First Nations. Extended family ties can protect by offering support or contribute to risk through enmeshment into dysfunctional patterns.

The Lakota have two concepts that represent the relational nature of the culture. *Tiospaye* (the collection of related families who are bound by blood) and *Hunka* (a traditional adoption ceremony that creates ties more sacred than biological kinship) support resiliency and strengthen and expand extended family ties (Yellow Horse Brave Heart, 2002).

Members of the Navajo share the holistic traditional views described earlier. The extended family system serves as an important source of resiliency for Navajo families. It is part of a larger network that is expected to actively support other members. Family groups are further clustered into clans that provide a strong sense of identity and govern acceptable relationships. As family members become acculturated into Western ways of thinking and behaving, tension can occur within family groups. Navajo families face some of the same risk factors described earlier, with consequent problems with alcoholism and family breakdown (McWhirter & Ryan, 1991).

Folk teaching engaged in by the family group and within the community can be protective (Cross, 1999). Sharing and generosity have been important values within many First Nations. These practices help maintain good relationships within the community and the extended family (Yellow

Bird, 2001). Brave Heart describes the cultural ideal of a generous person who puts the good of the community above one's self (2002).

Family Composition and Organization

Family organizational patterns vary widely depending on the group; for example, some groups like the Seneca are matrilineal. Brave Heart describes the traditional First Nations family as organized in terms of complementary gender roles. Unfortunately, some individuals have been influenced by European values of male domination with consequent devaluation of women and children. In some families this has led to domestic violence and child abuse (Yellow Horse Brave Heart, 2002). Forced separations of children from their families through boarding schools, child welfare programs, and the abuse experienced by children in these settings have also contributed to such problems in Aboriginal families (Kirmayer et al., 2006).

In terms of the holistic model described earlier, family stories and rituals represent potential protective factors. The active role of the father is also important (Cross, 1999). Warm, supportive mothers are a valuable protective factor for youth (LaFramboise, Hoyt, Oliver, & Whitbeck, 2006).

Indirect communication patterns can promote respect for family members. Parents may use stories rather than direct prescriptions of behavior (Winkelman, 2001). The use of silence demonstrates serious consideration of the words of others and is part of the pacing in communication (Winkelman, 2001).

Individuals

Protective resources reside within the mind and the spirit. These include faith, prayer, meditation, healing ceremonies, and positive thinking. Such activities counter negative practices and promote healing as well as group solidarity. Positive self-talk is also important (Cross, 1999). Yellow Bird (2001) describes spiritual practices as helping people gain a sense of meaning and wholeness within their lives. Issues of spirituality have been important sources of support and meaning and are described as an essential part of the First Nations member's being (Kirmayer et al., 2006). Traditional spiritual patterns were, however, long under attack by outside colonizers who sought to devalue and eliminate them. Gaining a sense of coherence and meaning about life in general has been associated with increased resiliency. In this regard, levels of cultural enculturation and self-esteem are important risk and protective factors in terms of the important problem of suicide and substance abuse (Kirmayer et al., 2006). Based on a study with youth of the Odawa and Ojibway nations, enculturation (identification with one's culture) interacted with self-esteem in terms of drug abuse. Youth with high levels of self-esteem and enculturation reported the lowest levels of alcohol and substance abuse. However, youth with low levels of self-esteem and high levels of cultural identity reported the highest levels of drug abuse. Among the elements of enculturation, the element of cultural affinity that reflects pride in one's background was positively associated with self-esteem (Zimmerman, Ramirez, Washienko, Walker, & Dyer, 1998). Higher levels of enculturation were associated with increased pro-social outcomes with Midwestern First Nation youth (LaFramboise et al., 2006).

Military Families

Although families with a member serving in the military belong to a wide range of ethnic and racial groups and include a variety of family arrangements, the military has a culture that influences these families, poses specific demands on families, and has codes that influence the type of help that is viewed as acceptable (Pryce, Pryce, & Shackelford, 2012). Military members and their families include those who are part of standing military units as well as reservists who are called up for duty in response to wartime needs. Recent wars have meant increased demands on individuals serving in the military and their families. In response, there has been renewed concern and research regarding the impact of these demands and ways to help them cope with these pressures. The following discussion identifies some of these demands and the associated risk factors, protective factors that enable families cope, and some of the programs that have been established to help families. In discussing risk factors, it is always important to remember the interaction that occurs among these. Factors that are closer to families (proximal risk factors) are influenced by those that are more distant (distal) (for example, the injury of a family member is influenced by the funding for health care for wounded warriors; readjustment back to the family and community is influenced by the job market in one's home community), and a combination or pileup of risk (cumulative/additive risk factors) exacerbates the stress experienced by a family.

The current profile of military families includes both men (85.7%) and women (14.3%) who are on active duty (Pryce, Pryce, & Shackelford, 2012). The majority of active duty soldiers (54%) are married and many (43%) are parents, typically with young children (40% under five years). Some soldiers are single parents (14% of women). Reserve members are usually older and married with families. Members of the military tend to have a higher education than the general population and come from middle class or higher income levels. In terms of racial/ethnic composition, in 2007, 65.5 percent were white, 13.19 percent were Hispanic, 12.82 percent were black, 3.25

percent were Asian or Pacific Islander, 1.96 percent were American Indian or Alaskan, and 3.42 percent were from several racial groups (Pryce, Pryce, & Shackelford, 2012). Recent changes in the Don't Ask Don't Tell policies that now open the door for gays and lesbians to serve openly in the military will further expand the horizons of families represented in the military.

Stress for military families in general can be particularly related to several phases of life in the military: relocation, deployment, and reunification because of the disruption in the family organization and support system that they create (Palmer, 2008; Pryce, Pryce, & Shackelford, 2012). The following discussion is organized in terms of the risk and protective factors present during these phases of military life.

Relocation

Military families, especially those with members on active duty, experience a series of relocations. Although earlier literature described this aspect of military life as problematic, more recent studies have found no evidence for problems in adjustment for military children. In contrast, children have learned adaptive skills. Frequent moves can be difficult for spouses in terms of their careers and require a commitment to the military as a lifestyle. The military community represents an important source of support for these frequent moves (Palmer, 2008; Park, 2011; Weber & Weber, 2005).

Deployment

Deployment during times of war can be an extremely stressful experience for military families. Deployment represents the reality of a time of uncertainty, absence, and potential danger for the soldier.

When adolescents were asked how they felt when they learned that their parents were going to be deployed, they voiced the following cognitive, emotional, and behavioral themes of stress: confusion about what this would mean, loss of their parent in the everyday life of the family, worry about when and if they would see their parent again, nervousness, anger, sadness, isolation, and fear. While positive feelings were infrequent, some referred to a sense of pride in their parent for what he or she was doing to protect us (Huebner & Mancini, 2005). Spouses of deployed service members were more likely to have diagnoses of depression, sleep disorders, anxiety, acute stress reactions, and adjustment reactions. Length and frequency of deployments increased the risk (Chandra, Sandraluz, Jaycox, Tanielian, Burns, Ruder, & Han, 2010; Huebner & Mancini, 2005; Huebner, Mancini, Bowen, & Orthner, 2009; Pryce, Pryce, & Shackelford, 2012). Families of National Guard members experience this without the organizational support typically available for active-duty family members (Pryce, Pryce, & Shackelford, 2012).

Further situational characteristics of the deployment situation that contribute to stress include financial stress (especially for reservist families), lack of access to supportive community resources, and media portrayals of the war scene. Related family and personal characteristics in terms of cognition, emotion, and family organization that further intensify stress include lack of understanding about the nature of the deployment (length and characteristics) and its impact on children, communication problems between the deployed family members and others within the family, problems in family leadership and structure (rigid, chaotic, new roles required), lack of a belief system that provides meaning for these life events, and pregnancy by the caregiving parent (Pryce, Pryce, & Shackelford, 2012; Saltzman, Lester, Beardslee, Llayne, Woodward, & Nash, 2011).

In addition to the stresses inherent in deployment, Pryce, Pryce, and Shackelford (2012) describe other difficult life events that pose additional problems for military members and their families both during deployment and the subsequent reunification period. Substance abuse and depression as a result of the war situation represent major problems facing many military members. Military personnel (especially women) have been sexually assaulted by fellow military personnel. They have frequently had difficulty seeking help for this problem within the military. There is currently growing recognition of the existence of this problem and the need to begin to address it. Physical wounds, including traumatic brain injury, can create major and lasting problems for soldiers and their family members. Post-traumatic stress disorder in response to the horrors of war can represent major difficulties for all parties involved. Suicide has become a major problem for active duty personnel as well as veterans. Approximately 6,500 veterans commit suicide every year (Pryce, Pryce, & Shackelford, 2012). Compounding these problematic situations has been a traditional reluctance to seek help, especially for problems related to mental health, for fear of being considered weak or risk jeopardizing one's career (Pryce, Pryce, & Shackelford, 2012). In this context, the role of the unit culture that encourages support as reflected in the commander's concern for families was especially important for families and their satisfaction with the situation in the military (Bowen & Orthner, 1993; Drummet, Coleman, & Cable, 2003; McCubbin, Dahl, & Hunter, 1976; Pittman, Kerpelman, & McFadyen, 2004).

Countering these risk factors are the following situational and family characteristics that serve to protect family members.

1. Adequate social and community support are important.

2. Protective family characteristics include the parents' ability to cope and adapt, supportive family communication patterns, strong marital bond, good parent and child relationships, and family role flexibility.

Young people described strong family ties as well as those with friends as important (Park, 2011).

3. A belief system that supports the military way of life helps families cope (Palmer, 2008; Park, 2011; Pryce, Pryce, & Shackelford, 2012; Saltzman et al., 2011).

4. The parent's ability to cope and adapt has been identified as the best predictor of the children's ability to cope. When the parent has problems coping, it not only fails to give children the support that they need but also makes them worry about their caretaker parent (Palmer, 2008). In contrast to earlier wars, soldiers today can frequently communicate on a regular basis with their family members. While an emphasis on problems can increase stress, this communication can be a real source of support for all family members (Pryce, Pryce, & Shackelford, 2012).

Reunification

Family reunification can be a source of joy and relief, but it can also pose problems. Everyone in the family has changed as a result of the situation and must now adjust to new roles. When family members come home with physical wounds, traumatic brain injuries, substance abuse problems, and posttraumatic stress disorder, major challenges can face families that exceed typical family coping resources. Family members can also experience the stress of trauma through the effect of secondary trauma—the trauma experienced by people who are close to people who have been traumatized (Pryce, Pryce, & Shackelford, 2012). Families with these issues are more likely to experience spousal and child abuse (Palmer, 2008).

Key protective factors have been identified that help family members cope. In terms of context, encouragement to use social service and health resources for problems by the military leaders is important to legitimize seeking this type of help given the historic fear that seeking help is a sign of weakness (Pryce, Pryce, & Shackelford, 2012). Finding support can be especially difficult for reservists because they are not part of the ongoing military establishment.

Support within the extended family and the community are important protective factors. Families are supported by a sense of hardiness by members—they have a sense of control over life and see changes as an inevitable aspect of life and as a challenge and opportunity for growth (Palmer, 2008; Park, 2011; Pryce, Pryce, & Shackelford, 2012).

Ambiguous Loss

One of the very difficult circumstances military families have to face is to have a loved one missing in action. In addition to loss, there is the ongoing pain experienced by families facing ambiguous loss because there is no official recognition of the reality of the loss that permits some type of closure. A study of adult children of soldiers missing in action during the Vietnam War revealed that family members still continued to experience ongoing pain, loss, and anger as well as the sources of resiliency in dealing with their painful situation. Drawing upon the resiliency model of family stress, adjustment, and adaptation described earlier, higher levels of family hardiness as reflected in a sense of control over life and commitment to the family was associated with lower levels of distress. The mother's leadership role of enabling the family to cope was also important (Campbell & Demi, 2000).

Based on her extensive work with families who have experienced ambiguous loss in terms of the military and other tragedies, Boss (2006) emphasizes the need to acknowledge with these hurting families the ambiguity of their loss and the inherent extreme difficulty of this situation. As in other traumatic situations facing families, exploring the family's sense of meaning regarding this event is crucial. Some approaches that can be helpful include spirituality, rituals, some positive aspect of the event (e.g., the person missing was engaged in a heroic or self-sacrificing action), and something that can engender hope. Boss also describes the burden that a strong sense of mastery can impose on families and the consequent need to temper this sense of mastery to learn lessons of acceptance. Such a view can help reduce some of the sense of self-blame that families can experience during times of painful loss. Acceptance in this context represents an active coping strategy, not passivity. Families also need to establish a new sense of identity that recognizes the ambiguous nature of their current situation.

Resources

The military has come to realize how critically important it is to promote resiliency among soldiers and their families. It has established programs to help address the stresses facing families and their members. Pryce, Pryce, and Shackelford (2012) provide a valuable resource in terms of descriptions and critiques of many of these programs and policies in detail in their recent book *The Costs of Courage: Combat Stress, Warriors, and Family Survival* published by Lyceum Press. One important program begun originally for National Guard families is the National Guard Family Program. Due to its effectiveness, it has been charged with providing family support and assistance for all military families not living in a Department of Defense installation. The program was created by a social worker and involves many social workers as state family program coordinators. The program works in partnership with communities and organizations to meet the support needs of military families throughout the deployment, redeployment, reintegration, bereavement, and loss stages (Pryce, Pryce, & Shackelford, 2012, p. 125). A curriculum entitled Operation Ready (Resources for Educating about Deployment and You) was designed and revised on a regular basis to prepare families for the process of deployment and to develop resiliency. These materials can be downloaded online at the Military Onesource (http://www .armyonesource.comn) (p. 127). According to Pryce, Pryce, and Shackelford (2012), the Veterans Health Administration is overwhelmed by requests for physical and mental health care.

Saltzman et al. (2011) describe the FOCUS program (Families Over-Coming Under Stress) designed to enhance resilience in families who have experienced trauma. The program is designed for families from culturally diverse backgrounds to help them deal with the challenges experienced during pre-deployment, deployment, reintegration, and long-term post-deployment. Based on evaluation of the program, certain aspects of family functioning appear to be most salient for improved family functioning and resiliency: communication, emotional responsiveness and involvement, role clarity, and problem solving (Saltzman et al, 2011). Huebner et al. (2009) argue for the importance of building support capacity within the community to assist families. They describe the importance of strengthening both formal and informal support networks as well as ways in which these two networks can support each other. They describe programs such as a 4-H for army youth that involves both the community and the military, Operation Military Kids for National Guard and reserve families, the Airmen and Family Readiness Center, and Essential Life Skills for Military Families. The Defense Center for Excellence for Psychological Health and Traumatic Brain Injury has created the Real Warriors project designed to help build resilience and support the reintegration process of those serving the military. Its website (www.realwarriors.net) has extensive information that encourages people to seek help and steps that service members and their families can take to promote resilience (www.realwarriors.net/family/change/family resilience/ php). The program also partners with a range of organizations to ensure that people are receiving adequate care.

Rural Families

Rural families are characterized by great diversity in terms of economic activities (for example, farming, fishing, mining, logging, tourism), racial and ethnic identity, and area of residence. Some of the earlier studies that address resiliency among rural African American families were discussed in the section about African Americans. This section will highlight issues related to rural families of the Midwest. While the economic situation in these areas has improved, recent hard times ("the farm crisis") revealed both vulnerabilities and resources. The following discussion emphasizes some of the lessons learned about rural family resiliency during the "farm crisis."

Social and Economic Context

Beginning in the 1980s, rural families and their communities experienced major financial hardship associated with a series of international and national developments. Rural communities lost their economic base (Van Hook, 1990a, 1990b). The economic stress had a negative impact on families (Conger & Elder, 1994).

Churches and schools represent key social institutions in these rural communities that serve as sources of community cohesion and identity. Youth also identify the important role of mentors in the community (Conger & Elder, 1994). Formal social services can be more difficult to access due to distances.

Extended Family

While rural families have traditionally been nuclear in organization, the heritage of farming from earlier generations and sense of obligation to this heritage had a powerful impact on families. Farming in this context represented not only a source of income but also a multigenerational way of life accompanied by a sense of purpose and meaning. As a result, the family circle represents both sources of support and the pressure of obligation when one cannot fulfill the obligations of the heritage (Conger & Elder, 1994; Elder & Conger, 2000; Van Hook, 1990b).

Family Patterns

Economic problems posed risk factors through their impact on the marital and parent-child relationships. These in turn strained the parent-child relationship and had a negative effect on young people (Elder & Conger, 2000).

When asked what helped their family to cope with these difficult times, young people identified the following sources of resiliency: the role of family cohesion mentioned earlier (family members pulled together) and flexibility (family gender roles became more androgynous—members did what they needed to do). For teenagers, being able to contribute to the solution in various ways was important to them (Van Hook, 1990a). Strong relationships with caring adults within the family (especially the father, supported by mothers and grandparents) were important (Elder & Conger, 2000). Young people were very protective of their families and sensitive to interactions that might cause them to reveal family financial difficulties (Van Hook, 1990a). Adult communication patterns that did not help young people understand what was taking place increased their anxiety (Van Hook, 1990a).

Individuals

The following protective factors emerged that helped young people cope. Young people were able to assume productive roles in terms of work and school that enabled youth to feel that they were contributing and gave them a sense of mastery. They also learned important work and organizational skills. Academic success was the most important factor in avoiding problem behavior. Such success was part of an interactive process. Young people who succeeded developed a greater sense of mastery and self-confidence. Doing well in school also helped young people gain greater access to other opportunities and mentoring relationships within the community. Religious involvement in the community was also protective (Conger & Elder, 1994; Elder & Conger 2000).

FAMILY STRUCTURAL ISSUES

Single Parents

Single parents vary widely in many dimensions. They are members of all cultural and social economic groups. They are single parents as a result of various circumstances, including death of a partner, divorce, adoption, or births that occurred outside of a stable relationship. Parents can be mothers or fathers by birth, adoption, or other family ties. The case illustrations in this book illustrate some of the diversity within this group of families. Recognizing this diversity, the following demographic information describes the demographic patterns of this group.

According to the U.S. Census report of November 2009, in 2007 there were 13.7 million parents who had custody of 21.8 million children under the age of 21 where the other parents lived somewhere else (Grall, 2009). Based on U.S. Census data, among all children, 26.3 percent of children under the age of 21 were living with one parent. Rates of single parents varied widely in terms of racial and cultural groups: among white children living in families, 22.4 percent of parents were living in single-parent arrangements, 25.4 percent among Hispanic families, a higher rate among black families (48.2%), and lower (16.2%) in the diverse group including Asian, First Nations, and Pacific Islanders.

In Canada an increasing percentage of children are born to single parents (Department of Justice, Canada, 2012). As of the 2006 census, 15 percent of families are single-parent families (Statistics Canada, 2007). Rates of single parents are substantially higher in the Inuits (22.5%), the First Nations (24.4%), compared with the Metis (14.0%) and non-Aboriginal families (12.4%). These rates represented a doubling for First Nations and tripling for Inuit families in the past ten years. Single mothers also tend to be younger among the Inuit and First Nations women (Quinless, 2010).

In the United States, single-parent families are primarily headed by mothers (82.6%) compared with 17.4 percent with fathers. The reason for being a single parent also varies by gender. About one third (34.2%) of single mothers had never married, 45.1 percent were divorced or separated, and 1.7 percent were widowed. Among fathers, 20.9 percent had never married and another 57.8 percent were divorced or separated. Race and ethnicity also varied by gender. Among mothers, 59 percent were white, 27 percent were black, and 18 percent were Hispanic. Fathers, on the other hand, were primarily white (71.6%), with smaller numbers in other groups (blacks, 11.4%, Hispanic, 12.1%).

Mothers were also overrepresented in Canada (87%) compared with fathers (13%). While death was an important reason for both men and women in the 1950s, divorce and separation have emerged as the most important reasons in recent years (Department of Justice, Canada, 2012).

Although single-parent families vary widely in terms of social economic status, as a group they are at greater risk for living in poverty and the risks associated with poverty, especially those living with their mothers. In the United States, among children living in single parent families, 24.6 percent were living in poverty (compared with 12.5% of children generally), including 18.2 percent who were receiving child support payments. Mothers with lower levels of education were less likely to have formal child support arrangements. Children living with their mothers are at greater risk for living in poverty (26.3% compared with 12.9% for children living with their fathers). Only 76.3 percent of parents who are due child support payments receive these payments and only 47.9 percent pay the full support due (Grail, 2009).

Single-parent families in Canada also shared this risk of poverty. They had incomes generally about half ($37,000) of those of two-parent families ($70,950), with this difference substantially higher in some of the provinces (especially the Northwest Territories and the Yukon) (Statistics Canada, 2012). Families headed by mothers who were employed had substantially lower incomes ($24,800) than fathers ($38,100). Gender and age emerged as important risk factors for Canadian single-parent families in terms of poverty. The vast majority (91.3%) of single mothers under the age of 25 had income rates below the low-income cutoff line. Rates were somewhat lower for mothers from ages 25 to 44—61.2 percent, and still high but less for those from 45 to 65 (41.1%), with a general rate of below the cutoff of 61 percent for female-headed families. This compared with 14.8 percent for families in general (Department of Justice, Canada, 2012). In recent years, the educational level of single parents has increased. As of 2008, only 15 percent of single mothers had not graduated from high school and 22 percent had at least an associate degree in the United States.

Single parents are represented throughout the child-rearing span: 25.8 percent are below the age of 30, while 39.1 percent are over forty years of age in the United States. Younger mothers were more likely to be living in poverty.

Employment also served as both a protective and risk factor for single parents. Parents who worked full time had a poverty rate of 8.1 percent compared with 57 percent for those who depended on governmental help. Over half (57%) of single parents balance family responsibilities with full-time employment. Fathers (71%) are more likely to be working full time than mothers (49.8%). Families have been caught in the economic decline at the same time as a change in policy regarding governmental benefits (a decline in participation from 22% in 1995 to 4.3% in 2007) (Grail, 2009).

In terms of risk and protective factors, some of the same personal, inter-personal, and contextual issues emerge for single- as well as two-parent families. Family appraisals played a critical role—especially whether or not the event represented a threat to the family. For example, in the study of African American single-parent families, the critical difference between adaptive and symptomatic single families "was that adaptive families tended to highlight positive events and to place less emphasis on the negative aspects of stressful events than did nonadaptive families" (Atwood & Genovese, 2006; Lindblad-Goldberg, 2006, p. 152).

Single parents are challenged to carry out the myriad of responsibilities that all families are expected to carry out (providing for the physical, emotional, and social resources of family members). As a parent myself, I have gained a greater appreciation for my mother, who had to raise two daughters following the sudden death of her young husband, and of the sacrifices that she made for us. These responsibilities can seem daunting at times for two parents and must be shouldered by one parent, often with limited economic resources. Single parents can face the challenge of role overload and feel overwhelmed (Lindblad-Goldberg, 2006). The ability of single parents to have effective coping strategies is an important protective factor (Baez, 2000; Lindblad-Goldberg, 2006).

Family leadership roles are also important protective factors. The family organization is crucial in dealing with these many responsibilities, especially the role of an executive subsystem. This can include the parent and one or more of the children or other adults in the family system. In Lindblad-Goldberg's study (2006) of African American single-parent families, this subsystem generally consisted of the parent and one or more of the children. It is crucial that the parent is the one in charge of this system and ultimately the family. In adaptive families, when grandparents were part of this executive system, they served as a supportive ally rather than assuming primary authority. Problems can emerge when the roles of individuals in this subsystem are not clearly defined or when children are given more responsibilities than the parent. Family boundaries between subsystems must also be clear. Family communication must be clear to create effective family functioning (Lindblad-Goldberg, 2006). Single parents must find ways to effectively set limits without another parent to support these efforts. Difficult decisions are often required without another partner to share concerns with (Atwood & Genovese, 2006). The parent needs to meet the needs of all the children within the family.

The challenge of trying to support a family financially competes with the other demands of parenting. The situation becomes even more challenging when the salary is low and thus requires two jobs or leaves no money for time-saving conveniences. This leaves little energy or time for single parents to nourish their own needs (Atwood & Genovese, 2006). Adaptive single parents were more likely to find ways to have a social life (Lindblad-Goldberg, 2006).

For some single parents, parenting offers an additional challenge because they lacked the opportunity to gain parenting skills through ongoing experience as a parent. Mr. Cole, for example, became an active parent when his wife died. Other parents have important parenting skills that serve as resources for single-parent families.

Feeling a degree of control over one's self was also protective for African American single parents while less adaptive mothers were more likely to feel that the world was controlling them (Lindblad-Goldberg, 2006). This fits with findings from studies of single parents living in poverty in South Africa where a sense of hardiness and sense of optimism emerged as protective (Greeff & Fillis, 2009; Greeff & Ilona, 2005). A related sense of self-confidence was important for middle- and upper-income single parents (Kjellstrand & Harper, 2012). Religious faith also served as a protective factor (Greeff & Fillis, 2009; Greeff & Ilona, 2005).

Social norms that support two-parent families as the ideal can also pose a challenge for single-parent families. As a result, when problems arise, single parents can feel blamed in ways that might not have occurred if there were two parents in the family (Atwood & Genovese, 2006).

Risk factors can also be associated with the circumstances that created the single-parent families. Divorce can for a time plunge a family into tension, uncertainty, and anger that creates problems for the parent and the children. Sometimes there is confusion in terms of the current relationship between an ex-spouse and the current family either physically or psychologically (Atwood & Genovese, 2006). Boss (2006) describes this as ambiguous loss as people are in a state of denial about the real end of the relationship. Family members can mourn their hopes and dreams for their family that has been shattered. Children can take out their frustration on the remaining parent. I remember working with a family in which a mother had left her husband because of his physical abuse and his infidelity. The children had not witnessed these aspects of the marriage and the mother had protected them from this information. The son had idolized his father and found his mother's decision intolerable. He was extremely angry and hostile toward his mother who had "taken him away from his father." It was only later that he was able to recognize the reality facing his mother and to accept her decision with sadness because he had to give up his idealized image of his father. Death brings with it feelings of grief on the part of children and the remaining spouse. This can make it difficult for family members to be available to others (Atwood & Genovese, 2006). Parents who previously were engaged in the external responsibilities of the family must now learn and assume new roles. Young people who become parents without a steady partner are often struggling with the challenges of young adulthood as well as the demands of parenthood and frequently lack the skills of parenting.

Single parents can find resources within the extended family and external community that represent important protective factors. Support from family and friends emerged as protective for single parents from a variety of cultural and economic backgrounds (Atwood & Genovese, 2006; Greeff & Ilona, 2005; Lindblad-Goldberg, 2006). Support from family improved the emotional life of single parents, which in turn helped them take a more active and leadership role in their families (Baez, 2000). In terms of the community, there are support groups for parents going through divorce, other types of loss, and single parents that can be valuable sources of information and relational support. Extended family in terms of grandparents and siblings can be potential sources of support. I know my grandparents and aunt were a great resource for my mother as well as for us. Parents who were previously involved in very destructive relationships can now feel freer to allocate these energies to their children. Friends and counselors who provide affirmation to single parents can be very important. All parents experience doubts and seek confirmation. Without a partner to share these matters, friends can be a powerful ally.

Members of single-parent families as well as two-parent families can bring to the family circle the important resources identified earlier in the literature as protective factors—for example, codes of family loyalty and affection, self-efficacy, a sense of coherence, hope and courage, role models of strength, flexible family roles, a sense of cohesion, clear communication, effective coping strategies, humor, and spiritual beliefs and practices. Family schemas can be created that are protective and positive as well as negative. I know my father's death created two positive belief systems within our family. The first family mantra in our family was that women need to prepare to support themselves financially because they cannot depend on a husband to do so. The second led me to treasure the time that I have with my family because we do not know how long they are going to be with us.

Because single-parent families differ on so many important dimensions, a variety of intervention strategies can be appropriate depending on the family and its circumstances. The following suggest some of the approaches that might be helpful depending on the circumstances. In helping single families overwhelmed by life events, a multisystemic approach can be particularly useful (for example, Mr. Cole). These families need an approach that enables them to play a role in the decision-making process, that emphasizes their strengths, that incorporates a wider systems approach to incorporate the resources of the extended family and community circle. Given the systematic disadvantage experienced by many single-parent families, ongoing efforts in the area of advocacy are also important. Families in which parents are having to assume new roles could potentially benefit from a social learning approach that enables them to learn and practice new skills and addresses the belief systems that enable them to implement them. Other families can be struggling with the problem of creating an effective leadership system and could benefit from a structural family approach. Some single-parent families have important basic resources and some of the necessary coping skills, but have become demoralized by their current situation. A solution-focused approach can help family members identify their views of possible paths toward solving their problems in a step-by-step approach that promotes hope. Other families like that of Mrs. James are struggling with the shadow of life events that are creating problem-saturated stories. A narrative approach can help them rewrite the family past and present script in ways that help them gain a more empowering perspective. Single-parent families can contend with serious illness in family members—a child or a beloved grandparent. A psychoeducational approach can be useful in helping them develop effective coping strategies and receive the support they need during this difficult time. Spirituality can potentially be an essential resource for single-parent families as they seek a sense of support and meaning and deal with the process of forgiveness. Past life scripts can be transmitted through family of origin that are making it difficult for people to address current relationships. A Bowenian systems approach and object relations might be helpful.

Divorced Families

Current high rates of divorce (approximately 50% of the marriage rate [Centers for Disease Control and Prevention, *Monthly Vital Statistics Report,* 2012b]) mean that many families consist of divorced parents and their children. Approximately 16.8 per 1,000 children under the age of 18 were involved in divorce. They tended to be living with their mothers—the mother was awarded custody in 72 percent of situations, joint custody was awarded in 16 percent, and the father was awarded custody in 9 percent (CDC, 2012b). These families must deal with the sometimes painful aftermath of the problems that led to the divorce as well as the circumstances of the divorce itself. As discussed in chapter 3, the King family's past experiences with divorce can have a lingering impact on the current family situation. Divorce typically brings pain to family members as they must face the challenge of adjusting to new relationships and structures. While some disruption is typical in family members experiencing divorce, most families are able in time to create a satisfying lifestyle for the members involved. Social workers must understand resiliency in this context not as lack of difficulties, but how families negotiate these adaptations and forge effective new meanings and structures. Hetherington and Elmore (2003) emphasize the basic requirements of developing age-appropriate competencies to address these challenges and satisfy basic needs. Financial stability is thus an important protective factor (Greeff & van der Merwe, 2004).

The nature of specific risk and protective factors facing children is strongly influenced by parental behaviors during this time. Parental behaviors associated with improved outcomes for children and the family unit include cooperation between the parents rather than an adversarial stance that involves disparaging the other parent (Hetherington & Elmore, 2003). A parental approach that is warm and includes appropriate use of authority and supervision along with family support and involvement in many aspects of the life of children gives children a sense of stability that reduces stress. Lack of parental involvement increases stress (Chen & George, 2005; Hetherington & Elmore, 2003). Ongoing involvement by both parents is valuable here. Parental support that is reinforced by extended family members and friends further supports resiliency (Greeff & van der Merwe, 2004). Open communication between parents and children is also useful (Greeff & van der Merwe, 2004). Siblings are frequently so involved in their own reactions that they provided limited support to each other. The role of peers emerged especially for teenagers (Grych & Fincham, 1997).

Drawing on a narrative account of mothers who were raising young children at least two years after divorce, a series of protective factors emerged that reflect those described above. A sense of effectiveness as a parent (self-efficacy) helped promote positive adjustment. While resilient mothers frequently faced situations similar to those facing other mothers, their interpretations of events helped them to cope in a more effective manner rather than become caught up in destructive and hurtful power struggles or abdicate their parental control. These mothers recognized the existence of problems and were confident in their ability to address them and generally felt in charge of the family situation. They were able to communicate sensitively with their children and to modulate their own demands on the children. They were able to place firm demands on their children in a flexible manner depending on the situation. These mothers were able to be empathic and to view the situation from the child's perspective as well as their own. At the same time they had expectations of their children. For many of these mothers, the process of parenting post-divorce has required them to adapt their parenting methods to fit with their new situation as a single parent.

In contrast, in families that reflected a poor adaptation, mothers described their sense of ineffectiveness and inflexibility in dealing with their children. They felt overwhelmed and seemed insensitive in communicating with their children. Many of these mothers felt unable to negotiate with their children and instead placed themselves in ultimatum and power struggle situations. Other mothers felt unable or reluctant to place demands on their children and used giving in as a typical strategy. These mothers also found it difficult to let their children express their sadness or anger for the situation and to be sensitive to their children's feelings (Golby & Bretherton, 1999).

While the focus is on the family unit, context also influences the nature of the financial and emotional support available to parents. How do extended family members and the relevant community view the divorce? What instrumental and emotional support systems are in place in the community?

These findings regarding divorce echo family resiliency themes in general of self-efficacy, effective communication and leadership, flexibility, parental coping skills, social support, and meaning systems that support the process of adaptation.

From the perspective of the children, a sense that they are to blame in some way for the divorce is extremely stressful and represents an important risk factor. It is also important that children experience being understood by their parents (Hetherington & Elmore, 2003). In Grych and Fincham's (1997) review of risk and protective factors from the children's perspective, children described the most stressful aspects of divorce as including their being blamed for the divorce, conflict between the parents, loss of relationship with one of the parents, and changes in their daily living arrangement. Post-divorce conflicts between the parents and situations in which children feel drawn into this conflict in ways that require them to demonstrate loyalty to one rather than both of the parents also create distress for children. Distance from the non-custodial parent emerged as a risk factor. Problems in parenting by the custodial parent due to her or his own emotional distress also were problematic. Changes in the living environment and economic problems were also risk factors (Grych & Fincham, 1997).

Protective factors included strong relationships with parents, preferably with both parents, and extended family members. Peers played a limited role until the teenage years (Grych & Fincham, 1997). Children who demonstrated better adaptation were also more likely to use active behavioral or cognitive coping strategies to understand or solve the problem and distraction by engaging in other activities. Children's sense of control over events was also protective. Avoidance (trying not to think about it) was linked with more problematic responses. The nature of the support that children could enlist from their parents and others in the environment was in turn influenced by the behavior of the child. Temperamentally easy children were better able to cope under conditions of stress (Grych & Fincham, 1997).

Assessment and Treatment

Studies regarding risk and protective factors have implications for family treatment with families that are dealing with divorce. These families vary widely so that the selection and implementation of specific treatment models must be tailored to the individual family and their social context. The following identifies themes that emerge in the research in terms of ways in which several models can address important risk and protective factors. Parental effectiveness that enables parents to respond with appropriate empathy and firmness is helpful to the children involved. Such effectiveness in turn promotes self-efficacy by parents in their parental roles. Separation and divorce frequently require parents to assume new parental roles as well as to deal with their own emotional pain and interpretation.

Social learning models combined with cognitive approaches can be useful in helping parents learn and apply new parenting skills as well as identifying and addressing their beliefs. As parents become more effective in their parenting role, they are better able to meet the needs of family members and to gain confidence in their new parental responsibilities. Structural models can be helpful in enabling parents to establish more effective parental structures that in turn give children a sense of security. Parents and children can also benefit from solution-focused approaches that enable both parents and children to identify which steps can help the family adapt in a more effective manner. Since issues of control and divided loyalty are important for children in coping, children can be given the opportunity to indicate the steps that are important to them in creating a new family arrangement. In discussing such steps, children have the opportunity to express their concerns about important issues such as divided loyalties and specific ways in which parents can give permission for their children to show their love for both parents. For some families, divorce is accompanied by serious economic and other social needs that require linkage with resources within the community. Family members can also identify members of the extended family or family of choice who can participate in the family sessions to support the family's adaptation.

Gay and Lesbian Families

Any discussion of gay and lesbian families must recognize that these families are very diverse. Family members have multilayered identities because they also belong to racial, ethnic, and socioeconomic groups as well as live in specific communities that play a role in who they are and the relevant risk and protective factors. While studies of gay and lesbian families have identified risk and protective factors that can influence family resiliency, any broad statement must always be paired with an individualized assessment in working with families.

External Social and Economic Factors

Social context plays a critical role with gay and lesbian families because they share a risk factor that is quite different from most other family groups.

Unlike families in general where the social context supports the legitimacy of families, gay and lesbian families frequently live in social contexts that deny this legitimacy and stigmatize them. While policy changes in terms of the repeal of the U.S. military policy of Don't Ask, Don't Tell and a growing number of states have legalized gay and lesbian marriages, this change has been controversial and efforts have been marshaled to prevent the change and continue to view these unions as outside the parameters of social and legal acceptability. The general social trend is toward greater acceptance of gay and lesbian family arrangements, but this varies greatly by community.

Lack of legal legitimacy has important repercussions for families that have to struggle with a context that in effect seeks to threaten the stability of the family relationship. Gay and lesbian parents, for example, have been threatened with loss of custody of children. Parents have been unable to be legally viewed as co-parents. Members of gay and lesbian couples have been excluded from the medical decision-making process for their partners. Family members have been unable to provide medical insurance for others through employee benefit plans. Current federal law still prohibits gay and lesbian couples from extending federal benefits to their partners (Ariel & McPherson, 2000; Bigner, 1996; Bos, Van Balen, & Van den Boom, 2005; Granvold & Martin, 1999; Hartman, 1999; Lott-Whitehead & Tully, 1999; Nichols & Schwartz, 1998), although some corporations and governmental bodies are extending partnership benefits to address this issue.

A recent study of parents in lesbian families indicated that while they generally did not experience high levels of rejection and stigma, those who experienced stigma felt a greater need to justify their position as mothers and were more likely to report behavior problems in their children (Bos, van Balen, van den Boom, & Sandfort, 2004). Social stigma has also led to violence against some gay and lesbian individuals with the consequent burden on family members (Granvold & Martin, 1999).

HIV/AIDS has been a significant health problem within the gay community. Despite the advances in medical treatment, this illness has taken a great toll on family members and their friends through loss and ongoing illness.

In some communities, gay and lesbian family members can be reluctant to seek help from health and service organizations because they fear discrimination or not being understood. The role of the church is also mixed, with some religious communities offering support and acceptance and others disapproval.

Social Support and Extended Family

The social support for gay and lesbian families can represent a mixture of risk and protective factors. The coming-out process with other family members can be problematic and leave ongoing tensions with extended family.

For others, this experience has led to support and affirmation. When an individual was married previously in a heterosexual relationship, the process of developing a family based on one's identity as a gay or lesbian individual has the added stress of dealing with the frequently very painful process of coming out with one's partner and sometimes children (Bigner, 1996).

Children living in gay and lesbian families indicated that their close friends were positive to the information that they had two mothers but that this was hard for some peers to understand (Bos, Van Balen, & Van den Boom, 2005). Peers can also serve as extended family as gay and lesbian family members participate in supportive social groups (Granvold & Martin, 1999; Muzio, 1999).

Family Structure and Organization

Many studies suggest that apart from the social context gay and lesbian families are more similar to heterosexual families than they are different (Bos, Van Balen, & Van den Boom, 2005). While the following differences emerged, they need to be set within the context of the great diversity within heterosexual and gay and lesbian families.

Gay and lesbian family members tend to be more flexible in their family roles than heterosexual families. While this represents a protective factor for many families, it can also create confusion and uncertainty in others. Lack of appropriate role models based on family background can be problematic (Granvold & Martin, 1999). Studies of lesbian families indicate that the nonbiological parent tended to be more involved with the children than was typical with families in heterosexual families (Bos, Van Balen, & Van den Boom, 2005).

SUMMARY

Cultural contexts influence the nature of the community context, the extended family, and appropriate social networks. Family members draw upon these relationships to gain a sense of meaning and strength to address life problems as well as for instrumental help. While the specifics of the cultural context of the preceding groups may differ, the theme of the importance of relationships in promoting resiliency—within the family circle and between family members and the social network in the community—is a consistent one for many groups. Flexibility within the family, affectionate ties, effective leadership, and appropriate communication help establish effective family patterns. The strength derived from these relationships helps family members develop a sense of confidence in their ability to cope.

At the same time, perceptions regarding the event can deter family efforts to seek help from those inside and outside the family circle. Efforts to enhance family resiliency thus transcend the specific family unit to include the nature of the community and the relationship systems within the community that can support families. Community context influences both the nature of the problem facing families, the presence of risk factors, as well as the type of resources that are available to promote resiliency. As with all group memberships, any broad strokes regarding the group must be balanced against information gained from individual members in terms of what fits for the members. This understanding in turn helps inform social workers and other counselors regarding approaches that are likely to be effective in the assessment and intervention process.

DISCUSSION QUESTIONS

Discuss ways in which cultural messages influence risk and protective factors (in general and also in terms of specific groups).

How does a history of oppression affect current members of racial and ethnic groups?

How can the extended family serve as both a protective and a risk factor in families (cultural groups, single parents, gay and lesbian families)?

How do cultural codes regarding gay and lesbian families influence these families?

Discuss the difficulties facing families during military deployments.

What are some of the issues that challenge families during redeployment?

Discuss some of the unique challenges facing families of National Guard members.

Discuss what are some of the helpful responses to military families in these different phases.

Discuss the economic challenges facing some single parents. What are the implications of these challenges for assuming the many parental roles?

Discuss the impact of the transition process (both positive and negative) facing single parents who were once in partnerships relationships.

From the perspective of the children, what are some of the family responses that are protective during the divorce and separation process?

Part II

Approaches to Social Work Practice with Families

INTRODUCTION TO FAMILY THERAPY MODELS

The following chapters discuss some of the important models of family therapy in terms of their theoretical framework, role of the therapist, and treatment techniques along with ways in which they promote family resiliency. As these chapters indicate, family therapy has a complex history with origins in a variety of theoretical orientations, professional traditions, and charismatic personalities. For some theoreticians and practitioners, the transition from thinking in terms of and treating families rather than a focus on individuals was a dramatic one. For others schooled in the social work tradition of family visitors and family casework, this was a natural way of thinking. These diverse theoretical models have contributed important concepts that have become part of the ongoing vocabulary of the field of family therapy. In many cases, the concepts are no longer limited to this particular school of thought. The following is not intended as a detailed history of family treatment but rather as a basic introduction.

Social workers in their role as family visitors early began the work of assessing and working with families to address the many problems facing the family. Furthermore, this picture included the wider social context of the family. This background helped contribute to the role of social workers as important pioneers and leaders in the field of family therapy (Nichols & Schwartz, 2001). Recognition of the role of external factors as well as the family unit also provided the basis for the multisystems family therapy model discussed subsequently.

While families are inherently more than a small group, certain elements of small group theory became part of the family therapy tradition. The themes of process and content described earlier in chapter 3 have been especially important in family therapy.

Role theory and its concepts of the nature of role prescriptions within the family unit helped in understanding the behavior of family members (Nichols & Schwartz, 2001). Roles within families can be complementary (different in ways that fit together) or symmetrical (similar) (Nichols & Schwartz, 2001, p. 38).

Virginia Satir, a social worker and important pioneer in the field of family treatment, identified the problem of family members trapped in constricting roles (for example, victims, placator, defiant one, rescuer) that created problems for family relationships and the person involved (Satir, 1972). She sought to find ways to help family members become free of these constricting roles.

The child guidance movement recognized links between the behavior of children and parents. For the most part, therapists continued to treat children and parents separately until Nathan Ackerman took the then bold step of seeing the entire family as a therapy unit. I remember as a student how shocked the psychiatrists at my internship were when we viewed a video of Nathan Ackerman seeing the family together.

Communication theory, especially influenced by studies of families with a member with schizophrenia, emerged as an important factor in the development of family therapy. Issues related to problematic or functional communication in families continue to play an important role in family therapy and illumine the complex nature of communication within the family system. Bateson developed the concept of "double bind" (a situation in which two contradictory messages are sent from one person to another in such a way that the person does not feel that he or she can contradict them and must act upon them) (Bateson, Jackson, Haley, & Weakland, 1956) Wynne developed the concepts of pseudomutuality by which family members deal with conflict and their fear of separation by creating a surface appearance of closeness that in reality blocks intimacy (Wynne, Rychoff, Day, & Hirsch, 1958). Jackson posited the concept of family homeostasis to describe family resistance to change (Nichols & Schwartz, 2001, pp. 36, 37). Related to this are family rules that help organize the behavior within families and maintain stability. Communication also operates on several levels, for example, words and nonverbal communication (meta-communication) that can either reinforce or contradict each other. As a result, one level of communication can qualify the message of the other level.

Systems theory, especially the concept of living systems, further contributed to the understanding of families. Living systems are open systems which interact with larger systems and are composed in turn of subsystems. What affects one member of the system reverberates throughout the entire system and in turn affects other members and the family unit. Bertalanffy stressed that while there are mechanisms in place for stability (homeostasis), they are also part of ongoing change (morphogenesis). Family systems are also able to reach goals by various means (equifinality) (Nichols & Schwartz, 2001, pp. 114, 115). Systems contain structures that shape the nature of the family, the roles of family members, and the communication system.

Boszormenyi-Nagy and Spark (1973) stressed the role of messages of loyalty that are transmitted and part of family life.

Virginia Satir linked systems theory with communication theory and saw in the family patterns a yearning for self-esteem and intimacy. She emphasized congruent communication and a climate of safety. Her goal for families was to help them find ways to enable members to fulfill these yearnings (Satir, 1972). With her general goal of promoting the positive aspects of the family, Satir was also concerned to find ways to uncover positive possibilities within the family through the communication process (Satir, 1967; Satir, 1972). Videos of Satir show her modeling this positive approach. In contrast to some of the family therapists of the period, she emphasized a collaborative approach with families.

Arising out of his training in psychoanalysis, Bowen's emphasis in systems theory related to differentiation of the self from the other family members. He saw family members reacting in an emotional way rather than using their intellects to create this differentiated self. His basic concerns related to the two life forces of togetherness and individuality (Bowen, 1976; Bowen Center for the Study of the Family, 2012; Kerr & Bowen, 1988) A differentiated self is able to relate to other family members while being comfortable with being one's self. Bowen developed the term *undifferentiated family ego mass* to indicate that the family "was like one chaotic conglomerate" due to emotional reactivity (Nichols & Schwartz, 2001, p. 119). He also developed the concept of the "multigenerational transmission process" to indicate that people are likely to become similar to their parents in terms of levels of differentiation. His concern for this transmission process led him to be concerned about family history and multigenerational patterns. The genogram that became an important tool in family therapy played a key role in this approach. In terms of the family system, Bowen was also concerned about family triangles by which two family members enlist a third member to reduce their anxiety (Bowen Center for the Study of the Family, 2012). Because he was concerned about the role of emotional reactivity, his emphasis was upon an intellectual process and his work was typically either with a single family member or emphasized the family member's conversation with the therapist rather than with other family members.

Subsequent work in family therapy that incorporated issues related to gender and culture began to question absolute criteria in terms of family triangles, signs of family differentiation, communication patterns, and appropriate family roles (Falicov, 1998b). It also stressed the importance of recognizing the interplay between the family and the wider sociocultural context (McGoldrick, 1999).

Object relations, another concept arising from the psychoanalytic tradition, became the basis for object relations therapy. This therapy also stressed the impact of earlier family experiences and the role of anxiety (Scharff & Scharff, 2003).

Minuchin (1974; Minuchin & Fishman, 1981) became concerned about family structure and leadership while helping families of young delinquents whose parents were overwhelmed and unable to provide adequate leadership. Issues related to family structure became the basis of structural family therapy as well as highlighting risk/protective factors for families generally.

A developmental perspective suggested the important role of the family life cycle, which influences the nature of family tasks and the roles of family members. It also poses the challenges of transitions from one stage to another as people must find new ways of coping in response to the demands from the outside world and the family unit (McGoldrick & Carter, 1982).

The focus on family problems and pathology that had permeated earlier work such as with families of schizophrenics began to give way to an appreciation for the strengths of family members. As Satir had earlier emphasized, addressing family strengths, finding ways for family members to tap into their yearning for closeness and caring, and attending to constructive aspects of the family were recognized as key elements in family therapy. The emphasis on family strengths created a strong foundation for brief therapy models and solution-focused therapeutic approaches (DeJong & Berg, 1998; deShazer, 1994). The strengths approach naturally fits well with the resiliency-based orientation of this book.

There was also recognition that families were essential in the care of persons with mental health and other illnesses. Psychoeducational approaches were designed to enhance family coping strategies through education and support. These approaches were designed to help families learn more about the nature of the illness and ways in which the family could help. In addition, families were also educated about the impact of the illness on the family itself and were supported in addressing the needs of the broader family system (Simon, McNeil, Franklin, & Cooperman, 1991; Solomon, 1998).

The behaviorist tradition contributed concern for family patterns that incorporated how family members learn behaviors and are reinforced for their performance of these behaviors. The related social learning tradition enhanced these concepts by examining how belief systems influence the process of learning and behavior (Bandura, 1977). The learning and performance process that includes models, reinforcements, and belief systems (including expectancies and self-regulation) has been an important tool for understanding family behavior and providing family members tools for change (Jordan, Cobb, & Franklin, 1999).

Belief systems have also played a role in more recent theoretical contributions. Constructionists and those concerned about the narrative tradition have emphasized the importance of understanding the meanings that family members create that both sustain problems and pose potential solutions (White & Epston, 1990).

While spirituality and faith issues have long been important for families, recognition of the value of incorporating these issues into the assessment process was a more recent phenomenon (Canda & Furman, 1999, 2009; Van Hook, Hugen, & Aguilar, 2002). This approach is not a treatment model but rather a potential portal into a further understanding families and identifying resources.

The following sections identify some of the key concepts in the intervention models described in the following chapters. They are primarily organized in terms of the basic emphasis, the major tenets, the role of the social worker, and ways in which the model supports resiliency. In highlighting key mechanisms, it is important to recognize that a positive change in one area, for example, improving family coping strategies, can facilitate the blossoming of other protective factors, for example, sense of humor, trust, a sense of coherence. Although cultural beliefs can play a role as risk or protective factors, they are not identified in the following sections because they typically emerge in terms of the family belief systems, the family organizational patterns, the potential support systems, and the community context.

Intervention Models

Social Learning/Cognitive Approaches to Family Counseling

Basic emphasis: Learning new skills, performing behaviors, modifying beliefs

Major tenets:

- Behavior is learned. Individuals learn from their social context how people behave and how others are likely to respond to them.

- Behaviors that individuals demonstrate are the product of their learning context.

- Belief systems influence the learning and the performance of behavior.

- Individuals behave in such a way as to maximize rewards. Consistent and immediate reinforcement is effective in influencing behavior.

- Inconsistent reinforcement is effective in maintaining behavior.

- Educating clients about the process of learning and performance and the role of belief systems is valuable.

Role of the social worker: Coaches, educates, encourages, helps modify belief systems.

Promotes resiliency by

- Addressing risk factors related to complex issues related to belief systems, family coping strategies, and family interaction patterns.
- Supporting protective factors by addressing belief systems, role models, and organizational patterns.

Belief systems: replacing negative belief systems with sense of self-efficacy and mastery, belief systems that promote use of appropriate coping strategies (including recognition of complex patterns, a developmental perspective, and what is possible), promoting sense of hope and courage, addressing negative beliefs from past life events, and allowing people to access potential sources of social support.

Role models: providing effective role models for families

Organizational patterns: helping family members develop effective problem-solving and coping strategies that improve the family organization, communication, positive interactions, and making room for affection and sense of humor

Psychoeducational Approaches to Family Counseling

Basic emphasis: Enable family members to cope more effectively with illness and other problems facing family members.

Major tenets:

- Families are the major support system for members with mental health and other types of illnesses.
- Family members are partners with the professionals.
- Families need the appropriate tools (information about the illness and the skills to deal with it).
- Family members need support in dealing with such a difficult life event in the family.
- In terms of mental illness, family members are not responsible for causing the illness. Tensions within the family can exacerbate symptoms but the family does not cause the illness. Some of the disruption in the family is in response to the distress created by caring for an ill family member.

- Family context and interpersonal relationships have an impact on the illness as well as being influenced by the illness.
- Family members can help identify potential signs of response and thus be helpful in preventing serious relapse.
- Culture helps define how illness is experienced and the nature of the response of family members.

Role of the counselor: Educates and provides support for family dealing with difficult situation.

Promotes resiliency by

- Addressing risk factors associated with lack of coping strategies to address illness-related stressors, stressors within the family, lack of support systems.
- Supporting protective factors by providing families with the information and support needed to develop self-efficacy in addressing a difficult situation, identifying what is possible, improving family leadership, developing effective problem-solving and coping strategies, and connecting with appropriate social supports. These supports promote family affection and family interaction.

Structural Family Therapy

Basic emphasis: Creating a more effective family organization.

Major tenets:

- Families are organizations with structural patterns that are important to the lives of the family members.
- Symptoms within families are signs of a family under stress. Assessment and treatment are organized to address the organizational pattern of the family.
- Structural dimensions include boundaries, alignment, and power. The interaction pattern demonstrated by the family in the family session is a critical source of information.
- Change occurs through active involvement of family members in alternative behaviors.
- The family session is used to enact new behaviors and family change.

Role of the therapist: Activist, stage manager—arranges for families to act out current and potential new scripts to create more effective family structures.

Promotes resiliency by

- Addressing risk factors associated with lack of effective leadership, family organizational patterns, and family belief systems that view problematic interaction patterns as inevitable.

- Supporting protective factors by improving family leadership, promoting appropriate levels of cohesion and boundaries, improving family coping strategies and positive interaction, and changing belief systems about the situation into those that contribute to self-efficacy.

Solution-Focused Family Therapy

Basic emphasis: Developing new solutions to problems or activating current possibilities.

Major tenets:

- The emphasis is on the future.

- Solutions are unrelated to how problems began, history does not provide the key.

- People tend to be locked into negative and pessimistic views of problem and themselves.

- People want to change. People are suggestible.

- People can come up with solutions for their family.

Role of the counselor: Using a not-knowing stance helps family members identify and implement solutions (family is the expert on the problem and the solutions).

Promotes resiliency by

- Addressing risk factors associated with belief systems that are negative and pessimistic about possibilities for the family and ability to meet family needs, and lack of effective coping strategies.

- Supporting protective factors by changing negative and pessimistic belief systems to those that give hope and enable family members to improve positive interactions, helping family members identify what is possible and to build on it, promoting family affection and appropriate coping strategies, improving family communication, and enlisting potential sources of social support as identified by the family.

Narrative Family Therapy

Basic emphasis: Transform problem-saturated stories into stories of hope and possibility—"victim to survivor."

Major tenets:

- Language shapes life experience.
- People construct stories that shape life events and how we experience life.
- Stories shape what we see and remember. Social context influences life stories.
- The emphasis in treatment is on the stories people create.
- It is important to expand life stories—new possibilities for growth and healing.
- Families contend with problems—families are not the problem.

Role of the therapist: Coedits the family story with the family to help replace their problem-saturated stories with those that offer possibilities for healing and growth.

Promotes family resiliency by

- Addressing risk factors of belief systems that are negative and demoralizing and thus maintain negative family patterns.
- Supporting protective factors by changing negative family belief systems to belief systems that provide hope and self-efficacy and sense of coherence. In doing so, it also helps improve positive interactions within the family.

Multisystems Approach to Family Therapy

Basic emphasis: Enable families to deal with multiple problems by linking with wider support systems and helping families cope more effectively.

Major tenets:

- Families live in complex multisystem environments that need to be incorporated into the assessment and treatment process.
- Family counselors need to use a variety of intervention skills to address families' multiple needs.
- Families need to be treated with respect and given decision-making power; they tend to be distrusting of counselor based on prior experience.
- This model focuses on the strengths of these already overwhelmed families.

Role of the family counselor: Assumes many roles in a flexible manner to create linkages with the external support system and enable family members to cope more effectively.

Promotes resiliency by

- Addressing multiple risk factors associated with lack of effective leadership and family coping, demoralization, lack of self-efficacy, ineffective communications, conflict, lack of social support, poverty and lack of community resources, and possible reactivation of past negative experiences.

- Supporting protective factors by helping family members develop effective coping strategies and problem-solving abilities, improving family organization, modeling effective leadership, providing role models of strength, and accessing social support and adequate resources. These steps can lead to increased sense of self-efficacy and affection within the family.

Bowenian Family Systems Therapy

Basic emphasis: Help family members differentiate from family of origin and develop appropriate relationships with current family members.

Basic tenets:

- Triangles are formed in families to cope with anxiety.
- The ideal state is one of differentiation—the ability to function autonomously, to balance thinking and feeling, to be intimate with others without sacrificing one's own individuality.
- Cutoffs and fusion are two ways in which failure to differentiate manifests itself.
- Parents can project their own struggles in an unconscious manner onto one of their children through parental projection.
- The process of differentiation is transmitted from generation to generation.
- Birth order plays an important role in families.

Role of the counselor: Coach to help people understand their family system and change their ability to relate to family members in a differentiated manner.

Goal of therapy: The primary goal is to help family members differentiate so that their behavior in the family is not based on emotional reactivity regarding current and family of origin issues.

Genograms play an important role in identifying intergenerational family patterns.

Promotes resiliency by

- Addressing risk factors associated with rigid family organizational patterns (cutoffs and fusion) and evidence of reactivation of past events.

- Strengthening protective factors by enabling family members to create positive interactions based on differentiation and possibilities within the current family reality that in turn can create a genuine sense of affection within the family.

Object Relations Family Therapy

Basic emphasis: Address interpersonal relationships issues with roots in earlier life experiences.

Major tenets:

- Family members bring to their current family the object relations system that was developed during their earlier life experiences.

- Individuals project their conscious and unconscious internal object relationships upon the spouse or other family member who in turn can fit and identify with this projection.

- Problems in the family occur when family members are unable to separate from these projections and members of the family are unable to grow as individuals.

- The task of the family therapist is to enable the family members to cope with their anxiety and begin to recognize and respond to people in a more open and healthy manner.

- Transference and countertransference are important tools in the therapeutic process.

Role of the family counselor: Enables family members to cope with anxiety through positive relationship and understanding regarding links between past and current relationships.

Promotes resiliency by

- Addressing risk factors associated with reactivation of unresolved past interpersonal relationships.

- Strengthening protective factors by helping family members resolve past interpersonal relationships and thus potentially creating positive and trusting family relationships based on realistic appraisals of the current relationships.

Spirituality

Basic emphasis: Addresses sense of meaning, values, and relationship with transcendence that can be part of many aspects of life.

Major tenets:

- Not a specific model of treatment but can be incorporated into various treatment models.
- Demonstrates respect for the dignity and value of family.
- Healing can occur at many levels even if events cannot be changed
- Issues of meaning and purpose can play important roles in life.
- Client is the expert in their spiritual journey, not the counselor.
- Counselor needs self-awareness.

Role of the counselor: Opens doors to possible spiritual dimensions. Acts as a partner, not an expert on the client's spiritual journey.

Promotes resiliency by

- Addressing factors associated with demoralization, negative aspects of spirituality, lack of social support, and fatalistic views.
- Strengthening protective factors by promoting a sense of coherence, hope, transcendent beliefs that promote a sense of meaning, and social support within a spiritual community.

5

Social Learning/ Cognitive Family Counseling

James Grant had to assume the roles of mother and father for three children (aged seven, eleven, and thirteen) when his wife died in a car accident. Prior to her death his responsibilities had been primarily on weekends because he worked long hours and his wife had the major responsibility for raising the children. The family was not only dealing with the grief of the loss of a wife and mother, but Mr. Grant was floundering in his role as a parent. He vacillated from feeling sorry for the children and thus imposing no limits on them and becoming overly strict when he felt that the situation was getting out of control. The children were further confused by his inconsistency and dealt with this by testing limits further. Discouraged in his role as a parent, he found excuses not to spend time with the children and volunteered to take on extra responsibilities at work. This was a world in which he felt competent. The children responded to his increasing unavailability by testing him further and seeking attention by negative behaviors. When the thirteen-year-old began to have behavior difficulties at school, the school social worker identified the presence of family problems and referred the family for further counseling. Mr. Grant was both defensive at the implications of failure on his part and relieved that some help might be at hand.

Sarah became a mother at age fifteen. Her boyfriend ended their relationship when he learned she was pregnant. Although there had been conflict with her parents, she continued to live with them while going to school and taking care of her child. She is now caught between the two worlds of an adolescent mother—trying to establish her separate identity from her parents and trying to learn how to be a parent herself. When her parents try to give her advice or other types of help, she interprets their actions as indicating they think she is still a child and resents their help. As a result, she finds it difficult to accept the help they offer. Her peer group of high school friends is no help in her new role as a parent and do not understand the pressures that she experiences. Sarah has become very discouraged about her ability to take care of her baby and feels overwhelmed by her responsibilities. She confided in the school social worker that while she loves her baby, she wonders if she had made the right decision to keep her baby and fears that she might hurt her child sometime when she becomes frustrated.

Jennifer and Martin have been married for six years. They met while both were attending McGill University and remained in the metro Montreal area where both were able to have work in their respective fields—Jennifer as a teacher and Martin as an engineer. They felt that their marriage was dissolving in ongoing tension. While they loved each other, they found themselves hurting each other as they tried to talk about the issues in their marriage. Both of them had grown up in conflictual family situations. Each of their parents had argued bitterly for years before finally getting divorced. Jennifer and Martin had both chosen McGill not only for its excellent academic reputation but also as a way to get away from their parents who lived in other communities. While Jennifer and Martin desperately wanted something different for themselves, they found themselves repeating the patterns of the parents. Jennifer would withdraw from Martin who in turn would shout at her. The more she withdrew, the more threatened Martin would become and the louder he would shout. Jennifer would then think that Martin did not love her and would withdraw further. Martin in turn interpreted her withdrawal as lack of interest in him and felt further threatened. When they finally sought counseling help for their marriage, they were extremely discouraged about their ability to save their relationship. They feared that they were about to repeat the pattern of their parents and doubted both themselves and their partner's ability to change.

Members of these families are struggling with troubling relationships and difficulties in carrying out their family responsibilities. While motivated to make things different, they find themselves repeating problematic patterns and unable to create effective new patterns. The vicious circle becomes more intense as they become discouraged about their ability to make things better and their efforts fail to make positive changes. In terms of the context of resiliency, these families lack critical coping skills to deal with the situation at hand and interpret their family situations in ways that intensify the problems. Although the family members are motivated to improve their relationships, lack of these skills has intensified the nature of the problems that they are facing and has destroyed their sense of mastery and self-efficacy. Skills and belief systems go hand in hand. Family members are also burdened by beliefs that are creating problems within the family. Family members lack a sense of self-efficacy regarding their ability to carry out important tasks and roles within their families and have become discouraged about their ability to do so. They also interpret the behavioral responses of others in ways that create further fears and difficulty. These belief systems represent a further burden in the relationship and make it difficult for them to use some of the skills that they currently have. In terms of protective factors, these families have adequate housing and the economic resources to meet their other essential basic needs. They are also motivated to improve their situations. Using a resiliency assessment of these families, a social learning/cognitive approach could be a valuable approach to helping them gain new skills and address their belief systems. It can help them develop a critical sense of mastery and self-efficacy and begin to replace their current dysfunctional belief systems with those that can be more productive within the family.

The social learning approach is essentially an optimistic and strengths-based approach that assumes people are able to learn. The current patterns that one sees in families can be understood in terms of the family members' past and present learning opportunities. The central approach within a social learning perspective is to provide effective learning opportunities that enable family members to learn and implement new coping skills. Family members might need to learn new skills, for example, in communicating, in parenting, in dealing with other community members, in addressing employment issues. While social learning approaches have some patterns that are general to the approach, the nature of the appropriate coping skills and reinforcement systems is tailored to the individual family that fit with their culture, the developmental stages of family members, and the many unique characteristics of the family. As a result, the approach can be adapted to people from a wide range of cultural backgrounds and contexts.

Belief systems can constrain people from learning new skills and using the skills they possess. Parents who believe that their children will not pay attention to them are not likely to try to exert their repertoire of discipline skills. Parents who believe that good parents must always have harmonious relationships with their children or fear the loss of their child's love can find it difficult to set appropriate limits. Children quickly learn the art of emotional blackmail of their parents. Partners who believe that if their partner loves them he or she should understand what they are feeling without being told might not use their existing communication skills and instead feel hurt and rejected when they are not understood by their partner.

The preceding families demonstrate this interaction of skills and belief systems. James Grant needs to learn more effective parenting skills now that he is a single parent and cannot rely on his wife to assume the major role of raising their children. He also feels so sorry for his grieving children that he is uncomfortable setting limits on his children. He feels defeated in his ability to effectively parent his children as the children push him to become more engaged through negative behavior. He misinterprets their actions and withdraws further. Sarah needs to learn the skills of parenting a young child as well as balancing her responsibilities as parent and student. She interprets her parents' offers of help in this realistically difficult situation as a message that they view her as still a child. As a result, she rebuffs what might be valuable help and feels even more alone in her situation. Jennifer and Martin have brought to their relationship a set of skills that are not helpful in meeting their relationship goals and need to learn the skills of communicating and facilitating a mutual relationship. Each interprets the actions of the partner as lack of love and responds in ways that only compound the misunderstandings and hurt.

Promotes Resiliency by

- Addressing risk factors related to belief systems, family coping strategies, and family interaction patterns.
- Supporting protective factors by addressing belief systems and organizational patterns, and offering role models.

Belief systems: replacing negative belief systems with a sense of self-efficacy, and mastery, belief systems that promote use of appropriate coping strategies (including recognition of complex patterns, a developmental perspective, and what is possible), promoting sense of hope and courage, addressing negative beliefs from past life events, and allowing people to access potential sources of social support.

Role models: providing role models for families.

Organizational patterns: helping family members develop effective problem-solving and coping strategies that improve the family organization, communication, positive interactions, and making room for affection and sense of humor.

Theoretical Background

Social learning approaches developed from behavioral traditions that emphasized the role of contingencies in maintaining behavior. From the perspective of operant conditioning, voluntary behavior is shaped by the consequences of this behavior. Change is organized in terms of changing the nature of responses to behavior. Reinforcement increases behavior; punishment or extinction (not responding) tends to decrease behavior (Skinner, 1953). In terms of family counseling, the social worker conducts a functional analysis of the behavior to identify the immediate antecedents (what occurs prior to) and the consequences (what occurs as a result of) the problem behavior. Parents might be asked to identify what was taking place when their child started sulking and what consequences followed this behavior. The consequences frequently become reinforcers that serve to maintain the behavior. In this process, parents could identify that they were perhaps inconsistent or in some way gave in to the child in ways that only perpetuated the behavior. They might be going to great lengths to find something that would make the child happy again and stop sulking and thus be inadvertently encouraging (positive reinforcement) the very behavior that they were trying to eliminate. Parents often engage in intermittent reinforcement—sometimes giving in and other times remaining firm. Behavior that has been reinforced in this manner is the most difficult to change. Using the results of this behavioral analysis, parents might be encouraged to alter their reinforcement system to reduce the nature of the difficult behavior. This model of working with families has been an important element in parental education programs as well as work with individual families.

Using the operant conditioning model, the behavioral assessment identifies a set of responses that influence the frequency of behavior. As indicated above from the Skinnerian model, positive reinforcements are responses that encourage behavior to occur more frequently. Negative reinforcements also increase behavior when a specific behavior results in the termination of something aversive. These two types of responses are frequently paired. The common situation of parents and children at the checkout counter represents this duet. When parents finally give in to the child's whining and buy candy, they are positively reinforcing the child's whining behavior. The child in turn negatively reinforces the parents by stopping the whining when the parents hand over the candy. Both parties are reinforcing the other for their part in the duet. Responses that decrease behavior are called punishment. Behavior is influenced most quickly if the response occurs shortly after the behavior and is consistent. It is most difficult to change behavior if the reinforcement system is intermittent. People continue to put coins in to the slot machine in hopes that the next coin will produce a larger payoff. Extinction occurs when there is no reinforcement for the behavior. Since the individual involved frequently escalates the intensity of the behavior at first in hopes of gaining the desired goal, extinction does not result in an immediate decrease in behavior. If parents finally give in to these louder demands, they inadvertently set in motion an intermittent reinforcement system.

The nature of these reinforcements is also idiosyncratic to the individuals and context involved. Over the years my children and I have frequently had very different sets of reinforcements in terms of music. While music by Bach might be a positive reinforcement for one person, Bob Dylan's music might work for another.

Stuart transferred this nature of behavioral reciprocity to work with couples using contingency contracting (Nichols & Schwartz, 2001; Stuart, 1969). Recognizing that couples with problems were caught up in a negative cycle leading to distrust and negative behaviors, Stuart focused on developing and enhancing positive behaviors by applying a reciprocity reinforcement paradigm (Stuart, 1969). Within this arrangement, couples would identify a positive behavior that they would like to occur, record the frequency of the behavior, and identify and exchange positive responses. For example, the husband might want his wife to call if she is going to come home later from work and the wife might want her husband to let her know when he has been delayed at the exercise center. Beginning with small steps identified by the partners helps make the arrangement successful and thus promotes trust.

Social Learning Paradigms

Bandura and colleagues moved beyond a system of reinforcers to identify how current behavior is not only shaped by the actual reinforcers but also by social context and cognitions, especially the person's expectations for such responses (Bandura, 1977, 1978). They also describe how complex behaviors are learned through the process of modeling. Individuals learn new behavior from others who demonstrate (model) this behavior. Models are especially likely to be emulated if these models are perceived as successful and their behavior is followed by positive consequences. Models viewed as similar are especially effective (Bandura, 1977). Younger siblings mimicking older brothers and sisters is an example of this pattern.

As a result of this broadened perspective, social learning focuses on the triad of learning opportunities, the reinforcement systems at work, and the thoughts of individuals that influence the nature of the behavior that is learned and the actual practice of adaptive or maladaptive behavior patterns. Cultural and unique individual life experiences shape relevant beliefs, learning opportunities, and anticipated rewards. Expectations regarding the impact of behavior are critical in the actual performance of behavior. If people believe that they are able to carry out a specific behavior (self-efficacy) and will be positively rewarded for this behavior, they are more likely to act in this manner. As described in the above situations, the thoughts and consequent interpretations of the family members in the previously described family situations play critical roles in the behaviors of family members. Mr. Grant does not feel confident in his parenting and withdraws from his children. His beliefs about the impact of the death of his wife and their mother further make it difficult for him to discipline the children. Sarah's interpretation of her parents' actions in the context of her own developmental journey causes her to rebuff her parents' often well-meant and potentially helpful advice. Jennifer and Martin's relationship is caught in a vicious circle of withdrawal and pressure that leads both of them to become discouraged about their relationship and thus to further withdrawal and pressure.

The family context provides a critical learning environment. Children learn the myriad behaviors that are necessary for their life as children as well as for adult responsibilities. They emulate their parents and their siblings as well as relevant extended family members. They watch how parents deal with older siblings and thus they learn how to deal with conflict and to communicate their wishes in effective ways. They learn patterns of violence or verbal negotiation. They learn to expect certain responses from others for their behaviors. They learn what is valued in their family context. As children become older, their models become part of their wider context of peers, neighborhood, school, and the media. As a result, family members who come for help represent a wide array of learning opportunities in their current and past relationships and belief systems that are relevant to their situation.

As people begin to believe that they can carry out various tasks effectively, they develop a sense of self-efficacy in this area. Parents who experience success in helping a child learn a new skill develop a sense of self-efficacy in the area of teaching their children. Parents who do not experience children as being responsive to their efforts to enforce limits begin to doubt their self-efficacy as parents in this area. Individuals thus both influence their environment and are in turn influenced by it—reciprocal determinism.

Cognitive Therapy Paradigm

Cognitive therapists have traditionally looked at the patterns of belief systems of family members as well as specific responses to individual situations. As described in the work of Hill in chapter 1, McCubbin and McCubbin (1996), and Beck (1976), these underlying belief systems (variously called paradigms, schemas, core beliefs) influence how family members view the world, themselves, and the family and thus shape the families' thoughts and behaviors in individual situations. These beliefs are shaped by the family origin as well as ongoing events within the life of the family. Cultural patterns profoundly influence these schemas. These schemas in turn influence the types of help that are valued or viewed as demeaning. Families with core beliefs that "You cannot trust anyone who is not family" would have great difficulty seeking supports beyond the family circle and would be very guarded if referred for counseling. Beliefs about what is appropriate behavior for men or women influence family options and probably played a role in the current problem facing James Grant where his wife had originally assumed the major parenting role. Life cycle development also shapes beliefs and makes it especially difficult for Sarah to accept help from her parents. Martin and Jennifer not only bring to the family desires for a better future but also fears that it will not materialize along with negative life skills that promote these fears. Helping family members identify these core beliefs, how they are affecting what is occurring currently, and examining their validity in the current situation can enable family members to adopt more effective ways of interpreting the world and behaving accordingly.

Social Learning/Cognitive Theory Major Tenets

From a family perspective, a social learning/cognitive approach has several key tenets that guide the assessment and intervention process. Drawing from operant conditioning models and social learning theory, these tenets address both the process by which behavior is learned and the motivation system that influences which behaviors will be demonstrated in a specific setting. They include both cognitions and behaviors.

1. Behavior is learned. Individuals learn from their social context how people behave and how others are likely to respond to them.

2. The behaviors that people demonstrate are the product of their learning context.

3. Belief systems influence the learning and the performance of behavior.

4. Individuals behave in such a way as to maximize rewards. As a result, they anticipate that the behaviors they demonstrate will accomplish this for them (based on their experience either personally or in terms of the models in their life setting—vicarious reinforcement). As a result, behavior is logical within the context of this learning experience and the current cognitions of the individuals.

5. Consistent and immediate reinforcement is effective in influencing behavior. Inconsistent reinforcement is effective in maintaining behavior.

6. Educating clients about the process of learning and performance and the role of belief systems is valuable.

These tenets shape the social learning/cognitive assessment and treatment approach with families. It is inherently a positive model. If individuals can learn one set of behaviors, they can learn others that are more effective in addressing their current situation. If people act in such a way as to maximize pleasure, then it is important to understand the context and their expectations. It also raises critical questions. If people continue to act in ways that would appear to have a negative impact on their lives, is it because they lack more positive ways to behave? Do they fail to anticipate the negative impact due to earlier learning experiences or are seemingly negative responses in reality positive for the person involved? What role are expectations and other cognitions playing in behavior that might otherwise seem self-defeating or having negative consequences? Children, for example, have been known to prod parents into yelling at them because being yelled at may be better than being ignored. People sometimes continue in abusive relationships because they fear the alternatives.

Goals of Treatment

The goals of the social learning/cognitive model are to enable families to meet the needs of members and to cope more effectively. Based on a paradigm that includes skills and motivation, the model seeks to promote family functioning by helping family members learn appropriate skills, promoting a motivation system that encourages family members to perform behaviors that meet the needs of family members, and addressing the belief systems that foster effective behaviors by family members. While the model includes interventions with negative behaviors and belief systems, the focus is on promoting positive changes. Changing negatives without finding positives and replacing these negatives with positives is not effective in the long run.

Role of the Family Counselor

In the social learning approach the role of the family counselor can be viewed as that of a coach. An effective coach helps individuals learn new behavior through modeling and other forms of instruction, provides opportunities for practice, offers feedback regarding the nature of the performance, and motivates individuals to learn and persist in the process of improving their performance through encouragement or other ways to promote positive cognitions. Since family members frequently do not understand the process by which behavior is learned and performed and the role of their belief systems, the social worker as coach helps educate family members about these important aspects.

Horne and Sayger (2000) stress the critical role played by the counselor's attitudes toward the family members in the therapeutic relationship. It is important that the counselor believes that each member of the family is "doing the best he or she can given the circumstances of that person and given the previous learning experiences that person encountered" (p. 472).

Viewed through the lens of resiliency, the family counselor provides a *model* of the new skills required and helps family members carry out these new skills. The counselor might serve as the model personally or identify other models in the life space of the family members. The counselor arranges for family members to have the *opportunity to practice these skills* in the counseling session and uses these occasions to give *corrective feedback* to ensure success. The counselor helps the family members *identify ways that they can practice* these skills in other settings to facilitate the process of generalization. The counselor *encourages* family members in terms of their ability to learn and the progress that they making. The family counselor helps family members *identify and alter cognitions* in ways that promote the family functioning. In the process the family members develop the critical skills needed to address their family situation and gain an appropriate sense of self-efficacy. The counselor is quick to help identify positive changes and encourage family members to take credit for these changes and thus promote self-efficacy.

For James Grant this means learning ways to parent his three children without vacillating between setting no limits and being overly strict. It means addressing some of his cognitions that prevent him from being an effective parent. It means gaining increased confidence in his ability to parent his children so that he does not have to retreat from parenting to the world of work where he views himself as successful. For Sarah it means learning how to parent her baby while balancing her own needs as a teenager. It also might mean learning ways to communicate more effectively with her parents. In the process Sarah can begin to accept the help her parents could give her and to view this help in rewarding rather than in negative terms. It might also mean working with the parents to help them understand Sarah's perspective and to offer their help in ways that might be more acceptable to her. For Jennifer and Martin it means learning new ways to communicate in their marriage so they do not continue to destroy their love for each other by their learned patterns of retreat and attack. It means beginning to learn to trust each other and their relationship.

Assessment

The assessment process from a social learning/cognitive perspective includes identifying issues in the following areas: skills, motivation system, signaling system, and belief system. Difficulties can arise in any of these areas, and the nature of the intervention differs depending on this assessment.

Skills. Family members or the family unit can lack the essential skills needed to address family issues within their current context and stage of development. These issues might include how to parent a toddler or a teenager, how to manage money, how to communicate with a partner, how to negotiate with extended family members, how to deal with a new culture, and how to adjust to changes in family roles due to illness or other major shifts, as well as various other family issues. Sarah and James Grant both struggle with lack of skills to parent their respective children. Jennifer and Martin's pain arises from their lack of skills in communicating with their partners.

As described previously, family members have typically learned their skills from past experiences; however, they might have had role models that were not appropriate for their current circumstances. What did they learn that could help in raising teenagers in the current world, in coping with circumstances in which the wife is the major wage earner, in dealing with the give-and-take of marriage, in caring for children as a single parent, in communicating between parents? While their previous models might have demonstrated coping skills that were effective within this context, families can be facing a disjuncture between these previous contexts and their current life. This can be especially critical for families that have moved from one culture to another (families in cultural transitions). In the rapidly changing world in which people move from community to community and the wider social context changes, such a disjuncture can be experienced by many families.

Motivation system. There can be a problem in the motivation system for the family or members of the family. Cognitions play an important role here because motivation is related to the perceived reward system within the family and the larger context. In terms of the parent-child relationship world, a child might know what to do but lacks the motivation to do it because the child gets more attention for misbehavior than for listening (a parent's version of punishment might thus be a positive reinforcement for the child). A parent might be reinforced by the child to just let things slide because the fight to get the child to listen is just not worth the effort given the other demands on one's time and energy. Almost every parent has reached this point at one time or another. A parent might be stymied by a child's emotional blackmail: "I hate you; my friend's parents are nice and you are mean." Another parent might give up on setting limits because the child tests extinction by pushing the limits harder. Parents might be setting opposite reinforcements in place—what the mother praises the father devalues and vice versa. Lack of self-efficacy can contribute to a person's difficulty in acting in an effective manner, for example, when a parent makes a hesitant request instead of a firm statement (and then is troubled when ignored by the child).

Cultural context is important in this reinforcement system. Family members who come from cultures in which extended family or relational issues are valued more than individual accomplishments might make choices that seem lacking in responsibility or ambition from the perspective of a more individualistic counselor. Another issue relates to the nature of the reinforcements and supports within the current cultural setting. People in cultural transition situations frequently live with cultural messages of what one should do (for example, care for older family members) but without the supports that enable one to carry these behaviors out in their current cultural context. Couples can experience tension if they come from different cultural contexts and expect behavior to be rewarded accordingly. Parents also must contend with powerful cultural messages from the media and the community that contradict family values. While parents might, for example, value academic achievement, the peer group of a teenager might place its value on athletic prowess.

Signaling system. There can be ambiguity in the current signaling system. People not only need to be able to carry out a certain behavior and be motivated to do so, they also need to be aware when such behavior is appropriate and required. Parents frequently stress this by saying words like

"I mean it now" as a signal that the parent is serious about what he or she is saying. Parents and teenagers often end up in arguments because the parents and the teenager interpret words like "don't be late" in very different ways (parent—11 p.m., teenager 1 a.m.). Children who have done well in structured situations with clear behavior clues often slip back into old ways of acting without the presence of these specific clues. As a result, helping parents develop clearer signals can be an important intervention. James Grant, for example, can be helped to develop some clearer ways of conveying his expectations of his children that can help the current vicious cycle.

Belief system. There can be problems and distortions in the belief system (cognitive part of the system) that in turn impede proper responses. The interaction between beliefs and the behavioral interaction between family members is often a cyclical one. A parent whose self-talk is "It doesn't do any good to tell the children what to do because they won't do it anyway" is not likely to assert one's self in an effective manner with the children. The children's disregard in turn only reinforces this belief system and further discourages the parent from acting in an effective manner. The individual who thinks that it doesn't do any good to tell the partner something because he or she wouldn't listen or care is not likely to communicate these wishes to the partner. Again, this individual is not likely to respond in an effective way and the partner's anticipated lack of response becomes a perceived reality.

Assessment process. The assessment process is a joint one with the social worker and the family members. Family members are encouraged to identify patterns to help them understand what is taking place. Tracking sequences of behavior can give important new insights. Parents, for example, can chart the patterns of what is occurring prior (A = antecedent) to a child's specific behavior (B = behavior) and the nature of the consequences (C = consequences). These categories can include belief systems as well as actions. They might discover that the child's whining occurs when the child is hungry or tired, or perhaps when the parents are busy with another child or other family responsibilities. They might learn ways in which they have been inadvertently reinforcing the behavior by redirecting their attention from the other children to this child in response to the whining and ignoring the child when he or she is behaving appropriately.

Family members can recognize that their beliefs are triggering issues or maintaining certain behaviors. Family members can be encouraged to identify their belief systems that are triggered or are antecedent to behaviors as part of the process of beginning to institute change. In counseling families, it is common for family members to be surprised at the thoughts evoked in each of the family members and how these belief systems are pushing them farther apart. Understanding these behavioral and cognitive patterns gives clues to the solution.

Family members need to be involved in the development of these tracking systems with an emphasis on trying to make them as simple as possible. If they are too complex and difficult for the family to carry it out, family members can become discouraged by the process and be viewed by their family counselor as resistant to change.

Including the family members as partners in the assessment process serves several purposes. First, they are in a unique position to identify what is taking place within the family context. Second, they are learning an important skill of identifying family patterns that can stand them in good stead in addressing future problems. Third, the experience of identifying patterns helps them in developing a sense of mastery that encourages family members in the process of change. Family members are helped to gain a sense of ownership over the nature of the problem and possible solutions.

Treatment Process

The following represent important steps and principles in the intervention process.

Build intervention efforts on the identified nature of the problem. If the social worker addresses motivation, for example, but family members lack the necessary skills, the result will only be frustration for all concerned because motivation without skills will not result in success.

> James Grant, for example, is struggling with lack of parenting skills because this is a new responsibility for him. He is also struggling with self-talk that makes it difficult for him to set limits on his children. As a result, this helps identify two areas for intervention. He has a strong motivation to be a good parent.

Identify positive changes. Families typically come for help because they want to change something wrong with their family or its members or because some outside party wants them to make these changes. As a result, the emphasis is upon something negative to eliminate. Families can easily spend the entire session complaining about what the other family members are doing wrong. One of the first steps in the counseling process is to help family members begin to think in terms of what are the positive changes that they want. Goals and the steps to reach them must be positive and clear in their direction. This step can be difficult for some families at first because they have become locked into their negative patterns and have not been able to envision other approaches.

Positive changes can give a meaningful direction to the efforts of family members. Parents, for example, can shift from "He has to get rid of that attitude" to "I want him to show a sense of responsibility by helping with the dishes without complaining." Sarah can identify ways that her parents can help her without making her feel that they are putting her down. Jennifer and Martin can identify something positive that they would like from the other one. As family members are helped to identify some positive actions, the counselor can help assess what further skills are needed to accomplish these changes and what reinforcement systems the family might put in place to encourage these positive steps.

> James Grant has to be helped to identify some specific positive behaviors that he is seeking from his children in clear terms. He can also identify some positive responses that he can demonstrate that show that he is being successful in not retreating from the parenting role. He can then reward himself for these steps (perhaps with just a "Good job, James").

Strategize for success. Family members usually come for counseling feeling defeated in their efforts for change. As a result, it is important for the counselor to help the family members identify changes that are realistic and can really be carried out. The counselor can problem-solve with family members about what small behavior would be realistic as a beginning step, ways to identify if it has taken place, and how to reinforce this positive change. By breaking down changes into understandable and manageable steps, the family is more likely to experience success and to gain important self-efficacy. Such an experience of success helps motivate the family members to persist and believe in the possibility of change.

Success is more likely if the identified behavioral steps are specific. "Doing better in school" is open to a multitude of interpretations by parents and their children with the potential for misunderstandings and consequent mistrust. "Raising the grade from a D to a C on the next science test" or "helping by loading the dishwasher after the evening meal" are specific and clearly understood by everyone. In the partnership context, "Showing that you care" is another ambiguous request. Helping partners identify what actions might reflect this leads to specifics such as "Ask me how it went at work/or with the kids today when you come home," "Read the children a bedtime story so I can get a break," "Sit with me to watch X TV show in the evening," which are understandable to the individuals involved. To be effective, steps must be realistic for the parties involved and the counselor can discuss this issue in the session with family members.

> James can identify some small steps that would be realistic for him in terms of his children and his actions with them. Breaking the goals into small manageable steps will help him avoid becoming overwhelmed and discouraged.

Educate the family about the learning process. A knowledgeable partner is a more effective one. Helping family members learn about ways in which behavior is learned and reinforced can give family members the tools to understand their family and to make additional positive changes in other areas and in the future. If parents understand that the first response of children to the process of extinction is to raise the volume of their whining, they will be able to interpret such behavior as a beginning sign of progress rather than the failure of their efforts. This knowledge can help parents persist rather than give in and create an even more entrenched pattern by their intermittent reinforcement.

James can be assisted in understanding how his children have learned to respond to his behavior as a natural part of the learning process of children.

Help family members develop needed new skills. Family members might lack the skills to carry out this positive change and will need help in learning and carrying out these new behaviors. The family counselor can use the family session to model the new behaviors and to enable family members to practice them. Jennifer and Martin, for example, have few skills in communicating with each other about troubling issues without their pattern of withdrawal and shouting. The counselor can model beginning steps of stating their views. The counselor then encourages the couple to practice these skills in the session in areas that are manageable for the couple. These practice sessions permit the counselor to give feedback about ways to improve their skills. Without this critical step, Jennifer and Martin are likely to go home and repeat the old troubling patterns and dig the hole of distrust and lack of self-efficacy deeper.

James can learn new parenting skills that have been part of his coping repertoire. In addition to counseling, he might be able to benefit from a parenting class.

Build in ways to generalize use of new skills and response patterns. Homework is a key element in helping people begin to generalize changes from the office setting to the daily life of the family. The social worker can problem-solve with the family members ways to practice these new skills in their daily life. James can be helped to begin to make changes in his behavior with his children or he and the children can identify steps that each of them will begin making. Sarah can be helped to identify a way she can handle a troubling situation with her baby more effectively. Jennifer and Martin can practice a specific new way of discussing an issue in their marriage.

Recognize that learning is a process. People have learned and practiced their current behaviors for many years so that these behavior patterns are well entrenched. Use of these old behavioral patterns is automatic, especially when people are under stress. It also takes time to generalize new behaviors from one setting to another. Family members can become discouraged by their responses or angry with other family members who slip back into old ways of behaving. The social worker can encourage family members to realize that learning and change is a process and thus that relapse into old ways is a normal part of change. They can also be encouraged to see signs of progress—the blowups occurred only three times instead of five times last week or the time of conflict lasted for only half an hour rather than an hour.

Sessions can be used to problem-solve with family members the nature of some of the challenges in responding in new ways. These challenges might be in several areas: an individual might still lack some of the skills needed. Motivation might be a factor, perhaps lack of confidence that the new behavior will really work, or worry how the other family members will respond (Will the children really listen if I do not threaten to hit them? Will my partner really listen?). Lack of clarity in the signaling system leads to confusion about what behavior is expected. It also takes time to generalize behavior from one setting to another—from the counseling office to the home, and from one aspect of life to another. Jennifer and Martin might find it difficult to transfer their new communication skills to another topic of concern for them. Based on this assessment, the counselor can both encourage family members that learning and change take time and identify some of the specific issues facing this family that can be addressed in the counseling setting.

James Grant might find it difficult to transfer his changes in response to the thirteen-year-old to the seven-year-old due to the differences in developmental needs. The counselor can help him problem-solve this issue to develop some new parenting approaches.

Help families reinforce positive behavior meaningfully for individuals involved. Family members need to find ways to encourage behavior that is identified as positive in order to help individuals maintain this behavior. If people do not believe (expectancies) that their positive changes will be favorably recognized (positive reinforcement), they will be less likely to continue these behaviors and to make them part of the life of the family. Frequently, troubled families have developed a pattern of negative comments about problematic behavior while positive behavior is ignored. Sometimes family members have grown up in families in which words of praise or other forms of positive recognition were uncommon (only criticism is spoken). There are thus several aspects to altering the reinforcement system depending on the specific family situation. If family members lack role models who have given affirmation, the counselor can serve as a role model for such behavior as well as educate family members about the valuable role of these responses. The counselor can problem-solve with family members about the reinforcements that would be meaningful and feasible within this family context and the ways to implement them in the life of the family. This new skill can be practiced within the session as well as in homework opportunities.

James Grant can be helped to identify what would be positive reinforcers for each of his children. As indicated, what would be desirable for one child might not work for the other one. He can also identify what would be rewarding for himself.

Help family members identify and counter destructive cognitions. Our belief systems influence whether we expect (expectancies) that it will be worthwhile to act in a certain way. As discussed previously, sometimes our cognitions prevent positive changes from occurring and trap us into self-defeating patterns. Recognizing and addressing some of these cognitions can help people begin to carry out new behaviors. For example, in terms of the discouraged parent who interprets the child's testing behavior as a sign that the child does not care about the parents, this cognition can be recognized and then reframed within a more benign developmental context: "You might be right that your child does not care what you want, or perhaps your child is like all other children that age, they try to test you because in their hearts they want limits. Being a parent at these times can be difficult." This cognition might reflect a more pervasive schema of not feeling valued by others generally.

Generalizing the intervention to this larger schema may be useful. When partners begin to make changes, one partner can dismiss this change with a comment that "He/she is just doing this because I asked for it." Sadly, neither of the partners experiences positive validation through this interchange. Helping people recognize that "doing something because the other person asked for it can be a sign of caring" might be another way of interpreting this new behavior that furthers the healing process. The family can also help in creating these changes. Sarah's parents might be encouraged to phrase their help in ways that can be less threatening to Sarah. Sharing with her their own uncertainty and fears when they were new parents might reduce her thoughts that she is being criticized. They can also comment favorably on things that she is doing in her care of the baby.

> James can be helped to realize that it is natural to become discouraged when you are trying to parent without the skills and background, especially if you are also facing the difficulties of the grief of the loss of a wife and mother. He can be helped to replace cognitions such as "I am a failure as a parent" by "I am making progress in learning how to parent my children."

Brock and Barnard (1999) describe three keys to success in teaching new behaviors within the context of family counseling. First, the counselor discusses the skill and presents a rationale for learning the skill to the clients. Second, the counselor demonstrates the skill. Third, the clients have the opportunity to practice and receive feedback while performing the skill (p. 84).

The family therapist needs to explain the nature of the skill, its importance, and how it will benefit family members. Encouraging further discussion between the family members and the counselor regarding the rationale is helpful in obtaining commitment to learning this skill. In the second stage of demonstration, the family therapist must ensure that the modeling gives an accurate picture of what is being taught and the context in which it will be used. Asking clients to explain what they saw you doing and discussing what occurred helps clarify any misunderstandings. The next crucial step is to have family members practice the new skill within the session. This can be difficult for family members not only because it is a new skill but also because the topics involved or the situation can be a highly emotionally charged one.

Brock and Barnard (1999) indicate the importance of having clients begin with situations in which the tension and threat are relatively low and gradually move to more emotionally charged ones. Jennifer and Martin can identify a situation that they feel most comfortable addressing.

Encouraging feedback is important. The therapist needs to let clients know that they are doing well. When there are problems in the performance, it is useful to stop and determine if there is need for further clarification of the skill that might require another demonstration or if the topic at hand is too emotionally charged to be appropriate at this time.

Application

Parent-Child Relationships

Parent-child relationships play important roles in supporting resiliency. As discussed in the earlier chapters, unfortunately external stressors on the family as well as the previous learning experiences of family members can jeopardize these relationships. Issues related to parenting play critical roles in terms of risk and resiliency factors regarding child maltreatment and positive child development. Protective factors include parental competencies in parental roles and related satisfaction in the parenting roles, while risk factors involve poor problem-solving skills, harsh, inconsistent discipline, and low nurturing skills (Thomlison, 2004).

Horne and Sayger (2003) describe the situation facing many level II parents as "relying on spanking, lecturing, or grounding to punish children for their behavior. These punishments are typically ineffective, particularly if the parent's authority is not secure or respected" (p. 125). Social learning approaches offer family members opportunities to learn new parenting techniques and strategies to implement them in ways that restore parental authority and respect.

There are several alternative strategies that parents can use to help shape the behavior of their children. These include time-outs, the Premack Principle, natural and logical consequences, assigning extra chores, and loss of privileges.

Time-outs involve sending a child to a non-reinforcing environment for an appropriate length of time to gain self-control. This technique provides a way for both the parent and the child to detach from an escalating situation. The length of the time-out is dependent on the age of the child because too long a length of time-outs for very young children quickly loses their sense of meaning. Parents also need to be aware of the potential reinforcements present in a setting. Sending a child to a room full of toys or computer games may represent a reward rather than a time-out.

The Premack Principle requires children to complete an activity they are less likely to choose before they can do something that they are more likely to choose to do. A child might be required to complete homework or a household chore before playing a video game. Naturally the parent has to ensure that the child has not rushed through homework or the chore at the expense of quality in order to get to the video game.

Natural and logical consequences is a means of teaching children that behavior has consequences through experiencing the results of their behavior. The child who impulsively spends his or her allowance on the first day will need to experience waiting until the next week before getting more money. A child who rushes through a task by doing a poor job will have to spend the extra time redoing it and missing out on some desired activity. A teenager who drives recklessly can be denied permission to drive the family car for a period of time.

Assigning extra chores involves giving additional tasks for older children who have violated important rules.

Loss of privileges involves taking away privileges that are important for a child (response cost) when the child has violated a family rule. These might involve use of the telephone, the car, or a weekend at a friend's house. As with all parenting techniques, it is important to respond in ways that match the loss of privileges to the severity of the behavior and the developmental stage of the child. If parents impose too severe a punishment, they might later feel the need to recall the punishment (thus undermining their future effectiveness) or generate serious resentment on the part of the child.

Use of contingency contracts is a useful technique for use between parents and older children. "A contract is negotiated wherein each participant specifies who is to do what for whom, under what circumstances, times, and places." The terms of the contract must be clear and precise. For example, the contract specifies that if the adolescent earns "a C or better on her weekly quiz," the parents in turn "will give $10.00 toward the purchase of her clothes for that week." As discussed, both sets of statements must be realistic for the parties involved. The contract opens the door to the opportunity for success in this specific interaction and helps build new ways of relating between the parties involved. Each of the parties reinforces the other to carry out their part in the contract. Hopefully the good results of this process generalize to other aspects of the family and thus help the family problem-solve and resolve conflicts generally.

Working with families requires more than educating parents about the nature and possibility of these alternative parenting strategies. Several important interventions can also be necessary. Addressing the belief systems of parents can be crucial. Parents who have grown up with physical punishment as the norm and have relied upon it as their primary means of discipline might be reluctant to try what they view as softer techniques. They might fear losing control of their children, perhaps based on a core belief they will lose control of their children and their children will get into serious trouble if they do not impose such punishments. The social worker may need to address their reservations by explaining the value of these new strategies.

It also means helping parents in the actual implementation of these new strategies. Since these are new techniques for parents, it will also be important to discuss ways to implement them given the developmental age of the child and the nature of the infringement. Ineffective implementations of these alternative strategies can reduce their effectiveness and fail to create the important parental authority and respect. A fifteen-minute time-out for a two-year-old can seem like an eternity and quickly loses its meaning. Upset parents can fall into the trap of creating overly harsh responses, for example, a loss of privileges for a month. After the parents have cooled off, they might rethink their actions. They are then caught between being inconsistent and unrealistic. Parents can frantically try a series of responses ("We have tried everything") without being consistent in their application. As a result, helping parents create realistic arrangements and ways to implement them consistently are important parts of the skill development with parents. Parents can also be helped to understand that the emphasis needs to be on positively reinforcing what the child is doing right rather than merely deterring negative behavior.

Parents who might fear losing the love of their children or at least alienating them might be reluctant to set limits that cause the child to become angry and make hurtful comments. Children quickly learn the power of words like "I hate you, you're not my friend" as well as the silent treatment. Parents need encouragement and positive recognition from the counselor for their own efforts to implement alternative parenting techniques. The family counselor needs to recognize small steps toward this goal.

It is also important to look at the support systems available to parents and other family members as they seek to implement new ways of behaving. James Grant, for example, might find a grief support group of other single parents who are facing some of the same issues that he is. Parents who find themselves being blackmailed by their children might be able to benefit from a parent support group to receive support from other parents and to realize that other parents are also facing this challenge.

Communication Skills

Communication skills are important in supporting family resiliency to help improve problem solving and create emotionally affirming relationships within the family. Many of the families who seek help have experienced a breakdown in communication between family members. Family members often report that they are not listened to or are misunderstood. The situation escalates and erodes the sense of trust within the family. As Jennifer and Martin illustrate, frequently family members misinterpret what is said or not said in ways that increases hurt. As a result, helping family members identify and develop valuable communication skills can be an important step in restoring family relationships and promoting resiliency. Again, this process requires assessing the current skill levels of family members as well as their expectations. If family members do not believe that other family members want to hear from them, they are unlikely to invest themselves in these efforts, and addressing these belief systems is important.

The counseling session is an important venue for teaching family members about communication strategies, identifying problems in the communication sequence, and giving useful feedback. By asking family members to carry out these activities in the session, the counselor can identify verbal and nonverbal messages and problems that impede the communication process. For example, while a family member might ask in the session why his partner does not believe that he is listening, observing him turning his eyes up to the ceiling while she talks gives an important clue to her reaction. The counselor might also discover that a parent states an expectation of children in such a tentative and hesitant way that it is very clear why the children do not follow these instructions and the parent feels devalued. As described earlier, such behavior reflects skills as well as belief systems.

Horne and Sayger (2003) describe the following steps in the communication process.

1. Speak your piece. Individuals must express their own thoughts rather than expecting others to understand their thoughts.

2. Find out what others are thinking. Family members are encouraged to ask others what they are thinking rather than making assumptions. Frequently in counseling situations, partners are surprised to learn what the other person was really thinking because it was far different from what they had assumed.

3. Show others that they are being heard. Demonstrate through words, eye contact, or other culturally appropriate behaviors that one is listening and hearing what is being said.

4. Ask questions when confused. Ask for clarification when family members are uncertain rather than making assumptions.

5. Stop and let others know when communication is breaking down. When the discussion begins to escalate with the danger of hurt statements, it is important to ask to stop the interaction and wait for a calmer moment. (pp. 125–126)

The social worker can model these behaviors and then problem-solve with the parties involved ways to implement them regarding a specific topic. Family members can be praised for changes that they are making (listening to the end of the sentence) as well as helped to identify behaviors that continue to disrupt communication (for example, not letting people complete their sentences before jumping in). The social worker and the family members can also problem-solve ways to implement these changes within the home context and possible challenges in doing so. Using the principle of strategizing for success and beginning with small realistic steps, they can identify issues that are realistic to communicate about using these new techniques and other issues that might be too explosive to tackle without the presence of the counselor at this point in time.

Anger control can play an important role in family communication, especially if angry comments have escalated and created major conflicts. Jordan, Cobb, and Franklin (1999) describe a sequence of steps to help families learn to reduce these negative interactions. The first step in this process is to educate family members about the nature of anger and ways in which anger can escalate through the family system through the interaction among the family members. The next step is to engage family members in agreeing upon another way to deal with handling these angry interactions. Family members must be willing to recognize when the situation is escalating. When this occurs, family members agree to give each other a sign agreeable to all that indicates "I am getting too angry to continue this discussion and I need a break and cool off" (p. 81). The discussion then stops for a period of time but resumes again later, enabling the family to resolve the issue. The request for the time-out occurs again if needed while the family works on the issue at hand. Family members learn new skills of handling conflict with the accompanying sense of being able to control anger within the family (Jordan, Cobb, & Franklin, 1999).

Problem-Solving

The ability to problem-solve is a critical aspect of resiliency. Problem-solving requires family members to assess the problem facing them and to identify possible steps that can help resolve it. Gaps in the problem-solving process can create further difficulties within the family and relationships with the external world. Within the social learning approach, the social worker can help family members problem-solve more effectively by modeling more effective problem-solving skills or helping family members carry out these steps in addressing a specific problem facing the family.

Family members might lack skills in problem-solving generally or demonstrate this ability in some contexts, but lack specific skills pertinent to the family situation. James Grant demonstrated effective problem-solving skills at work but lacked critical ones in the area of parenting. Sarah might have good problem-solving skills in terms of dealing with her girlfriends, but feels lost in her parent role. A further assessment of Jennifer and Martin might have revealed problem-solving skills in other areas of life that were not being tapped in their marital relationship. Using a strengths-based perspective, the social worker can help family members identify ways they are solving problems effectively in other areas of life and possible ways that they can transfer these skills to the family arena. This approach helps build an important sense of self-efficacy as well as improving family problem-solving skills.

Horne and Sayger (2003) identify four key questions to help families guide their problem-solving efforts.

1. What is your goal? What would you like to see happen?
2. What are you doing to achieve this goal?
3. Is what you are doing helping you achieve this goal?
4. If not, what are you going to do differently? (p. 127)

These questions can help family members identify the steps in generating and evaluating possible alternatives to reaching family goals. It also helps translate problems (negative) into goals (positive).

Evaluation

The social learning/cognitive approach provides opportunities that enable family members to develop more effective coping strategies and relate to each other in more positive ways. Jordan, Cobb, and Franklin (1999) reviewed the literature on family counseling derived from behavioral learning principles and found them to be effective in addressing parent-child and marital issues. Increasing communication skills has been one of the most effective aspects of couple therapy (Nichols & Schwartz, 2001). Parent-child issues have also responded well to programs combining cognitive and behavior components (Jordan, Cobb, & Franklin, 1999, p. 91). Parental education has emerged as helpful for the targeted behavior but as having less impact on other behaviors, thus suggesting limitations in generalizability (Nichols & Schwartz, 2001). While parental education has demonstrated effectiveness in addressing conduct disorders with children, families with many risk factors show less improvement than do families with fewer risk factors. Length of treatment (especially more than ten sessions) and the therapist's knowledge of social learning principles and skills were also associated with increased effectiveness of this approach (Sexton, Robbins, Hollimon, Mease, & Mayorga, 2003).

Summary

The social learning/cognitive approach to counseling with families can be effective in helping families learn and practice new skills and alter belief systems that contribute to dysfunctional patterns within families. The approach is strength-based in that it assumes that people are able to learn more productive patterns of behavior. The counselor acts in the role of a coach helping families learn and practice behaviors that are adaptive and identifying and altering belief systems. The implementation of the model is tailored to the unique circumstances and cultural context of the families involved.

Discussion Questions

Discuss the importance of identifying whether the problem is in the area of skills, motivation, or signals.

What are ways in which cognitions can make it difficult for people to carry out their skills?

How can we help people create changes in their behavior that continue past the therapy hour?

Discuss what steps in the treatment process help give people needed encouragement to keep trying.

Discuss why it is important to identify desired changes in positive and clear terms.

6

Psychoeducational Family Counseling

Gregg (aged nineteen) became ill during his sophomore year in college. He began to experience voices telling him that his roommate and others on his residence hall floor were trying to hurt him and that he should avoid them as much as possible. He found it difficult to concentrate on his studies as a result of the voices and his fears of what might happen to him. He gradually stopped going to classes because he found it too difficult to concentrate and could sometimes be found pacing about one of the quieter spots on campus. During the night he would fight sleep by walking the hallways because he feared what would happen while he was sleeping. His residence hall counselor became concerned and insisted that Gregg see someone at the student health center. This visit led to a meeting with staff members of the counseling center, where Gregg was diagnosed with schizophrenia. Because he felt so threatened by the college situation, he left school and returned home to his parents, where he began receiving help from the local mental health center. Gregg's parents were bewildered and frightened about what had happened to their son. They were unsure about the nature of the illness and how they should respond in ways that would be helpful.

Lillian (aged seventy-eight) was the matriarch of the family. Her married children lived in the area with their children. The family gathered at her home on a weekly basis and this gathering was the centerpiece of the family ties. Lillian was free with her advice for her children and they respected her suggestions. She had been widowed for the last ten years and supported herself through Social Security and her own and her husband's pensions. Suddenly everything in this family changed. Lillian had a serious stroke. She could speak with difficulty and needed help in taking care of herself. Her emotions changed rapidly and this once proud and independent woman would find herself crying even in the presence of her family. Her adult children found this change troubling and puzzling.

Bradley (aged thirty) rode his motorcycle to work and joined his friends on weekend rides. One day coming home from a ride with his friends, he skidded at a turn and his bike turned over and he hit his head. Unfortunately, he was not wearing his helmet. While Bradley survived the accident, he suffered a severe closed head injury that left him with major cognitive and emotional disabilities. His wife and parents were relieved that he had survived the accident but were now distressed about the changes that they were seeing and uncertain about how they should react to Bradley.

All these families (as well as the Patel and Rodriguez families discussed earlier) share a major change in terms of one of the family members. The above individuals and their families are struggling to cope with a difficult health situation of a family member. Family members are uncertain about the consequences of the illness or disability, what they can expect, what effective treatments are, and how they should respond in ways that are helpful. The health problem of one family member is a source of distress for the entire family.

Psychoeducational approaches are designed to help family members cope with these and other difficult circumstances. While the specific nature of the programs varies in terms of content and format, psychoeducational models share the following components: education involving information about the nature of the illness or specific problem, symptoms and signs of relapse, and treatment options; ways that the family members can cope and help the person with the problem and about the potential impact on the family members; skills to cope more effectively and emotional and social support for the family members. Families can also be empowered to take on an advocacy role as appropriate for the family. Psychoeducational treatment of families can occur with individual families or in multifamily groups. The term *psychoeducational* is used in the broad sense as an approach that contains the above elements rather than referring to specific treatment models for specific health issues. Such a treatment approach has a wide applicability with families and serves a preventive as well as a treatment function.

Theoretical Background

Psychoeducational models in the field of mental health, specifically schizophrenia, grew out of an understanding that some of the problems evident in families in which a family member had a mental illness were in response to the distress created by the disruptions of living with an ill family member rather than the cause of the illness. While these patterns did not cause the illness, they could create stress with the potential to increase the risk of relapse. Psychoeducational models were also created in the context of a growing appreciation of the crucial role the family plays in caring for individuals with illness. As Simon, McNeil, Franklin, and Cooperman (1991) describe in their classic article regarding psychoeducational approaches, this trend was accentuated by the deinstitutionalization in mental health. The very short-term stays in hospitals for all illnesses generally place family members center stage in caring for their members. As important as the mental health and general health care systems are in providing care, it is the family that typically assumes the ongoing responsibility for the person.

Despite the important role of the family, in various studies family members reported that they had not received any information about the nature of the illness and ways to cope. In addition to being burdened down by worry and lack of knowledge, families with a member with schizophrenia felt blamed by the professionals and stigmatized by the illness (Simon, McNeil, Franklin, & Cooperman, 1991; Solomon, 1998). As a result, ignorance and blame increased their already difficult caretaking burden.

Rather than view the family as the cause of the illness of the family member, the new approach has conceptualized family members as potential resources who need information and skills in order to carry out their important responsibilities. Recognizing the cyclical nature of stress and distress, psychoeducational approaches seek to reduce the distress of family members and to help family members respond more effectively to the ill family member. These changes can in turn reduce the ill family member's experience of distress that can contribute to relapse or a worsening of symptoms. Psychoeducation with family members is now viewed as an evidenced practice model in adult psychiatry (Dixon et al., 2001).

Early models of psychoeducational approaches with families in the field of mental health were generally organized especially around the need to help families decrease their level of expressed emotion (high EE), referring particularly to critical and hostile comments and climate, and included a rather lengthy process of family counseling (Solomon, 1996). Solomon also describes family educational models based on a coping-adaptation model designed to offer family members information to enhance their self-efficacy (Solomon, 1996).

Research in the area of chronic disease also supports the value of psychoeducational approaches. An ecological perspective has emerged as the most effective treatment model of chronic disease, whose care and management make up the largest single cost to the health care system (Fisher & Weihs, 2000). Rather than focusing on the patient, the intervention addresses the social setting in which disease management occurs. The social context generally is the family. This approach emphasizes the "relational context in which the disease takes place," includes the family environment, addresses the broad needs of the patient and family members, views the disease as an ongoing process, and includes the patient and the family in the assessment of outcomes (Fisher & Weihs, 2000, p. 562). Fisher and Weihs (2000) describe examples involving a range of health issues including children with cystic fibrosis, type 1 diabetes, and older adults at risk for rehospitalization.

The psychoeducational approach mirrors resiliency-based research in terms of how family members cope with difficult illness in the family as discussed subsequently in the chapter "Families Coping with Difficult Life Circumstances." These include studies related to families with children with chronic illnesses, family members with dementia, HIV/AIDS, and mental illness. Parents and family members attempted to cope by increasing their knowledge through seeking information about the illness from the medical system and by seeking social support.

The National Working Group on Family-Based Interventions in Chronic Disease identified potential mechanisms by which relationships within the family influence disease management and risk and protective factors (Fisher & Weihs, 2000). First, the emotional climate within the family influences the physiological systems of the patient. Secure attachments among family members have positive effects while family hostility and criticism impact negatively on the "hormonal, immunologic, and other biological systems that are linked to the outcomes of chronic disease through the physiologic stress responses" (Fisher & Weihs, 2000, p. 562). Family relationships also influence the disease process through the patient's self-care behavior. Fisher and Weihs (2000) point out that many "chronic diseases require tedious, repetitive, and at times invasive management procedures that force major changes in family life style, allocation of power, personal autonomy, role functioning, and decision making" (p. 562). Family response can either lead to family members working together to encourage effective disease management or undermining it by their responses and actions. Thus the family's response affects the disease process directly as well as the emotional lives of all the family members.

Linking research between family resiliency in general and protective family factors related to chronic disease, the following characteristics have been identified as playing a protective role in disease management: "family closeness and connectedness, problem-focused coping skills, clear family organization and decision making, and direct communication among family members related to the chronic diseases" (Fisher & Weihs, 2000, p. 562). Risk factors included "intrafamily hostility, criticism and blame, psychological trauma related to the initial diagnosis and treatment of the disease; lack of an extrafamilial support system; family perfectionism and rigidity; and presence of psychopathology with onset prior to the chronic disease" (Fisher & Weihs, 2000, p. 562). While improving protective factors is valuable, reducing family risk factors is especially important (Fisher & Weihs, 2000).

Major Tenets

1. Families are the major support system for members with mental health and other types of illnesses.

2. Family members are partners with professionals.

3. Families need the appropriate tools (information about the illness and the skills to deal with it).

4. Family members need support in dealing with such a difficult life event in the family.

5. In terms of mental illness, family members are not responsible for causing the illness. While tensions within the family can exacerbate symptoms, the family does not cause the illness. Some of the disruption in the family is in response to the distress created by caring for an ill family member.

6. Family context and interpersonal relationships have an impact on the illness as well as being influenced by the illness. Family relationships can serve as both risk and protective factors in terms of disease management.

7. Family members can help identify potential signs of relapse and thus be helpful in preventing serious relapse.

8. Culture helps define how illness is experienced and the nature of the response by family members.

Goals of Treatment

Psychoeducational family therapy seeks to help family members provide effective care for a family member with special needs while at the same time ensuring that this effort does not sacrifice the welfare of the family as a whole and the other family members. The approach includes information and emotional support for family members.

Promotes Resiliency by

- Addressing risk factors associated with lack of coping strategies to address illness-related stressors, stressors within the family, and lack of support systems.

- Supporting protective factors by providing families with the information and support needed to develop self-efficacy in addressing a difficult situation, identifying what is possible, improving family leadership, developing effective problem-solving and coping strategies, and connecting with appropriate social supports. These supports promote family affection and family interaction.

Role of the Counselor

The family counselor creates a working alliance with family members as partners in addressing the special needs of the family member. The family counselor assumes the dual role of educator and provider of emotional support. The counselor ensures that family members receive adequate and accurate information about the nature of the illness, appropriate types of treatment, available resources, and signs of relapse. The family counselor sometimes conveys this information personally or arranges for other professionals to communicate this information. The counselor also serves as a guide in terms of the many sources of information currently available. The counselor also helps the family learn effective ways to respond to the individual with the illness. The counselor helps the family identify potential resources within the family and the external world. The counselor also helps the entire family recognize and attempt to meet the needs of the family as a whole and other family members. Families in these situations risk ignoring the needs of other family members in ways that are harmful to all concerned. The counselor helps family members identify ways in which the situation is creating negative responses within the family and to cope in more effective ways for the entire family. The counselor provides social support for the family in meeting their relational and emotional needs and helps link the family with other sources of support.

Treatment Process

The following represent important steps in the treatment process.

Create a working alliance with family members as partners. Such an approach recognizes the critical role that family members play in providing essential care for their family members. The family counselor seeks to empower the family to carry out this role as effectively as possible.

Assessment. What are the issues that relate to stress within the family as well as the person with the health problem? In terms of the family, such stress can take various forms depending on the situation and the family, for example, the loss of Lillian's effective leadership within her large family, the grief that Gregg's parents feel as they see their son unable to cope with college and life, and the worry of Bradley's parents and wife as they realize that he will not be able to care adequately for himself, much less provide for his family. The Patel family is worried about their son and his future. The Rodriguez family is concerned about how to provide adequate care for their father and how to continue the success of the family business.

These stresses are paired with those experienced by the person with the problem. Gregg's illness has plunged him into a world of fear and anxiety, compounded by his inability to pursue education as he had planned and his fears for the future. Lillian's stroke has robbed her of a role that was central to her identity and has compromised her ability to control her emotions in ways that further diminish her family leadership. Bradley faces a period of major rehabilitation with a guarded prognosis about his ability to assume his prior life, compounded with the stress of ongoing problems in cognitively and emotionally processing life events.

What are the resources that the family brings to this situation? The assessment includes an exploration regarding how the family members are coping both with the current situation and how they have coped in the past. Sometimes the shock of a current stressor prevents families from accessing and demonstrating their potential resources. Identifying past evidence of coping can help identify these potential resources for the family. Such an exploration also helps identify patterns of coping of the family that can be used to address the issues at hand. Identifying past and present coping strategies serves as valuable information to support current coping efforts and to identify the appropriateness of these efforts given the immediate situation.

Maximize the family coping resources. Several elements help maximize the family coping resources to deal with a realistically difficult situation.

Families need accurate information in order to cope. As a result, providing the family with information about the nature of the illness, the symptoms and the meaning of symptoms, treatment possibilities (medication, therapeutic modalities), and the signs and circumstances of relapse is an essential part of the model. The specific information will depend on the nature of the situation. Social workers can arrange for an expert in the illness to provide this information or provide it personally—depending on their expertise and the resources involved. Written material that is culturally and educationally appropriate for family members is valuable so that family members can study it later at home and share it with pertinent others in their support system. With the explosion of information on the Internet from sources ranging from sound and trustworthy to commercial ads, it can be important to provide the family with some guidance in sifting through such sources of information. Families are also seeking information in terms of what the future is likely to hold—the prognosis.

In terms of the family's coping efforts, the social worker can help Gregg's parents realize that he is having difficulty processing multiple stimuli and to reduce this in their conversations with him. Gregg's parents can be helped to identify how he can realistically function at this time and to adjust their expectations accordingly to reduce the context of criticism. Bradley's family can be helped to realize that his closed head injury makes it difficult for him to deal with abstract concepts and to identify more concrete forms of discussing issues with him. Lillian's family might be helped to understand that Lillian still treasures her importance to the family and her dignity but to reduce the numbers of people who are meeting with her in order to help her currently compromised language ability. They can be helped to realize that her emotional instability is probably part of the impact of the stroke and to find ways to prevent overwhelming her emotionally.

Important information can include the nature of the types of available treatment and how families can access this help. Families need information about the relevant health care or rehabilitative system, the related social services that can be helpful for the family, and ways in which the family can connect with these services for their family.

Families also need information about the impact of these changes on the other family members. A family systems perspective suggests that what happens to one family member has an impact on every member of the family. Helping family members identify the stresses that they are experiencing and ways to meet the needs of family members is an essential part of the psychoeducational approach. Family members can try to deal with the emotional stress in many ways. Some of these can be problematic, for example, by denying the seriousness of the illness, by submerging their own needs, by overly compensating for the ill family member, or by becoming angry with the ill family member or the health care system. Caregivers can become overwhelmed and thus begin to experience their own stress and finally become ineffective in their caregiving role. Families can be helped to find ways to maintain a normal family life as much as possible under the circumstances rather than letting the entire family revolve around the illness of a family member. Counseling family members to cope in ways that reduce these negative responses can be helpful for both the family and the ill family member.

Family members need information about signs of potential relapse and the type of help that would be appropriate in these circumstances. This information can help reduce some of the damage that might occur due to this behavior and to recruit help as quickly as possible.

Arrange for supportive help. Family members are facing a difficult situation, and ongoing support through groups, family meetings, and other formats can be essential in dealing with this. Meeting with other family members facing a similar problem can be extremely supportive emotionally as well as providing family members with potential coping strategies. Arranging for other members of the community to be part of an informed support system can also be useful.

Cultural Issues

Because culture influences how families experience life events and family caretaking responsibilities, it is important to understand the cultural context of families when designing psychoeducational approaches. The medical explanatory model that has been supported by the traditional psychoeducational programs does not do justice to some of the varying cultural interpretations (Guarnaccia, 1998). Designing culturally appropriate psychoeducational approaches needs to consider how the relevant illness or life events are viewed within the culture, the nature of the family system, and the cast of influential individuals within the community that can be supportive of these efforts and the family. Specific implications regarding culture are included in the subsequent discussion of applications.

Applications

Mental Health

As discussed earlier, some of the first models were developed regarding families who had a member with a serious mental health problem, especially schizophrenia. The focus at this time was to reduce negative expressive emotion. The following models address several mental health concerns.

Dixon and colleagues (2001) identify the following fourteen principles for working with families of individuals with mental illness. These address the treatment needs of the individual and equip the family to respond more effectively and to meet their own needs:

- Coordinate all elements of treatment and rehabilitation to ensure that everyone is working toward the same goals in collaborative, supportive relationships.
- Pay attention to both the social and the clinical needs of the individual.
- Provide optimum medication management.
- Listen to families' concerns and involve them as equal partners in the planning and delivery of treatment.
- Explore family members' expectations of the treatment program and expectations for the individual.
- Assess the strengths and limitations of the family's ability to support the individual.
- Address feelings of loss.
- Provide relevant information for the individual and his or her family at appropriate times.
- Provide an explicit crisis plan and professional response.
- Help improve communication among family members.
- Provide training for the family in structured problem-solving techniques.
- Encourage family members to expand their social support network (e.g., participate in family support organizations such as NAMI).
- Be flexible in meeting the needs of the family.
- Provide the family with easy access to another professional in the event that the current work with the family ceases. (Dixon, McFarlane, Lefley, Lucksted, Cohen & Falloon, 2001, p. 904)

Children with Mental Illness

Caring for children with various types of mental illness can take a toll on the mental and physical health, the social life, work responsibilities, and family life of parents. They have the responsibility of addressing many difficult experiences as well as grieving for the loss of their hopes for their children. While some families report a growing closeness of their families, many families experience the strain created by dealing with this issue. As a result, programs have been developed to provide parents with education about the nature of the illness, resources, ways to cope with the problems that they are facing, and stress management for the family (Mendenhall & Mount, 2011). In a review of programs for families, the following represent psychoeducational programs that have been effective with parents of children with mental health disorders (Mendenhall & Mount, 2011).

- Family-focused treatment (FFT; Miklowitz et al., 2004) is designed for adolescents diagnosed with bipolar disorder and their families. It included twenty sessions over nine months. The program includes three components: psychoeducation, communication enhancement training, and problem-solving skills training. These are modified from the adult FFT model to respond to the developmental needs of adolescents. Both adolescents and parents reported progress over a one-year period.

- Family psychoeducation (FPE; Sanford et al., 2006) uses a multiphase model, including the home setting, to address issues affecting adolescents with depression and their families. It included eight ninety-minute sessions with separate parent and children groups. Parents reported satisfaction and improvement.

- Multifamily psychoeducational psychotherapy (MF-PEP; Fristad, 2006) uses a group setting to provide education and support to children with mood disorders and their families. It included twelve 1.5-hour sessions at home with one booster session and a three-month follow-up. Participants demonstrated improvement.

Goldberg-Arnold, Fristad, and Gavazzi (1999) developed a six-week psychoeducational group for parents. The nature of these sessions is similar to others in their basic outline: understanding mood disorders and their symptoms, treatment medication, interpersonal aspects of the illness on individuals and families, effective parenting techniques, communication strategies within the family and external organizations (e.g., schools), problem solving, and review of family issues. The specific problems and issues vary depending on the families involved in the group. A follow-up with parents revealed that information, coping skills, and support were important for families and remained important for months following the group. During this six-month period, parental attitudes toward their child and the illness became more positive. Goldberg-Arnold et al. (1999) hypothesize that as family members replace shame and stigma with empowered thinking they might be more active in seeking support and begin to think more positively of their child and the illness. Such programs thus reduce caregiver burden.

Parents with Major Depression

Papalos (2002) describes a five-session psychoeducational approach that includes the individual with the affective disorder and other relevant family members. During these sessions, information is shared about how the family members have experienced the illness; the nature, symptoms, and course of treatment of the disorder; the effects of it on the relationships within the family; and strategies to respond more effectively. The approach is designed to help the individual with the disorder and family members to accept that a family member has an illness that could be recurrent and to educate them about the nature of the symptoms. Family members are helped to understand the impact that this has had on the relationships within the family and ways to resolve these more effectively. Information is shared about signs of potential relapse and ways to monitor treatment and the course of the illness (Papalos, 2002).

Beardslee and colleagues developed a program to help children whose parents had mental health problems and to improve the parenting behavior. This program became the basis for subsequent psychoeducational programs. The goal of this approach is to help family members, especially the children, gain a better understanding of the nature of the illness experience as well as improve the parents' behavior in terms of their children (Beardslee, Salt, Porterfield, Rothberg, Van de Velde, & Swatling, 1993). This approach was based in part on previous research regarding the resiliency of children whose parents had affective disorders. Resilient adolescents were able to be aware of their parents' illness, thought about their parents, and understood their parents' illness. They realized that they were not the cause of the illness and were able to see themselves separately from their parents. It was important to understand how family members, especially the children, had experienced the illness of their parents.

The format of the intervention consisted of six to ten sessions with individual meetings with the parents, meetings with each of the children, and several family meetings. Children were also given age-appropriate literature about depression and children of parents with depression. Family members had access to a clinician as needed. Didactic information about depression, risks to children, and ways to support resiliency was presented to the family. This information was linked with the family's own experience of the illness. Parents were helped to understand the impact of depression on the children. A plan was developed with the family in terms of ways in which the family could cope and create a life separate from the illness of the parent. According to the authors, the following components are core to the intervention: factual information is presented in a way that links it to the experiences of the family, there is a focus on the resiliency of the children, and concrete plans for the future are developed (Beardslee et al., 1993).

Given the prevalence of affective disorders in adults and the impact on the children involved, a clinician-led intervention was compared with a lecture format. Both approaches included information about the nature of the illness, the risk and paths to the resiliency of children, the general experience of a family in terms of the illness, and ways to cope. They also received written material. The clinician-led group also included establishment of a therapeutic alliance and discussion on the specific impact on the individual family and ways to address it.

While participants in both groups reported a decrease in distress following the intervention, those of the clinician-led group reported higher levels of helpfulness, an increased understanding of the illness, as well as behavioral changes in terms of greater communication within the family and more adaptive coping strategies. As in the previous model, linking the discussion to the specific family situation seemed to be useful here (Beardslee et al., 1993).

Depression by mothers can ripple throughout the family system. Drawing in part on the work of Beardslee described above, a recent ten-session program combining aspects of psychoeducation along with cognitive behavior and post-modern approaches of solution-focused and narrative family therapy models (described subsequently in chapters 8 and 9) was designed for women suffering from depression and their family members. The program used the multi-family approach described previously. Parents and children met together in groups and also separately. The program was based on earlier findings regarding the stress created in the family as a result of the mother's depression resulting from diminished communication, lack of parental warmth, inconsistent discipline, decreased pleasant activities, family stress, and maternal withdrawal. Support by the partner or other caretaker is an important protective factor for the family. The ability of the parent to participate in positive parenting is another protective factor. Participants learned about depression and were helped to alter their negative views of themselves and their families with an emphasis on the strengths and capacities of the family members. They were encouraged to have home activities that created behavior change and encouraged the mother to view herself as a capable parent. Solution-focused approaches were used to highlight exceptions and to identify strengths. Narrative approaches were used to help family members understand their family's unique experience. Participants reported improvement in family functioning and in the health of the mother (Riley, Valdez, Barrueco, Mills, Beardless, Sandler, & Rawal, 2008; Valdez, Mills, Barrueco, Leis, & Riley, 2011).

Beardslee's Preventive Intervention Program for Depression was also modified to meet the needs of low-income Latino families. The program was offered in settings that fit with the needs of the family members. These adaptations included the following:

- Bilingual providers
- Sessions translated into modules that allowed for great time flexibility
- Expanded history-taking that included information about immigration/migration history, adaptation to dominant culture
- Expanded emphasis on alliance building and collaboration by
  - Transparency regarding goals and interventions
  - Demonstrate respect for family members
  - Ensure family members feel heard
- Expanded role of psychoeducation—including cultural models
- Children aware that their mother supports their participation
- Parents prepared for family meetings
- Modified family meeting to meet cultural expectations
- Follow up-review of cultural transition issues
- Address family crises as they occurred

Family members typically described the program as helpful. The mothers with depression rated the relationship with the program provider very highly. The program contributed to family resiliency. Family members felt empowered and better able to handle family difficulties. They reported feeling that their voices had been heard by members of the family and thus they were better able to address family concerns. Family members described the family meeting as the most important part of the program. A bilingual prevention provider was important because he or she was frequently needed to interpret between the generations—both in terms of language and understanding of cultural issues. Understanding the immigration story and what this meant for family members was also important (D'Angelo, Lierena-Quinn, Shapiro, Colon, Rodriguez, Gallagher, & Beardslee, 2009).

In addition to the previous suggestions for adapting a psychoeducation model for Hispanic families, Guarnaccia (1998) suggests other concerns in terms of implementing programs with these families. It is important to understand that the illness can be interpreted in a spiritual way. As a result, when families seek help from spiritualists, it is helpful to encourage them to do so as a parallel path to the mental health system. Spirituality can be an important source of support. It is also important not to confuse spiritual behaviors with mental illness. Close family relationships within the Hispanic family can be mistaken for problematic overinvolvement. At the same time, mothers can become overly involved with their ill sons and sacrifice their well-being to the detriment of themselves and their sons. The counselor can help by indicating that good mothers also take time for themselves (Rivera, 1988). Given the importance of the extended family in Mexican American families, including them in the treatment process can be valuable (Jordan, Lewellen, & Vandiver, 1995).

Hispanic families frequently have high stimuli contexts in terms of people, music, and other activities. These high levels of stimuli can be overwhelming to a person with a chronic mental illness. Helping families to problem-solve different ways to reduce these stimuli can be useful.

Counselors need to be aware that the mutual help-giving that is part of Hispanic culture means that people are ready to share their medications with other people and thus people might be taking additional medication than prescribed. As a result, care needs to be taken to support the family's intent but to educate family members about the need for proper medication and the potential problems in combined and shared medications (Rivera, 1988).

Bipolar Disorders

Brennan (1995) describes a closed-entry multifamily group program that included individuals diagnosed with bipolar disorder and their family members. The program consisted of fourteen sessions in which some of the sessions included the individuals diagnosed with the illness and the other family members and other sessions were divided into groups of individuals with the illness and groups with other family members. He describes the value of having both the individual with the illness and other family members in most of the sessions to ensure that all parties are receiving the same information and to enhance the understanding of the impact of the illness on all of the parties involved. Session topics included the nature of the illness, medications and treatment, the impact of the illness on the parties involved (individuals with the illness and the family members were in separate groups twice during these weeks), signs of relapse, the nature of the mental health system, information provided by a guest psychiatrist, suicide, managing symptoms, guidelines for managing the illness, and topics of interest to the parties involved. Participants indicated that although they were apprehensive about the group at first, they found it very helpful. They were especially likely to describe content about the illness and ways to manage it as helpful as well as the awareness that they were not the only families facing this problem. The group facilitated communication among family members, including the person with the illness, about the illness and the family (Brennan, 1995).

Borderline Personality

Gunderson, Berkowitz, and Ruiz-Sancho (1997) describe a psychoeducational program created for families with a member with a borderline personality disorder. Such programs were slower to develop than programs for families with a member with schizophrenia because these families were less likely to be viewed as partners in the care of the family member. The family situation related to a borderline disorder is frequently characterized by underinvolvement by the parents, sometimes to the point of neglect. There can also be a history of conflict with high levels of dysfunction within families.

The program was developed through a process of exploring with adults with a borderline disorder and their parents the nature of the burdens that they wish to have addressed. Both agreed that the major issues were communication, and the problems of conflict and anger within the family. Parents were concerned about suicide by the adult children (Gunderson et al., 1997). Parents described their families as healthier than did their adult children. In this context, individuals with borderline personality disorders can have a pattern of characterizing others who have cared for them in negative terms. Unlike other mental health problems like schizophrenia where the theme has been on the etiology as a brain disease, the emphasis in these sessions is on how to cope with the problem rather than etiology.

The counselors first meet with the families individually to join in a non-threatening manner and to provide them with relevant information. Families then join together in a larger group for a review of information about the illness followed by a discussion of ways to solve common problems. Sessions include a social time followed by a problem-solving period. The intent is to reduce the crisis orientation of the families and to replace this with more stable patterns and relationships not tied to threats and rages. Families are helped to listen to the anger of their adult children without retaliation while at the same time learning that they can limit the length of time that they are willing to permit this exchange to take place. The treatment approach is not designed to treat the borderline condition, but rather to reduce the stress within the family that might serve as a trigger for an outburst. This family approach is relatively lengthy (can take place for a year or longer) (Gunderson et al., 1997).

Indochinese families. Vandiver and Keopraseuth (1998) describe some of the cultural considerations in conducting psychoeducational efforts with Indochinese families (especially those from Vietnam, Cambodia, and Laos) who are caring for a relative with mental illness. While there are differences among the groups representing the Indochinese people from Southeast Asia, there are also some similarities that influence the nature of treatment.

The extended family with an emphasis on "family obligations, filial piety, respect for one's parents and siblings, harmonious interpersonal relationships, interdependence, and collective responsibilities and decision making" (Vandiver & Keopraseuth, 1998, p. 77) is important. Children learn early that their behavior is a reflection on the entire family. The stigma of mental illness thus means that the illness of one person brings shame on the entire family. At the same time, the disruptions experienced by many members of these groups along with isolation from family and relatives have contributed to higher levels of depression and post-traumatic stress disorder. Many of these families have experienced major losses both prior to and after their move from their homeland. The stigma associated with mental illness leads families to be reluctant to admit that a family member is ill. Given the shame attached to mental illness, these problems are frequently described and viewed in terms of somatic complaints. Traditional healers are important resources for family members. Families that have a member with mental illness frequently lack knowledge about the problem and feel isolated from sources of support (Vandiver & Keopraseuth, 1998).

Cultural patterns tend to make these families hierarchical, with respect due to older members of the family. As a result, aspects of caring for older family members by younger members can be problematic because older individuals might be unwilling to accept instructions from younger members about medication compliance and other issues (Jordan, Lewellen, & Vandiver, 1995).

Given the importance of the extended family setting, it can be important to engage the wider family circle in these psychoeducational efforts (Jordan, Lewellen, & Vandiver, 1995). Recommendations in terms of the format for family sessions vary. Given the context of stigma, some families might be reluctant to participate in a group setting. As a result, providing psychoeducational services to the family privately or in the context of their home would fit with their cultural preferences (Vandiver & Keopraseuth, 1998). In terms of Laotian families that have a member with a mental illness, Jordan, Lewellen, and Vandiver (1995) describe the benefits of using a multifamily group model organized as a social event and the importance of involving people with credibility within the community and knowledge of the culture. Social workers thus need to explore with individual families what would be appropriate for them.

Direct comments about needed lifestyle changes of family members can also convey messages of family weakness and cause family members to lose face. Consequently, Vandiver and Keopraseuth (1998) suggest the value of using indirection or making suggestions regarding alternative behavior that the entire family can try. Coping efforts that involve the entire family and comments regarding how well the family is doing are supportive of the important role of the family.

Counselors also frequently need to serve as cultural brokers with the family. For some families, this might mean education about survival skills for functioning in their current society (Vandiver & Keopraseuth, 1998).

Chronic Illness

Studies of psychoeducational approaches for helping families cope with illness suggest the need to look at two basic types of chronic illnesses. The first type includes illnesses that begin with an acute or traumatic episode that can lead to remission or potential recurrence (e.g., heart disease, cancer). The second type includes illnesses that begin slowly but are ongoing and progressive and require routine management practices (e.g., Alzheimer's disease). The first type of illness typically involves crisis management, post-traumatic stress management, and invasive disease management. The second type involves the process of caregiving, management of the disease, and the risk that over time the disease will take over the lives of family members (Fisher & Weihs, 2000). As a result, psychoeducational models need to look at the nature of the illness and the impact of its pattern on the family.

Diabetes. Diabetes represents a potentially life-threatening chronic illness with extensive lifestyle demands. The following is an example of a program designed to address diabetes with attention to cultural adaptations. The First Nations communities have experienced an epidemic of diabetes. Mendenhall and colleagues addressed the challenge of developing a family education program for members of American Indian groups in the Minneapolis area. The project first began with extensive consultation with community leaders in terms of the health issues of concern to the community and ways to address it. This was a two-year process. The Family Education Diabetes Series (FEDS) participants included not only individuals with diabetes, their family members, and health professionals but also respected community leaders. Meetings began with an important health marker—members checking and recording each other's blood sugars and weight, and conducting foot checks. Participants cooked and ate meals together, a culturally appropriate feature. This led to discussions regarding meal ingredients, cost, availability, portion size, and relevance to diabetes. It was followed by an educational sequence (including basic diabetes education, health care, stress management, family relationships, community and health resources). The program included talking circles, music, drumming, creative arts, impromptu theater, and time for informal sharing and support. While the biweekly series was scheduled to last for three hours, most participants arrived early and stayed late. Follow-up data revealed improvement in health markers (Mendenhall et al., 2010).

A brief educational intervention with adolescents and their parents during the regular visits for medical care proved useful in terms of the medical care of the adolescent with type 1 diabetes and reduced parent-child conflict (Anderson, Brackett, Ho, & Laffel, 1999). Parents and their adolescent children who participated in this program showed better disease management and less conflict than families who were not part of the program.

Alzheimer's disease. Alzheimer's disease is a devastating chronic disease that creates distress for the family and the individual with the disease. Mittelman, Ferris, Shulman, Steinberg, and Levin (1996) conducted a psychoeducational approach with families with an elderly member with Alzheimer's disease. Family members included the spouse, adult children, and other involved family members. They attended a six-week session of meetings that provided members with information about the nature of the disease and its management. Family members learned skills to resolve family conflict, enhance family problem solving, and identify signs of emotional overload by caretakers. Families received follow-up treatment for several years to help them deal with ongoing problems. Compared to a control group that did not receive this service, caregiver mental health was better and placement into nursing homes occurred later in the illness.

Evaluation

As indicated in the previous discussion, there is extensive evidence that psychoeducational approaches that combine education with support and problem-solving results can be an important adjunct to treatment for a variety of problems and can help decrease relapse. Family members are helped to become more effective partners in caring for the individual, develop greater self-efficacy in their ability to handle the situation, and experience reduced levels of distress.

Summary

Psychoeducational programs that provide family members with information and support can be valuable in helping family members cope with a variety of illnesses. Social workers can take an active role in arranging for family members to receive appropriate information, to cope more effectively, and to meet the needs of the entire family through various sources of support within the family circle and the extended circle of informal and formal support networks. Including cultural consideration in the design and implementation of programs can be important to their success.

DISCUSSION QUESTIONS

Discuss the protective factor of self-efficacy as it relates to psychoeducational approaches.

What does it mean to view the family members as the partners in psychoeducational approaches?

In what ways does psychoeducational family therapy serve as a prevention strategy?

How might culture influence the psychoeducational process?

7

Structural Family Therapy

Alicia and Matt were discouraged with their family life. They felt beaten down in their role as parents. Their three boys, aged five, eight, and twelve, had clearly gained the upper hand in the house. The family was in turmoil. When Alicia and Matt would shout at the boys to try to get them to behave, the boys typically would not listen to them. Alicia and Matt would throw up their hands in despair and walk away or turn on the TV louder to drown out the sound of the boys' fighting. When things got too bad, they would order the boys to their rooms but would quickly give in when the boys began to cry or shout at them. Alicia and Matt would argue about which parent was to blame for what had gone wrong. Matt had grown up in a family in which his father was clearly in charge, almost to an abusive manner, and Matt wanted his children to feel closer to him rather to fear him as he had feared his father. Alicia's father had left when she was a small child and she had grown up very close to her mother. She had felt responsible for taking care of her mother and had never really challenged her own mother. She felt overwhelmed by her boys who were constantly testing their parents. Out of their frustration, Matt and Alicia were constantly criticizing each other in their handling of the boys. They were especially frustrated with their twelve-year-old son who they felt was modeling defiant behavior that the younger boys were imitating. They were not sure how to regain their parental leadership and ended up blaming each other for not making this possible. When the family finally contacted the local center for help, the parents indicated that they no longer felt in control of the family and were trying to find some way to restore their parental leadership.

From a resiliency perspective, this family has important protective factors including an adequate financial basis, a safe home, and a sense of commitment to the family. The parents are motivated to maintain their family, but their lack of effective leadership skills have left them overwhelmed in trying to establish their sense of authority in this family. Their earlier life models did not provide them with the opportunities to learn parenting skills that would be effective in their current situation. The parents almost abdicated their authority to the children, who in turn continue to push their parents by testing whatever limits the parents still attempt to set. The situation escalates as the children's efforts to search out and test the limits create further turmoil while the parents' inability to establish leadership contributes to the boys' difficult behavior.

> Valerie is a single parent of three children, a girl aged five, a boy seven, and a boy thirteen. She seeks help because she is feeling overwhelmed by the boys, especially her thirteen-year-old son, who has started to increasingly ignore her instructions. She fears that he will also start getting in more difficulty in school if the problem gets worse. Valerie and the boys' father were never married and he left the family three years ago. He has no contact with the family and only pays child support when forced do so by the court. Valerie works as a health aide at the local hospital. Her income is adequate to meet the basic needs of the family but not enough for any extras. She has several sisters and brothers in the community and spends time with them on a regular basis. They also have school-age children. Valerie attends her local church when she can (her work requires her to work some Sundays). During the session, the social worker notices that Valerie's tone of voice varies from angry to resigned when her older son speaks in a defiant manner to her or ignores what she is saying to him. She speaks with greater confidence with the two younger children, especially the daughter. She describes many effective parenting tools that she has learned and used in the past. In an exhausted manner, she indicates that she is very tired from her long hours at work and feels so discouraged with her son that she finds herself often not trying and just letting things slide. She fears that the other children will soon start following in his path.

Valerie loves her children but finds it difficult to be an effective leader in this family. While Valerie has a knowledge of effective parenting skills and is able to use them more consistently with the youngest child, she has become so tired and discouraged that she is no longer able to assert herself as an effective family leader with her oldest child. The family is experiencing a vicious cycle because the more Valerie becomes resigned to this situation, the more her son disregards her authority, and thus the more Valerie becomes discouraged about the family situation and her ability to create order. This pattern is also beginning with the middle child.

In addition to Valerie's knowledge of parenting skills, this family also has other important resources. Valerie is a capable worker who earns at least an adequate salary. The father could potentially be required to pay additional child support. The family has an extended family that lives nearby and plays a regular part in their lives that offers them emotional and social support. The family members attend church when they are able to do so and thus have spiritual support and the potential support of the church members.

Structural family therapy can be a viable option for families like Alicia and Matt and Valerie and their children where an effective leadership structure is currently lacking. Effective family leadership represents an important factor that contributes to resiliency, while lack of such leadership is a risk factor. Effective leadership enables family members to meet the myriad needs of family members occasioned by external circumstances and family development stages. Helping families develop appropriate leadership skills can be extremely important for families in which the leadership structure is ineffective and needs strengthening.

Structural family therapy is an important model of family therapy that looks at the family as an organizational structure with the goal of helping the family create a structure that can more effectively meet the needs of family members. The emphasis in structural family therapy is on the organization of the family, the reoccurring behavioral patterns that reflect the organizational structure of the family. Symptoms in families are a reflection of the stress and strain experienced by the family. The role of the family therapist is to help the family experience and establish more effective organizational structures by means of a series of active interventions. The family therapist focuses on the healing capacities of the family to transform its organizational structure and view of the family reality (Minuchin & Fishman, 1981; Minuchin & Nichols, 1991).

Theoretical Background

Structural family therapy began with Salvador Minuchin and his work with the boys at Wiltwyck School and their families who came primarily from poor areas. These families were typically headed by single mothers who were overwhelmed by their lives. The role of fathers in the lives of the boys was frequently minimal. "The youngsters themselves did not have a clear sense of family rules, hierarchy of authority, or whom to depend on within the family for help with life. The model sought to bring effective organization to the family so that its members could find better solutions to their problems" (Aponte, 2003, p. 104). Based on his experience with these families, Minuchin developed a treatment strategy that was action-oriented and relied heavily on engagement (enlisting families to bring their family behavioral sequences into the therapy session). The focus was on using the active role of the therapist in this setting to alter the structure and related interaction patterns of family members (Aponte, 2003; Minuchin & Fishman, 1981; Minuchin & Nichols, 1991).

Minuchin was joined by colleagues who helped to develop the clinical strategies and organizations in which structural family therapy was developed and implemented. From its origin in the 1970s, it has developed into a widely used and highly regarded form of family therapy whose value has been recognized as applying to families facing an array of problems. Given the context of the early families treated, structural family therapy has also looked at the social environments of families. Recognizing that spirituality can be a resource for demoralized families, Aponte (1994, 2002, 2003) expanded the model to incorporate ideas of values and spirituality.

Major Tenets

Structural family therapy is based on six tenets.

1. Families are organizations with structural patterns that are important to the lives of the family members.

2. Symptoms within families are signs of a family under stress (Minuchin & Fishman, 1981).

3. Understanding the organizational patterns of families as they relate to the problem at hand is essential to the assessment and treatment process. Families include subsystems. The three basic structural dimensions of families include (Aponte, 2003):

   - Boundaries. Who is in or out of a family relationship vis-à-vis the focal issue, as well as what their roles are in this interaction

   - Alignment. Who is with or against the others in the transactions generating the problem

   - Power. What is the relative influence of the participants in the interactions that create the problem?

Triangulation can be a destructive form of alignment within families when family members with greater power compete for the alignment of a family member with lesser power. The family member with less power is really not in a position to refuse to play a role in this part of the family dance. Parents who are in conflict can seek to align one of the children on their side so the child is forced to choose between one of the parents and does not feel that he can opt out of this arrangement (Minuchin, 1974).

4. The interaction pattern demonstrated by the family in the family session is a critical source of information and more reliable than a family member's self-reports.

5. Change occurs through active involvement of family members in alternative behaviors.

6. The family session is used to enact new behaviors and family change.

Goals of Treatment

The goal of structural family therapy is to change the structure of the family in order to enable family members to "free the symptom bearer of symptoms, to reduce conflict and stress for the entire family, and to learn new ways of coping" (Minuchin & Fishman, 1981, p. 29). In order to respond to internal or external demands on the family, these changes can include developing a more effective leadership subsystem, reducing overly enmeshed family patterns, or encouraging closer relationships among family members. By using an active approach, structural family therapy also seeks to change the family's view of reality regarding its members and context and thus create opportunities for new behavior and family structures.

Promotes Resiliency by

- Addressing risk factors associated with lack of effective leadership, family organizational patterns, and family belief systems that view problematic interaction patterns as inevitable.
- Supporting protective factors by improving family leadership, promoting appropriate levels of cohesion and boundaries, improving family coping strategies and positive interaction, and changing belief systems about the situation into those that contribute to self-efficacy.

Role of the Therapist

With the goal of changing the structure of the family, the family therapist plays a very active role in joining with family members and enabling family members to experience new patterns of behavior. The therapist's active involvement in the family serves as the basis for the assessment process as well as for the interventions. The therapist joins the family dance (interaction patterns) but creates new patterns in this process. The therapist sets in motion new patterns of behavior by family members through active use of the therapist's self. The family therapist in many ways acts as stage manager with the family—arranging for family members to act out their current and potential new roles. This role is critical because active engagement of family members in their changed behavior in the therapy session is a key element in structural family therapy.

To be effective, the family therapist must first join with the entire family so that the family members will trust that the therapist is "working with and for them" (Minuchin & Fishman, 1981, p. 32). Joining requires the therapist to be sensitive to the culture of the family (Minuchin & Fishman, 1981). Culture here refers to the unique patterns of this family as well as to membership in a specific cultural group. Is this a family that tends to understate, or to express thoughts in a dramatic manner, or to rely on silence? The therapist in turn adapts one's manner to this manner of communication. The therapist imitates the family in some key ways to solidify the therapeutic alliance. The therapist activates parts of the self that facilitate the joining process. This can occur through sharing aspects of the therapist's life that link with the family (e.g., a shared enthusiasm for soccer or music) or assuming behavioral patterns that reflect the family. The therapist also identifies strengths within the family and uses confirming statements regarding members of the family. The therapist enables family members to feel that the therapist understands them and looks for strengths within the family. While joining the family system, the therapist also remains an outsider and thus has the freedom to respond in different ways that challenge the family's typical interaction patterns.

Assessment Process

Assessment and joining of the family are intricately linked in structural family therapy. The therapist observes the family's organizational pattern during the sessions. As a participant in the system, the family therapist experiences the family and uses this information in the assessment process of the family's functioning. The family therapist attempts to create a map of the family that identifies the positions that family members take in terms of other family members. "This map reveals coalitions, affiliations, explicit and implicit conflicts, and the way family members group themselves in conflict resolution. It identifies family members who operate as detourers of conflict and family members who function as switchboards. The map charts the nurturers, healers, and scapegoats" (Minuchin & Fishman, 1981, p. 69).

In this process, the family therapist identifies possible areas of strength or dysfunction in the family. For example, as the social worker joins with Alicia and Matt and their boys, the worker sees how the parents view themselves as unable to exert control over their boys. The social worker can also observe how the boys have mastered the divide-and-conquer strategy so that Alicia and Matt end up undermining the efforts of each other rather than supporting each other as fellow parents. As the parents begin to criticize each other for what they are doing wrong or not doing, the children are left free to disregard their parents' authority. The social worker is also able to observe both how Valerie is able to be effective with her youngest child and her sense of defeat and resignation with the older son that undermines her leadership.

Dysfunction can typically involve either overaffiliation (too much closeness) or underaffiliation (lack of adequate closeness). In families in which there are inadequate boundaries between individuals and overaffiliation is present, members of the family often speak for others in the family session. Lack of adequate closeness can be revealed through bodily posture, nonverbal gestures, seating arrangements, lack of knowledge regarding the other family members, or other signs that indicate the separate nature of the lives people in this family lead.

The therapist also assesses the family in terms of areas of flexibility and rigidity. Families need both a degree of flexibility to address changes in life and stability to give members a sense of security and coherence. More information about these issues emerges as the counselor engages with the family in the change process. As the family is encouraged in the session to assume new patterns, areas of flexibility and rigidity become clearer as the family responds by their ability or willingness to make changes (Minuchin & Fishman, 1981). This information is thus used by the therapist in planning for future intervention needs.

Treatment Strategies

Minuchin describes three main strategies of structural family therapy. These strategies relate to actions of the therapist in terms of the family dance: challenge the symptoms, challenge the family structure, and challenge the family reality.

Challenge the symptoms. Families typically come to the session with one person identified as the problem. From the perspective of the therapist the problem lies in the interaction patterns rather than in the client. The family therapist seeks to help the family reframe the problem in terms of the family structure (Minuchin & Fishman, 1981; Nichols & Schwartz, 2001). While Alicia and Matt might blame each other for being ineffective or blame one of the boys whose behavior had been the most difficult to control, the family therapist looks at the organization patterns that play a role in creating and maintaining the problems. The task of the therapist is to "challenge the family's definition of the problem and the nature of their response" (Minuchin & Fishman, 1981, p. 68). The goal is to "reframe the family's view of the problem, pushing its members to search for alternative behavioral, cognitive, and affective responses" (p. 68). Instead of Alicia and Matt dealing with the problem by blaming each other in ways that only serve to undermine the parental coalition, they can be helped to begin to support each other in setting limits on the children. This change thus counters their original view of their reality that the parents cannot exercise leadership, or that one of the parents is to blame, or that they have a set of impossible-to-control children. Valerie can be encouraged to assert herself more forcefully with her older son rather than speaking in a manner that is already resigned to being ignored or defied. By doing so she can begin to create change within the family and thus challenge the original view of the family.

Useful techniques to help reframe the family's view of the situation include *enactment, focusing, and achieving intensity* (Minuchin & Fishman, 1981). Enactment occurs as the family therapist sets the stage for the family to reenact the family patterns within the counseling session. The therapist can ask the family to discuss a specific matter of concern within the session (Aponte, 2003; Minuchin & Fishman, 1981). The therapist can also use spontaneous interaction in the family session to identify and transform patterns.

The therapist changes the meaning of these events and "suggests alternative ways of acting that become actualized in the therapeutic system" (Minuchin & Fishman, 1981, p. 77). When Alicia and Matt describe their situation as impossible because the children are not able to listen to them, the therapist can challenge this interpretation in terms of their children doing what comes naturally to children, testing out their parents to see if they will actually follow through on what they say. The symptom is challenged as family members try these alternatives and experience their family members and the family in different ways.

As the family therapist suggests alternative ways to view and experience the interactions, he can present this information in such a way that it heightens the intensity of the experience. The family therapist can intensify the family's response by insisting that they persist in reaching a goal rather than giving up or by exaggerating the expected behaviors. For example, when the children do not listen to Alicia and Matt—as is typical and the parents follow their usual pattern of throwing up their hands and giving up on making a difference—the therapist can encourage the parents to come together in the session and to persist until they have evidence that the children are listening to them. Valerie is encouraged to speak in a firmer tone with her children and to insist that her son listen to her when she is talking to him. The family's response to this intervention reflects the flexibility of the family patterns. The therapist's pressure to persist rather than giving up as they do at home raises the intensity of the situation. Change in the behavioral patterns within the family are also used to change the meaning that family members have given to this situation. The use of enactments can address some of the core dynamics in families (Fellenberg, 2004).

The family therapist uses focus to organize the data around the theme. The therapist selects a specific pattern of interaction and focuses the session on this aspect. The therapist tracks with the family the sequence of behavior related to these themes as part of the assessment and treatment process. By changing the outcome of the pattern of interaction during the therapy session, the therapist has begun to challenge the previous reality and replace it with a more effective one (Minuchin & Fishman, 1981). As Alicia and Matt and Valerie are able to be more effective with their children in the sessions, they can begin to challenge their previous hopeless view of reality and replace it with a view of themselves as more effective parents.

Challenge the family structure. Family life is organized along long-standing patterns. The long-standing nature of these is often reflected in comments made by family members (She has always been that way; He never listens to me; That's the way it has been with us; She has always been a stubborn kid). Dysfunctional patterns can involve the range of overaffiliation (overinvolvement) or underaffiliation (lack of appropriate closeness). The social worker uses both her role in the family system and her relative freedom to challenge the structure and support the development of other structures. The family therapist can challenge the parents' view that they are powerless by supporting the parents' joining forces to insist on setting limits on the children during the session. The therapist can help Valerie identify some consequences that are in her control in asserting her leadership and point to potential sources of support within her extended family members. The therapist can insist on talking with the family isolate whom the other family members ignore and thus potentially alter the role of this person within the family structure.

The therapist uses a strengths-based perspective to highlight and reinforce positive areas of functioning within the family interaction. The therapist can comment on even small examples in which Alicia and Matt are joining together and thus punctuate the interaction cycle in a positive manner. Valerie's therapist can comment on the way in which she demonstrates her authority with the younger children. The therapist seeks such opportunities within the session and stops the current action (*punctuates the action to give meaning*) to highlight such a positive family dance step. Such strengths-based approaches help alter family patterns and negative views of reality about the family.

The family therapist tries to avoid doing for the family what the family members can do for themselves. When the therapist takes over for the family members, the inadvertent message can be that the family members are incompetent. Thus instead of the therapist "helping the parents" by setting limits on the children in the session (which translates into the message that the parents are incompetent to do so), the therapist sets the stage so that the parents begin to take these steps and are confirmed by the therapist for their actions. As a result, instead of the therapist's setting limits on Alicia and Matt's children, the therapist would continue to find ways to encourage and support the efforts of Alicia and Matt and highlight what they are able to accomplish.

Minuchin and Fishman (1981) describe the techniques of boundary making, unbalancing, and teaching complementarity. Boundary making helps family members create meaningful subsystems that enable the family to function more effectively. Unbalancing refers to "altering the hierarchical relationship of the members of a subsystem" (Minuchin & Fishman, 1981, p. 161). The counselor temporarily takes sides to change the family interaction or broadens the focus of the situation.

Alicia and Matt have had difficulty creating an effective parental subsystem. Not only have they been overwhelmed by the children, but they have been quick to criticize each other rather than to work as a team. Like all intelligent children, their children have long learned the route of divide and conquer to prevent the parents from creating a firm stance. The social worker helps the two parents join forces (boundary making) despite the efforts of the children to continue the older patterns. As the children, led by the oldest son, try to distract the parents and interrupt the parents' discussion, the social worker acts to keep them focused on their discussion rather than being distracted. This intervention helps to establish boundaries around the parental subsystem. As the children continue to try their well-tested divide-and-conquer maneuvers in the family session, the worker uses her influence to support the alliance between the parents and their right to set limits on the boys (unbalancing). In this process the parents begin to give each other increased support and begin to exert more effective leadership with the children. As the parents do so, the social worker also highlights this interaction to help the family perceive itself in a more positive manner and the parents to view themselves as a more effective team.

In another family system, the social worker might observe that one of the family members is consistently absent from the family conversation or perhaps his comments are disqualified by other family members. In this situation, the worker might alter the family structure by engaging this isolate in conversation or carefully attending to the words of this person.

Teaching complementarity refers to understanding that problems within the family result from family patterns "to see their behaviors as part of the larger whole" (Minchin & Fishman, 1981, p. 194) rather than residing within one member of the family. Rather than simply defining the children as "uncooperative" or defining Alicia or Matt or Valerie as an "ineffective parent," family members can begin to experience the ongoing reciprocity of the pattern that occurs within the family with consequent possibility for change.

Repetition plays an important role in structural family therapy because long-standing patterns become habitual and do not change immediately. The family therapist identifies other areas in which similar patterns occur and seeks to change the family interaction pattern in these settings also. Through such repetition change in the family structure emerges. Alicia and Matt might unite initially around one issue with the older son. The therapist would then help them practice similar strategies with the other boys as they relate to other issues and find ways to solidify their own relationship. Valerie might begin by not letting her son interrupt her so that she can finish her sentences. She can then be helped to practice her leadership skills by insisting that he listen to what she is saying or by placing consequences on his making derogatory comments about her. The therapist's focus on this interactional pattern and the structure that it supports thus gains increased power through repetition.

Challenge the family's reality. As family members change their structure and patterns of behaving, they also begin to experience their family and context differently and cognitive changes occur within family members in terms of the family. Such an experience is part of altering the family's view of reality. Alicia and Matt can begin to shift from viewing their children as impossible to control and each other as ineffective parents. Their therapist highlights these new views of reality by emphasizing the evidences of strength. Valerie can begin to view herself as a parent who can assert some control over her children. As indicated earlier, the family therapist actively seeks out constructive patterns as well as attempts to encourage them in order to replace the family's negative reality with more constructive conceptions of the family. Symbols and metaphors can be used to capture this new view of reality (Minuchin & Fishman, 1981).

Treatment Principles

Aponte (2003) describes the following basic principles of intervention that provide the foundation for structural family therapy. These principles can help families develop and strengthen the effective leadership that contributes to resilience in families.

Focus on concrete issues. The counselor should direct the therapy to that which the family views as urgent and important to the needs of family members. "Structural therapists look for concrete issues rooted in current life experiences which carry the deepest investment and motivation for change in the life of clients" (Aponte, 2003, p. 108). Because this issue affects the family in this manner, it also helps mobilize the family's efforts to try to address it. Change can be difficult for families with hard choices and changes to make. Addressing important problems helps provide adequate motivation to mobilize people to make these changes. Motivation is also supported by the moral and spiritual beliefs of family members.

Locate in the present. The past is embedded in the present of family relationships and is thus amenable to change through the present. Selecting issues that are meaningful in the present carries these messages from the past. As a result, by working through current issues, the counselor can address the deeper structural and dynamic forces.

Mediate interventions through the client's experience in the session. "The principal field of intervention for the SFT is the family's enactment of their issues in the session" (Aponte, 2003, p. 108). Enacting family issues within the session activates both the intellectual and emotional aspects of the family members. The therapist either takes advantage of spontaneous situations that arise in the session or creates such opportunities within the family session. As family members enact new behaviors in the session, they experience new aspects of themselves and their family relations and thus potentially begin to revise the structure of the family and their view of the family.

Reorganize the structure of relationships. "Structural therapists intervene to resolve conflict, repair brokenness, and build new strengths in the underlying structure of issues that clients present" (Aponte, 2003, p. 109). Therapeutic interventions are designed to realign family structures that create family distress and to replace them with structures that are more effective in meeting the needs of family members.

Build on client strengths (Aponte, 2003, p. 109). Structural therapists search for strengths within family members and seek to build on the power of change within the family to create more effective family patterns. They seek to tap whatever strengths are involved within family members, the immediate and extended family system, the support system, and the community to enable families to create and maintain these patterns. The social worker can highlight family strengths by punctuating the interaction after family members have demonstrated an effective interaction. The therapist uses her stage manager role to stop the action at the end of an interactional sequence that demonstrates strength on the part of a family member and that supports strengthening family leadership. The family therapist acknowledges the power of the family members to make critical decisions for the family.

Aim at palpable outcomes. "The family therapist enters the family's struggle through the enactment, the actual reliving of the family drama in the session" (Aponte, 2003, p. 110). The therapist seeks to create within the family session opportunities for family members to interact with each other in new ways that offer more promising alternatives and outcomes that contribute to positive change within the family.

Homework is used to supplement the actions that are taking place within the session. People have further opportunities to experience these new interaction patterns. "When people experience a change in a new, palpable experience, it reaches deep, taking root more profoundly in the heart of the psyche and the relationship" (Aponte, 2003, pp. 110–111). Alicia and Matt are given homework that includes activities that they view will strengthen their relationship as a couple, as man and wife, and also as parents. Valerie is given homework on specific ways that she can continue asserting her authority at home. If she feels in need of support from another adult, she can be given the homework of seeking out support from one of the members of the extended family to help strengthen her role as a parent. Matt is given homework in terms of ways that he can support Alicia in her leadership role.

Intervene through the active involvement of the practitioner with the family (Aponte, 2003, p. 111). The family therapist engages the family in new ways of relating and relates with the family in ways that promote these new behaviors. The therapist begins this process through joining with the family in order to create trust and to enable the counselor to begin to make changes within the family structure. Counselors use themselves in a creative and active manner to challenge old patterns, unbalance rigid structures, and encourage more adaptive patterns. Such active use of the self requires a careful knowledge of the self by the counselors.

Spirituality as a potential resource. Aponte (2003) also describes the important role of spirituality in terms of family strengths. Spirituality gives some family members valuable resources in term of a sense of meaning as well as potentially faith communities and a relationship with God (p. 110).

Nichols and Fellenberg (2000) identify elements of implementing enactments that seem to be associated with a positive shift in the family interaction process. Unsuccessful interactions are those in which there is no evidence that change has occurred. The strategies of the therapist are examined in terms of initiating, facilitating, and closing the enactments.

Initiate the enactment. Successful enactments were more likely to occur if the therapist took a directive stance in terms of getting the individuals to talk with each other and specifying the topic of the conversation, and at the same time removing the worker's own chair away from the interaction. Unsuccessful enactments included not positioning people to talk with each other, not specifying the topic or the way to talk with each other, and not moving the counselor's chair away.

Facilitate the enactment. Once the family members began with the enactment, the following actions by the family therapist were associated with productive enactments. Positive actions of the therapist included not interrupting family members once they began talking with each other, and engaging family members to continue speaking to each other rather than the therapist. When enactments began to bog down, two kinds of interaction seemed helpful: "pushing family members to keep talking or to explain themselves more fully or digging beneath the surface of defenses, for example, probing deeper into clients' feelings or points of view, encouraging family members to try harder to understand what each other was feeling" (Nichols & Fellenberg, 2000, p. 146), and offering encouragement to family members. On the other hand, problematic interventions included the counselor's interrupting family members prematurely or interjecting oneself before clients had a chance to communicate with each other.

Close the enactment. In line with efforts to help family members challenge their current reality, it is helpful to close the enactment by the therapist's helping the family to recognize the meaning of this event for their understanding of their family life. Thus family members are able to recognize the meaning that this interaction has for the future possible interactions between family members. For example, following an enactment in which Alicia and Matt were helped to stop blaming each other and instead to join forces and insist that the children listen to them, the therapist could point out the problematic dynamics that occurred when they would blame each other and the positive changes that occurred when they joined forces. The therapist could praise them for their efforts and emphasize the need for future efforts in this regard. In contrast, closing the enactment without commentary is not helpful (Nichols & Fellenburg, 2000).

Nichols and Fellenberg (2000) suggest three major lessons. (1) Family therapists must guard against interjecting themselves too quickly. "The important thing is that family members test their resources, get past the point where they are tempted to give up, and feel the pressure to speak up and to listen until they get somewhere" (p. 152). Family therapists need to help families keep the dialogue going rather than intervene too quickly. (2) When family members seem to bog down in unproductive blaming or bickering, it can be effective for the counselor to probe deeper into the feelings— frequently to get to the hurt behind the anger. Once family members open up with these feelings, the therapist again backs away to encourage the family members to continue their conversation. (3) The process of family members' improving their ability to communicate was more important than whether or not they agreed with each other. Interventions that enabled family members to learn something about themselves and clear guidelines for continued improved communication were important in enactments.

Cultural Adaptations

Families seeking help come from a wide variety of cultural backgrounds that influence family patterns. The Spanish Family Guidance Center in Miami was established to offer services to the local Hispanic community and subsequently broadened its services to families from other cultural backgrounds. In the process, the center adapted the structural family model to be responsive to families from different cultures. The counselors recognized that family structures were also impacted by social systems external to the family (e.g., school, neighborhood) and thus that the intervention needed to include the interactive patterns between families and these systems as well as patterns within the immediate family. The treatment approach thus began to incorporate a multisystem approach as well as a structural approach within the family itself. This broadened approach is called Structural Ecosystems Theory. Similar to structural therapy described earlier in this chapter, this model includes the concept of the need to look at repetitive patterns of interactions between parts of the system with the goal of identifying and changing maladaptive patterns of interactions that keep the family from reaching its goals (Kurtines & Szapocznik, 1996). The following is a discussion of some of the cultural adaptations involved in using the structural family therapy model with families from different cultural groups.

Cultural context and norms are important considerations in the assessment process. Cultures that value the extended family and kinship networks might have different patterns of the executive system than families that emphasize the nuclear family. Such patterns can occur and be very adaptive, for example, within Hispanic, Asian, and African American families. The grandmother/mother subsystem in which a single mother lives with her mother can represent the executive subsystem. Within Asian American families, the husband's mother can play an important role in shaping the behavior of her daughter-in-law in a culturally sanctioned manner. The important question is—what arrangement is functional given this cultural context? What do cultural norms support as adaptive? (Kurtines & Szapocznik, 1996).

Joining with the family is also influenced by the culture of the family. In the process of joining, the counselor must respect the culturally influenced nature of the family. For example, in families from Hispanic and Asian communities in which respect for those with power in the family hierarchy (especially the parents and grandparents) is important, Grant (1999) stresses the need for the therapist leadership role not to usurp their power. The therapist must also respect the family's definition of who are family members in terms of those who participate in the session. Fictive kin, informal adoptions, godparents, and others who are engaged in family roles all can play key roles in the family treatment process.

The amount of closeness between family members varies depending on the cultural context. Hispanic family members, for example, tend to be closer than are members of Anglo families. When family members interrupt and speak for each other, it could reflect cultural patterns that value closeness rather than signs of problematic enmeshment. Whether or not it is problematic depends on its function within the specific family rather than any abstract concept regarding what are appropriate levels of cohesion, and so on (Kurtines & Szapocznik, 1996).

Developmental issues that influence family roles and structure also vary depending on culture. These differences also vary within cultural groups depending on subgroup membership. Kurtines and Szapocznik (1996) describe intracultural differences, for example, "in a Hispanic migrant family, it might be expected that an 8-year-old girl miss school to work with the family in the fields. Yet, in an urban context in some Latin American cities, a 16-year-old girl may not be allowed to date unchaperoned" (p. 678). Cultures also differ in terms of the extent to which children are expected to provide support for parents and extended family members.

Conflict resolution styles also reflect cultural differences (Kurtines & Szapocznik, 1996). Hispanic families, for example, frequently use conflict diffusion rather than conflict emergence with resolution.

Reframing, one of the key strategies in restructuring families, is also influenced by culture. The meaning of events varies between cultures and thus what is considered as admirable within one culture might be given a different meaning in others. A graduate student belonging to one of the First People American nations indicated to his Anglo professor that he was going to take a break in writing his dissertation because he needed to be home to take care of his ill father. From the perspective of his culture, caring for family members was an essential priority. The student described his hurt and anger when his faculty advisor accused him of not taking his studies seriously.

Working with boundaries and alliances is another key strategy in structural family therapy. Again, culture influences the nature of adaptive boundaries and appropriate alliances. In working with single-parent families within, for example, the Hispanic and African American cultures, the counselor might be able to take advantage of opportunities within the extended family to support the mother (Kurtines & Szapocznik, 1996). As indicated in the chapter on culture, this depends on the assessment of whether or not the extended family supports or undermines the mother in her authority role.

Evaluation

Structural family approaches have been useful in working with families presenting with a variety of problems. Jordan and Franklin (1999) describe it as demonstrating more effectiveness with families that are enmeshed rather than disengaged. There has been extensive support for the value of structural family therapy with families dealing with anorexia, various psychosomatic problems (Minuchin, Rosman, & Baker, 1978), and drug addiction (Aponte, 2003). Structural family therapy has been an effective approach with Latino families (Grant, 1999; Romeo, 2000) and African American families (Grant, 1999). Early versions of structural family therapy have been criticized as being too rigid in terms of gender roles, especially in terms of supporting a patriarchal view of family hierarchy that disadvantaged women (Jordan & Franklin, 1999). At the same time, the model offers the opportunity to use the basic techniques in ways that are supportive of flexible gender roles that meet the needs of the family.

Summary

Structural family therapy can be a useful family therapy approach because it helps develop and support the leadership structures within families that are needed for meeting the needs of family members. Efforts to create appropriate leadership systems can enhance the organizational patterns of families that contribute to family resiliency, while lack of such leadership represents an important risk factor. These efforts also alter the family's view of the situation. An understanding of cultural patterns is important because they influence the nature of these organizational patterns and thus the approaches that are appropriate. Structural family therapy sessions emphasize the active role of the therapist along with the present life of the family and change that occurs within the sessions themselves.

DISCUSSION QUESTIONS

Discuss what it means to call the therapist a stage manager.

Describe the interaction between family beliefs and behavior in the change process in structural family therapy.

Discuss ways in which the therapist can use herself or himself to alter the family interaction process.

When might there be times in which the therapist would abandon a position of neutrality?

8

Solution-Focused Family Therapy

As discussed in chapter 3, Mr. and Mrs. Norris have begun to define their relationship in terms of the difficulties and tensions that are present and have lost sight of other possibilities in their family relations. The solution-focused treatment model could be appropriate for this set of risks and resiliency factors. Mr. and Mrs. Norris are discouraged and have begun to view their family relationships as marked by tension and disagreements. This family situation suggests the need to create hope for the possibility of change. The couple has some realistic problems to address but have become discouraged by their disagreements and have come to define themselves and their family in these terms. Their negative and discouraged view of the situation has hindered their ability to envision and create new alternatives and thus to address their problems in an effective manner. Helping them recognize the presence of exceptions and enabling them to identify steps that will help solve their family problems can be important for this family. Such steps can help change their definition of the reality of family and thus enable them to use their creativity to begin to solve family problems.

Martha Martin and Joyce Kimble have been living together for the past year and a half. Martha has an eight-year-old daughter, Megan, from her marriage to George Martin. About four years ago she began to feel that her marriage to George did not fit her increasing identity as a lesbian. The process of revealing this to George was a difficult one and there is ongoing tension between the two. Her parents were distressed at the time but gradually came to support her decision. George's parents have remained distant from her although they continue to send cards and gifts to their granddaughter. George initially threatened that he would deny Martha custody of their daughter but came to terms with the situation and the two now share custody. In the meantime George has remarried and his second wife is pregnant. Both families live in the same community. Martha and George share the parental roles in important ways, including support when discipline was required. Martha works as a computer programmer. George is a teacher and contributes financially to the care of Megan. Joyce has a twelve-year-old daughter, Stephanie. She and her first husband have been divorced for over ten years and he subsequently died of cancer. She has ongoing contact with her extended family, who initially found her lesbian identity difficult but after a few years became reconciled and have recently been supportive of her. Her husband's family has stayed distant. Joyce is an office manager of a medical office. The two met through mutual friends and were friends for about a year before living together. They are members of a support group of lesbian mothers in their community.

Martha and Joyce contact the office because they are having difficulty creating an effective family group. While the two women care deeply for each other and their children, they have had difficulty in working out their parenting styles with the girls. Joyce and her daughter have been extremely close during these years. In many ways, the two became the chief support for the each other and Joyce found it difficult to set limits on her daughter. While extremely organized and able to deal with difficult people at work, as a parent she assumed more a best friend rather than parental role. Martha and Megan moved into Joyce's house because it is larger and each girl is able to have her own bedroom.

Stephanie has found it very difficult to accept her mother's new relationship with Martha and Megan. She shows her resentment toward both of them in many ways. She vocalizes her unhappiness about having to share the house with them. She refuses to accept any of the limits that Martha sets for her and is openly critical of Martha. Faced with this situation, Megan withdraws or tries to avoid spending time home and turns more to her father. She has started asking her mother if they can return to their old home. While Martha and Joyce want their new relationship to succeed, this tension is causing them to question if this arrangement is a good one. The two have begun arguing increasingly about how to co-parent. They turned for help to their support group, who have been sympathetic and encouraged them to seek professional help.

This family has some important risk and protective factors. In terms of protective factors, Martha and Joyce have a strong commitment to each other and to their daughters. They have employment that gives them an adequate economic base. Their work performance demonstrates their intelligence and ability to relate effectively with others. They have a support group of friends as well as extended family members. Risk factors include their socially marginalized status as a lesbian family. While they receive support from friends, there is no legal support for their relationship and thus separation remains more of an option. They are struggling with the skills of co-parenting with each other, especially because their parenting styles are quite different. Stephanie is fearful of the loss of her close relationship with her mother at the same time she is entering into the developmentally insecure world of pre-adolescence. They have become demoralized and discouraged about their ability to cope with the current situation.

Solution-focused therapy offers them an opportunity to regain a sense of hope that their relationship can survive by identifying times in which things are going better. It mobilizes their energy to focus on potential solutions to their situation. It further looks at the small steps that can make this possible.

Theoretical Background

Solution-focused family therapy is an important school of treatment within the brief family treatment model. Solution-focused therapy emphasizes the family's strengths and sources of resiliency to promote positive change. The focus on solutions and the value of small changes has enabled solution-focused therapy to be viewed as a brief therapy model. With a focus on the future, treatment is organized around successfully achieving the identified goals rather than understanding the origin of the problem. Families are helped to draw upon their coping strategies and to expand their repertoire to meet their goals. With the belief that people and families are constantly changing, the emphasis is on helping families envision and create positive changes within the family. The therapist engenders hope by identifying signs of previous successful functioning as evidence of the potential for future progress (Berg & Dolan, 2001; Homrich & Horne, 2000; O'Connell, 1998). Berg and Dolan (2001) summarize the philosophy of solution-focused therapy as "the pragmatics of hope and respect" (p. 1).

The solution-focused approach enables family members to focus on the solutions that have been or might be helpful in creating new realities for the family. From this perspective, family members are doing the best that they can. They may lack the skills, or more likely, lack the awareness that they have the skills to engage in solving the problem and thus feel stuck (Homrich & Horne, 2000; Koob, 2003). Recognizing that families frequently come to treatment with a reduced sense of self-mastery about their ability to address their situation and are concentrating almost exclusively on the problems that they are facing, solution-focused therapy places the spotlight on family actions that can solve these problems. It expands the family's vision of reality to incorporate the possibilities that can enable them to reach their desired goals. Such efforts can enhance hope. The emphasis is on creating solutions (emphasis on future possibilities) rather than solving problems (emphasis on problems) (Berg & Dolan, 2001; Butler & Powers, 1996; Koob, 2003; Nichols & Schwartz, 2001). The approach has grown extremely popular in a world in which brief treatment is valued by managed care as well as by family members.

The founders of solution-focused treatment began their work at the Brief Family Therapy Center in Milwaukee. I remember attending early workshops with one of the leaders, Steve de Shazer, whose theme in these presentations was to "find out what is working with the family and help the family do more of this." Important contributors to the development of the clinical aspects of solution-focused treatment include Insook Kim Berg, Eve Lipcheck, Michele Weiner-Davis, Scott Miller, Peter DeJonge, John Walter, Jane Peller, and Bill O'Hanlon (Nichols & Schwartz, 2001).

Major Tenets

Solution-focused therapy is based on seven tenets.

1. Solution-focused therapy places its emphasis on the future—what in the future will be different or what can be different. The emphasis is on the future because it is in the future (rather than the past or the present) that problems will be solved. As a result, envisioning the future is an important first step.

2. The solution to a problem can be unrelated to how the problem began. As a result, one does not need history as a necessary guide to solve the problem. Understanding the past does not necessarily provide the key to changing the future. Problems can develop a life of their own unrelated to their origin.

3. People are hindered in their efforts to solve problems because they are locked into negative and pessimistic views of the problem and feel unable to solve the problem. They have focused so much on problematic events and aspects of the family that they have forgotten times in which problems did not occur or result. They have become so trapped into the negative meaning systems that they cannot look at the positive alternatives or new ways to attempt to solve their problems. Instead of trying new approaches, they continue using their old methods. When these do not work, they redouble their efforts to try to make things improve.

4. People really do want to change. Solution-focused therapists do not view the family as ambivalent or resistant to change. When family members do not cooperate, it is their way to guide the therapist into more appropriate ways to be helpful. Problems are not viewed as serving some hidden purpose within the family.

5. People are suggestible. People can thus be highly influenced by the theoretical orientation of the counselor. As a result, the interpretations that occur in the sessions between the therapist and the family tend to be influenced by the orientation of the therapist. To avoid this situation, the solution-focused therapist comes to the therapy session with a perspective of not knowing and seeks to identify how the client perceives the nature of the problems and the possibilities for solving them.

An example of how easy it is to view one's own theoretical formulation as the answer occurred when I taught solution-focused therapy to my graduate social work students. Many of them expressed initial frustration with the counselor on the video because she was not addressing the problems that the students were sure were important. Instead the counselor was asking questions of the family members in terms of what was important for them and following up on these issues. These students became further frustrated when the family members did not identify the solution that their (the students) theoretical formulation indicated should be the solution. As the session continued the power of allowing family members to formulate their own views of the key problems and means to solving them emerged. The students then began to realize how the solution-focused approach had empowered individuals to create viable and relevant solutions predicated upon the family's interpretation of key problems and helpful solutions.

6. Language is powerful in shaping reality. Solution-focused therapy is influenced by the constructionist tradition that believes that language shapes reality (deShazer, 1994). As a result, the important task of the therapist is to change the way people talk about their problems. People who have suffered a great deal can thus be described as either victims or survivors. Rather than encouraging clients to continue to talk in terms of their problems, the therapist seeks to have them talk about potential solutions (from problem talk to solution talk).

7. People judge what is important and thus select their own goals. They are the experts on their family. Solution-focused therapy does not prescribe a specific way of living one's life. It recognizes that families choose different ways of life and thus what is appropriate and acceptable for one family may not be so for other families (Nichols & Schwartz, 2005; O'Hanlon & Weiner-Davis, 1989).

Goals of Treatment

Solution-focused therapy seeks to help families reach the goals that they define. Solution-focused therapists have faith that the family can define the appropriate goals and have the skills in order to work toward this goal. Problems occur when people are unable to use their skills because they have lost sight that they have these skills or have become overwhelmed by the problem at hand. Helping families focus on what they are doing right and expanding their own ability to use these skills can be very effective. Such an approach expands the family's vision of their possibilities. Families can also find it difficult to use the skills that they have used in the past because for various reasons these skills are no longer part of their current behavior pattern. As a result, the therapist needs to find ways to help the family members begin to restore these skills and use them to address their problem.

Goals in solution-focused therapy represent the presence of something positive, rather than the absence of something negative. Goals are also most effective if they are phrased in concrete behavioral terms (what someone will be doing differently) that are measurable (DeJong & Berg, 1998, p. 74). A related process goal is to help family members shift from talking about problems to talking about solutions. Families who can make this shift can begin to build on the solutions that emerge from these new conversations.

Solution-focused therapy is organized around accomplishing modest goals. The very step of helping individuals set goals that are clear and achievable represents an important intervention. It is part of the solution-focused approach to help individuals think about their future and how they want it to be different. The assumption is that such an effort sets in motion the possibility for ongoing positive change in the family. These small changes can alter the direction of the change that is ongoing within the family in a positive manner. These changes also influence the way in which the family envisions itself and the future (Walter & Peller, 1996).

Promotes Resiliency by

- Addressing risk factors associated with belief systems that are negative and pessimistic about possibilities for the family and ability to meet family needs and lack of effective coping strategies.

- Supporting protective factors by changing negative and pessimistic belief systems to those that give hope and enable family members to improve positive interactions, helping family members identify what is possible and to build on it, promoting family affection and appropriate coping strategies, improving family communication, and enlisting potential sources of social support as identified as helpful by the family.

Role of the Therapist

The therapist assumes a not-knowing stance with family members as the experts regarding the family and their solutions. The stance of the therapist is one who asks questions to elicit the family's goals, their view of potential solutions, and behavior patterns that exemplify exceptions to the problem stance.

The following represent some possible questions:

"What do you think the problem is now?"

"How will you know when the problem is solved?"

"How will you know when you don't have to come here any more?

What will the signs be?" (Nichols & Schwartz, 2005, p. 238).

While clients often begin talking about what others will be doing differently, the therapist can gradually expand this set of questions to include what the clients will also be doing differently (DeJong & Berg, 1998, p.74).

The counselor also works toward a related process goal of helping the family members shift from talking about problems to talking about solutions. As discussed previously, the counselor also recognizes the importance of accomplishing modest goals because doing so can create significant family change.

The therapist also acts as an encourager for the family. The therapist comments in an affirming manner about any evidence that family members can change in a positive manner and are able to solve their problematic issues (DeJong & Berg, 1998). The twin major roles of the therapist are to provide acknowledgment and possibility (Butler & Powers, 1996). Acknowledgment refers to the therapist's being with the family in their life circumstances. The therapist makes comments that convey to the family members that the therapist understands and empathizes with their current situation. Possibility refers to the therapist's orientation to the future when the current problems are resolved. The therapist brings a stance of curiosity to learn how the family will solve their problems. Possibility also conveys to the family the therapist's view that such positive change is possible in the life in the family.

As in all models of family therapy, therapists must always tailor interventions to the individuals involved and to the matter of timing. Technique is only effective in the context of an empathic collaborative relationship between the therapist and the family. As in other therapy models, this can mean ensuring that family members feel understood in terms of the reality of their situation. Clients might need to express their pain and fears and feel that their therapist understands this aspect of their lives before they are able to take the next step to look at the future and solutions. Failure to do so can make these potentially effective techniques appear mechanical. I taught for a brief time in a community in which solution-focused treatment was very prominent. Students reported that their clients would sometimes say, "Oh no, not another miracle question." While I could not interview these individuals, I wondered if their comments reflected their sense that the technique had been and was being applied in a rather mechanistic way without giving them the opportunity to feel understood and validated. Thus any discussion and implementation of treatment of any type must be understood with this caveat in mind.

Treatment Process

Treatment is organized around the goals, resources, and exceptions to the problem. The family therapist seeks to identify solutions that are already part of the repertoire of the family members and to expand upon these. Exceptions are evidence that the family can address their problems in more effective ways.

The process of expanding on solutions is a collaborative effort on the part of the therapist and the family members. The solution-focused therapist is willing to work with the members of the family who are willing to come.

Identification of positive elements (compliments). The therapist focuses on already existing family strengths. Complimenting the family members for positive elements (for example, they are still together, they came for help, the children are in school, the children are neatly dressed, a parent is employed, a spouse listened to the other partner, a parent set limits appropriately with a child) represents an important strength-based approach. Identifying these positive elements can lead to transformations that can be enhanced through more specific solution-focused approaches. Berg and DeJong (2005) describe three types of compliments: direct—observing something useful in clients and bringing it to the attention of the family members; indirect—asking questions from the perspective of others familiar with the family; and self—phrasing questions that result in family members describing a strength—perhaps for the first time.

In addition to the general emphasis upon looking for interactions that represent an exception to the problem and a focus on the family's view of potential solutions, several key techniques have emerged in solution-focused treatment. These techniques take the form of questions, with the family as the expert on the family.

What do you want to continue? (Formula One). Following the first session, family members are asked to observe their family during the next week (or until the next session) to identify what happens in their family they would like to continue (the Formula One questions). This homework assignment places the family members in the role of looking for exceptions to the problem and positive aspects about the family (DeJong & Berg, 1998; Nichols & Schwartz, 2001).

The miracle question. The therapist formulates the miracle question to help family members begin to develop their solutions (Nichols & Schwartz, 2001, p. 376). "Suppose one night you were asleep, there was a miracle and this problem was solved. How would you know? What would be different?" This question is designed to help family members look beyond the immediate problem and to visualize what it is that they want. The emphasis then becomes one of helping family members construct the steps that they view would enable them to make these changes possible. The counselor asks a series of questions designed to identify what small and manageable step would indicate that things were different. As people are able to take more steps that move in the direction of the desired goal, the problem itself becomes less of an issue.

DeJong and Berg (1998) remind therapists that asking the client to imagine how life will be changed when the problem is solved can be difficult. Use of the miracle question represents a major shift in the client's thinking. They suggest several techniques that can be helpful to make this transition in using the miracle question with families. The first involves the therapist's use of the voice. Speaking slowly and softly helps the client make the shift from the problem to a solution focus. Introducing the miracle as something unusual or strange marks it as a new approach. Using future-directed words helps the client think in terms of the future—"What would be different? What will be signs of the miracle?" (DeJong & Berg, 1998, p. 78). Repeating a phrase during the follow-up questions, such as "a miracle happens when the problem that you brought here is solved" (p. 78), helps to reinforce the transition to solution talk. Refocusing the client's attention to what will be different when the miracle occurs can be helpful when the client returns to problem talk (DeJong & Berg, 1998).

The exception question. This question is designed to elicit from the family members the times in which the problem did not exist or occurred to a lesser degree. In the case of Mr. and Mrs. Norris, exceptions would occur when were they able to agree on their son, to support each other in dealing with a problem, to come together on ways to help Mrs. Norris's father. For Martha and Joyce it might represent a meal in which the four were able to talk about what happened that day without it turning into a verbal battle or Stephanie walking away from the table in anger. For another family the questions might revolve around when they could discuss finances without a fight (or a lesser degree of conflict) or show the other party that they appreciated them. Exploring these times opens the door to examining how these exceptions occurred. This information enables family members to begin expanding these times. As family members are able to expand their exceptions, they are able to develop a greater self of self-efficacy and mastery in dealing with the problems (DeJong & Berg, 1998).

Scaling questions. Scaling questions can help enable individuals to identify more clearly what they want, to move them beyond all-or-nothing thinking, and to think in terms of small steps. Family members are helped to identify what small changes can make a difference in the life of their family and ways to accomplish these changes. Scaling questions can relate to family members' perceptions of the seriousness of the problem and of their confidence that they can make changes. Family members can be asked these types of scaling questions.

First, family members are asked to indicate on a scale from 1 to 10 how *serious* they view the problem. One can be described in terms of just terrible and no hope while 10 can represent the lack of any problem. If family members describe themselves at 4, they can be asked what might make it possible for them to see their family situation at 5. This question sets the stage for engaging family members in strategizing what steps or actions would make it possible for this change to occur.

A second scaling question relates to the issue of *motivation*: How motivated are you? How hard are you willing to work to help solve this problem? Family members can be asked what could help increase their motivation. This information can be used to identify sources of motivation and ways to enhance it.

A third scaling question relates to the issue of *confidence:* How confident are you that you can do what has been identified? Answers to this question can identify what might be blocking one's being able to change or issues that can facilitate it. Family members can be encouraged to identify small steps that might help address these issues to support confidence (DeJong & Berg, 1998).

The family therapist takes a hopeful and encouraging approach to families. This hopeful approach supports the possibility side of the solution-focused approach. The family therapist acknowledges evidence of small positive changes, successes, and efforts to respond in new ways. The therapist continually seeks evidence of exceptions and elicits information about how the family members make this possible. During the session and in the end-of-session-feedback the emphasis is upon the competencies of the family.

Solution-focused therapy distinguishes between *customers* and *complainants*. In this context customers are concerned about the problem and are willing to change to make things better. Complainants are concerned about the problem but are not yet willing to change to improve the situation. One of the challenges of the solution-focused therapist is to move complainants into customers. A useful strategy is to help individuals identify the advantage to them of this change. For example, an adolescent might see the advantage of gaining the trust of his parents because he would have more freedom. A family might view less intense supervision from the Department of Children and Families as worth the effort. *Visitors* are individuals who are neither concerned about the problem nor willing to change (DeJong & Berg, 1998).

Application: Case Illustrations

The following describes a prototypical two-session therapy scenario using solution-focused therapy (Koob, 2003).

Session 1. The family therapist seeks to identify who in the family are customers because these individuals will help ensure that change will occur. This may be evidenced by the family member who speaks first or who made the contact with the agency. A useful technique is to ask the family "Who is most concerned about resolving this problem? Who is second? Who is third?" (Koob, 2003, p. 136).

As described earlier in chapter 2, the therapist joins with the family by listening in an empathic manner to their concerns, identifying the nature of the problems cited, and asking family members how they have managed to cope. This combination serves to help the family members feel that they have been heard and understood as well as places the focus on the potential strengths of the family. The conversation regarding how the family members have coped also helps them identify positive exceptions in the current life of the family. The therapist expresses (compliments) these positive elements with the family.

If family members are able to engage in solution-focused conversation, the therapist can ask the miracle question described earlier in this chapter. The therapist can then pursue the answers given by family members to identify clearly what are the specific changes and actions that would represent the desired change and the solution.

Family members are then asked to rank by scaling questions how close they are to reaching this miracle. The therapist can comment favorably if they indicate that they are at least halfway there. The therapist can comment on any step beyond one—how despite all the many problems you describe have you managed to keep up some hope for things becoming better? Since solution-focused treatment is based on encouraging the family to at least make small changes, the therapist asks family members what would have to happen for them to move ahead from 5 to 6, or a fraction of a number if this seems too great a change. This latter part helps move the family members into a solution-focused conversation. Family members can also be asked how motivated and how confident they are about being able to do so. Answers can be used to identify what would help family members become more motivated or confident as well as what enables them to be as motivated and confident as they are now.

The therapist then takes a break to consider the issue and to consult with a team located behind the one-way mirror (if such resources exist). The therapist returns with a message that includes the following components: compliments for the family, normalizations, reframes (positive). The therapist then prescribes the strength-based Formula One: this homework assignment requires observation on the part of family members. "When people enter therapy, they begin to change. There are things in your life, however, that you do not want to change because they are positive. So between now and the next time we meet, pay attention to those positive things in your life, and we will discuss it next week" (Koob, 2003, p. 137).

Session 2. The therapist follows up on the first session by exploring what the family has identified that they want to keep in the family. The therapist also explores positive changes that are described in terms of whether or not this is a new behavior, what made it possible, and how it can be encouraged in the future. If family members do not identify anything positive, the therapist explores in detail to discover any evidence of small signs of positive changes. The family is again asked to scale their situation. Positive changes are marked by asking what made this possible and how it can be kept going. When situations are either the same or worse, the therapist can ask what the family did to prevent things from getting even worse.

The therapist also uses *presuppositional* questions. These questions involve asking the family members to identify circumstances that occur either before or after the exceptions that might enhance such exceptions. These questions have a strengths-based focus. They emphasize what family members did to make the difference that helped the family members reach their goals. What did your husband (wife) do that made you feel that you could work together as parents? What did your parents do that helped you feel that they understood how difficult school is for you right now?

Solution-focused therapists can use several other techniques to help family members reach their goals. These are *behavioral tasks* organized around types of actions by the family members. Such tasks are particularly appropriate if the family members have identified clearly defined goals. The specific nature of the tasks involved depends on the goals identified and information about previous behaviors that have been identified as helpful (DeJong & Berg, 1998). The following represent several behavioral tasks.

Do more of what works. This task draws on already identified effective coping strategies within the family. When family members describe something that has helped, family members are encouraged to do more of these actions; for example, "If you are able to talk better when you both take a ten-minute break to cool off, do this when you are getting angry trying to solve this problem in your family."

Do something different. When families report their failed attempt to address a problem, the therapist can encourage them to experiment and think of some other approach. This task encourages families to discover their own solutions. It also helps family members break out of rigid and ineffective patterns.

Go slowly. In order to help families overcome any fear of change, the solution-focused therapist can encourage family members to change slowly. The therapist can ask the family, "Could there be any advantages to things staying the way they are?"

Do the opposite. If family members report that their current solutions are not working, they can be encouraged to try the opposite. This technique is based on the idea that current solutions can be maintaining problems. A parent who has been using scolding to correct the behavior of a child can be encouraged to try praise for good behavior.

Prediction task. The therapist instructs the family members "'each night before you go to bed, predict whether or not things will be better. At the end of the day, examine if your prediction was correct. Account for any differences between your prediction and the way the day went and keep track of your observations so that you can come back and tell me about them'" (DeJong & Berg, 1998, p. 124). This task can help people gain a sense of patterns that are associated with improvement and increase their expectation for change.

The following cases illustrate the application of solution-focused family treatment. This discussion is quite detailed in order to show how the worker can grant the family the position of decision maker in the counseling process (goals, methods to reach these goals) while at the same serving as the leader to guide this process.

Application: The Norris Family

As described earlier, Mr. and Mrs. Norris's relationship has become organized around disagreements regarding their son and his disappointing academic achievement and ways to provide help for Mrs. Norris's father. Mr. and Mrs. Norris have begun to define their relationship in terms of these two concerns and points of disagreement.

Session 1. Mr. and Mrs. Norris arrive for the first session somewhat nervous about whether or not therapy can really help their difficult problems. Since Mrs. Norris in her role as mother and daughter has felt the burden of the problems on her shoulders more than Mr. Norris, she made the call and speaks up first in the session. The social worker asks both Mr. and Mrs. Norris how the therapy session can be of help to them—how will they know if therapy has been helpful to them. Framing the question in this way permits the family to express their concerns regarding their family but sets the stage for a forward stance in terms of the therapy effort. Mrs. Norris begins to describe their worry about their son as well as the burden she is feeling in terms of her father. The social worker is careful to ensure that Mr. Norris also has the opportunity to express his concerns.

The social worker listens empathically to the concerns of both parties— their worries about their son, their frustration about being unable to talk about and reach any agreement on how to handle the situation, the tension about Mrs. Norris's father and how to handle this trouble. Mrs. Norris describes their concern about their son Jason who is not doing well in college. They are afraid that he will drop out of school. She describes how she and her husband have become angry with each other because they are so frustrated and do not know what to do. As a result, they end up blaming each other and accusing the other partner of contributing to the problem because of the way that they have treated the son. Mr. and Mrs. Norris then begin to start blaming each other because of an incident last night. Mrs. Norris goes on to say that she also feels under pressure due to her father and does not feel supported by Mr. Norris because he thinks that she could help solve the problem by taking his advice. This then prompts a brief sharp interchange between the couple. Mrs. Norris accuses Mr. Norris of not understanding and Mr. Norris accuses Mrs. Norris of talking about problems but never wanting to hear any advice. The social worker listens empathically to this exchange but recognizes that the session could easily be consumed by this couple's well-rehearsed negative exchanges. The worker delineates the concerns expressed by Mr. and Mrs. Norris about the son in terms of their shared concern that their son not waste his talents and do well in school and the difficulties in knowing what to do to help an elderly parent.

The social worker moves on to explore and underscore what they hope the therapy session will contribute and what would make them think that their time here was worthwhile. The couple indicates that while they are concerned about both their son and Mrs. Norris's father, they realize that there are some additional community resources that they could use to help with Mrs. Norris's father, and their primary source of contention and worry now is their son. They would like to concentrate on this. Respecting the family's choice of the priority issues, the therapist not only explores further about the nature of the problem but also probes for exceptions—times in which the parents see eye-to-eye about their son. While the parents have limited control over the actions of their son, they are able to control how they view each other as parents and their ability to act as a united front. These questions can also explore times in which they were able to relate to each other as husband and wife rather than anxious parents. The therapist can also explore with the parents any possible times in which their son shows some signs of more responsible behavior.

Recognizing how difficult these situations are for concerned parents, the therapist uses acknowledgment to affirm their role as concerned parents and asks how they have managed to cope as parents with this situation. When Mr. and Mrs. Norris seem puzzled, the therapist explores further how they have managed sometimes to find a way to agree on how to handle their son or at least have handled their differences without the other party feeling put down.

After further listening to the concerns of the family and identifying them so that the family members realize that their concerns have been heard and that they have been acknowledged, the therapist asks the couple if they would be willing to try something different and introduces the miracle question. After some thought, Mrs. Norris states, "I would know that something was different because my husband would listen to my concerns without minimizing them. When he minimizes my concerns, I feel he doesn't respect me and I in turn press the issue further. I find myself then criticizing how he handles our son." Mr. Norris states, "I would know the miracle occurred when my wife would acknowledge that at least I am trying." The therapist asks both to describe exactly what they mean so that everyone can have a clear picture. When asked to describe their view of the seriousness of the problem on a scale from 1 to 10, Mrs. Norris describes it as 5 and Mr. Norris as 6. The therapist then asks each of the parties what it would take on everyone's part to move their view up one step. Mr. and Mrs. Norris are then asked to identify some small step that would make this difference and what would be different if this small step occurred. The emphasis here is on a small step that might be realistic for each of the individuals to accomplish. After the couple is asked to identify how confident they are that they would be able to carry out this step, the therapist explores with them what would help them to be able to do so and what might prevent them from doing so. This provides the basis for further discussion on possible solutions to these barriers. They are also asked how motivated they are to make these changes and both express a high degree of motivation (steps 6 and 7).

The therapist then explores any possible times recently in which Mrs. Norris feels that Mr. Norris shows an appreciation for her concerns and that Mr. Norris has felt that his wife gives evidence that she thinks that he is trying. Small and fleeting examples are noted and then explored in terms of what the couple thinks helps make them possible. The social worker asks further questions to amplify information about what occurred prior to these times and the impact that this had upon their relationship. These examples are discussed with the family in terms of evidence of coping strategies that the family already possesses and has been able to use.

Toward the end of the session, the therapist indicates the need for a break to consider what would be the recommendation. The therapist comes back and compliments Mr. and Mrs. Norris for their love and concern for their son and their commitment to their family. The therapist then normalizes the situation by indicating that it can be painful and frustrating when grown children appear to be going in directions that cause concern and it can be difficult to handle this new stage of parenting when children become young adults. The therapist also recognizes their stress as being part of a sandwich generation with responsibilities for two generations in addition to their own. The therapist comments on the frustration experienced by both of them as a sign of their commitment to their son (reframing). The therapist then gives a version of the Formula One session task. The Formula One task asks people to focus on things within the family that people do not want to change. The counselor can give a homework assignment that asks people to identify these elements. "When people enter therapy, they begin to change. There are things in your life, however, that you do not want to change because they are positive. Between now and the next time we meet, pay attention to those positive things in your life, and we will discuss them next week" (Koob, 2003, p. 137).

Session 2. Mr. and Mrs. Norris both indicate a positive thing that they want to keep is their investment in their son despite the pain that it sometimes gives them. Mr. Norris states, "I appreciate her caring manner in general even though sometimes it creates tension in the family." Mrs. Norris states, "I appreciate his hard work on the job that has helped us meet our financial obligations, especially since my own family often struggled to make ends meet." The therapist then asks them to scale their current situation. Both rate the situation as slightly better. The therapist then explores individually with Mr. and Mrs. Norris what happened during this past week that helped make this difference. Mrs. Norris: "My husband was able to listen to me without pressuring me to stop worrying too much." Mr. Norris: "My wife was able to talk to me about our son without implying that I was in some way at fault for his actions and had even gone further and commented positively on something that I had said to him last week." They reported that while these changes had not yet made their son become more responsible, they felt that the problem was not pulling them apart as much as it had been. "We are starting to feel like we are a team again instead of arguing with each other all the time. This is important to us because we used to be able to talk about things. This used to be an important part of our marriage that has been lost."

Application: Martha and Daughter Megan, and Joyce and Daughter Stephanie

Several possible treatment models might be appropriate for this family. There are structural issues in terms of the two parents finding it difficult to create a parental coalition. As a result, a structural approach might be useful. A solution-focused approach can help the family claim and enhance some of the positive aspects of the family relationships that have become buried in the tensions of the present and the transitional process of this family. The following discussion relates to the use of a solution-focused approach with this family.

As with the Norris family, this family has become organized around a set of defeatist beliefs and family interactions. As the problems intensify, Martha and Joyce have begun to question the wisdom of their new family situation. Their relationship has started being defined in these terms so that they are considering separation. While encouraged by their friends to seek help, they have become discouraged and demoralized.

Session 1. The therapist begins the session by asking the family how the counseling session can be of help to them and how they will know if counseling has been helpful. The therapist is careful to listen to all the family members as they tell their story—Martha and Joyce's wishes to be a family, their current tensions, their fear that this new family will not work out; Stephanie's comments that she would like to have her mother back like old times; Megan's complaints that Stephanie hasn't given her and her mother a chance and her wish to have things peaceful again.

The therapist listens to their accounts of the situation while aware that the session also needs to highlight some of their hopes and goals for positive change. The therapist delineates the concerns raised by all the members—their hopes for having a family together, their fears that it will not work, the unhappiness of Stephanie with the current situation and wish to return to the old times, and Megan's wish that Stephanie would give them a chance or if she cannot do so, that she and her mother have peace again.

The therapist acknowledges with the family that creating a new family from two separate families is a difficult thing to do because every family has its own ways of doing things and what is important for them. The therapist also comments favorably on their willingness to come to work on their family situation.

While listening to these problem-oriented accounts, the therapist also explores for exceptions—times in which the family managed to overcome this very difficult task of blending two families together (times in which all the family members were able to get along, times in which Stephanie still felt that she was special for her mother, times in which Martha and Joyce were able to relate to each other as a couple rather than as frazzled parents, times in which the parents were able to agree on how to handle the children, times in which Megan found home a peaceful place to be). The therapist uses this information to affirm the efforts and ability of family members to handle this realistically difficult situation.

After listening to the concerns of the family members and identifying them so that all the family members recognize that their concerns have been heard and have been acknowledged, the therapist asks them if they would be willing to try something different and introduces the miracle question. After some thought the family members say what this would mean to them. Martha states, "I would know that something was different because when I come home from work Stephanie would say something nice to me rather than making me feel like I was unwelcome in her house." Joyce says, "I would know that something was different because Martha and I would be able to enjoy being together rather than spending our time talking about the problems we were having with our daughters." Stephanie jumps in with a comment that if they just moved out they would not have this problem. Her mother indicates that they are here to work things out, not to just move out. Stephanie first said, "I would know a miracle had happened because my mother would tell me that we were moving out." When her mother says that this is not the plan and asked her to come up with a miracle that does not include moving out, Stephanie quietly states, "I would know a miracle happened because my mother would ask me to go to a movie with her like we used to do—just the two of us." Megan says "I would know a miracle had happened because people would be sitting in the family room together watching TV rather than arguing." Each of the family members is asked to clarify what they mean by these statements so that the other family members understand what they are trying to say.

The social worker then asks the family members to mark on a scale of 1 to 10 how serious the problem is. Martha indicates 7 and Joyce 8. Stephanie indicates 2 and Megan 4. The therapist comments on the relatively favorable perspectives of Martha and Joyce. The social worker then asks each of the family members to think of something that would help move their view of the situation just one step up and what would be different if this small step occurred. The emphasis was upon a small step that would be realistic for each to accomplish. Martha indicates that she would know that a small step occurred if Stephanie would at least stay in the room for a couple of minutes when she entered rather than walking right out. Joyce says, "I would feel a small step has occurred if Martha and I could talk about something other than the problem with our children for a few minutes during the evening when we are together like we used to do before we moved in together." Stephanie says, "I would know that a small step occurred if my mother would ask me what I would like for supper the next day like she used to do when we were together." Megan says, "I would know that a small step occurred if we could at least watch part of one TV program together one night during the week." After ensuring that all of the family members had heard the comments of the others, the therapist asks them if they would rank from 1 to 10 how confident they were that they and the other family members could carry out this step. After obtaining this information, the family discusses what would help them be able to do these things and what would prevent them from doing so. They are also asked how motivated they are to make these changes. In this discussion, both parents indicate a strong motivation (8), Stephanie a relatively low motivation (3), and Megan a 5. The therapist comments on the commitment of Martha and Joyce to improve their own relationship and that of their family as a whole and their children.

The therapist explores times in which the family currently has been able to act in ways that at least approximate these steps. Even small and fleeting examples are noted and family members are asked to think about what has made these possible. The therapist asks further questions that amplify information about what occurs prior to these times and the impact that this has had on their relationship. These examples are discussed in terms of evidence that the family already has some coping strategies and ways in which they can be amplified.

Toward the end of the session the therapist indicates the need to take a break to consider what would be an appropriate recommendation. After returning, the therapist compliments the family members for coming to deal with what is a very difficult situation. The mothers are complimented on their commitment to their children and to each other. Stephanie is complimented on her concern for her mother and her wish to maintain a close relationship with her mother (positive reframing of her needs). Megan is commended for her wish to have a peaceful family.

The therapist then gives a version of the Formula One session that helps individuals focus on the things within the family that they do not want to change. "When people enter therapy, they begin to change. There are things in life, however, that you do not want to change because they are positive. Between now and the next time we meet, pay attention to these positive things in your life, and we will discuss them next week."

Session 2. Family members are asked to identify positive things in their family that they do not want to change, why these are important, and how can they be encouraged. Martha indicates that she is able to spend time with Joyce, someone who is very important to her. Joyce indicates that she has felt quite alone with her daughter before and now has another adult to share her parenting concerns. Stephanie is reluctant to mention anything that she would like to continue, but finally adds that her mother does not seem quite so worried about money now that she can share expenses with another family. Megan said that she had wanted a sister and hopes that Stephanie will someday want to be a sister to her. Family members are then asked to scale their current situation. If it improved, they are asked to indicate what helped it improve. When asked to rate their current situation compared with last week, all the family members rated it as slightly higher except for Stephanie. Family members were encouraged to identify what had happened that made them rate it somewhat higher. In terms of Stephanie, the therapist explored what helped prevent things from getting worse. Her mother also jumped in to remind Stephanie that she had done what Stephanie had asked earlier—get her input regarding the menu for dinner one night and that she had tried to fix her favorite food. Stephanie grudgingly admitted that this had helped make her feel better that day.

The therapist acknowledges with the family the important efforts that they have been making. Recognizing the tension between responding to the wishes of some family members for rapid change and the reluctance and fear of others (especially Stephanie), the therapist encourages the family to remember that addressing an important issue like theirs cannot be done overnight. It is important to move at the speed at which people feel comfortable. Family members can also be asked if there are any advantages for things staying the way that they are to elicit some of the ambivalence.

Another possible intervention with this family is that of prediction. Members can be asked to predict the night before if the next day will be better. This information can be then used to explore what are the patterns related to improvement.

These sessions set the stage for building on the strengths of the family members in the context of what is important for the individuals involved. Family members are encouraged to identify ways in which the family can gradually bring their miracle to life through small steps.

Applications for Specific Problems/Family Issues

The following section describes some basic elements of using solution-focused therapy for specific problems. The basic theoretical approach described also applies to these applications and is not repeated in detail. The readings cited give further description of the assessment and treatment process.

Families Involved with Protective Services

Insoo Kim Berg and Susan Kelly (2000) provide an excellent guide for adapting a solution-focused approach for families who are involved with protective services. Their approach draws upon a collaborative approach with families in addressing potentially very serious problems related to the children in the family. Their approach further expands beyond the individual worker-family relationship to the entire agency culture that supports a collaborative, strength-based way of working. The premise of the book is that in order to bring about lasting change, workers "need to join with families in respectful partnerships that result in safe and adequate care for children" (p. 44). Such a partnership moves beyond compliance to collaboration. "The reality is that, unless the solution is the family's solution, the best that will occur is compliance—until no one is looking" (p. 44). The worker's challenge and the opportunity is to create a context in which the worker and the parents are genuinely working together to further the welfare of the children and the family. There is no universal solution but rather solutions that make sense for the individual family.

An important key in engaging families and creating a collaborative partnership is listening, listening, listening. Although the discussion of the multi-systems approach in chapter 10 is not specifically solution-focused, several of the themes discussed in that chapter also apply in a solution-focused approach to working with families engaged in protective services. These include the importance of involving clients in the decision process, acknowledging and building on the strengths of families, enabling family members to identify goals, and ways of behaving in the home visit in such a way that it conveys respect as well as aids worker safety.

In conducting the interview with the family, some questions are especially useful because they can provide useful information and also be affirming and help family members think about ways to reach their goals. The questions following these basic categories might fit, for example, with a mother of young children who has been so overwhelmed that she has been neglecting herself and her children.

Coping questions: These questions convey an appreciation for the challenges facing the parent and draw on some potential strengths: "Caring for three little children by yourself can be really tough? You stuck with them when your partners left? How did you manage to do that?"

Relationship questions: These questions ask about how others would think about them. "You mentioned your girlfriend. What do you think she would say about how you have managed to stick by your children despite all the problems you have faced?"

Exception questions: These questions ask about times in which the problematic behavior did not occur. "Tell me about a time when despite being really down you managed to get up and help get your children dressed."

Scaling questions: These questions help identify the degree of confidence, assurance, willingness to take steps. "I realize that you want to start giving your children breakfast and that you have some cold cereal in the house. How confident would you say you are that you will be able to put some cereal on the table tomorrow for the children?" (on a scale from 1 [not at all confident] to 10 [absolutely sure]). This can then be used as a way of exploring how the mother could feel more confident.

Miracle question: The miracle question is followed by a series of questions related to how this might occur and what might be the effect. For example, "I would be giving my children breakfast every morning instead of just letting them fight because they are hungry." "So what would you be doing differently? What do you think would help you in doing this? How do you think your children will be acting differently if they get breakfast? Are there any ways that they could help you make this happen?"

Substance Abuse

Solution-focused therapy addresses the problem of substance abuse by focusing on what is right—the strengths and resources of the individuals and the family. This translates into a search for and focus on times in which family members are able not to drink or abuse other substances and ways to increase these times. The emphasis is on the possible resources within the client, the family, and context that support not drinking to excess or abusing substances. The role of the family therapist is to elicit from family members "those strengths, resources, and healthy attributes that are needed to solve the presenting problem" (Berg & Miller, 1992, p. 5). The therapist guides the therapeutic conversation to identify the family's potential solutions to addressing the problem. Solution-focused therapy does not take a particular theoretical framework toward a substance-abuse problem. Instead it accepts the family's way of explaining and defining the problem and the solutions related to this explanation. This approach helps build a therapeutic relationship based on genuine cooperation (Berg & Miller, 1992).

As in other problematic issues, the therapeutic-client relationship can involve a customer (recognizes the problem and willing to work on it), a complainant (recognizes the problem and is not willing to personally work on it), or a visitor (no agreed-upon problem). Understanding the nature of this relationship is important for success because these relationships require different approaches. In terms of people who are complainants or visitors, the therapist needs to identify goals that are relevant to the person involved. In terms of substance abuse, while individuals might not be a customer for their drinking problems, they might be willing to be one for other issues in life (Berg & Miller, 1992), for example, to keep their driver's license, their job, their family. Motivation to make a difference in these life issues can enlist the individual as a customer.

As with solution-focused therapy in general, establishing goals and criteria for success is another important step. The very process of identifying goals can be therapeutic. Effective goals fit the following characteristics: important to the family members, small and manageable, realistic and achievable, concrete and specific, and positive. Creating goals that are important to all the family members can be complicated because family members can have different goals and the family therapist has the challenge of identifying goals that family members share. Such characteristics enable family members to have a clear picture of the steps involved. They also encourage people because progress is realistic.

It is also important to help families recognize the importance of the goals that represent steps along the way in moving toward the final goal. Specifying what are the first steps toward accomplishing this final goal helps create manageable action steps and reduces people's fear that they are being asked to do the impossible. Being able to meet these steps along the way promotes a sense of mastery and hope rather than discouragement because the final goal seems too far away. As a result, the family can concentrate on helping the family member deal with their strategy for the office party next week (two beers with food rather than five mixed drinks) instead of feeling that they need to cope with the years of sobriety ahead.

The family therapist also acknowledges the reality of the hard work involved in creating change. Such an acknowledgment reflects the realistic nature of the difficulty in making such changes and thus also promotes the dignity and respect of the individuals involved (Berg & Miller, 1992). It is important to identify times that the client was able to hold off temptations (Berg & Kelly, 2000).

The miracle question is used with family members to identify potential future goals and the small steps to begin the journey toward accomplishing them. Recognizing that the challenge in treating individuals with substance-abuse problems is to help them maintain progress and prevent relapse, solution-focused therapy emphasizes the times and circumstances during which the client is not demonstrating this problematic behavior. The therapist searches for small steps of progress and seeks to identify how family members managed to accomplish it. The therapist is very supportive and affirming of these efforts and steps of progress and the hard work involved. When relapse does occur, the therapist maintains the focus on seeing prior success and encouraging the client to return to the current goal as soon as possible rather than letting the family become bogged down with feelings of failure and shame (Berg & Miller, 1992). Such an approach is compatible with helping individuals deal effectively with relapse when individuals become so discouraged by a slip back into their old patterns that they give up their efforts to change.

Grief and Loss

Butler and Powers (1996) describe the value of using a solution-focused approach in helping families cope with grief. The role of acknowledgment that validates the client's experience of the problem plays a critical role. When clients feel validated regarding their feelings of grief and loss, they are also able to begin to think about possibilities and recovery from loss. Once family members feel understood and acknowledged, the miracle question can be a helpful tool in enabling them to think in terms of the possibility of emotional healing. Questions related to coping can be useful in identifying exceptions—times in which either the problem is not present, is less intense, or handled in a way that the individual feels better. When the family members are asked how they coped, it adds focus to the possibilities that they might be able to use in their current situation.

The scaling questions also provide a way to explore with family members ways that they are able to move in positive directions toward their goal. Since the approach is set within the coping resources and strategies of the family members, it enables family members to identify resources within their own framework. Butler and Powers (1996) have discovered that families will often identify spiritual resources.

Tasks represent a further healing strategy. Family members might, for example, identify a special ritual that they could carry out together that would help bring healing, or they could identify a cause that had been dear to the family member who died and think about ways that they could contribute to the work of this cause. Another family might conclude that they had not been adequately attentive to the young children in the family whose laughter their departed family member had loved. As a result, they might organize a fun time for the young children. The family therapist assesses whether action-oriented, thinking, or observational tasks would be most appropriate for the clients. "Whatever the task, the message is designed around the basic acknowledgement-possibility paradigm" (Butler & Powers,

1996, p. 240). While pacing is always important in working with families, this is a particularly critical issue in therapy with families dealing with grief. Therapists need to be attentive to the messages that families are giving them in this regard (Butler & Powers, 1996).

Evaluation

Butler and Powers (1996) describe the importance of validating hurtful and painful aspects of the client's feelings through an example of working with a woman with a long history of depression. When counseling a woman who was suffering from depression in response to recent losses, the therapist listened in an empathic manner rather than asking about the future. During the second interview, the woman again told of her long history of depression and loss. This time the therapist recognized with the client her many losses and used this to introduce a solution-focused question: "When I look over this long list of losses and consider what you've been through, I can't but wonder how you keep it from getting worse" (p. 230). Waiting to introduce the solution approach in this manner helped the woman feel understood and ready to listen to a strength-based approach.

Gingerich and Eisengart (2000) reviewed a number of studies evaluating the effectiveness of solution-focused treatment. Outcomes in terms of individuals experiencing problems including depression, antisocial behavior, and orthopedic health problems indicated that solution-focused therapy was helpful. A study of parents indicated improvement of parenting skills for participants in solution-focused treatment. Other studies using clients' perceptions of progress revealed that about 75 percent of the clients had made substantial progress in meeting their goals and that this progress was maintained for at least the eighteen months of the follow-up period (O'Connell, 1998). A meta-analysis of solution-focused brief therapy revealed small but positive treatment effects with such treatment. It was only statistically significant for internalizing behavior (Kim, 2008).

In follow-up studies with couples that had received solution-focused therapy, family members and therapists reported somewhat different versions of what was helpful. While the therapists focused primarily on the techniques that they used, the family members were more likely to attribute this to their relationship with the therapist (Nichols & Schwartz, 2005). This fits with evaluation regarding the effectiveness of treatment generally that the context of mutual respect and collaboration plays a vital role (Friedlander, 1998).

Some have raised the question of whether or not solution-focused therapy is genuinely collaborative or directive in the positive approach (Nichols & Schwartz, 2005). As discussed earlier, therapists can err in being too insistent in emphasizing the positive aspects of the lives of families. Critics have raised the question whether families have genuinely moved into a more positive mode or have stopped raising these concerns given the strong positive message from the therapist and disregard for anything negative (Nichols & Schwartz, 2005).

In seeking to create a balance between theoretically based techniques and the reality of working with families, Nichols and Schwartz (2005) quote Michele Weiner-Davis's confession that she doesn't always practice what she preaches. "My clients cry and express pain, anger, disappointment and fears just as they might in any other therapist's office. And I respond with compassion. . . . My therapy story [what she presents in workshops] is not the total picture of how I do therapy" (p. 157). Her comments reveal the essential need to join and acknowledge as part of the process of eliciting solutions and future possibilities from family members.

Summary

Solution-focused therapy has emerged as an important brief family therapy model that helps families focus on their strengths and on ways to solve problems more effectively. Family members are viewed as the experts regarding their goals and ways to accomplish them. By using a future orientation, it enables family members to envision possibilities and to identify the small steps that they can take to create these changes. By searching for exceptions to the problems, it helps family members identify potential skills in problem solving and enhances the self-efficacy of family members.

DISCUSSION QUESTIONS

Discuss the role of the future in solution-focused family therapy.
What role do small changes play in solution-focused family therapy?
Discuss the concept of the family as the expert in solution-focused family therapy.
How can compliments lead to changes in the family?
What is the role of the Formula One question in solution-focused therapy?
Discuss the role of a future orientation in solution-focused family therapy.

9

Narrative Family Therapy

As discussed in chapter 3,

> Mrs. James and her children, Marie and John, come to the counseling center with the family still dealing with the scars created by the children's sexual abuse by their stepfather. Mrs. James has taken a courageous stance to leave her husband and support her children during this difficult time as well as arrange for the children to receive the help that they need. In important ways the James family can be characterized as a problem-saturated family— the problem has become the dominant story of the family, and healthy aspects of the family are not incorporated into this family narrative. Mrs. James has great difficulty seeing the positive signs in John and in herself as a parent. Instead of Marie's outgoing adaptation reassuring her mother, it only serves to confirm the mother's worries about John in their current family narrative. Encouraging words from the teacher have also not found a place in this problem-saturated story.

Narrative family therapy builds on the assumption that family problems and solutions rest in large measure on the meanings that people attribute to life events. Human beings are by nature meaning-making creatures. Families create stories that help make sense of past and current events as well as influence their expectations for the future. No family gathering is ever complete without family members telling stories about family events. Families maintain their sense of continuity and identity through the stories that are told. The stories that families create and tell are strongly influenced by their social and cultural context as well as specific life events. Narrative therapy uses a strengths-based approach to reconstruct family stories.

From the perspective of narrative family therapy, families become stuck due to problem-saturated stories. As a result, family members keep repeating old problematic patterns. Families seek help when their life story does not meet the current needs of the family (White & Epson, 1990). The central theme of narrative therapy is to empower families to create stories that liberate them from these problem-saturated versions and in the process to recreate new and more empowering meanings. These alternative stories are strength-based and highlight the resources of family members. From a resiliency theory perspective, the meanings that families attribute to life events are critical in terms of both risk and protective factors. Meanings influence how life events are interpreted and experienced and the coping strategies that are deemed appropriate. These interpretations promote self-efficacy or a sense of powerlessness within family members. As a result, helping families create meaning systems that enable them to cope and to meet the needs of family members represents an important therapeutic effort that supports family resiliency. From the perspective of narrative therapy, "the question for the narrative therapist isn't one of truth but of which points are useful and lead to preferred effects for clients. Problems aren't in persons . . . or relationships. . . . Problems are embedded in points of view about individuals and their situations" (Nichols & Schwartz, 2001, p. 316). Since problems are embedded in points of view reflected in the language of story, the narrative therapist seeks to help the family reexamine and alter the family story to become a more empowering one. Changing the story enables individuals to change their behavior and family relationships.

Narrative therapy provides a means for the James family to claim its identity as survivors rather than as "damaged goods" and to thus envision the strengths that are present in the family. With this altered view of the family reality, the actions of family members and their responses to each other will also be shaped and altered in accord with their new story. For example, when Mrs. James is able to view John as a healthy boy with a more introverted temperament than Marie's and to recognize that some of the behaviors that she sees can be attributed to the development stresses of being thirteen years old, she will be able to hear the affirming words of the teacher and Marie about John. She will also be more able to relinquish her burden of guilt and sense of failure. She will be able to be more accepting of John as he is and reduce the pressure on John to be more extroverted. As John begins to feel that he not a disappointment to his mother, he will regain some of his self-confidence in the social realm. He will also not have such a need to escape into his own room and will be able to be more sociable with his family. As Marie is no longer used as a standard for John to meet in order to feel accepted, the strain in their relationship can decrease and the two siblings can be a stronger support system for each other.

Theoretical Background

With its suspiciousness of the power of ruling meta-narratives, deconstructionism has opened the door to look at ways in which ruling narratives can maintain oppressive structures along with ways in which liberating narratives can be constructed. In the context of this background of seeking liberation from oppressive ruling narratives, narrative therapy grew out of the social constructionist movement that argued that social interaction rather than objective descriptions of reality plays a powerful role in generating meaning for people (Hoffman, 1993). Cultural beliefs and patterns strongly influence how people view their world, their narratives. It is thus important for therapists to understand their own social context and that of the families they serve. Language emerges as an important vehicle for change because it is the means by which people share their view of reality. Cultural group membership as well as family and individual life experiences shape the language that gives meaning to life events. Social constructionists also assert that therapy should be collaborative in nature because "no one party has a corner on the truth and new realities emerge in the process of the dialogue" (Nichols & Schwartz, 2001, p. 316).

Michael White, Cheryl White, and David Epston were the original developers of the narrative movement in family therapy. They were influenced by the French theorist M. Foucault, who questioned the dominant assumptions underlying humanism and psychology and also addressed issues of meaning, subjectivity, and power (Besley, 2002). In the spirit of re-creating family stories and meanings, they developed narrative metaphors and techniques to help families re-create their stories in order to move from problem-saturated stories that burden families to ones that empower and free families from this burden (White & Epston, 1990). Nichols and Schwartz (2001) provide an excellent discussion of the theoretical journey of the founders of narrative family therapy. Other early contributors include Jeffrey Zimmerman, Gene Combs, and Vicki Dickerson (Freedman & Combs, 1996; Zimmerman & Dickerson, 1996). Currently narrative approaches are used with a variety of family situations.

Major Tenets

Narrative therapy is based on these basic tenets:

1. Experience is shaped by the language we use. Language helps us create the meaning of life events and thus is an important avenue for change.

2. We construct stories that shape our life events. How we experience life events is inherently shaped by the stories that we construct.

3. Our stories shape what we see and remember. As we live our lives, what we see and how we remember it are shaped by our stories. These stories in turn are further influenced by perceptions of subsequent life events. My husband and I joke that it seems as if we take separate vacations because the stories that we tell and the memories that we share following

trips are so different. Family therapists discover that family members sincerely give very different accounts of what happened the previous evening.

4. Social context has a profound influence on the stories that shape life events. Culture shapes values, social roles, gender relationships, concepts of justice, and many other aspects of life. Therapists need to understand ways in which cultural narratives trap people into stories that create problems in their lives and to promote alternate stories that can be strength-affirming.

5. Stories don't mirror life, they shape it. Our stories do not represent reality, they shape how we experience life. The emphasis is on stories rather than a search for facts. As a result of the way in which family stories shape life, incidents and meanings that do not contribute to this problem view of the individual or the family are lost and do not actively counter the problem focus. People continue to react to this problem-focused view of life, their family, and family members. Strengths and positive ways of viewing life are lost in this process. Parents who are worried about one of their children may focus on the reports of teachers who describe problems in the classroom and give less credence to the reports of teachers who give positive reports.

6. It is important to expand our life stories. Current life stories can be too narrow and fail to include possibilities for growth and healing. Problems can occur when we accept cultural or familial views that are narrow. These views thus limit alternative interpretations or alternative ways of responding. Problem-saturated stories begin to represent the family reality.

7. Families are not the problem, families experience problems. Instead of viewing problems as within the family structure or system or members of the family, it is important to view the family as contending with a problem rather than being a problem. This view offers the possibility of uniting family members to address the problem facing the family (White & Epston, 1990; Zimmerman & Dickerson, 1994).

Goal of Treatment

The goal of narrative therapy is to alter the family's interpretation of themselves and their situation to ones that are more liberating. If family members are able to change the meaning of life events, they are also able to change their responses. Nichols and Schwartz (2001) describe the goal as transforming "clients' identities from flawed to heroic" (p. 397). Narrative therapy thus seeks to enhance resiliency through the beliefs of family members about themselves and their ability to cope with life—replacing problem-saturated beliefs with empowering ones that enable family members to identify and claim their strengths and resources.

The family therapist seeks to create these alternatives through several specific strategies:

- *Externalizing the problem.* By separating the family from the problem (the family has a problem but is not the problem) the therapist can help unite the family to fight this common enemy.

- *Finding unique outcomes or sparking events.* The therapist helps the family search through the family history to find the outcomes and events when the family resisted the problem or behaved in ways that contradicted the problem story.

Promotes Family Resiliency by

- Addressing risk factors of belief systems that are negative and demoralizing and thus maintain negative family patterns.

- Supporting protective factors by changing negative family belief systems to belief systems that provide hope and self-efficacy and sense of coherence. In doing so, it also helps improve positive interactions within the family.

Role of the Therapist

The family therapist plays the role of a *coeditor* of the family's stories rather than an outside expert who manipulates people to make specific changes. The therapist helps the family deconstruct their problem-saturated stories and reconstruct more empowering stories. The therapist assumes a collaborative relationship with family members. The therapist takes a non-knowing stance with the family and thus embarks upon a series of questions with the family as the expert. The task of the therapist is to engage the family in ways that give room to new meanings (the role of the coeditor). The therapist seeks to help the family develop healing narratives. The family is treated with great respect in this process and the counselor remains optimistic regarding the family's potential resources. Guided by these principles, the therapist asks the family members a series of questions to help identify exceptions and examples of resourcefulness. These examples help to separate the family from the current problem-saturated narratives that have dominated the family's view of reality and the family.

The therapist also engages the clients in *externalizing conversations* to separate them from the current negative narratives. The therapist can help conceptualize the problems facing the family as an externalized entity (e.g., "damaged goods" for the James family). Given the impact of social forces on family narratives, the therapist also explores with the family ways in which cultural themes can be limiting (e.g., cultural messages regarding gender) in order to create possible alternative realities. The therapist must be aware of her or his own cultural or personal narratives because they could influence viable alternatives for the family. The therapist must also be aware of her professional authority and its potential to shape clients' stories as well as her own cultural narratives.

Treatment Process

Narrative therapy is organized around a series of questions designed to elicit from the families their current problem-saturated stories and to edit these stories to free family members from the dominance of these negative stories and to reconstruct more empowering stories. The following discussion describes the steps in this process.

Listen to the family tell their problem. The therapist begins by a respectful eliciting from each of the family members of a picture of the current family life through a series of questions. These questions are designed to encourage family members to tell their story—their description of the problem and the situation that prompted the family to come for help. In addition, the therapist explores their life further to gain a broader picture of the life of family members. The focus is not limited to the problem world of the family but a broader and richer picture of the family life and members. Such a conversation not only helps establish rapport so that family members feel understood, but also enables the therapist to begin to identify some of the resources and accomplishments of the family. Learning about the son's role in the school band, the father's leadership in church, the mother's role in the community choir is a critical part of the family story. This information helps expand the view of the family beyond the problem-saturated story. The initial conversation also helps establish a collaborative relationship with the family members.

Externalize the problem. Based on the assumption that the problem does not reside within the family but within the family's narrative account, the narrative therapist seeks to help the family members detach themselves from the problem by externalizing it (White & Epston, 1990). The family contends with the problem but the problem is not equated with the family. The problem is portrayed as an "unwelcome invader that tries to dominate family members' lives" (Nichols & Schwartz, 2001, p. 401). White describes a family that has become dominated by their child's smearing his pants. This problem becomes externalized as "sneaky poo" (White & Epston, 1990). The James family can be helped to externalize their problem in terms of damaged goods. The children in this family experienced the pain of abuse by their stepfather and this family has been contending with both the direct effect of this series of events and the fears of what this effect might be. If a family has many angry shouting arguments that tear the family members apart, the problem could be externalized as "the storm cloud." The process of externalizing taps the creativity of the counselor and the family. The therapist suggests this term to the family and it is offered for their input rather than being imposed as a label by an expert. Externalizing the problem takes the burden of blame off the family members and helps unite the family to address the problem.

Map the influence of the problems and of the persons (relative influence questions). Once the problem is identified and the process of externalizing has begun, the counselor asks each family member to discuss the effect of the problem on the family members. The important message here is that the problem is not equated with the individual or the family. Family members can be asked both how the problem influences them (influence of the problem) and how they have influenced the problem (influence of the individual). Family members can be asked a series of questions that explore these two dimensions: how has the problem made them do things they might not ordinarily have done; how did they fight back against the problem; how has the problem tried to sneak up on them; how has it affected them as a parent/spouse/daughter; how have they held out against the power of the problem?

The James family for example, could be asked "What message does 'damaged goods' send you about your family, about you as a mother? How has this made you think about yourself and your family" "Are there times when it just sneaks up on you when you are not expecting it?" "How have you been able to talk back to it, to tell it that it's wrong about you and your family?"

In his latest work, White (2007) describes a pair of maps—the map of action (what happened) and the map of identity. As the family members create these new maps and fill in the information, they are drawing together a new story line that includes many overlooked life events. The therapist can help family members draw conclusions about these life events that can contradict the existing deficit-focus stories that have dominated their lives. White reminds therapists that because this is such a potentially powerful intervention, they have important ethical obligations toward the family.

Relative influence questions. These can be asked to indicate the type of relationships that exist with the problem and that underline the difference between the problem and the family members themselves (White & Epston, 1990).

These relative influence questions map out the interplay between the family and the problem. Mrs. James can be helped to identify the impact her belief that the family members are damaged goods has on her relationship with Marie and John. She can be asked to discuss when she has been able to push back that thought and take pride in her accomplishments for the family. John can be asked to talk about his response when he is pressed because of the fear of damaged goods. He can describe how he turns up the radio louder and hides out more in his room. He can also describe how he also enjoys doing things with his friends and feels a part of the group when asked to join them. Marie might indicate how she spends more time with her friends where she does not have to deal with it. She can also describe how she sometimes encourages her mother to view John as a normal thirteen-year-old boy going through what is frequently a difficult time in life.

The following strategies are important ways of mapping the impact of the problem on the family and the family's ability to fight back against the problem.

1. Search for a unique outcome. Using a strengths-based approach, the therapist seeks to identify with family members times in which they have managed to win against the problem or at least were able to be less controlled by it. Family members can thus be helped to identify times in which they, not the problem, took charge over what happened. Since family members have been dominated by the problem-saturated narrative, family members have frequently overlooked these times. The therapist seeks to identify and validate these times in order to help the family begin to construct a new story (White & Epston, 1990). As in all counseling efforts, the therapist must be sensitive to timing because people need to feel heard and understood and will resist moving forward until they feel understood.

The therapist can ask Mrs. James when she was able to fight back against viewing her family as damaged goods. The therapist can thus help Mrs. James recognize times in which she did not let her fears win and has been able to accept John's more introverted personality without becoming alarmed. She can recall feeling temporarily relieved after a positive conference with the teacher. John can describe times in which he went out with his friends or watched TV with his mother. He can also report how his recent report card was good. Marie can describe times in which she enjoyed spending time with her mother and brother.

2. Ask spectator questions. These questions explore how family members speculate how other people might experience them. This technique is designed to gain a wider perspective on the narrative account (Williams & Kurtz, 2003).

Mrs. James might be asked how her other family members or friends would have explained how she found the strength and courage to leave her husband and make a new life for her children. She might also be asked what information the children's teachers have used as the basis for the good reports that they have given them.

3. Collapse time. Family members can be asked to explore the issue over time. This exploration includes both the past and the future (Williams & Kurtz, 2003).

Mrs. James and her children might be asked if damaged goods is a greater problem for them now than it was last year. Perhaps the children would agree that their mother is gradually fighting back more effectively (or less so as the case may be). Family members could then be asked what would be happening in the family in the next six months if they continued to push it back, or let it get the best of them.

4. *Predict setbacks*. The therapist can help family members prepare for setbacks in ways that will not demoralize the family. This technique recognizes that the process of reconstructing a narrative and changing life circumstances is an ongoing process with inevitable ups and downs. As a result, the family finds a way to incorporate setbacks in the family story without becoming overly discouraged and feeling defined by these problems.

The James family members might be asked how they will fight back if damaged goods manages to strike back and makes their mother worried again, or makes John want to avoid others in the family by staying in his room, or encourages Marie to stay away from her family by spending all of her time with her friends. The family can be helped to identify such events as part of the ongoing life story and help them find ways to fight back against the problem.

5. *Reauthorize the story in terms of the family members (significance questions)*. The therapist now uses the exceptions that have been identified as evidence to change the views held by family members about themselves, others in the family, and the family as a group. If a family member has been able to withstand the pressure to cave in or to refuse to become defeated by the problem, what does it say about the person?

The therapist asks family members questions that make them reflect on what it says about themselves that they were able to withstand the pressure of the problem. The answers to these questions help people reclaim the strengths evident in their actions and to define themselves in terms of strengths rather than the problem-saturated stories. Questions can also be asked in terms of the family as a unit in terms of identified exceptions.

"What does it say about you, Mrs. James, that you were able to conquer your fears and hear good reports from the teacher?" "What does it say about John and Marie that they are able to be such good students?" "What does it say about your family that you can have these good times together?" (a specific example described by family members).

6. *Identify cultural messages that support problem-saturated stories*. Since family stories are influenced by the cultural context, it can be important to help family members identify the cultural messages that shape these narratives. Some of these messages might relate to gender prescriptions or family power roles. What is the impact on the family when young women are valued in terms of their sexual appeal to men, when boys are supposed to be athletic, when mothers are supposed to feel responsible for everything related to their children, when men are supposed to be strong and not express their fears? Are these messages that have had an impact on the family story, are these messages that the family has accepted or has managed to resist? How do these messages help the family meet the needs of family members, or have they created burdens for the family members?

If Mrs. James comes from a cultural background that views women as needing to keep a family together despite the odds or one in which women are expected to be submissive to their husbands, this cultural message could have made it difficult for Mrs. James to leave her husband. It could also have influenced the nature of the supports that were available to her during this difficult time. Cultural messages that suggest that John's more introverted personality does not fit with a masculine identity could make it more difficult for Mrs. James to accept John's personality as normal rather than a sign of damaged goods. "Did you grow up with messages from your family and your community that made it difficult for you to leave your husband? Did you get messages that boys are supposed to be outgoing and sociable?" "Did you grow up believing that as a mother you are totally responsible for your children's personalities?" The therapist can thus help the family look at ways in which cultural messages have shaped the alternatives available to the family and the family's interpretation of life events. For Mrs. James, such an understanding could be used to emphasize the courage that she demonstrated in the face of these cultural constraints. Broadening of the cultural message regarding John could help decrease the problematic interpretation of the current situation.

7. *Create ways to reinforce the new narrative.* The therapist can help family members identify others within the community or extended family members who can support the family and their reconstructed narrative. Are there other women, friends, or extended family members that Mrs. James can turn to for support when she is fighting back her fears and guilt? Can Mrs. James ask for another visit with the teacher to learn more about John's current school performance that could be supportive of this more strength-based narrative?

8. *Communicate with the family by letters from the therapist.* Letters from the therapist can be used to support the reconstructed narrative. Summary letters following a session can be used to reinforce the issues raised in the session, especially as they relate to the possible alternatives to the problem-saturated story. These letters are available for the family to read on an ongoing basis. The therapist could write the following letter to the James family following an early session.

> Dear Mrs. James, Marie, and John,
>
> I have been thinking about our session today and our conversation. Please let me know if I missed some important things or need to understand anything more accurately.
>
> You described how you escaped from an abusive family situation to create a new family group without your husband and stepfather. Mrs. James, I understand that this took a great deal of courage on your part because you had to find a way to support the family and risked the anger of your husband. I understand that you helped Marie and John receive counseling to deal with being abused by their stepfather. Marie and John, I realize that you both took advantage of this opportunity as shown by how well you

have been doing in school. I realize from our meeting that the three of you have a great deal of love for each other and have been doing the best that you can to make a new life for your family.

I also learned that you have been struggling with the problem of "damaged goods." This has affected all of you in different ways. Mrs. James, you have been afraid that you failed Marie and John by letting them be abused by their stepfather and by not protecting them enough. You worry that both Marie and John, and especially John, are still carrying serious scars from it. I learned that "damaged goods" becomes especially strong when John spends time in his room rather than going out with his friends or being with his mother and sister. John, I understand that when your mother worries about you, you feel that you are not living up to your mother's expectations. You then spend even more time in your room, watching TV or playing video games. When your mother compares you with Marie, you begin to doubt yourself and "damaged goods" gains more power. Marie, I understand that your mother is not as worried about you because you go out frequently with your friends.

I also learned about times when your family is able to put "damaged goods" in the background. Mrs. James, there are times when you are able to relax and hear good news from the teacher. There are also times when you are able to feel that you have given both John and Marie the help that they need. Marie and John, there are times when you are able to have a good time together—quite an accomplishment for a thirteen-year-old brother and a sixteen-year-old sister.

I wonder how you have been able to be such a strong family and show such care for each other. I wonder how you managed to push back the power of "damaged goods" when you did? Where did you find this strength?

I know I will have more questions next week when I learn more about ways that you are continuing to push back "damaged goods." I will be glad to discuss this with you further as I remain your partner in your important efforts.

9. Use a reflecting team. The reflecting team as developed by Anderson (1991) consists of several other therapists who listen to the family session and are invited to give their input to the therapist and the family. For narrative therapists, reflecting teams join with the family to help the process of developing new narratives—both deconstructing the problem-saturated descriptions and helping shape more positive and strength-affirming alternatives (Freedman & Combs, 1996). In contrast to the Milan approach in which the team behind the one-way mirror remained unknown to the family and spoke only to the therapist, the reflecting team speaks openly to both the family and the therapist as befitting the egalitarian and strength-based approach of narrative therapy (Goldenberg & Goldenberg, 2000). The precise way in which the process is organized varies from therapist to therapist.

In general the members of the reflecting team speculate about the nature of the problem and the family's response to it. They seek to identify further exceptions. The team uses language in accordance with the presence of the family members. The team members are respectful and strength-affirming in their comments:

> "I wonder how the family managed to stick together despite all of their long history of difficulties."

> "I am impressed by the way the family has managed to fight back against the problem of distrust that might have torn another family apart."

Family members are encouraged to ask questions of and dialogue with members of the team. The team also raises questions about possible alternatives:

> "What did the family expect to happen by choosing this path? Are there other routes that your family could take?"

> "Have you thought about any of these other possibilities? How might you talk about some of these other paths?"

The questions and comments of the team members can encourage family members to consider new possibilities.

Transparency is another aspect of the narrative model. The reflecting team members reveal aspects of themselves that can offer healing to the family members. I remember Anne Hartman at a National Association of Social Workers conference describing her experience serving as a member of a reflecting team while working with Michael White. The mother in this family had struggled hard to keep her children together. Anne had been hospitalized with polio as a child and had experienced the fears and sense of aloneness of being hospitalized for a long period of time as a young child. She was encouraged to use this personal experience to further support the value of the mother's struggles in this family. She described how sharing this information with the mother had served to validate the mother and her efforts in a powerful manner.

The reflecting team could join the James family and the therapist after learning about the situation facing the family. They could ask questions: How did Mrs. James find the strength and courage to leave her husband when she learned about what was happening to the children? She did not have a steady source of income and her extended family did not approve of her taking this action. This took a great deal of strength and it would be helpful to learn more about how she went about seeking support to make this move.

> "How have the children been able to do so well in school?"

> "How does a family with two teenagers do things together as a family? I wonder how they manage to do so" (refer to specific events).

"What would happen if Mrs. James could feel more relaxed about John spending time in his room when the thought of damaged goods sneaks up on her?"

10. Using certificates and celebrations. The counselor can mark victories or the creation of new meanings through celebrations or certificates. White and Epston (1990) describe ways in which certificates can be used to validate progress. The certificates designed by White include the new individuals or family narrative combined with a dash of humor.

The social worker can create a certificate for the James family that would acknowledge their success in creating a health-affirming family narrative. There could be a celebration of their growing success in defeating "damaged goods" and replacing it with "doing fine."

11. Definitional ceremonies. White (2007) subsequently developed a concept of "definitional ceremonies" to affirm the new family narrative. These are ceremonies attended by the family and carefully chosen participants. After the family members have shared their current family stories, participants engage in dialogue about what they have observed and how this resonates with their own life experiences.

Narrative Therapy Applications

The following represent applications of narrative family therapy with several common issues facing families.

Blended Families

Shalay and Brownlee (2007) describe the use of narrative family therapy with blended families and the special challenges that they face. These can include risk factors associated with expectations such as the adjustment process will take a brief time, or the new family will make up for past losses and pain; societal views that blended families are in some way inferior to nuclear families; confusion regarding family rules; and ambiguities in family roles. Family members can be asked questions to learn the influence of these risk factors on the family and ways in which they are responded.

For example, family members can be asked

- How do you think what you see on TV has influenced what you think about families?

- If you were a nuclear family, how do you think things would be different?

Views of about what family life should be can be called "old views" and people can then be asked how this view affects their family life.

"How is old view getting in the way of your present relationships?"

"How is old view getting you to argue with each other?" (Shalay & Brownlee, 2007, p. 26).

"What do you need to do to guard against old view gaining the upper hand?"

The authors use the metaphor of gates to look at issues of boundaries within a blended family. Depending on the specific nature of the family, a term can be coined that captures something about the family and externalize the family situation as described earlier. Family members can then be asked about its effect on them, how they have fought back, and so on.

Families with Children with PTSD

Bernandon and Pernice-Duca (2010) describe the use of narrative family therapy with children suffering from post-traumatic stress disorder (PTSD). This approach also draws upon trauma recovery principles. The treatment approach involves the entire family system to create more empowering belief systems on the part of the child and family members. In this context, the child has a problem, rather than being the problem. Trauma can have an immobilizing effect that further silences communication on the part of the person who has been traumatized. Incorporating the child into a collaborative family approach helps prevent the child from being immobilized. By externalizing the problem, looking at its effect on the family and ways that they have been able to fight back (exceptions), the family can be helped to create family stories that reduce the sense of being a powerless victim. This also increases communication within the family. Drawing from the recovery literature, it is also important to maintain a sense of structure to help reduce the anxiety of the child. Although the James children described earlier did not manifest PTSD, they did experience the trauma of abuse. The family thus illustrates the use of narrative therapy to create meaningful systems that promote healing and a sense of family strength.

Families That Are Without a House or Apartment

Fraenkel and Shannon (2009) describe a creative use of a narrative family approach with families living in shelters in New York City. The participants are primarily African American and Latin American. This approach uses a group format that gives family members further support. Recognizing that a family approach only addresses some of the multiple challenges facing these families and the importance of taking a broader community-based strategy, this approach is designed to address some of the negative, defeatist views of family members. This group intervention was set within the context of a program called Fresh Start for Families that attempted to engage family members as experts in the program design generally. Family group members begin in a game format by which they identify constraining factors and their impact on the family. Many of these include stigma about being homeless. Family members are helped to externalize "homeless" or the term appropriate for the family members and identify ways in which they are able to put "homeless" in its place and to regain pride in themselves and their family. Family members are also engaged in an exercise by which they describe their preferred future. This helps family members begin to look at what might be possible for them and engages them in the process of looking at steps that might make this future a reality. The broader group aids in this process. Family members also write a letter to the future to further help make this possibility real. Although implemented in a shelter setting, such an approach could be useful for economically marginalized families who also face stigma and defeat.

Families with Youth Coming Out as Gay, Lesbian, Bisexual

Saltzburg (2007) describes how narrative therapy can be used to address the social roles of power and privilege (frequently negative) in terms of what it means to be gay or lesbian in current society. The impact of these story lines on the family narratives can be identified and then questioned as described through the techniques cited previously. It thus enables families and their members to rewrite the family story in a positive manner as they come to terms with this change within the family.

Adolescents with Eating Disorders

Manley and Leichner (2003) describe a narrative approach that helps young women who are feeling despair in their context of eating disorders. The approach of externalizing the eating disorder can help reduce feelings of guilt and powerlessness. The future orientation also helps give hope. Involvement of the parents in terms of education and counseling in a manner that promotes communication within the family is an important aspect of this treatment.

Evaluation

There are limited outcome data related to narrative therapy, especially studies using objective outcome measures. Most of the outcome information is impressionistic. Part of this limitation relates to the social constructionist nature of the therapy that resides in the subjective perceptions of families.

In a study using ethnography to identify the experience of eight families regarding narrative therapy, the clients found narrative therapy to be helpful. They reported that the presenting problem was reduced. The clients also appreciated the respectful approach of the therapists, the recognition they received from the team members to overcome their problem, and the reflecting team's helpful comments (O'Connor, Meakes, Pickering, & Schuman, 1997). Another small (six families) single-subject evaluation of narrative therapy used to improve parent-child conflict revealed significant improvement (88–98%) in conflict in five of the families (Besa, 1994). Another small study revealed more mixed results. Four clients indicated that they were able to see the problem in a more helpful way and another four indicated that they were not able to do so (Coulehan, Friedlander, & Heatherington, 1998).

An evaluation of narrative family therapy conducted in Iran (with 30 families—15 with narrative therapy) revealed that couples who received narrative couple therapy improved their family functioning, although it did not influence enmeshment (Sadeh & Bahrami, 2008). A recent study evaluated narrative family therapy from the perspective of the therapists who were conducting therapy using this model of treatment. Based on ethnographic observations and interviews with eight therapists, the following themes emerged. All eight of the therapists indicated that the narrative approach was helpful to their clients. They attributed this success to three reasons. First, narrative therapy promoted "personal agency" in clients. Second, the therapist demonstrated respect to the clients and did not pathologize clients or place them in categories. The third reason was a weaker one—clients became more able to deal with their problems. They viewed narrative therapy as unburdening the therapist and the family and opening up new pathways for growth. Therapists also expressed the limitations due to the requirement for specialized training, the time- and resource-consuming nature of the model. The last was especially an issue when the reflecting team was used. While the reflecting team was viewed as helpful in terms of opening new possibilities, it could also be overwhelming to both the family and the therapist (O'Connor, Davis, Meakes, Pickering, & Schuman, 2004). On the other hand, findings from several other studies suggest that the reflecting team helped the family make positive changes and that the multiple perspectives were viewed as helpful (Biever, Gardner, & Bobele, 1999).

Reservations have been voiced about the fit of narrative therapy for some families. There are families where the members might not be able to be successfully encouraged to join together to fight the problem by means of the techniques of this model. Nichols and Schwartz (2001) raise the question whether externalizing and searching for unique outcomes necessarily mean that the family will be able to join forces in this way.

The relativism of the social constructivist basis of narrative therapy also poses questions and potential problems. There is the dilemma that occurs when the issues at hand are difficult to place in relative terms. Violence within the family has been raised as particularly problematic in this context (Laird, 2000; O'Connor, Davis, Meakes, Pickering, & Schuman, 2004). The latter also reflects the controversy within narrative therapy about how to deal with cultural patterns that could be viewed as oppression in the family. According to Laird (2000), some narrative therapists consider "bringing culture into the therapy room in a way that challenges dominate ethnic practices or cultural discourses as an imposition of personal politics" (p. 352). Others, including Laird (2000), "argue that clients need to be helped to deconstruct not only their self-narratives, but the dominant cultural narratives and discursive practices that constitute their lives" (p. 352). According to Laird (2000), "deconstruction means to explore how these dominating discourses are shaped, whose interests they serve and whose they may subjugate, to explore the marginalized possibilities" (p. 352). She also raises the issues of how the presence of both dominated and subjugated narratives influences the stories that are available to clients in their situation. The therapist does not deal with this issue by delivering his or her own views as truths but by being aware of the voices that are silenced due to lack of power and by helping these voices find a way to emerge (Laird, 2000).

Nichols and Schwartz (2001) in their critique of narrative family therapy ask if the therapist is not more directive than the model purports to be. Although the therapist engages the family in a series of questions rather than giving answers, these questions are targeted to leading people in certain directions.

Laird (2000) describes narrative therapy as well-suited to culturally sensitive practice. "The therapeutic stance—a stance that is highly respective, collaborative, and nonhierarchical—is one that encourages the expression of multiple ideas and possibilities. It avoids blame or pathologizing; searches for strengths, rather than defects; is grounded in a value stance; and fosters transparency by the therapist" (p. 350). Such an approach requires the therapist to be self-reflective regarding his or her own narrative.

Summary

Narrative therapy has emerged as a major school of family therapy arising from the social constructionist perspective. Narrative therapy seeks to make changes within the family by helping families replace their problem-saturated stories with alternative ones that include examples of strengths and success over problems. Such a model of therapy can be especially helpful for families for whom the meaning that they have attributed to life events has become problematic for the family.

DISCUSSION QUESTIONS

Discuss what it means to say that the family isn't the problem but contends with a problem.

What does it mean to describe the family therapist as a coeditor?

How does the search for exceptions help alter the family story, and why is this search necessary?

Discuss ways in which the therapist can help solidify change.

Discuss how culture influences the family's narrative and the ways that it can be addressed in narrative family therapy.

10

Multisystems Family Therapy

Miss Kenisha White (age 24) contacts a crisis social service program. She and her children have been living with her mother for the last few months after she left her partner of five years who had been abusing her, especially when he was high on drugs. Miss White has three children: Tyrone, aged eighteen months, Anthony, four years, and Karmella, seven years. The two youngest are by her previous partner and the oldest is by another man who has lost contact with the family. Miss White's mother is not able to keep the family on a long-term basis because she has very limited room in her apartment, and the addition of Miss White and her children puts her at risk of losing her apartment. Her mother also has Miss White's high-school-age brother and sister living in the apartment. While her mother used to work, serious health problems have forced her to stop working and apply for disability benefits. Miss White's father died due to a work-related accident when she was in high school. Miss White's children have been frightened by the events of the past months and cling to her. Karmella has been reluctant to go to school—a situation complicated by a school change caused by the move to her mother's apartment. Miss White fears that Karmella might have to change schools again when they move. Miss White has applied for assistance with the local Department of Children and Families as well as a program for families that need help in finding housing. Miss White has been staying at home taking care of the children because Tyrone has a chronic health problem. She fears that she will have to go to work to support the family and is worried what she will do about child care for Tyrone. She dropped out of high school when she became pregnant with Karmella and has held minimum-pay jobs in the intervening years. Her mother has been active with the local church but Miss White has drifted away from it. Miss White tries to be a good mother to the children but sometimes gets very discouraged about her situation. At these times, she finds it hard to be patient with the children and will either snap at them verbally or withdraw from them. She has been able to turn to her mother and friends for support during these difficult times, but it is important now for her to try to find a place for her own family to live.

The White family has important risk and protective factors. In terms of protective factors, Miss White is committed to the welfare of her children. She also has the emotional support of her mother, her siblings, and friends. Her mother is active in church that might be a source of resources for Miss White. She currently has a place to live. There are potential community resources to be explored. Miss White had the courage to leave her partner who had been abusing her and taking drugs.

There are also a series of risk factors that place this family at great risk for not having basic family needs met—safe housing. This stress is taking its toll on the entire family system. Her mother has taken the family in temporarily but cannot provide ongoing housing. Miss White has been under great stress and has reacted at times by becoming potentially verbally abusive or withdrawing. The older child, Karmella, has recently been reluctant to attend school. Tyrone has serious health problems that require additional care. Miss White has a limited education and job skills.

The Alvarez/Colon family contacted the crisis center for help to find housing after they had been evicted from their apartment for nonpayment of rent. The family consists of Mr. Alvarez (aged twenty-four), who does unskilled labor when he is able to get employment, and his partner Miss Colon (aged twenty-three), who does housekeeping at a local motel. They have a son, Jose, eighteen months old. Due to problems in the economy, Miss Colon's work hours have periodically been reduced. When she does not work full time the family lacks medical insurance, but they do have insurance for their son through the state insurance plan. The couple met when both moved to the area to find work. They have lived together on and off for three years but have been together steadily for the past year. Neither Mr. Alvarez nor Miss Colon graduated from high school.

Their relatively poor reading skills have posed employment problems for them, but they work hard when they are able to find employment. One of their current problems now relates to their car, which needs frequent repairs. Because they do not live near a bus line, they have problems getting to work when their car does not work. As a result, Mr. Alvarez lost his last job and the salary of Miss Colon was not enough to pay the rent. Their extended family members live out of the area and lack the financial resources to help out more than with occasional funds. They have some friends in the area, but these friends are also struggling financially. Mr. Alvarez has been taking care of Jose while the mother works. Miss Colon has been worried about Mr. Alvarez's temper when he gets frustrated with situations like their present one. While he has never hit her or hurt Jose, she is afraid that his increasingly short fuse will cause him to hurt the boy. She is also worried that he will begin drinking again—a problem that he had earlier in their relationship. She has been afraid to say anything to Mr. Alvarez about it. While she is nervous about this situation, she is also worried that if she says too much that he will leave as he used to do in earlier times before Jose was born. As a result, she has been very tense and finds herself shouting at Jose when he makes too much noise. Despite the family's financial problems Jose is dressed very nicely in clothes that Miss Colon has found at garage sales. He is a friendly little boy who seems especially attached to his mother but appears to be comfortable with his father. He is beginning to use words and developmentally seems to be on track. In terms of the community, there are few housing options for families with low incomes or limited economic resources.

This family and its members demonstrate some key resiliency resources along with risk factors. In terms of resources, both parents have a good work ethic when they are able to find work that matches their skills. Despite recent pressures Mr. Alvarez has not relapsed in terms of drinking and has been able to handle life events without turning to alcohol. The parents have demonstrated some effective parenting skills as demonstrated in the way in which their son relates to people and is dressed. The family roles are flexible enough so that either parent can take care of Jose depending on their job commitments. Although Mr. Alvarez shouts when he is angry, he has not resorted to hitting either Jose or Miss Colon and Jose does not seem afraid of his father. Miss Colon is resourceful in terms of finding clothing at garage sales. Although the couple had an unstable relationship in the past, they have been together in recent months since the birth of their son and seem to have developed a close bond. Jose demonstrates qualities of resilience in terms of a friendly personality, age-appropriate development, and good relationships with his parents, especially his mother. They have family members and friends who are interested in their well-being even if they cannot help financially.

The family is also struggling with contextual, organizational, and personal risk factors. At the community level, recent economic problems have limited their employment options and there is little in the way of low-income housing. Transportation is also a problem. This combination caused them to be evicted and is making it difficult for the couple to get back on their feet and provide an adequate living and stable housing for the family. Their support system cannot be of any consistent help financially. Although the parents have a good work ethic, they lack some essential employment skills (especially in the area of reading) and have not graduated from high school. There is a history of instability in the relationship. There are also relationship and communication problems as reflected in Miss Colon's reluctance to express her concerns out of fear that Mr. Alvarez will leave. Mr. Alvarez has a history of alcohol abuse and tends to lose his temper when under pressure.

Miss Colon has begun to shout at Jose as a result of her frustration. In addition to the specific problems cited, the combination of issues facing this family creates a situation of additive risk factors.

This family illustrates the need for a multisystems approach useful with families in a state of crisis and with complex needs. The family is in a crisis situation that needs to be addressed (safe housing). Family members would also benefit from some longer-term efforts to strengthen their ability to meet the needs of family members and to reduce the likelihood of similar future crises. Recognizing the need to do a risk assessment process to ensure the safety of Jose in these circumstances, Grigsby (2003) emphasizes the importance of taking a strengths-based perspective with families like Mr. Alvarez and Miss Colon who are already overwhelmed with difficult circumstances. As described earlier in the summary of resources, this family does have some important resources that can be identified with the family. Family members can sometimes lose sight of these strengths because they risk being overshadowed by the difficulties facing them. As part of this strengths-based approach, it is important to create a situation in which family members identify the issues that are important to them. In this context Grigsby also discusses the need to provide emotional support to deal with the stresses involved as well as advocacy to identify and connect families to these needed resources. Such families can also need help in dealing with conflict and communicating in such a way to help resolve conflicts. Case management models (Greene & Kropf, 2003) can also be useful in helping these families connect with resources to address the immediate crisis and strengthen family coping.

This family could benefit from an improvement in their life skills. Addressing the needs of this family might involve linkages with community resources as well as counseling. Housing is clearly a pressing key issue here so that help in this area is critical. Employment issues are also important. The low reading levels of Mr. Alvarez and Miss Colon will continue to make this family economically vulnerable. Using a case management approach, they might be linked to community programs in which volunteers tutor people in their reading skills. Although their extended family members and friends are not in a position to offer any substantial financial help, they might be able to provide some needed emotional support for the parents. The couple might be helped by some counseling focused on improving their communication skills to help provide needed support for each other and to strengthen their relationship. The parents might also benefit from some help in stress management as they are coping with a realistically difficult situation. This help can reduce some of the strains in their relationship and between the parents and Jose. The counselor can identify ways in which Mr. Alvarez has managed to cope without drinking as support for his maintaining sobriety. With the pressure facing this family, such an assessment might identify further resources within the family that can be tapped. While this assessment identifies a variety of possible approaches, an essential part of the assessment process will involve the family in identifying their priorities.

As discussed earlier in chapter 3, Mr. Cole is struggling with his fear of being evicted, his sense of being overwhelmed as a parent, his problem of depression, and a son with difficulties in school. He too is struggling with a host of problems that make his family a good candidate for the multisystems approach.

As illustrated by the preceding families, many families that seek help from social workers are experiencing multiple problems. These families either do not have some of the basic resources of life that other families take for granted or are at great risk of losing them. They lead lives that are frequently on the edge of survival and typically have experienced a series of crises. These are the families described by Kilpatrick as Level I families where the basic foundational needs of the family are in jeopardy. This in turn jeopardizes the family's ability to meet the emotional needs of family members (Kilpatrick, 2003). Such families are at heightened risk of neglecting or abusing their children (Thomlison, 2004). Children in these situations face many risk factors for serious childhood social problems (Fraser, Kirby, & Smokowski, 2004). In looking at these vulnerable and overloaded families at high risk for future serious problems, Walsh (1998) urges counselors not to "view them as 'problem families' but families struggling with many problems which are largely beyond their control and often not of their own making. Crisis situations are often embedded in problems in the community and the larger society, which must be addressed. Crises may also be fueled by reactivation of past traumas, which need to be understood and integrated for greater resiliency" (p. 238). As a volunteer at a program for homeless families, I marvel at the strength shown by some of these families as they contend with such difficult life circumstances. I wonder how I would cope.

The goal is to empower the family to be able to meet the needs of the family members more effectively on an ongoing basis. Addressing only the issues within the family system fails to meet some of the essential needs and ignores some of the potential resources available to these families. As illustrated by the three preceding families, these needs involve many aspects of the community and its wider support systems (e.g., housing, employment, the school system, child care, transportation, health care, extended family and friends). Using a risk and resiliency perspective, these families face a variety of risks derived from their wider context. These environmental risk factors interact with potential risk factors related to the family (e.g., organizational instability, poor problem-solving skills, negative interpersonal interactions, low educational level or job skills, and low self-efficacy of family members). From a resiliency perspective, the social worker seeks out potential resources (protective factors) within the family and the larger environment to strengthen the family and its ability to meet its needs and to enhance the resiliency of the family. The family counselor recognizes the over-whelmed nature of the family and tailors the intervention accordingly.

In looking at the importance of using a larger community lens in under-standing and addressing the needs of these families, Aponte (1994) uses the analogy of the "canary in the mine"—their suffering is a warning of the toxic-ity of our social environment. The situation of these poor families makes us recognize that we need to work to restore health not only to these families but also to the community and the larger society.

As a result, while the focus of this book is on working with families, it remains important to recognize that social and economic policies selectively advantage and disadvantage members of groups in ways that have important implications for the families that we serve. Policies that define what consti-tutes a legal family, who are eligible for employer-based health plans, on what basis does a society grant health insurance, what are the levels of bene-fits provided for people with disabilities, and what types of support for health care or housing are present in the community all play critical roles in the lives of many people. Social codes that influence the nature of wages comparable to the cost of living in the community as well as laws regarding the minimum wage have a major influence on many families. As a result, family practice at the micro level cannot be divorced from concern for social and economic policies and general efforts to create change in these areas.

A multisystems model of treatment helps social workers address these complex family needs. In doing so, the worker assumes a variety of roles in terms of the family itself, the extended family, and wider community sys-tems. As described earlier in the introduction to family therapy models, multisystems family therapy has a broad vision of supporting resiliency within families that requires these diverse roles.

The multisystems approach is defined as "a problem-solving approach that helps families with multiple problems to focus and prioritize their issues and that allows clinicians to maximize the effectiveness of their interaction" (Boyd-Franklin, 2003, p. 4). This definition emphasizes the active role that families play in the decision-making process (prioritizing their issues) as well as the multifaceted aspect of the treatment model. Described by Boyd-Franklin in terms of African American families, the model is applicable to members of all ethnic groups living with multiple needs (Boyd-Franklin, 2003; Grigsby, 2003; Thomlison, 2004). The multisystems model recognizes that the organizational structure of the family and the internal processes of the family are profoundly shaped by the wider systems in which the family lives. Resolving family issues will probably require addressing issues within the wider system and enlisting members of wider systems to make a differ-ence. The roles of advocate and mediator between families and community organizations can be important. Kilpatrick (2003) describes one of the jobs of the social worker with these families as to "marshal the troops" (p. 5). The following discussion draws extensively on the work of Boyd-Franklin

(2003) with African American families, the work of Walsh (1998) with vulnerable multi-crisis families, multisystemic treatment designed for antisocial behavior in children (Henggeler, Schoenwald, Borduin, Rowland, & Cunningham, 1998), the treatment discussions related to Level I families generally (basic family survival needs) (Grigsby, 2003), and of multi-stressed families by Madsen (2007).

Theoretical Background

Multisystems models of treatment built on the earlier work of a variety of family therapists and theoreticians. Boyd-Franklin (2003) describes its foundation in terms of the following three theoretical approaches that illumine the organization of the family and the ongoing interaction between the family and its environment. As such, the multisystems model is an integrative model.

First, the *structural family system* model (Minuchin, 1974). This model views the family from the perspective of an organizational structure. The approach is active and present-focused. The therapist joins with and thus enables the family to solve their problems more effectively. This approach also promotes leadership and effective family organizational patterns.

Second, the *ecological approach* (Bronfenbrenner, 1979). This approach places human behavior in an ongoing interactional context between the person and the environment. Bronfenbrenner (1979) portrayed this process through a nesting of concentric circles leading from the individual through the family, the community, and the larger social contexts (microsystems, mesosystems, macrosystems, and ecosystems). Families are understood in terms of the interaction among three dimensions: life transitions, interpersonal processes, and environment (including both the physical and social) (Holland & Kilpatrick, 2003). Assessing and addressing the transactional process between families and these larger systems is critical. Hartman and Laird's (1983) work on family treatment within this ecological framework has been helpful.

Third, the *ecostructural approach* (Aponte, 1994). Looking at the wider social structure in which people lead their lives, several elements are important in working with people who are struggling economically.

- Options and power—people need to feel control over their own lives rather than be treated as if they were powerless.
- Purpose and meaning in life—people need to reach for purpose and meaning in life that is rooted in psychology, family history, and cultural and spiritual origins.
- The personal ecosystem's multilevel structural organization—communities are crippled through chronic economic deprivation and cultural supports, leading individuals to feel incompetent. (p. 10)

Madsen (2007) stresses a collaborative relationship approach in working with multi-stressed families. It also recognizes the importance of addressing larger contextual issues.

Major Tenets

1. Families live in complex, multisystem worlds that need to be incorporated into the assessment and treatment process.
2. Family counselors need to use a variety of intervention skills to address these multiple needs. They must be flexible in their roles in working with these families.
3. Families need to be treated with respect and given decision-making power in the treatment process. While this assumption is true for all models of effective treatment, the counselor needs to recognize that many of the families with multiple problems have frequently experienced interactions with wider systems that have left them feeling disrespected and unable to make crucial decisions. As a result, families frequently anticipate such behavior from their current counselor.
4. The focus is on the strengths of families who are already overwhelmed by their current life circumstances and are frequently in crisis. Searching for strengths within the family and the wider context provides clues for addressing the problems facing the family without further overwhelming them. As Walsh (1998) describes, "When treatment is overly problem-focused, it grimly replicates the joyless experience of family life, where problems seem all-pervasive. Interventions that enhance positive interactions, support coping efforts, and build extra-familial resources are more effective in reducing stress, enhancing pride and competence, and promoting more effective functioning" (p. 241).

Goals of Treatment

The goals of multisystems treatment are to enable families that are being overwhelmed by issues within the family and their relationship with their larger context to meet the needs of family members. The approach has a strong dual focus on the family and the wider context. The family counselor seeks to enhance the resources available to the family. The approach is strength-based and action-oriented.

Promotes Resiliency by

- Addressing multiple risk factors associated with lack of effective leadership and family coping, demoralization, lack of self-efficacy, ineffective communications, conflict, lack of social support, poverty and lack of community resources, and possible reactivation of past negative experiences.

- Supporting protective factors by helping family members develop effective coping strategies and problem-solving abilities, improving family organization, modeling effective leadership, providing role models of strength, and accessing social support and adequate resources. These steps can lead to increases in a sense of self-efficacy and affection within the family.

Role of the Counselor

The family counselor needs to be flexible in the use of the self and assume a variety of roles within this multisystems framework. In terms of relationships between the family and the larger system, the counselor may be acting as an advocate for the family, as a broker between the family and the larger system, and as an educator with the community. Within the family the counselor may be acting as an encourager and as a role model. The family therapist typically uses an action-oriented approach rather than an emphasis upon reflection and insight.

The counselor takes a strength perspective, helping the family identify potential resources within the family and their context and seeking to help the family mobilize these resources. The location of counseling is flexible and may range from the office to the home or other relevant location.

Treatment Process

The multisystems model includes treatment organized around the family and the wider social context. Interventions can be office- and home-based. The following discussion draws on the work of Boyd-Franklin (2003) with African American families, Level I families described by Grigsby (2003), families with major problems (Henggeler, Schoenwald, Borduin, Rowland, & Cunningham, 1998; Thomlison, 2004), case management (Greene & Kropf, 2003), collaborative therapy with multi-stressed families (Madsen, 2007), and strength-based family-centered services (Walsh, 1998). Although the details of the implementation vary, these models all share a strength-based approach, a flexible holistic approach to treatment, attention to both the family and the wider context, and a collaborative approach with family members and others in the community. Working with the family requires the counselor to join and engage the family, to assess the needs and resources, and to help the family gain the needed problem-solving skills and organize the family in such a way that it can address the multiple issues facing it.

Treatment is organized around four steps: joining, initial assessment, problem solving, and restructuring the family.

Joining. While joining is always important with all families as discussed in chapter 2, it is especially critical with these families because of their past history and sense of being overwhelmed. The strength-based approach is valuable in this process for several reasons. Most of these families have had prior experience with the social service or related systems. It is not uncommon that these encounters were judgmental and deficit-based. Family members frequently did not feel like they were engaged in a collaborative relationship. As a result, family members are likely to expect this of their current encounter and will be wary that their present counselor will be yet another person in this negative chain. In addition, family members who are feeling overwhelmed by their situation are also likely to feel hopeless and defeated. Such an emotional state makes it even more difficult for family members to mobilize themselves to problem-solve effectively and thus the negative cycle becomes even more intense. Listening to their past encounters with the social-service system, including their problematic experiences, can help reveal some of the reasons why they are wary and also offers the counselor opportunities to explain how he or she hopes to work with the family. This information suggests some of the reasons why the family is pessimistic about counseling and why the family members feel discouraged and defeated. The counselor can use this opportunity to identify potential strengths within the family that can facilitate the joining process as well as explaining how the counselor seeks to work with this family.

Families are also frequently sent for counseling by another organization rather than seeking help for a problem that they have identified. The joining process can thus be especially difficult. The National Family Preservation Network (2012) states the importance of listening, listening, and listening as an important step in joining with these families.

Grigsby (2003) reminds us of the importance of the social work mantra "Start where the client is" in this process. Asking the family members what is important to them indicates respect and gives a message that they are partners in the process. With the myriad problems facing families, it also helps begin to prioritize the most important ones.

Treating family members with respect translates into the myriad details that are involved in interactions with others. How the counselor conveys dignity and respect (or fails to do so) through the ways he or she addresses or dialogues with people is critical in this joining process. The counselor has the responsibility to build the bridge over the potential chasm created by differences in education, social class, and other life opportunities offered the counselor and the family members. The following represent some examples.

Addressing adults with Mr., Mrs., Miss connotes respect and dignity. Asking people what they would like to be called sends the message that they are respected partners who share in the decision-making process.

Using vocabulary that is meaningful and understandable to the people involved sets a collaborative tone in addition to facilitating communication. If people do not understand the counselor's vocabulary, they might be unwilling to ask for clarification and could feel demeaned by having to make this request.

Behaving as an appreciative guest during home visits is strength-affirming. Body language here is as powerful as words. Many years ago, our family was dealing with a realtor who taught me this lesson in a vivid way. At the time we had four young children and so she seemed to assume that every chair in the house would be dirty. Before she sat down on any of our chairs she would always turn around and carefully wipe off the chair. No matter how diligently I cleaned the house before she came, she always went through this same routine. I was offended and felt that she was nonverbally labeling me a dirty housekeeper. I felt demeaned by her actions. Certainly I never joined with her in a trusting manner. However, it gave me an understanding of the power of these nonverbal gestures and the messages they convey and a determination to find ways not to repeat this with others.

Simple steps can also help build bridges. I remember working with a young couple with two small children, a baby and a first grader who was in a class for children with special needs. I was a social worker assigned to this class and thus represented the school system. Neither of the parents had had positive experiences during their own years as students. As such, there was a strong sense of distance as I represented this intimidating authority. During a home visit, the mother was busy pitting cherries. I asked her if I could join her because I had always enjoyed doing this. As we pitted the cherries together, she visibly relaxed and began sharing her concerns in a way that created the beginning of a collaborative relationship—two people who shared a concern for her son. While this represented a unique situation, there is both the challenge and the opportunity to look for cues in the setting that can create a bridge that affirms the family members.

The counselor might also need to reach out to others within the broad family circle to recruit them into the counseling endeavor. Boyd-Franklin (2003) discusses the importance of reaching out to family members within African American families because key family members might be unwilling to come in to the session. Negative past experiences with other helpers can contribute to this reluctance. In some situations, it can be useful for the counselor to do so directly either through telephone, letters, or home visits rather than giving this task to other family members. These actions by the counselor can help set a new tone for this encounter. From my experience in working with families, the preceding comments also apply to families belonging to a wide range of cultural groups.

Boyd-Franklin (2003) also discusses the importance and challenges of reaching out to men within African American families. The history of discrimination experienced by many African American men generally with accompanying personal experiences of being slighted and negatively stereotyped can make these men even more reluctant to become involved with yet another member of a system that might be demeaning. Although the man might not be living in the home currently, he might have a potentially important relationship with the family or the child that can be a resource for the family. For example, Kenisha White's high-school-age brother might be a resource for her boys who have lost their father/stepfather under difficult circumstances. The counselor needs to send messages about his importance. Walsh (1998) reminds counselors that questions pertaining to the men who have been part of the lives of women and children are important in working with families generally. It might be the father of the child, an uncle, or a grandfather.

The counselor can also explore with the family others in their life space that might be valuable resources. Boyd-Franklin (2003) describes seeing a counselor "walk into a waiting room and invite the 'family' in for a session and leave the friend or neighbor they have brought along sitting outside" (p. 231). Rather than ignoring these individuals, their presence provides an opportunity to explore their place in the life of the family. It is possible that including these individuals in the session with the family's permission might reveal a gold mine of resources for the family.

Initial Assessment. The assessment process begins with the counselor's initial observation of the family and then proceeds to the communication that occurs between the family members and the counselor. While the assessment process identifies some of the pressing problems and risks facing the family, an emphasis on the strengths of the family, their coping abilities, and the potential resources available to the family is essential. The assessment process is also an ongoing one and is influenced by new information. While the emphasis on strengths is important, it is also essential to assess the risk of abuse and neglect within such overwhelmed families in order to ensure that the appropriate help is offered to everyone involved (Thomlison, 2004).

As in other family models, verbal and nonverbal messages of families offer valuable clues to the family. Selection of seating patterns can reflect family alliances and boundaries. Certain individuals can emerge as family spokespersons. Family communication patterns reflect whether family members are able to listen to each other in ways that demonstrate mutual respect and caring or reflect scapegoating and hostility. Such behavioral patterns also reveal family leaders or isolates. Issues of power and leadership within the family emerge as family members defer to those with power or perhaps hesitate to make decisions without the presence of a family member who is not present in the session.

In addition to assessing the family, it is also important to assess the process of joining between the family and the counselor and the nature of this collaborative relationship. Boyd-Franklin (2003) identifies a series of valuable questions to organize this assessment. Again, while she frames these in terms of African American families, these questions can be important for other groups who have also experienced being marginalized or oppressed.

How is the family responding to the therapist?

Are key family members beginning to trust the therapist? Should the issue of race (or class) be raised at this point?

Who referred the family? Has the therapist made a distinction between her or himself and the referral agency?

How does the family feel about being in therapy? How do other key family members (not represented at the meeting) feel?

Why does the family believe they are coming to therapy and what do they want from the process? (p. 232)

Walsh (1998) reminds us that "assessing whether overwhelmed families are motivated poses the wrong question. Rather, we need to ask ourselves how we can help them keep their heads above water to take on efforts for change" (p. 253). This assessment also helps identify what the family can realistically take on at this time. Asking the family to take on responsibilities that are unrealistic for them will only result in a further sense of failure and reduced self-efficacy.

While problems such as poor housing, loss of jobs, and economic poverty are realistically important to families, Aponte (1994) urges family counselors to look beyond these concrete signs of poverty to signs of poverty of the spirit that robs people of a sense of meaning, purpose, and hope. Ongoing experiences of being denied opportunity and power by society can lead to a pervasive sense of injustice, helplessness, and anger. Such poverty of spirit represents a major risk factor in contrast to a sense of coherence and meaning that promotes resiliency. Assessment of this aspect of life is most effectively accomplished in the context of the trusting and respectful relationship described earlier.

Acknowledging how difficult the situation facing the family can be while at the same time looking for evidence of strengths can enhance the therapist/family relationship. "After just an hour of pandemonium in a session, or hearing about the myriad of problems they are facing, we can use our own overwhelmed reactions to identify with their predicament and applaud them for hanging in there all week" (Walsh, 1998, p. 253). The presence of a children's book or toy, family pictures on the wall, the presence of a child's picture on the refrigerator all represent possible clues for evidence of strengths to pursue.

The counselor must be sensitive to timing in terms of the assessment process. Information can be valuable to create a collaborative working relationship and solving problems. Families need to trust why the counselor needs this information and what he or she will do with it. While these words apply to all families, they have special meaning for members of these families. In this context, it can be useful to explain to family members why you are asking about specific information and what you plan to do with this information.

Boyd-Franklin (2003) discusses the importance of waiting until trust is established to use tools such as the genogram with African American families lest families view the counselor as "prying into their business" (p. 21). Families are likely to withhold important information and become more distrustful of the social worker. This caveat applies also to other families with negative prior experiences with counselors or those who are so overwhelmed with their current crisis that the genogram is not viewed as meeting the family needs. When the family has gained trust in the counselor, genograms can be useful. Genograms can be created jointly with the family or developed by the counselor with information obtained.

When family members are experiencing great turmoil, it can be valuable to identify times of peace and healing and individuals who have contributed to this period (Walsh, 1998). The counselor can explore some of these times in the course of creating the genogram. This information can help in several ways. It gives family members a sense that life can be better and can also suggest possibilities for restoring some of this in the life of the family currently. Such information can be used later in the counseling session to help the family in their problem-solving process.

When family members seek help because they are overwhelmed by problems, the counselor needs to use the assessment process to identify the strengths (protective factors) of families as well as the nature of problems facing them. The counselor seeks to frame a balanced picture of the family and their situation by seeking information about ways in which family members have coped in the past; ways in which they are still managing to cope; ways the family members can still enjoy each other; and possible resources within the immediate family, extended family, friends, and the wider community. As discussed earlier, sharing these assessment observations with the family can be strength-affirming for the family as well as enhancing the collaborative nature of the relationship. The fact that the family is there to work on the problem is a strength. Identification of such resources also provides clues for future work with the family and creates a foundation for a strength-based approach to families. Use of the risk and resiliency framework helps identify strengths as well as organize the potentially chaotic picture.

While tailoring one's questions to the social context is always important in the assessment process, it can be especially a sensitive issue with these families. Boyd-Franklin (2003) suggests asking people "Who lives with you or who lives in your household?" (p. 236) rather than the standard set of questions regarding what might be viewed as typical family structure. This question enables the family to tell its unique story without creating inappropriate categories of family relationships for this family. Other useful questions to learn more about the family and their context are, "Who helps you out?" "Who can you turn to?" (p. 236). Asking about grandparents and their relationship with the family can tap another potential resource.

Problem solving. Families characterized by Level I functioning typically are overwhelmed by a series of problems—where to live, how to support the family, how to deal with a health problem, how to guide the children, how to deal with school problems, and the list can go on and on. The situation is further compounded because the executive function of the family is often compromised because the parents are overwhelmed or lack effective parenting skills.

Mr. Alvarez and Miss Colon and their family have at least the following set of problems to contend with: eviction from their home, loss of a job, lack of transportation, fear of potential abuse and return to substance abuse, and lack of viable job skills. This is a list long enough to make the strongest family feel under great stress. Miss White and her children are struggling at a minimum with housing, health problems for the youngest child, school adjustment issues, the trauma of abuse, and economic stress. Mr. Cole and his children are contending with his problem of depression, limited job skills, lack of confidence as a parent, loss of the children's mother, and the son's poor performance in school. The list of these problems that is rather typical for many families would challenge any of us. Furthermore, beyond these concrete problems Aponte (1994) reminds us that families can also experience a sense of helplessness that destroys the spirit.

It is important to engage the family in the process of prioritizing the problem that is especially important for them or the problem whose solution would make an important difference for the family. Engaging the family in this decision-making process grants the family needed respect. Selecting and prioritizing a problem helps make the situation more manageable because no one can work on many problems at once. Working with the family to address the identified problem helps create a sense of teamwork and grants the counselor and the counseling process credibility. Mr. Alvarez and Miss Colon's family might identify housing as their critical priority issue. Mr. Cole might indicate either his own depression or perhaps the school situation with his son. Miss White might prioritize a place for the family to live.

In terms of selecting and prioritizing, families also need to recognize what cannot be changed and to focus on "their capacity to right themselves and move forward" (Walsh, 1998, p. 259). This capacity enables families to master the art of the possible—an important element of resiliency.

> Miss White blamed herself for having become involved with her last partner: "I should have known he wasn't any good. He started being mean to me when I got pregnant with Anthony. My girlfriends told me to get rid of him. Look what this has done to my kids." Miss White cannot undo the past. She can look at what this means for her future and what she can now do for herself and her family.

In designing problem-solving strategies, "action-oriented, concrete problem-solving approaches work best with overloaded families" (Walsh, 1998, p. 258). It is especially useful to develop specific, concrete goals with realistic steps to reach them. Small steps help make success possible with the accompanying increase in confidence and self-efficacy to address other family problems.

It is useful to prepare families for setbacks as well as to help them identify ways in which they will cope if a setback occurs. Such an approach is consonant with the premise of resiliency that "failure is not falling down but staying down" (Walsh, 1998, p. 259). Mr. Alvarez, Miss Colon, and Miss White might not find housing in their first attempts. The counselor can empathize with their discouragement and praise them for their efforts. The counselor can problem-solve with them how they will handle these setbacks if they occur so that they will be able to persist in their efforts and their discouragement will not damage other parts of their lives.

Collaboratively developing specific tasks to address the concrete goals the family established gives a sense of dignity to the parties involved. Being able to accomplish small steps successfully begins to address their sense of powerlessness and helps them feel that they are able to make a difference in their lives (a key aspect of family resiliency). Mr. Cole and his son might use the session to talk about ways in which they will deal with the school situation. The worker can encourage Mr. Cole to think of ways he can discuss the situation with the teacher that separates his role as parent from his earlier life experiences as a youth. The worker can use role-play as a way to help Mr. Cole gain confidence in his ability to handle the situation. As Mr. Cole is able to take steps in this area, he begins to experience himself as a more effective parent.

The therapist's active involvement in the daily activities of the family can be useful. This approach provides needed nurturing for the parent and also serves as a role model for carrying out these activities. These in vivo demonstrations that occur within a trusting relationship can be very helpful for parents' nurturing (Grigsby, 2003). As discussed in terms of Mr. Cole, the steps of educating through role modeling can be helpful in learning and implementing new skills.

The use of enactment, prescriptions, and tasks can be helpful. Drawing from the structural approach, encouraging the family members to interact with each other and to enact their family drama in the session involves family members in the therapeutic process. It also helps create ties between talking about and acting to solve problems. If Mr. Alvarez and Miss Colon select housing as their priority issue, the counselor can encourage them to discuss how they are going to go about solving this within the session. The worker can use enactment to enable the couple to discuss this critical issue more effectively and to problem-solve some very specific tasks that they can work on to address the problem. It can also be important to give people a constructive experience if family sessions have been used in negative and demeaning ways in the past.

Boyd-Franklin (2003) stresses the importance of thinking in terms of empowering rather than helping. "When a process is initiated whereby the family does the work in the session and members speak directly to each other rather than through the therapist, the likelihood of generalization outside of the actual session is far greater" (pp. 234–235).

Restructuring the family. Restructuring efforts with the immediate family and the support system represents an important treatment strategy. As indicated in the resiliency literature, families need an effective organizational pattern with leadership that helps family members meet their needs. Looking at the family's interaction in the session as well as at information obtained through other avenues suggests ways to strengthen the family structure. Family members who have leadership responsibilities might be overwhelmed. Others in the extended family might be able to serve as resources or might be undermining their leadership ability. The leadership coalition might be compromised due to conflict, or an inability to communicate. Members of Level I families may lack the skills of conflict resolution and thus minor conflicts are not resolved and can escalate into further problems (Grigsby, 2003). Active involvement of the family can be useful in helping people gain and practice these new skills. The following represent some ways that the leadership structure in these families could be strengthened.

> Mr. Alvarez and Miss Colon have two critical important problems to solve—housing and employment. Difficulties in discussing family issues hinder their problem-solving efforts and their alliance as parents. Miss Colon is afraid to bring up issues because she fears that Mr. Alvarez might leave her or return to drinking, therefore she does not bring up her concerns. The counselor can use the family sessions as a way to help the couple communicate in a problem-solving manner about steps to address these important issues. This strategy not only helps the family in their problem-solving efforts but also strengthens the parental subsystem and the relationship of this couple. The experience of being able to do this successfully in the session can empower the couple to begin doing so at home.
>
> Miss White is now separated from her partner and is responsible for her three children. She is feeling overwhelmed by the trauma and the difficult situation facing her. While she wants to be a good mother, the stress of the circumstances is compromising her parenting ability. Although she cannot continue to live in her mother's apartment, the counselor can explore ways in which the mother and the siblings can be a stronger support system for her. Miss White and these other family members could join together in the session to discuss ways these family members can strengthen each other. There might also be friends who can serve in this role. Perhaps someone in the wider support network might have some leads for housing.

Mr. Cole is also feeling overwhelmed in his role as a parent, especially in dealing with the school system. He fears becoming depressed again and is not taking his medication. Perhaps his sister with whom he has a good relationship can be a support in his role as a single father. She might be able to encourage and problem-solve with him in dealing with the school system as well as helping him resume his medication.

Home visits as well as home-based counseling can be valuable in working with families (Boyd-Franklin, 2003; Boyd-Franklin & Bry, 2000). Such visits give a picture of the life of the family that hours of conversation in the office can never reveal. Some of the stresses faced by the family in the neighborhood and the physical condition of the home emerge as well as the inability of the family members to organize a household. Dirty laundry scattered about the house and dishes piled around the kitchen reveal a great deal about the family's current ability to organize family life. Family resources also emerge. In addition to major problems, during home visits I have discovered hidden creative talents by family members, good organizational skills, and family warmth as well as other family strengths that had not emerged in the office visits. Sometimes the counselor can find signs of efforts by family members that can be used in later family sessions—a book for the child, pictures by children on the refrigerator, pictures of the children with a grandparent. Boyd-Franklin and Bry (2000) also describe the value of these visits in terms of engaging family members with power who have not come to the office-based sessions.

Boyd-Franklin and Bry (2000) give six important guidelines for home visits that have special relevance for families with multiple problems, although the guidelines can be helpful in general.

1. Counselors must recognize "how they would feel if a stranger came to their home asking painful, difficult, and sometimes intrusive questions" (p. 38). The situation is further complicated if the family has not been in control of this decision and they have had to comply with an outside authority. Since family members are likely to feel wary and uncomfortable, the counselor should be extremely gracious to help put people at ease. Counselors should also be aware of the risk of violating confidentiality in terms of their presence at the home of the family.

2. Counselors must recognize they "are on the client's home turf" (p. 39). Families are likely to be engaged in a variety of family activities so the counselor needs to be able to "go with the flow" (p. 39) and take advantage of this opportunity to get to know the family better.

3. Counselors need to spend time joining with the family in the ways that are culturally appropriate. Such activities can be important in bridging barriers between the family and the counselor. Failure to do so can create major problems in joining. If the family welcomes the counselor by asking her or him to join in eating something, the family may feel devalued if the counselor turns this down. Engaging with the children can be helpful.

4. Counselors need to recognize the power of genuine praise. This can be especially important for people who are overwhelmed with problems and a sense of defeat and hopelessness.

5. Counselors need to understand and be able to use themselves in an effective manner. Home visits can evoke powerful feelings from counselors that require self-knowledge. Dressing in such a way that combines a degree of professionalism with easy-to-care-for clothing (clothing that can withstand a little dirt if necessary or does not create a needless distance from the family) can be important in maintaining a trusting relationship.

6. "Empowerment is the goal" (p. 42). The goal is not to fix or help things for the family but to enable the family to address their issues. Part of this process is to ensure that family members are given credit for the change that has taken place (Boyd-Franklin & Bry, 2000).

Social workers and family counselors need to ensure their personal safety in home visits. Representatives of the organization should know their plans. Cell phones can be important for protection. The worker does not want to dress in a way that makes her stand out in the community any more than is necessary. The family members should be expecting the worker. Family members can also give further guidance in terms of location and any potential risk factors (e.g., do not park in front of the blue house). Social workers need to have an understanding of the area where they are going, including the potential risks in the neighborhood. Agencies need to give permission not to enter the home or to leave if there are any hints of danger. The mantra "Be aware of your surroundings" is an essential one in making home visits.

Multisystems Levels

The counselor takes an ecological systems approach to identify the potential resources and strains in the wider context of the family. Family members might come to counseling already connected with wider levels. Sometimes these connections are supportive, other times people might be working at cross-purposes, or these connections are only adding burdens to families. The White and Cole families have important issues related to their connections with the school system. Working with families in terms of this wider system requires the counselor to assume a variety of roles.

The following represent key multisystems (Boyd-Franklin, 2003).

Level I: Individuals
Level II: Family subsystems
Level III: Family household
Level IV: Extended family
Level V: Non-blood kin and friends

Level VI: Church and community resources

Level VII: Social service agencies and other outside systems.

The social worker can work directly with the family to seek to create change within this wider social context or work collaboratively with the family to link the family to resources within this context or to advocate for families.

Level I: Individuals

Recognizing that change in one part of a family system can create changes in the larger system, coaching individual family members to create change represents an important treatment strategy (Hartman & Laird, 1983). Coaching includes a discussion of the change sought, problem solving regarding how to try to institute this change, and rehearsal regarding the action involved. Family members can be coached regarding ways they can try to create desired changes in terms of relationships with significant other people within the family circle. This process can be used to help family members establish more effective roles within the wider family system. Family members also need to be aware that families will exert pressure on members to retain their original roles within the family system. As a result, the coaching efforts need to include how the family members will respond to these pressures. Hartman and Laird (1983) remind counselors of the importance of making sure that clients understand that no one can guarantee what the response will be from other family members and that people can ultimately only be responsible for their own actions.

> Mr. Cole might express a wish to have a better relationship with his sister from whom he has been alienated. He and his sister had once been close but there had been a falling out several years ago at the time of the divorce. His sister was very close to his wife and he did not think that she had been willing to hear his side of the story. As a result, he has shut her out of his life. Now that his wife is dead and he is struggling to raise the children alone, he is interested in reaching out to family members both for his own sake and that of his children. The counselor problem-solves with Mr. Cole ways to approach his sister and what might be her possible responses. When Mr. Cole decides that he would like to begin with a phone call, the counselor role-plays possible scenarios with him. They also discuss how he will handle it if his sister really is not willing to resume a relationship with him.

Levels II and III: Family System

Depending on the family's needs and goals, techniques drawn from other strengths-based models can be used to support the family organizational structure. As described earlier, structural family therapy approaches that strengthen parental leadership in the family can be useful when the parental subsystem is having difficulty assuming appropriate leadership. Mr. Cole, for example, can be helped in this way to assume a more effective parental role. Family members can be helped by learning more effective leadership skills. Miss Colon and Mr. Alvarez, for example, can be helped to problem-solve together. The family counselor can model more effective behaviors. Parents can learn how their responses to their children shape their children's behavior and possible alternative responses. Family members can be helped to break down major issues into smaller and more manageable steps. The counselor can use the family interaction in the session as a way of strengthening family leadership roles. A solution-focused approach can help people identify changes that are important to them, and the small steps that would represent this change. Family members can be involved in a solution approach that asks people to imagine the changes that would help make things better and what small steps would represent this change.

Exploring the nature of the immediate and wider family networks can be valuable in identifying potential solutions as well as the dimensions of the problem. What the concept "family" truly means is influenced by culture and individual family patterns. In some African cultures, for example, the word *cousin* is not used to describe the children of your siblings. They are called brother or sister and the word *cousin* is viewed as an inappropriate sign of distance. Many cultural groups have a strong sense of obligation for the extended family system, such as African American (Boyd-Franklin, 2003), Latino (Garcia-Preto, 1996b), First Nations (Sutton & Broken Nose, 1996), Arabic (Abudabbeh, 1996), Italian (Giordano & McGoldrick, 1996), and Asian Indian (Almeida, 1996). Informal adoptions can take place as individuals view others as members of the family group.

Boyd-Franklin (2003) suggests exploring by using questions such as "Who helps you with the children?" "Who lives in the house?" "Do you have a special person in your life?" "How many children live in the house or stay over often?" (pp. 244–245). She also describes the sensitive issue of discussing the paternity of children in African American families. Miss White might have been reluctant to explain that her oldest daughter had another father. Boyd-Franklin suggests the importance of exploring whether grandparents might still be interested and involved in the lives of the children even if the father is no longer involved with them.

Levels IV and V: Church, Community, and Social Service Networks

Family counselors can enable family members to access appropriate services within the community. An assessment of their current and past relationships with community services can be important in designing interventions with families in order to access appropriate resources and to avoid repeating prior ineffective efforts (Imber-Black, 1988). This issue is discussed in greater detail later in this chapter in "Family-Focused Case Management."

As indicated, such steps can involve the counselor in various roles. The counselor might only need to link people with services by informing family members about the services and ways to access these services. The counselor might need to go further and advocate for this family with the service delivery system. In some situations, families have burned their bridges with this service in the past and the counselor needs to advocate to give them another try. Family members can also be reluctant to turn again to agencies where they did not receive services or perhaps felt demeaned by workers. Level I families can easily be victimized by people in the community. This can make them suspicious of the social worker's intentions as well as the staff of other helping groups. Helping family members in these situations can be important.

The counselor may need to play a mediator role between the family and community services because of tensions between the family and the organization. Children can be quite adept at pitting the school and their parents against each other so that two parties who need to be partners are working at cross-purposes. The counselor then serves as a mediator who tries to establish an effective partnership. Relationships between the school and the family can be especially critical because studies reveal that school performance represents the most important predictor of the child's future (Boyd-Franklin & Bry, 2000). Learning how to handle the school situation provides important coping skills for the later world of work. Confidence that one can do well in school (academic self-efficacy) buffers adolescents from other stresses (Boyd-Franklin & Bry, 2000).

The counselor may also need to serve as an educator, especially in helping community members understand more about the family in terms of its culture and unique needs. This information can enable others to respond in more appropriate ways to the family and thus make services more effective. This need can be especially important in helping families who have come to the community from very different cultures (for example, refugees).

In other situations, the counselor might need to organize with community members to create a new set or arrangement of resources within the community to meet emerging needs, for example, when families from different cultural groups and with new sets of needs move into communities or in situations in which economic changes place new burdens on community families. Old arrangements for services are no longer adequate to address these new needs. Given the rapid changes occurring in many communities, this has become a rather common occurrence.

While informing families about services can be adequate for some family members, others may require more help in being able to take this step.

> Mr. Cole is reluctant to contact the school system because of his own bad experience as a child. His reluctance not only prevents him from addressing an important family issue but also reduces his self-efficacy as a parent. The counselor can work with Mr. Cole to help him separate his experience as a child from that of his current role as a parent. At the cognitive level, the counselor can help Mr. Cole view himself through the lens of an adult rather than the student he once was. Given Mr. Cole's lack of confidence regarding his ability to take on this parental task, the worker might need to model this action with Mr. Cole and then role-play the respective roles of parent and teacher with Mr. Cole until he feels more comfortable with this step. The social worker identifies Mr. Cole's interest in trying to contact the teacher as a strength and later affirms his efforts. The worker can further emphasize how difficult this has been for Mr. Cole given his past experience and thus how much this represents a real strength on his part.

Exploring with families why they have not received services in the past with an agency can be helpful in identifying strategies for success. It might be that the way the family presented their situation did not fit with the agency's criteria or they did not have the necessary documentation.

> Miss White sought help for her family because of the chronic illness of her youngest child. She met with the agency representative and was denied the help. When the social worker explored the situation and identified the requirements for the service, she realized that Miss White did not bring proper medical documentation from the doctor.

The counselor can work with families to identify ways to present their needs in a more effective manner. Sometimes the counselor learns that family members have been reluctant to state their needs or have acted in such an attacking way with the agency representatives that their needs were not recognized. Again, such efforts are useful not only because they result in the family receiving needed services, but also because they represent areas of success (for the family and the counseling endeavor) and opportunities for the family to learn how to problem-solve in this area more effectively in the future.

Social workers also need to be aware of services that are working at cross-purposes and that sometimes end up giving families mixed messages. Workers can also use their general understanding of the community to recognize services that are especially likely to offer help or subtle barriers that limit access.

As potential resources within the community, the church family can be important for families from various religious traditions. Churches provide an array of programs for families in the community. Most religious traditions have long emphasized charitable efforts, and congregations frequently offer programs for families in the community, for example, Christian (Van Hook &

Aguilar, 2002), Hindu (Singh, 2002), Muslim (Nadir & Dziegielewski, 2002), and Jewish (Friedman, 2002). Spirituality and the church have been strong resources for African American families over the years (Boyd-Franklin, 2003; Grant, 2002; Hines & Boyd-Franklin, 1996). Exploring whether or not this is a potential resource for the specific family can be useful. Some families may also have become alienated from the church community for a variety of reasons.

Family Preservation Models

Family preservation models were developed in order to prevent children from being removed from their homes and to address the needs of families with the multiple problems that made children at risk for such placement. These models represent a type of multisystems approach because they address issues between the family and the larger community context. The approach is short-term and intensive with a combination of home- and community-based interventions. The following section describes family preservation in more detail. A discussion regarding specific programs that have been identified as effective is included in the appendix. The National Family Preservation Network (www.nfpn.org) is an excellent resource for updated information about assessment tools, service models, and research regarding serving these struggling families.

Family preservation models share some major tenets, several of which are reflected in the previous discussion. These include

- Children should remain with their families if at all possible.
- Families are active agents in the change process.
- Families are doing the best they can given the circumstances, but they need help in order to provide better care for their children.
- Intervention should be based on family strengths.
- Therapists should be nonjudgmental and accept families "as they are rather than emphasizing deficits."
- Intervention takes place through engagement with a helper, who assists the family in identifying and building on inherent strengths. (Grigsby, 2003, pp. 75–76)

Family preservation models for families in crisis typically share the following characteristics while the specific details of individual programs vary. With the goal of maintaining the family unit when children are at imminent risk for out-of-home placement, the response is an immediate one. The focus of assessment and treatment is on the family unit and its community context. The goals and objectives are limited. Services include both concrete and psychological interventions and are offered on a short-term (6–12 weeks length) intensive (5–20 hours a week) basis. Services are offered in the home and the community. The family counselor is available outside traditional office hours. Caseloads are small to enable the intensity of services (Grigsby, 2003).

Several core treatment elements of family preservation have been discussed in terms of multisystems therapy with families because these elements are important for counseling with crisis-prone families. The engagement process is critical and must take into consideration the family's suspicion of the counselor given the circumstances and prior experiences with the social service system. Enlisting family members in terms of what is important for them helps establish a collaborative partnership relationship with family members. Searching for the strengths of families and using these as a basis for a strength-based approach helps empower families. The counselor needs to give family members emotional support. This support can take the form of active involvement in the daily life of the family, helping model new ways of responding to family members, and encouraging positive changes. The counselor serves as a positive role model for the family members, especially the parents. The counselor also helps family members learn and practice more effective conflict resolution strategies. The counselor may also need to advocate for families in terms of the broader social service system as well as teaching family members ways to advocate for themselves (Grigsby, 2003).

Thomlison (2004) identifies family preservation and parent education models that have demonstrated effectiveness with at-risk children and their families. These models along with a brief description and citations to obtain more information about specific models are included in the appendix.

Family-Focused Case Management

Family-focused case management represents a valuable intervention approach for families with multiple problems by connecting families with important community resources. According to Greene and Kropf (2003), the purpose of the case management is to provide the family with "service options that promote group and individual functioning" (p. 95). Using a strengths-based approach, "the goals of family case management are to mobilize a family's strengths, to marshal resources, and to maximize family functioning capacity" (p. 85). As discussed in multisystems treatment with families, the case manager assumes a variety of roles in connecting families with services. These include client-focused roles (e.g., educator, enabler), coordinating roles between the family and the services (e.g., service broker, information gatherer), and advocacy roles (e.g., mediator, community organizer) (Greene, 2002).

Case management includes some of the important steps described earlier. The case manager must seek to engage the members of the family system in a relationship characterized by trust. This process includes explaining the case manager's role and the nature and purpose of the information requested. The case manager assesses the family and the relevant context from appropriate sources. The case manager uses a strengths-based perspective in this assessment process. The case manager develops a case plan that is agreed upon collaboratively with the family. The next step is to link the family with relevant services using the roles described above. Service delivery must then be monitored to ensure that services are coordinated and effective. The case manager troubleshoots as necessary to ensure that these are delivered in an appropriate manner. The case manager may need to advocate for services for individuals and for groups in the community with needs. The system of services is evaluated in terms of their effectiveness for the family. Evaluation of services includes attention to the availability and accessibility of services, the services that are available but not used by families, the needs that are going unmet, and providers that might potentially offer services to meet unmet needs (Greene, 2002). Case management can be appropriate for families facing a variety of problems that require linkage and coordination of resources within the community.

Mr. Cole and his family meet with a family case manager. The case manager explains his role in terms of helping link families with services in the community that can be helpful. Mr. Cole identifies some key problems facing the family, especially his concern about the school situation and his son, his worry about his depression, and his wish to obtain better-paying employment. The case manager also assesses strengths and resources within this system, including the daughter's good adjustment to school, Mr. Cole's sister, and the concern of family members for each other. The case manager helps the family identify some of the primary goals and concerns lest the family become overwhelmed with a variety of tasks and persons. The family identifies Mr. Cole's fear of relapse of his depression and the son's school problems and indicates that help in these areas is especially important. The case manager learns that Mr. Cole has discontinued his medication because he has been worried about the cost of the medication and thought that he would try to see how he could do without it. The case manager offers to see if there could be some way to help with the costs of the medication if Mr. Cole's physician suggested that he resume the medication. The case manager explores whether Mr. Cole would like to meet with the school social worker who could work with the family in terms of the school situation. The case manager explains the role of school social workers and how they frequently help families in which there are problems in terms of children in school. With the agreement of the family, the case manager arranges for Mr. Cole and his son to meet with the school social worker. The case manager assures the Cole family of his ongoing interest and that he wants to make sure that the services that they need are working out for the family. He also lets the family know how to contact him if there are needs in the future or if the family later wishes to work on some of the concerns that they identified today.

Evaluation

The families described in this chapter and other literature related to multisystems approaches, including family preservation models and case management, need a multifaceted approach to address their multiple needs both within the family and the larger context. Multisystems family therapy has emerged as effective in improving parenting practices and changing the family environment (Thomlison, 2004) and in addressing adolescent externalizing behavior problems (Sexton, Robbins, Hollimon, Mease, & Mayorga, 2003). In families where abuse and neglect are the key issues, intervention strategies that combine a focus on improving parental skills through providing cognitive, emotional, and behavior competencies that are tailored to the specific needs of the family and their cultural values and creating collaborative partnerships with the parents and other support systems in the community are especially effective (Thomlison, 2004).

Family members who had received services because their children were having serious behavior problems were asked what contributed to positive change. They identified the following elements: a holistic approach that included both the immediate family and the wider context; a relationship with the counselor that included empathy and was based on a person-centered, collaborative, and practical solution-focused approach. Parents reported an increase in parental skills. They also indicated initially being very apprehensive and reluctant to engage in the counseling effort because they were exhausted and feeling great stress. As a result, the caring, empathic approach was especially important. Parents also reported a need for some ongoing help past the formal treatment period (Tighe, Pistrang, Casdagli, Baruch, & Butler, 2012).

Family preservation models have been evaluated primarily in terms of prevention of out-of-home placement. Berry (1999) reviewed the outcome literature on a variety of family preservation models on this dimension. Typically the majority of children were able to remain in their homes. While the numbers ranged from 50 to 90 percent in terms of children in imminent risk of placement, definitions of "imminent" also differed. "Family preservation services were associated with the following changes during services: improvements in behavior, material resources, family structure, family

dynamics, emotional climate, perceptions of problems, community perceptions of the family, information support network, and community involvement" (Berry, 1999, p. 212). Children also improved in terms of school
adjustment, delinquency behavior, and behavior at home (Berry, 1999). Lack
of control groups in most of these studies is a limitation. Berry (1999) further
analyzed the service components that contribute to success: the amount of
time spent in the home; the provision of concrete services "such as teaching
of family care, supplemental parenting medical care, help in securing of
food, and financial services" (p. 213); and being linked to formal social supports (e.g., day care, respite care, medical care). The amount of time spent
in terms of these formal support services was more important than the particular service used. The ability to maintain a clean home emerged as a particularly important life skill. Other more recent studies, however, have revealed
less favorable outcomes, and some families with difficult circumstances have
even shown a deterioration in their ability to provide adequate care for their
children (Cash & Berry, 2003). In evaluating these specific models of treatment, it is important to remember that poverty continues to be a problematic
circumstance for families. Thomlison (2004) has identified a number of models with demonstrated effectiveness that are described in the appendix.

Despite the demonstrated effectiveness of these models with some individual families, it is important not to overlook the ongoing challenges facing
these families due to poverty and other environmental difficulties. As
described earlier, efforts with individual families need to be paired with
those at the community and social policy levels. Prevention at the community level includes addressing social and economic structures that systematically disadvantage families.

Case management has emerged as a valuable approach with families
facing a variety of problems that involve negotiating complex service systems. This approach has been helpful with families and the health care system (Greene & Kropf, 2003), older adults with a variety of needs, individuals
with mental illness and issues associated with housing, employment, and the
mental health and social service systems. In order for case management to be
effective, the case manager needs to be knowledgeable about the relevant
systems, and the systems, in turn, need to have the required resources.

SUMMARY

Models of treatment using a multisystems approach to counseling with families assume a variety of specific forms while sharing a perspective that effective help involves addressing the family and its social context. These models
promote resiliency by addressing the family and its relationship to the

broader social structures. Treatment models are strength-based and action-oriented. Social workers and other family counselors use themselves in multifaceted ways.

Discussion questions

Discuss why taking a strength-based approach is especially important for these families.

What are some of the roles that social workers need to play?

What are some of the barriers to bridging the distance between family members and the counselor (and what are some ideas for bridging them)?

Discuss why you might need to explain why you want some information.

How might you want to phrase your requests for information so as not to make people feel defensive?

While looking for strengths, why is it also important to be aware of potential safety risks for members of the family?

11

Bowen Family Systems Therapy

James and Valerie Mathews have been married for 12 years and have three children: a daughter, Sarah, age 11, and two sons, Mark, age 7, and Bill, age 5. James is an engineer with a local firm and Valerie is a teacher. James views himself as independent and separated from his parents and his siblings. He is very reluctant to spend holidays with his family although the children are unhappy that they are able to see their grandparents so infrequently. The grandfather was very successful financially and loves to treat his grandchildren. Valerie is very close to her parents, who live in the same community. Valerie and the children visit her parents frequently, although James often gives work as his excuse not to be part of the visit. James's mother has recently become quite ill with a chronic illness and his father and sisters have been pressuring him to visit more often. He always finds some reason why he is needed at work and declares these requests to be unreasonable. Valerie notices that these requests leave James anxious and irritated in ways that create tension within the family. Even the children are starting to dread the days when their grandfather or an aunt call the house to speak to their father. The children have learned to tell the grandfather and aunt that their father is not at home although they feel like traitors to their grandparents in doing so. Both James and Valerie have been telling their eleven-year-old-daughter their frustration with each other. She listens to both but feels torn because she cannot take either side without alienating one of her parents. Valerie turns to her usual resource, her parents, and begins seeking advice from them on how to deal with this situation. When James learns what Valerie has been doing, he becomes extremely angry with her and calls her a traitor to her marriage. Not knowing what else to do, Valerie secretly contacts her parents again for advice. The children are also becoming tense as they see this scenario playing out in the family. The seven- and five-year-olds begin to escalate their teasing and physical tussles until Valerie begins to get worried about the impact of their tension on the children. When the behavior problems of the seven-year-old spill out into the school setting, Valerie becomes concerned and tries to enlist James to seek help for the family. As a teacher she is especially attuned to the needs of this child and begins spending additional time with her son. James in turn has been spending less time at home and more time at the office and has been uninvolved in this family drama.

This family has several important protective factors in terms of adequate financial resources, parents' ability to carry out their challenging professional roles, and the presence of caring grandparents. The couple has been married for over twelve years and until recently the family had settled roles that met most of the family needs. Valerie is generally attentive to the needs of the children. At the same time, there are risk factors in terms of the marital relationship, which is characterized by tension arising most recently from the inability of James to respond to the requests by his parents and sister to attend to his mother's needs. This tension has rippled throughout the family system as evidenced by the behavior of the younger children. The eleven-year-old daughter has been triangulated into this arrangement by both her parents and feels helpless to escape this no-win situation. While James views himself as independent of his family, his behavior reflects a pattern of being strongly influenced by his parents. The more they seek to draw him closer to them, the more he withdraws. In stark contrast to James, Valerie is very close to her family. In fact, she views them as her most reliable source of support and turns to them despite the wishes of her husband and the likely tension that it creates. There are serious communication problems in terms of Valerie and James, especially as it relates to their respective relationships with their parents.

Bowen systemic family therapy addresses the interpersonal world of family members, especially in terms of the shadows created by relationships between generations. These families have their basic needs met but relationships are troubled by family patterns.

While James views himself as independent from his parents and sister, in reality he is very emotionally reactive to his family. As they make requests (pursues), he retreats and pulls away further (distances himself). In fact, his behavior might also be characterized by a pattern of whatever they ask of him, he does the opposite. He has mistaken independence for an emotional cutoff. In reality a person who is truly differentiated can choose to be close to his parents, can choose to agree, can choose to be part of the family. For James, these are not options that he views for himself. Valerie, on the other hand, manifests lack of differentiation in the opposite manner, being very involved with her family even at the price of creating tension within the family. While their behaviors are very different, in reality both of them have had difficulty truly differentiating from their families of origin. From a systems perspective, James and Valerie have married individuals at similar levels of differentiation. Both parents have also pulled their daughter into a situation of triangulation whereby she feels that she must listen to both of them and yet cannot take either side (despite implicit demands by both parents that she agree with them).

Goals of Treatment

The primary goal is to help family members differentiate so that their behavior in the family is not based on emotional reactivity regarding current and family of origin issues. This process enables family members to relate in a manner that provides for one's individuality as well as connections. A related goal is to reduce family anxiety that fuels problems with differentiation and the existence of triangles within the family system.

Major Tenets

1. Triangles are formed in families to cope with anxiety.
2. The ideal state is one of differentiation—the ability to function autonomously, to balance thinking and feeling, to be intimate with others without sacrificing one's own individuality.
3. Cutoffs and fusion are two ways in which failure to differentiate manifests itself.
4. Parents can project their own struggles in an unconscious manner onto one of their children through parental projection.
5. The process of differentiation is transmitted from generation to generation.
6. Birth order plays an important role in families.

Theoretical Background

Murray Bowen was one of the leading pioneers in family systems theory. His own professional background was psychoanalysis, and this approach helped inform his understanding of families. Daniel Papero (2000) and Nichols and Schwartz (2001) provide excellent descriptions of Murray Bowen's professional journey and its impact on his theory and practice.

Bowen viewed the family as a system occurring over time. He was concerned about how people exist both as individuals and in relationships as well as the role of anxiety within the family system. As a result, he developed the following theoretical concepts that are the cornerstones of his theory. These concepts and the related technique of the genogram have been influential in other theoretical approaches that address family organizational issues. The following concepts are included in publications regarding Bowen's family systems theory (for example, Bowen, M. [1978], Walsh & Harrigan [2003], and the current web page of the Bowen Center for the Study of the Family [www.thebowencenter.org/pages/concepts.html, 2012]).

Triangles. Triangles are formed when two members of the family enlist a third member in such a way that the third person really cannot escape and does not feel that he or she can comment. Such a triangulation process is a response to anxiety within the two individuals who in turn create anxiety within the third party through the process of triangulation. James and Valerie have triangulated their daughter. She wants to please both parents and does not feel as a child that she can refuse to play the role in the family that they have assigned her.

Differentiation. Bowen's concern was the ability of family members to be both together in relationships and to be individuals. The ideal state is one of differentiation—the ability to function autonomously, to balance thinking and feeling, to be intimate with others without sacrificing one's own individuality. In terms of behavior, failure to differentiate can be manifested either in people who conform at great costs or who act reactively in an opposite manner. For example, James is so caught up in his need to distance himself from his parents that he cannot respond to the illness of his mother and reflect on the cost of his actions to his family. Valerie is so close to her parents that she cannot find other sources of support that will not create tension within her family.

Emotional cutoffs. Family members can deal with their lack of differentiation by being emotionally distant from family members. The quality of this distance is emotionally reactive in nature. As indicated earlier, James has dealt with the emotions created by his family of origin by cutting himself off from this family and instead burying himself at work.

Emotional fusion. This represents the other side of emotional cutoffs. Here individuals are so connected with others that they in effect lose their own individuality. Their feelings and thoughts are in essence those of others.

Individuals who are undifferentiated are also less able to handle anxiety and stress. This tension can result in (1) "marital conflict," (2) "reactive emotional distance," (3) "physical or emotional dysfunction in one or more of the spouses," and (4) "projection of problems onto the children" (Nichols & Schwartz, 2001, p. 142).

Family/parental projection. Parents can project their own struggles in an unconscious manner onto one of their children through parental projection. As parents are unable to address their own relationship, children are pulled into the situation. The child's behavior in turn enables the parents to focus their anxiety on this child—for example, James and Valerie's seven-year-old son who "needs" his mother's expertise as a teacher.

Multigenerational transmission process. The process of differentiation is transmitted from generation to generation. Anxiety within the family situation reduces the level of differentiation. The situation is compounded because people are likely to marry individuals at similar levels of differentia-tion. Valerie and James, for example, are both emotionally reactive to their families, although the manifestation of this is at opposite poles.

Family birth order and sibling position. These play important roles in the development of a child, especially as the children fit into the broader family system. Each of the children of James and Valerie is influenced in different ways by the family situation. James's role within the family birth order had a powerful effect on this family role.

Promotes Resiliency by

- Addressing risk factors associated with rigid family organizational patterns (cutoffs and fusion) and evidence of reactivation of past events.

- Strengthening protective factors by enabling family members to cre-ate positive interactions based on differentiation and possibilities within the current family reality that in turn can create a genuine sense of affection within the family.

Role of the Counselor

Bowen described the role of the family therapist as a "coach" (Walsh, 2003, p. 158). The therapist serves "as a model for rational interaction" (Walsh & Harrigan, 2003, p. 387). Bowen viewed the role of the counselor as remain-ing neutral and objective. In order to reduce the excessive anxiety and reac-tive emotion with the family members, his approach is based on facts and thoughts rather than feelings. The attention is on process rather than the content to avoid getting caught up in the hotbed of emotionally laden con-tent. The therapist engages in dialogue with individual family members in the presence of the other family members. The coach helps family members identify triangles within their current family as well as family of origin.

The neutral approach of Bowen was altered by followers who were concerned about gender issues within the family and thus addressed issues related to power differentials or gender scripts that influenced power within the family system (Nichols & Schwartz, 2001, p 158).

Assessment

The genogram. The genogram plays a critical role in the assessment process within family systems therapy. As described and illustrated in chapter 3, "Assessment of Families," the genogram is a diagram of the current family as well as the family of origin. While ideally it should include three generations, this is not always possible. The genogram not only includes the names and birth dates and death dates of family members but also concise descriptions (type of work, personal style) and alliances within the family tree. This assessment tool is designed to help family members recognize patterns and messages that are transmitted from generation to generation.

As described in chapter 3, the Loden family members recognized messages that were transmitted regarding illness and health that were controlling current reactions to the health situation of their son. A genogram of Valerie and James also reveals messages. The following genogram information, expressed in words, is organized in greater detail in terms of James, but in therapy this genogram would also trace the family line for both parents.

James's paternal grandfather had been a tool and die maker who had provided a good living for the family (including James's father and his two older sisters). His grandmother had been a homemaker who cared for the family until she became quite ill and was no longer able to do so. The two daughters were then enlisted into this role. The grandfather became very anxious and found it both difficult to concentrate on his work (essential for his very precise work) while at the same time retreating to the shop to deal with the pressures at home.

James's father's anxiety created by this family scenario translated into a determination to protect himself and his family by becoming a successful businessman. He viewed this as a way of controlling life circumstances. He made good on this determination, obtained a graduate education in business, and did very well in the field of business. James's father and mother had had two daughters before a boy was born. This child was born with congenital abnormalities and died as a toddler. James was born two years later. His mother hovered over James, afraid that something might also take him away from the family. The message was one of danger. The father placed on James the expectation that he would follow in the father's footsteps and carry on in the family business. He was critical of the mother's hovering approach, urged James to become more physically adventuresome with him, but never directly challenged the mother's overprotective behavior with her son. As a result, James felt contradictory messages directed at him. James's sisters were close together but older than James so he did not feel a close sibling-type of relationship with them—instead they were more like junior parents.

James disappointed his father by not wanting to follow in the family business. Instead he became very interested in how "things worked," and began to think about engineering. From the perspective of his father, this was following in the footsteps of the grandfather and not a safe journey. Father and son had many heated arguments. The mother stayed out of these arguments but was anxious about James leaving the family to go away to school and expressed her worries to him. James did not feel that he could share his wishes and concerns with his sisters because he viewed them as allied with his parents.

James responded to these messages of "you are weak," "you are not living up to family expectations" by cutting himself off from the family. His badge of honor of independence from his family is in essence a cover-up for his inability to differentiate from family messages. Family visits served to reactivate anxious feelings so the safe path was to avoid family contact. The illness of his mother and pressure from his father and siblings to become engaged again in the family, especially in response to family need and illness, have set in motion increased anxiety that he is dealing with by distancing himself further.

Valerie grew up as an only child in her family. Her mother had had two miscarriages prior to her birth and one following her birth. Valerie was born premature and struggled as a baby with a heart problem that was addressed through several surgeries. Her mother was very protective of Valerie and attentive to any potential signs of heart issues. Valerie's father was also very close to her. Both parents tended to shield Valerie from stressful situations. She could count on them as a safe haven during potentially stressful times. She grew up feeling very vulnerable and close to both of her parents, whom she tended to rely on for strength when she felt overwhelmed.

While James's and Valerie's behaviors in terms of their families of origin are very different—Valerie very attached and James in a cutoff stance—both share problems in becoming comfortably differentiated from their parents. Illness is also a very potent source of anxiety within these families and carries messages of threat, loss, and vulnerability.

The information provided by the genogram thus provides a means by which family members can identify messages from family of origin that are influencing current family tension. The therapist can ask questions that help family members identify current patterns as they relate to these earlier messages.

Treatment Process

Providing a setting that is safe to explore family patterns without emotional reactivity. This context is important because family members are likely to replicate in the session the emotional reactivity and related behavior patterns that have maintained the problem. Bowen frequently worked only with one of the family members, typically the family member who was the most differentiated and thus willing to consider change.

Genogram. The genogram serves both as an assessment and a treatment tool. Constructing the genogram provides the family an opportunity to understand its family messages that are continuing to play a role and creating problems. As described in the Loden family and Valerie and James, the genogram provides a visual tool for recognizing how these patterns have developed and are continuing.

The genogram is also an important tool for other elements of family treatment: helping family members gain insight, educating members about family issues in general, reducing triangulation within the family scene, creating new attachments with others, and changing old relationships with family members.

Insight. Insight is important for understanding and change. Insight can be directed toward the current nature of interpersonal relationships (family triangles, family themes) and the developmental nature of family relationships over time (Walsh & Harrigan, 2003).

In terms of James and Valerie, the genogram and associated conversation helped family members develop insight into their family and use this to begin to make changes within the immediate and extended family system. This insight is part of a step to enable people to begin the differentiation process. The first step is further understanding and insight into the family system. The second is to use this understanding to reduce the emotional reactivity involved. The third (and potential) step is to try to make changes in relationships with others within the family system. The word *try* is used here because individuals must realize that they ultimately cannot control the reactions of other people. The following illustrates these steps.

> Valerie has gained a better understanding of the anxiety created by the current situation in James's family. This has helped her not to take his response so personally. Valerie has begun to understand how her own dependence on her family, as evidenced by her sharing with her parents these issues, is increasing tension within the family. She has also begun to explore other possibilities for support than her parents. James and Valerie can problem-solve ways that they can address this situation without pulling their daughter into it. James has gained insight into the pulls that he is experiencing in terms of his mother's illness, especially given the context of worries of illness over the years. He has begun to recognize ways in which his father's expressed disappointment regarding his career choice was partly a way to protect his family rather than a mark of failure on James's part. James identifies his relationship with his younger sister as less emotionally toxic as the one he has with his parents. Recognizing that his sister might respond as he hopes that she will, he reaches out to his sister to learn more about what is happening in the family. He is fortunate that she is receptive. His conversation with his sister gives him further understanding of the family story. He explores with his sister ways that he can reconnect with his parents without being pulled into the earlier roles and emotional reactions.

Evaluation and reinforcement of progress. Walsh and Harrigan (2003) describe several clinical approaches that the family therapist can use to evaluate the progress of family members and to help reinforce progress. These techniques can aid family members in examining how behavior has changed as a result of therapy and ways to help sustain it.

- The use of dual genograms: one regarding how they see themselves and the others as they wish to be. Family members can be asked to create genograms periodically during therapy to examine how the current situation is approaching what people would like it to be. These can also be used by the therapist to summarize the nature of progress.

- Observations and experience of anxiety in the session: the therapist can observe behavior patterns of interaction that reflect on more positive interactions as well as his own experience of anxiety with the family. During the process of termination, this information can be shared with the family. Family members can be asked what they think contributes to the therapist's decreased sense of anxiety as a way to test changes in interaction patterns.

- Changes in relationship patterns: the therapist can ask family members to share their plans for maintaining these changes.

- Evidence of insight: the therapist can ask the family members to review what they have learned about themselves and their family.

- Rituals: rituals can be used to affirm the progress the family has made and to integrate this new understanding and behavior into their daily life. Family members help develop rituals that are appropriate for their family life experience.

Evaluation

Bowen and his colleagues were typically more concerned with theory and related practice than in conducting evaluations of therapy. One study did indicate that the treatment was associated with statements that reflected greater degrees of differentiation (Winter, 1971 as cited by Nichols and Schwartz, 2001, p. 171). The treatment as designed and implemented by Bowen appeared most appropriate for families that were relatively enmeshed and not troubled by financial difficulties (Nichols & Schwartz, 2001). At the same time, the concepts of "family system" and "triangulation," have proven very valuable, and the genogram is a useful tool for family therapists using a variety of approaches.

SUMMARY

Family systems theory was one of the early attempts to bridge individual and family concepts and to understand ways in which early family relationships impact on current family systems. It developed important concepts such as the genogram, triangles, differentiation, and fusion/emotional cutoffs. Therapy was organized around helping persons individuate from their family of origin so that they could develop authentic relationships with family members while retaining their own sense of individuality. The focus in the sessions is upon intellectual understanding rather than emotions. Families typically have their basic needs met and do not need additional services.

DISCUSSION QUESTIONS

Discuss how problems in differentiation can manifest themselves in completely opposite behaviors.

How does the genogram facilitate both the assessment and the treatment process?

How does triangulation help mitigate anxiety for some family members and increase it for others?

Why is it important for the family therapist to assume an emotionally unreactive manner in the therapy process in this model?

12

Object Relations Family Therapy

Lewis and Emily Wilson are seeking therapy because Emily has been struggling with severe anxiety during the past year. They have been married for three years and would like to begin a family. They are seeking help to relieve Emily's suffering and because they do not think that it would be a good idea to have a baby while she is experiencing such disabling anxiety. While anti-anxiety medication has been somewhat helpful, they have also felt that there has been a strain in their relationship and do not want to risk Emily's becoming dependent on such medication. Emily wants to return to her old self, the cheerful engaging person that she was when they got married and that Lewis fell in love with. Lewis is disappointed because Emily is not the loving person that he thought he had married because her anxiety makes her withdraw from many of the activities that they used to enjoy together. Lewis works long hours as an accountant for a local business and is able to support the family adequately through his work. Sometimes he finds himself working even longer hours than necessary because he does not know how to handle the current situation at home. He then feels guilty and becomes more solicitous toward Emily. Emily has worked as a receptionist but has found it difficult to work in a steady way since her anxiety has become more severe. Both Lewis and Emily had mothers who suffered from illness (depression and cancer) and want to spare their children this pain. They met during college. Lewis was two years ahead of Emily. They married after he graduated. She found work as a receptionist and did not continue her education. Her engaging personality made her a good receptionist until she began to become so anxious.

Lewis grew up in a family in which his mother suffered from chronic depression that made her unavailable to her child. His father was burdened down with the financial responsibilities of the family and tried to meet the bills by working two jobs. Lewis was an only child and did not have siblings that would help buffer his sense of aloneness. His grandparents did not live in the area. Lewis developed internalized objects (internalized concepts of himself and others) that included his anger toward his parents for their emotional unavailability and a longing for closeness, along with a fear of loss and a sense of self that did not view himself as worthy of his mother's love. He coped by trying to be very mature and good (the false self) in order to try to win his parents' love and to protect himself against his own anger and longing. His appearance as a young adult in the dating world was that of a pleasant and self-assured person who was attentive to the needs of others. When he met Emily in college, she was an engaging young woman who was impressed with his maturity. He in turn was impressed with her warmth and eagerness to be close to him.

Emily was looking for a source of strength because she too had struggled with early experiences that left her feeling unsure of herself. She was the youngest of four children and the only daughter. Her mother had been ill with cancer for much of her childhood and was in and out of hospitals until she died when Emily was beginning middle school. While her mother was very loving when she was home and feeling better, her illness was very disabling for much of the time. Her father was the strong parent in the family and Emily felt safe when she was able to be with her father, but his responsibilities also included financially providing for and caring for the other three children in the family. Emily grew up with internalized objects that included a fear of loss of her mother, longing for closeness and protection, and a sense that women were weak and could only be safe by being close to a strong male. While Lewis coped by appearing very mature and attentive to the needs of others, Emily coped by trying to be very engaging to her father and other men to keep them attached to her and a source of protection.

While this young couple has many protective factors in terms of adequate financial resources, their intellect, ability to cope with education and work, and commitment to each other, their relationship has become severely strained in response to Emily's anxiety and Lewis's uncertainty about how to cope with it. They are currently in a cyclical pattern. Lewis is alternating between being solicitous to Emily and distant in response to feeling overwhelmed. Emily, in turn, feels anxious when Lewis becomes distant. She is ambivalent about his solicitous response because it both sends a message that he cares and can lend her his strength but also that she is a weak person who is unable to cope and thus cannot survive without him.

Goal of Treatment

Object relations therapy seeks to enable family members to relate to each other in a genuine manner that fosters individual growth as well as satisfying connections within the family. The therapist seeks to do so by helping family members reduce the anxiety that keeps them bound to the types of relationships created to deal with earlier needs and conflicts. Object relations theory recognizes that human relationships occur between our internalized concepts of others and ourselves that are created through time. Through object relations therapy, individuals are helped to move beyond the shadows cast by the object relationships created earlier in life that have been projected in a problematic way onto their current family members. Symptom relief and behavior change are viewed as by-products of the resolution of underlying conflicts.

Object relations family therapy addresses the interpersonal relationships within the family. From the perspective of object relations theory, relationship problems have their origin within the early life experiences of family members and are played out in the framework of current core family relationships. This process shapes ongoing family relationships. Many of the early pioneers of family therapy had their original training and orientation in psychodynamic theory and their work grew out of this perspective. Object relations family therapy draws upon object relations theory to understand the interpersonal world occurring within the family context. From the perspective of object relations theory, relationships with others represent a core need so that life is an ongoing story of the need for connection with others as well as the need to be a separate individual. The term *object* in object relations theory has implications for the relationships between individuals; however, objects are not equivalent to other individuals. Objects represent the internalized perceptions of others and thus never truly match the reality of the other individuals. These internalized objects include not only the actual behavior of the other individuals but also how this behavior is perceived and integrated into the already existing framework (Goldstein, 1995). Such internalized objects influence subsequent relationships with others. As discussed in the following section, the child deals with frustrations in the course of development through a process of repression (removal from consciousness) and splitting (separation of the perceived good and bad). Object relations family therapy seeks to reduce the need for splitting and repression and thus to modify the problematic projective systems in place within the family (Scharff & Scharff, 2003).

Theoretical Background

Object relations theory and family therapy come from several different theoretical approaches to human development. From the perspective of attachment theory, the infant is born both dependent upon the mother for survival as well as with the competencies to engage the mothering person (Bowlby, 1969). Research with infants has revealed that even young infants have remarkable capacities to discern the interpersonal world around them. By two to three months of age the infant appears to relate in an integrated manner suggestive of the development of a core self (Stern, 1985). Scharff and

Scharff (2003) describe the infant as born "able to use relationships for survival and for the pleasure that relatedness brings" (p. 60). According to Fairbairn the child is born with a fully formed and differentiated ego that permits the child to relate to others and at the same time to be autonomous, that is, be an individual and a member of a family group. Typically the mothering person is able to respond to the child well enough so that the child can cope with the pain during times in which the mother is unable to respond. When the caregiving adult is chronically unable to respond or the child is constitutionally challenged, the child can become overwhelmed by the experience (Scharff & Scharff, 2003). This experience of frustration creates a differentiation within the child's ego into unconscious and conscious parts. When this sense of frustration is overwhelming, the ego deals with this by the defense of "splitting," dividing the frustrating experiences into bad and the satisfying ones into good. The ego then becomes a complex internalized structure composed of three elements: (1) the central ego that is conscious, connected to the ideal object and feelings of satisfaction; (2) the libidinal ego that is unconscious, connected to the need-exciting object and feelings of emptiness, neediness, longing, and craving; and (3) the anti-libidinal ego that is unconscious, connected to the rejecting object, and filled with feelings of outrage, anger, and hurt. Although the self seeks to be whole again, the central ego continues to repress the other aspects of the self in order to protect itself from pain (Goldstein, 1995; Scharff & Scharff, 2003). As the child has ongoing interpersonal experiences, the central ego remains open to new experiences that can modify this original configuration. If the central ego has been significantly compromised because the splitting is so severe, the process of being open to new experiences and modifying in response becomes problematic and personal growth is stunted.

Winnicott emphasizes the essential infant-mother bond and identifies two aspects of the mother: the environment mother who holds the infant and the object mother who engages the infant through eye contact. According to Winnicott, infants need "good enough mothering." Problematic patterns occur if mothers are too distant or do not permit their babies appropriate separation. When the infant is unable to receive mothering or experiences serious problematic patterns, the child develops "the false self" that is erected to please others and protect the child from pain (Goldstein, 1995; Scharff & Scharff, 2003). Traumatic experiences can be especially problematic in terms of the child's attachment patterns and development of the sense of self (James, 1994).

Klein took the concept of splitting further by describing how the child projects onto the mother both the child's aggressive, death instinct (the bad mother) and the child's life-affirming views (the good mother). Such a process protects the infant from his or her anger and destructive impulses. She used the term "projective identification" to describe this process (Scharff & Scharff, 2003). This process of projecting has emerged as one of the pillars of object relations family therapy. Bion (1970) viewed the infant's anxiety in terms of how the mother processes it. The mother takes the anxiety of the infant and processes it in a structured way that is manageable for the infant. As the infant identifies with the mother and her processing of anxiety, he or she develops his or her own psychic structures for coping with anxiety (Scharff & Scharff, 2003). The mother's difficulty in processing anxiety can thus be transmitted to the infant in the developmental process. When young children become angry or frustrated, they can lash out at their mothers or fathers with "I hate you" and other similar words. A mature parent can help the child deal with his or her strong feelings by words to the effect that "I know you are angry with me but I still love you." Sadly, some parents are unable to respond in this manner and either lash out in turn or turn away and reject the young child—leaving the child with no way to resolve and cope with their own anxiety and anger.

From the perspective of object relations theory, these early life experiences contribute to the relationships within the current family. The shadows of the past become incorporated into the current object relations context and individuals relate to others accordingly. Individuals whose object relations are characterized by fear of rejection bring this into their current relations and respond to others accordingly. Individuals with an anxious attachment pattern will fear loss and respond to others in ways that are governed by this fear. They might compromise other important personal needs to maintain a relationship and avoid the danger of loss. The core couple relationships consist of a union between two complex phenomena: (1) the central ego system of each individual and (2) the split-off and repressed internal object relationship—either the exciting or rejecting object. The process is further compounded by the process of projective identification identified by Klein (Nichols & Schwartz, 1998; Scharff & Scharff, 2003). In this process, the individual's conscious and unconscious internal object relationships are projected onto the spouse; for example, a sense of personal weakness and accompanying need to have an all-protecting person creates in turn a need to see the partner as very strong with no personal doubts and vulnerabilities. Problematic patterns occur when the other partner is unable to separate from these projections and cause them to reflect reality in a more accurate manner. In the preceding example, the partner acts as if he or she has no vulnerabilities and never seeks support from the spouse or others. Scharff and Scharff (2003) describe unhealthy marriages as those in which instead of reality altering the projections, the other partner behaves in such a way to confirm these projections and both partners are unable to grow as individuals. The projective identification process is really a dance between the two partners with a joint process of projection and collusion occurring at the same time. For example, Lewis projects his anxiety and fears onto Emily, who in turn accepts this projection and becomes increasingly anxious.

From the perspective of object relations family therapy, Emily and Lewis demonstrate a set of projections and identifications. As a result, their conscious needs for an adult close relationship that will allow them to become genuine partners and parents are not being met. At the unconscious level, however, this arrangement meets some important needs for both individuals that cause them to remain stuck in this pattern. Both Emily and Lewis grew up with object relations that reflected fear of loss combined with a longing for closeness. Lewis is able to project onto Emily his fear of loss and weakness that in turn fits with her own fears of loss and view of men as strong. Emily is able to project onto Lewis her fears of loss and sense of aloneness created both by her mother and her father and her insecurities about women and the parallel strength of men. Emily's anxiety keeps her safely dependent on Lewis and thus close to him. His own sense of weakness that he has defended against by his image of maturity and strength is projected onto Emily, who in turn responds by becoming anxious. Emily's view of fear of loss is projected onto Lewis, who in turn needs to care for her. His strength and care for her confirms her view of men as strong and herself as weak.

The challenge for this young couple is for each of them to separate their current relationship from the shadows and unmet needs of the past. Both Emily and Lewis have strengths that can contribute and needs that can be met without the cost of Emily's anxiety and Lewis's burden of the total responsibility of the family. Emily will no longer need an overall powerful man to take care of her. Lewis then can relax that Emily will not abandon him if she is able to be strong.

Scharff (2006) further describes the ongoing process that occurs within the immediate family and the wider circle in which it lives. Children and their parents both develop sets of introjected (incorporated into the self) objects. Children introject objects based on their experiences with their parents. Parents in turn both project onto their children aspects of their own parents and develop internalized objects of their children. Parental projection onto children can result in children's becoming scapegoats. Parents who are struggling with their own aggressive aspects can project these onto their children, who cooperate by acting in a delinquent manner. Other parents can project their own anxiety and sense of weakness and these children can accept these projections in the form of fear of going to school. Parents can project onto their children their own unresolved sexual needs and these children accept these projections in the form of sexual promiscuousness.

Using a family development perspective, Scharff describes family development as set within a nest of concentric circles that hold the family: the mother who holds the child and is held by the child, the father who holds both of them and is held by them, the wider nuclear family that in turn both holds and is held, that in turn is held by the extended family. This family group is then held by their relevant social circles, that in turn is held by the wider society.

Major Tenets

1. Family members bring to their current family the object relations system that was developed during their earlier life experiences.
2. Individuals project their conscious and unconscious internal object relationships upon the spouse or other family member who in turn can fit and identify with this projection.
3. Problems in the family occur when family members are unable to separate from these projections and both members of the family are unable to grow as individuals.
4. The task of the family therapist is to enable the family members to cope with their anxiety and begin to recognize and respond to people in a more open and healthy manner.
5. Transference and countertransference are important tools in the therapeutic process.

Promotes Resiliency by

- Addressing risk factors associated with the reactivation of unresolved past interpersonal relationships.
- Strengthening protective factors by helping family members resolve past interpersonal relationships and thus potentially creating positive and trusting family relationships based on realistic appraisals of the current relationships.

Role of the Therapist

Scharff and Scharff (2006) describe the role of the therapist as the "new attachment figure" that enables people to deal with their anxiety in a healthier manner (p. 31). Through the therapeutic relationship, the therapist seeks to enable the family to transform its anxiety into an emotional experience that can be tolerated, thought about, and thus managed differently in the future. The therapist "bears the family's anxiety, reflects on the experience of being with that family, and puts anxiety into words" (Scharff & Scharff, 2003, p. 66). Frequently family members experienced painful events that were handled either by repression or by emotional amplification by important family members in the past (Scharff & Scharff, 2006). In contrast, the therapeutic situation creates a situation in which family members can tolerate and experience painful events, past trauma, and anxiety in ways that can be integrated in a manageable way. Through this process, family members are able to develop their own ability of self-regulation by identifying with the family counselor and thus no longer need the presence of the therapist to do so (Scharff & Scharff, 2006). The emphasis is upon the therapist's relationship with the family and the members of the family with each other. Family therapists need to have a good understanding of their own personal issues to order to be helpful to the family. The family therapist behaves in a calm and helpful manner—friendly and yet professional.

Assessment

Scharff and Scharff (2003) describe a structured assessment process of one to four sessions. The arrangement is carefully structured and attempts to alter this structure are explored in terms of their therapeutic meaning. The therapist seeks to hear from all concerned. The focus is on identifying any transference manifestation of treatment and exploring them in terms of anxiety about treatment. The family therapist is also attuned to his or her countertransference toward the family and uses it as a tool for understanding the family. By being aware of issues within his or her own internalized objects, the family therapist can come to a better understanding of the family (Scharff & Scharff, 1987, 2003). If the therapist begins to feel a need to protect one of the family members, it might be in response to an internalized object of weakness by a family member and the need to create relationships in which one is cared for.

The therapist focuses on the relationships among family members and between the family members and the therapist. The therapist attends to the signs of transference that take the form of resistance to treatment. As part of helping the family members begin to deal with their anxiety, the therapist brings the family's distrust of therapy into the session in a non-defensive manner that can contribute to trust.

The interview follows the family members' account of their story with attention to pauses and possible omissions that serve as clues to the unconscious of the family members. The therapist explores with the family the meaning of possible omissions. The therapist also attends to strong emotional exchanges that occur and explores with the family members if these were anything like what they had experienced in their family of origin. Intense emotions are viewed as a replay of past experiences that cannot be remembered, only reenacted. By bringing these core emotional exchanges into consciousness, family members can be helped to come to terms with them and to decrease their current toxic power (Scharff & Scharff, 2003). The calm and non-judgmental presence of the therapist enables the family members to discuss their private life in a way that encourages understanding. As family members describe the problem, they begin to reenact family patterns that reveal their defensive patterns within the sessions in ways that can be explored within therapy. Scharff and Scharff (2003) describe transference and countertransference as the key to therapeutic action. As the therapist recognizes how the family affects her in terms of her own countertransference issues, she can begin to work with the family from this perspective.

Treatment Process

Several treatment approaches are important in object relations family therapy. Scharff and Scharff (2003), Nichols and Schwartz (1998), and Kilpatrick, Kilpatrick, and Callaway (2000) describe the following approaches. Given the intensely private nature of the content that can occur, the therapist is very conscious of appropriate family boundaries. For example, sexual relationship issues are discussed between the couple separate from their children.

Interpretations that link events and contribute to insight are valuable. These interpretations identify relationship patterns, especially those with a "because" clause. Scharff and Scharff (2003) describe these as addressing the multilayers of relationships—the relationship that is openly required, the one that is avoided, and the calamity that it fends off. The family's response to these interpretations also serves as an assessment of whether or not the family is interested in understanding their family problems in a psychologically insightful manner or if another approach is more appropriate at this time (Scharff & Scharff, 2003).

Transference and countertransference issues are critical in the ongoing treatment process. They give clues in terms of the early experiences of family members.

Empathic listening involves waiting for people to say what they want to say and imagining the situation facing them. To facilitate empathy and understanding, family members are asked to tell more, to draw a picture of the family, or to describe a dream. Empathic listening gives support to family members. As in other models of family therapy, listening includes nonverbal as well as verbal communication.

Clarification comments by the therapist are shared with all family members to ensure that everyone hears the views that have been expressed.

The therapist also makes "*shaping comments*" to bring together the process to date. Development of a shared narrative experience occurs when the therapist puts conflict into words. By describing the repetitive patterns, family members can begin to face their underlying anxieties. The therapist uses countertransference to experience these conflicts.

Identification of unconscious projections based on the family patterns is a first step toward helping family members begin to own their projective identifications. Family members can be helped to recognize how their own repressed wishes are reflected in the "problematic" behavior of the other person.

Use of adjunctive methods. Object relations therapy recognizes that interpretations are not always adequate to address important patterns like substance abuse or mental illness. Therapists encourage families to seek help from programs like Alcoholics Anonymous and other appropriate forms of help.

Brief Object Relations Family Therapy

Stadter and Scharff (2006) describe focal psychotherapy, a brief therapy approach using object relations theory with emphasis on the joint projective process within the marital relationship and a psychodynamic model of brief therapy. This approach emphasizes four key elements:

1. Each individual, family, and therapeutic relationship is unique and therapy must be tailored to this uniqueness.
2. People are helped to identify the past patterns that continue to repeat themselves so that people can be helped to create new patterns.
3. A positive therapeutic relationship is critical for success.
4. It is important to study the ongoing patterns within the relationship (transference and countertransference) as well as to combine them with interpretations as appropriate to enable people to develop new ways of relating.

Stadter and Scharff (2006) describe eight strategies but caution that there are two critical elements in such brief therapy efforts: (1) strategies must be set within a positive therapeutic relationship, and (2) a clear focus must be established to organize the therapeutic effort.

Strategy 1. Establishment of the therapeutic alliance is the critical first step and involves the therapist's empathic understanding, non-judgmental approach, and interactions that convey respect. It is important not to let the pressures for brief treatment force this process to proceed faster than family members are ready. This positive therapeutic relationship is fostered by several actions of the therapist: directing attention to and demonstrating understanding of the client's pain, taking a history in a way that creates a shared process of discovery, collaboratively setting a focus, and attending to the transference and countertransference reactions in ways that permit one to use the client's internal language.

Strategy 2. Create a dual focus on symptoms and dynamics. Ideally it is valuable to be able to link symptoms to the dynamics of the individuals. For example, "Your intense anxiety about taking your final tests seems to be linked to your ongoing fear that you will not live up to your father's expectations." "Your fear of bringing up issues with your wife/husband seems to be linked to your fear of losing someone important as occurred when your mother deserted the family when you were a child."

*Strategy 3. Obtain historical information related to family members'
object relations patterns.* This process can help individuals see patterns in
what previously was experienced as random, for example, understanding a
history of fearing that one is not living up to one's father's expectations and
a pattern of fearing to face situations in which one could be judged even if
it means giving up on otherwise desired goals. Several important aspects in
a history can include the following:

- Family members' impression of parents and other key family members or others that influenced their personality

- Ongoing patterns of interpersonal relationships—backing away from intimacy, abuse

- Best and worst levels of functioning

- Family history of problems and dysfunction

- Previous suicidal thinking and other disturbed thinking, health issues

- Previous therapy (Stadter & Scharff, 2006, p. 424)

*Strategy 4. Engage family members in looking at the way in which they
and the family therapist are relating.* This provides family members a way
of looking at their past relational patterns and ways in which they are occurring in the present. Recognizing the anxiety that this can pose for clients,
the therapist can invite members by asking about their response to certain
interactions.

Strategy 5. Interpret dynamics and patterns when possible (Stadter &
Scharff, 2006, p. 425). The presence of transference and countertransference
within the therapeutic situation provides the opportunity to look at these
patterns. The therapist might notice ways in which the couple avoid dealing
with painful issues by quickly changing the subject. When this occurs, the
therapist can wonder if they are fearful of what might happen if they should
explore this further because they sometimes appear to be fearful with each
other. If previously revealed historical material might reveal trauma or other
life experiences that have made such conversations anxiety-producing
because it makes the individual feel weak or threatened, the therapist can
further link these patterns with such earlier life experiences.

Strategy 6. Use non-psychodynamic techniques as appropriate. The
therapist can draw upon techniques from other traditions to enhance the
efforts. The therapist must be aware of the impact on the relationship of the
use of other techniques and ways in which transference and countertransference issues can play out in such recommendations. Therefore it is crucial
to be aware of the family members' inner world in making such recommendations.

Strategy 7. Therapy can be thought of in terms of segments, so that clients can return for ongoing work as needed.

Strategy 8. Arrange for clients to have "a new ending for an old experience" (Stadter & Scharff, 2006, p. 428). The therapist can offer new outcomes for old patterns of clients in order to allow them to experiment with new ways of relating. For example, a client who has always related to people who viewed her as incompetent can find in the therapist a person who looks for evidence of her competence and relates to her as a competent adult rather than a child in an adult body.

Stadter and Scharff (2006) describe the following client characteristics as indicative that brief therapy would be appropriate:

- the ability to define a clear focus
- the ability to develop quickly a positive relationship with the worker
- the ability to tolerate the frustration involved in a brief treatment
- the positive response to typical interventions
- the history of at least one good relationship
- psychological mindfulness
- motivation for more than symptom relief

Individuals facing externally imposed or developmental crises might be good candidates for brief treatment.

Application

Emily and Lewis seek counseling because Emily is suffering from anxiety to the degree that they are hesitant to become parents and their marital relationship is suffering. During the session, Lewis and Emily sit close together and Lewis places his arm around Emily in a protective and caring manner. Lewis takes the lead in explaining the situation, indicating that just talking about the problem makes Emily anxious. Several times Emily begins to explain what she has been feeling but then hesitates and seems unsure of herself and turn to Lewis for support. Lewis then picks up the conversation and speaks for Emily. Emily visibly seems smaller as Lewis continues to speak for her. This pattern continues as the therapist leads the couple in describing their reason for seeking help. The social worker attends to this pattern of protection by which Emily seeks strength from Lewis who in turn acts in a protective manner. The social worker also reflects on personal life experiences in childhood in which she felt overwhelmed and turned to her older siblings for help in dealing with the death of her mother. The therapist comments to the couple that she knows how difficult it can be to express feelings of anxiety as they are trying to do in the session.

As Emily and Lewis continue to talk about their current life and the frustration that they are feeling with the impasse that they have reached, their emotions become more intense. The therapist uses this as an opportunity to explore with them whether their current feelings are similar to any of their prior experiences as they were growing up.

The therapist comments on the pattern that she is seeing—that Emily seeks support and protection from Lewis who in turn behaves in a very protective manner. Emily finds it difficult even to describe her own feelings and turns to Lewis for strength, who in turn becomes the pillar of strength in their relationship. The social worker wonders who Lewis can turn to when he needs support in dealing with problems at work and other life challenges. The couple seem receptive to an approach that helps them understand their relationship and the current situation.

Using empathic listening and clarifying comments that are shared with the couple, the therapist continues to help the couple explore the connections between their current relationship and the family patterns growing up. The therapist is aware of the anxiety that both must be experiencing now as well as in their past and conveys a sense of calm strength. The couple describe their experiences with their own families and how important it is for them to be able to protect their children from going through what they experienced. Emily is gradually able to connect her current need for strength from Lewis as related to the little girl she once was who felt so alone and scared with the illness and subsequent death of her mother. She could only feel safe with her father by her side taking care of her. Her anxiety has kept her from being the engaging person who used to attract people and she fears even more that Lewis might leave her. When Lewis is gone she is even more frightened. Lewis is gradually able to link his own feelings of loss and loneliness as a child because of his mother's depression and his father's absence to his way of dealing with the world—be strong and do not let yourself or others see that you have needs. He was attracted to Emily because of her warmth that made him feel loved. Her anxiety has given him an opportunity to feel strong and put behind him his own needs for protection.

As the couple is able to cope with their anxiety about these painful shadows of the past and their ties to the present, Emily is gradually able to become less anxious and dependent on Lewis. Lewis is gradually able to share more of who he is with Emily. The pain of loss and fears that they both shared in their youth has become part of their conscious connections to the present. As a result, they are able to have empathy for each other without emotionally locking their partners and themselves into these rigid roles that protected them from the shadows of the past. Initially these changes occurred primarily in the sessions with the therapist present and gradually began to permeate their life together outside of the counseling session and the presence of the therapist. Sessions were spaced farther apart to give the couple the experience of being able to maintain these new patterns with reduced support from the therapist.

Evaluation

The goal of object relations family therapy is more than symptom relief and behavioral change and views them as by-products of resolution of the underlying conflicts. It seeks to accomplish reconstructive psychotherapy. The family therapist seeks to help family members relate to each other in a genuine manner that fosters individual growth as well as connections. These goals are difficult to operationalize in measurable ways that fit current outcome evaluation paradigms. Outcome studies within this model are primarily case studies (Kilpatrick, Kilpatrick, & Callaway, 2000). The world of managed care and expectations for brief treatment has also been problematic for object relations family therapy because of the typical length that this model entails. Implementation of this model of family treatment requires social workers and other family counselors to be very aware of their own personal issues because countertransference plays such a critical role in the treatment process. Many of the families seeking help from social workers are looking for more immediate symptomatic relief or have pressing life problems that make it difficult for them to engage in the type of lengthy insightful exploration involved in object relations family therapy.

SUMMARY

Object relations family therapy is a model of treatment designed to address the complex interpersonal issues that have their origins in past family relationships. The treatment is intended to enable family members to reduce their anxiety so that they can reclaim portions of themselves that they have projected onto other members of the family. Family members are helped to relinquish these rigid family roles and to grow as human beings.

DISCUSSION QUESTIONS

While self-understanding on the part of the counselor is important in all treatment approaches, discuss why it is especially important in object relations family therapy.

Drawing from object relations, what are some of the pathways by which early life experiences influence current family relations?

How does insight play an important role in object relations family therapy?

What role does the family therapist play in reducing the anxiety of family members in object relations family therapy?

13

Spirituality

As a social work student working in a secular mental health program, I was reminded of the crucial role that spiritual issues can play in family life events.

> Mrs. Joseph contacted the clinic because she had become very depressed following the birth of her last child. The baby was born without eyes. Exploration with Mrs. J. revealed that while having a child born with such a serious disability could be distressing to any parent, the condition of this child had special meaning for her. Mrs. J. was a devout Catholic who had been raised in the church. She had been married as a young woman and was subsequently divorced without the sanction of the church (before Vatican II). She later remarried, but was unable to marry within the church or to participate in the sacrament of Reconciliation. While this did not trouble her husband, she was unable to hear his reassurances and found herself waiting for God's punishment. When her son was born without eyes, she was convinced that this was God's punishment and she was responsible for her son's blindness. Her husband did not share this perspective but could not change her mind and she continued to suffer. Fortunately, my supervisor knew of several valuable resources within Mrs. J.'s religious community. The first was a group of Catholic religious sisters who worked with children with disabilities. With Mrs. J.'s permission, they came to visit her and assured her that her child's condition was not God's punishment. They also offered to help her with her son. The other resource was an understanding priest. Again Mrs. J. made the decision to meet with him. He also helped her understand that her son's condition was not God's punishment. The assurance and support of these parties within her spiritual tradition were profoundly meaningful and comforting to Mrs. J., who was then able to attend to her son's needs without her own suffering of depression and guilt.

There is an increased recognition by social workers and other helping professions of the importance of understanding the spiritual and religious perspectives of individuals and families as part of holistic models of practice (Canda & Furman, 1999, 2009; Carlson & Erickson, 2002; Frame, 2003; Kilpatrick, Becvar, & Holland, 2003; Van Hook, Hugen, & Aguilar, 2002; Walsh, 1999, 2006). Studies have shown that the majority of people prefer to have their spiritual practices and beliefs integrated into their counseling (Walsh, 1999). While the physical resources of life are important to people, so are the aspects of the spirit, of a sense of meaning. In a world in which people are sometimes valued by the money they earn, the possessions they have, or the work they can do, people can begin to hunger for a deeper sense of meaning and purpose and a sense of being valued for who they are rather than what they produce. Studies set in various traditions have identified spirituality as a potential resource for people addressing life challenges (for example, Aguilar, 2002; Bell-Tolliver & Wilkerson, 2011; Bradley, 2011; Canda, 2002; Friedman, 2002; Grant, 2002; Han & Richardson, 2010; Haynes, 2002; Nadir & Dziegielewski, 2002; Singh, 2002; Van Hook, 2002; Yellow-Horse Brave Heart, 2002; Young, 2010). Spirituality can also help provide a moral compass to guide people in making the myriad of difficult decisions in life (Aponte, 2002). This chapter on spirituality does not represent a specific model of treatment but rather potential ways to incorporate an aspect of life that can emerge in various treatment approaches.

Spirituality, described both in a religious and non-religious context, is being recognized as playing a vital role in the helping process (Aponte, 2002; Canda & Furman, 1999, 2009). For many people, spirituality in a variety of forms represents a very important way of coping. A nationwide survey conducted in the United States after September 11 found that turning to religion (prayer, religious or spiritual feelings) was the second most common way of coping (90%) (Schulster et al., 2001 as cited in Peres, Moreira-Almeida, Nasello, & Koenig, 2007). Canda and Furman (1999) describe "spirituality as the heart of helping—the heart of empathy and care, the pulse of compassion, the vital flow of practice wisdom, and the driving force of action for service" (p. xv). In recognition of the important role that spirituality and religion frequently play in the lives of people, the National Association of Social Workers, in its Code of Ethics, requires that social workers be culturally competent in several areas, including those of spirituality and religion. The Council on Social Work Education has included knowledge of spirituality and religion as part of the content of the social work curriculum.

Nature of Spirituality

Although spirituality refers to a specific domain of life, it permeates all aspects of life. It influences how people view and experience life events. Recognizing that spirituality can be based on a supernatural deity (typically expressed in religion) or on a philosophical, non-supernatural foundation, Aponte (2002) identifies three basic elements of spirituality: "morality, meaning, and the nature of the individual's relationship to the world" (p. 16). Spirituality shapes issues of meaning and purpose, how suffering and healing are understood, and appropriate ways to resolve life struggles. Canda (1988) identifies three aspects of spirituality: values, beliefs, and practices organized around "a person's search for meaning and purpose, developed in the context of the interdependent relationship between self, other people, and the nonhuman world, and the foundation of being itself" (p. 43). Spirituality has been linked to people's relationship with the transcendent. Religion, on the other hand, involves an institutional, organizational, and community framework with accompanying patterned belief systems and traditions. While spirituality can be separate from religion, it "takes on religious meaning when the centers of value, beliefs, images of power, practices, and master stories of one's faith— the central dynamic of one's search for meaning and purpose—are grounded in the creeds, texts of scripture, rituals, and theologies of a particular religious tradition" (Hugen, 2002, p. 11). As a result, incorporating spirituality into an assessment of families involves an understanding of the belief systems of families, their sense of values, and practices related to their sense of meaning and purpose. When family members' spirituality is grounded within religious traditions, understanding the basic beliefs and organizational nature of the faith community can also be important to understand the meaning of life events and potential resources for these families.

In terms of family counseling, spirituality is not viewed as a distinct model of counseling like structural or narrative family therapy. Instead, an appreciation of the ways in which the current and past spiritual journey of family members are influencing how people are experiencing life events and potential resources for healing can be infused in a variety of family counseling models.

Such an appreciation of the potential role of spirituality and religion in the lives of families must take into consideration the complex nature of this role. While these aspects can represent a source of comfort and meaning for some people at difficult times in their lives, they can also be the source of guilt, conflict, struggle, and sense of alienation (Pargament, 1997). Family members can also be in very different places in terms of their spirituality and religion and these differences can be the source of conflict or tension. Such integration can also require an understanding of how specific religious and cultural traditions shape people's spiritual experiences, their search for meaning, and their perception of appropriate strategies for addressing issues in life. Even if families are no longer affiliated with a particular tradition, earlier life experiences can cast lasting shadows in these important areas of life. For example, a family's perception of serious illness within the family could vary greatly depending on whether the family's views were shaped by their Christian Science, Catholic, Hindu, Islamic, or Buddhist traditions. Different beliefs about life after death and the rituals associated with this somber period of life can have profound meaning to families facing this difficult period of the life cycle. The increasing diversity of religious/spiritual communities makes it even more important for social workers and other counselors to be sensitive to these potential differences.

The term *healing* is important in a discussion of spirituality. Walsh (1999) describes the role of healing in family treatment as the core of a resiliency-based model of practice. Healing is the process of becoming whole or finding some way to adapt and compensate for losses. Healing in this context "is seen as a natural response to injury or trauma" (Walsh, 1999, p. 33). It recognizes that people can heal physically but not heal emotionally. It also recognizes that "we can heal psychosocially even when we do not heal physically or when a traumatic event cannot be reversed" (Walsh, 1999, p. 33). These multiple layers of healing permit counselors to foster resiliency even in situations in which it is impossible to solve the problem or when such a problem might reoccur. Many families who seek help from counselors are facing current or past issues that cannot be changed, but must be faced and coped with, for example, past abuse or death in the family. Suffering is also part of the human journey. It frequently causes people to raise questions of meaning and other spiritual concerns. Healing draws upon the resources of people and their context. Incorporating spirituality into counseling with families can be instrumental in this healing process. It can address past events as well as enhance the sense of meaning, purpose, and connection that can be protective in terms of current and future life events. Recognizing the brokenness of relationships in the lives of many of the families who seek help, Walsh describes as a spiritual endeavor the work of counselors to help clients seek "reconciliation to heal wounded relationships and encourage them to forge more meaningful personal and spiritual bonds" (Walsh, 1999, p. 49).

As discussed in chapter 1, aspects of spirituality can represent important protective factors for family members. Religion in terms of beliefs, rituals, and the organizational context can be protective as well as accentuate risk factors for families and individuals (Van Hook & Aguilar, 2002; Koenig, 1999; Pargament, 1997; Van Hook & Rivera, 2004; Walsh, 2006). Walsh (1999) describes spiritual beliefs and practices as strengthening "the ability to withstand and transcend adversity. Such keys to resiliency as meaning-making, hope, perseverance, and connectedness are all enhanced by spirituality" (p. 38). Further supporting resiliency is "being able to give meaning to a precarious situation, having faith that there is some greater purpose or force at work, and finding solace and strength in these outlooks" (Walsh, 1999, p. 38). Crises in people's lives can become opportunities to develop spiritual dimensions (Walsh, 1999). Understanding the nature of these risk and protective factors and enhancing the protective factors can promote healing in families.

Goals

The goal of this chapter is to enable counselors to help family members identify potential healing forces within their own spiritual and religious traditions that can be used to address their family issues and to strengthen the family as well as to identify roadblocks in the process of healing. It is not designed to equip social workers and family counselors to be religious counselors. Critical family issues can be a result of the current situation facing the family members (e.g., illness of a family member, economic crisis, parent-child or marital conflict) or can be the result of emotional scars due to past life events (e.g., emotional or physical abuse, abandonment, losses) that can be coped with but cannot be changed. As discussed in chapter 1, current events can also reactivate past life events with added distress for the family members.

It is also beyond the scope of this chapter to provide information about all of the many religious traditions and the implications of social work practice in working with these families. Several resources include Van Hook, Hugen, and Aguilar (2002), which contains chapters written by social work experts regarding a variety of religious traditions; Walsh (1999), which includes chapters about various religious traditions and traditions associated with racial and ethnic groups; and Canda and Furman (2009), which describes various religious and spiritual traditions. These works also provide a more extensive treatment of the use of spirituality in social work practice than is possible in this chapter.

Promotes Resiliency by

- Addressing factors associated with demoralization, negative aspects of spirituality, lack of social support, and fatalistic views.
- Strengthening protective factors by promoting a sense of coherence, hope, transcendent beliefs that promote a sense of meaning, and social support within a spiritual community.

Role of the Counselor

The role of the counselor is one of opening the door to this potentially important dialogue regarding spiritual issues and life issues between the family members and the counselor as well as among relevant family members. Given the past divide between social work and other forms of family counseling and spiritual issues, family members might be reluctant to raise this issue in the counseling session because they do not think their concerns will be valued or viewed as relevant, or fear they are not being understood by the counselor. In this regard, the interview is a two-way street, with family members assessing the counselor to see if they can trust the counselor with this very important aspect of themselves. One of the initial steps of the counselor is to open the door by asking appropriate questions about potential issues related to meaning, purpose, and the spiritual and religious aspects of life events. This exploration helps legitimize bringing these issues to the counseling situation for those families who view the spiritual as relevant. Family members thus have the choice of whether or not they view these aspects as germane to the issues at hand. Hospitals have taken this message to heart and questions related to spiritual needs are frequently part of the admission process.

In this context, Walsh (1999) describes an earlier clinical experience in which she was working with a family in which the father and husband, a beloved minister, had died in an auto accident. She had counseled the widow and the children regarding their grief and loss without ever raising any issues related to spirituality. When later asked why she had not done so, she reflected on the great divide between spirituality and family counseling and its negative impact on the true effectiveness of a family counselor.

Walsh (1999) describes spirituality in terms of the very fabric of the family counseling situation in ways that transcend specific treatment models. The counselor's faith in the family's potential can help restore hope. Incorporating spirituality into the counseling process requires the counselor to be able to create important and respectful connections with family members. "Valuing connections, we help our clients to seek reconciliation to heal wounded relationships and encourage them to forge more meaningful personal and spiritual bonds" (Walsh, 1999, p. 49). Wright (1999) goes further to use the term "reverencing" in terms of her relationship with clients (p. 63). Reverencing involves a sense of profound awe and respect for the family members. The ensuing reciprocal connection between family members and counselors can lead to important changes in thinking, behavior, and the experience of suffering. This attitude further grants dignity to people (food for the spirit).

Incorporating spirituality into the counseling process requires the counselor to have a deeper understanding of him or herself. Aponte (1994) reminds us that in order to address others about the spirit, we must first examine ourselves in terms of what gives us meaning and purpose in life and how this affects our views and relationships with others. While self-awareness is important in any counseling effort, it can be especially critical in this arena because our own spiritual and religious traditions can have a profound impact on our work with others. Without intending to, counselors can find themselves reacting in ways that impose their own beliefs on clients or at least make it uncomfortable for clients to bring up certain spiritual or religious elements. It is essential for counselors to be aware of their own spiritual beliefs and how they can influence their counseling efforts. This raises several questions. As counselors, what are our spiritual and religious beliefs and experiences? Can we appreciate other spiritual traditions and their role in the lives of families? Can we give room for people to question and doubt spiritual or religious issues that are deeply important for us?

Such self-awareness can help counselors guard against the danger of using the counseling session to proselytize or try to persuade family members to accept the counselor's spiritual or religious stance on life (Canda &

Furman, 1999, 2009; Frame, 2003; Hugen, 2002; Sherwood, 2002). Sherwood (2002) stresses the ethical importance of not using the vulnerability of a client's situation to impose one's own spiritual or religious perspective on others. Aponte (2002) describes the importance of counselors understanding their own spiritual journey in ways that permit them to use aspects of themselves to gain empathy for their client's stories and to engage in needed professional closeness without "infringing upon the boundaries of the client, and not allowing their own boundaries to be trespassed" (p. 21).

Several years ago when I was conducting workshops for social workers and mental health counselors regarding the role of spirituality and religion in working with clients, it became clear that many of the individuals in the audience were responding out of their own life experience. While general comments regarding spirituality generated positive comments, when the topic moved more specifically to the religion of family members, the comments became more heated. Some of the attendees described in great detail and with considerable emotion their own negative experiences as proof that religion could only be damaging and a source of pain for *all* families. Others spoke of the support they had received as something that might be valuable for *all* families. While social workers would be quick to realize that their personal experiences regarding marriage or divorce would not necessarily be applicable to others, it appears that it can be more difficult for people to create these appropriate boundaries between their own personal experiences and that of others in the area of religion. Because these issues have not traditionally been part of many social work curriculums, people have also had less preparation for doing so.

The role of counselor is one of a partner rather than expert. Addressing issues related to spirituality is as a partner between the counselor and the family. Aponte (1994) further reminds us that we are "companions on a journey, their journey. We do not own expertise about the spirit. As therapists, we are not the new priesthood" (p. 246). The family counselor does not enter the arena as a spiritual or religious expert, as a religious or pastoral counselor, but as a person who can help family members identify or connect people with resources within their spiritual journey. This requires the counselor to gain an understanding of the religious and spiritual tradition of the family members. The counselor uses his or her knowledge of or at least willingness to learn from the family about their spiritual or religious tradition to understand the family more effectively, and to help identify potential resources, not to guide them in terms of their belief system.

Being a partner on this journey can also mean being truly with people during times of suffering, offering compassion, helping family members reach out to each other, helping family members identify their beliefs or practices that can be meaningful, and connecting them with others who can be helpful at this stage of their life. Helping people recognize the spiritual dimension of their lives can also help lend dignity and value.

Assessment

Assessment of the family's spiritual or religious situation is an important aspect of incorporating spirituality into family counseling. Such an assessment means opening the door to this important topic as well as asking specific questions that can help understand the family. Before discussing specific ways to assess spirituality and/or religion in the lives of people, it is important to recognize that this process belongs to the arena of "knowing" rather than mere "information." Knowing pushes beyond a set of facts to the meaning of these facts in the life of another person, which creates a sense of understanding. For example, a statement on a face sheet of an agency that someone is Catholic or Hindu is not the same as inquiry that pertains to the meaning of this religion in the life of the person and how this meaning in turn relates to the current situation. If a family member is dying, issues related to important rituals prior to and following death or interpretations of the possibility and nature of life after death become extremely relevant in the knowing process. The assessment process can take the form of a guided interview (a conversation) as well some recently developed visual tools.

Social workers cannot assume that all members of racial or ethnic groups share similar religious and spiritual views because of the diversity within groups. African Americans, for example, belong to virtually every religious group and some have no religious perspective. At the same time, members can share a profound spiritual sense of the purpose of life despite such religious differences (Boyd-Franklin & Lockwood, 1999; Martin & Martin, 2002).

Hodge (2003) describes the guided interview—the therapeutic conversation as a spiritual anthropology. As family members describe their family, counselors can explore some relevant questions about the issues the family members are presenting as well as the solutions that they are considering. To ask about spirituality in this manner is strength-based and demonstrates respect for the client's right to self-determination. These questions open the door to exploring issues of spirituality and religion in more meaningful ways than a simple notation in the record that a person is Catholic, Jewish, Hindu, nonreligious, and so on. The counselor naturally needs to be sensitive to whether or not families wish to explore these issues further and to respond accordingly. Recognizing that not all issues are relevant or apropos for all families or situations, some potentially important questions could include one or more of the following. The following are phrased in a general way and would be modified for the specific family and their situation.

Are any faiths, religions, specific spiritual beliefs and practices important to the family members (both currently and in the past)?

How, if at all, does the spiritual or religious tradition of the family members give meaning to the issues facing the family and their options for addressing them?

Have the family members sought to address their current situation in part through their concept of spirituality, their religious beliefs or faith, or their religious or spiritual community, and if so, with what results? (This question can elicit potential resources, family coping strategies, and possible experiences of alienation and distress.)

Are there any rituals associated with the spiritual or religious tradition that the family views as appropriate or helpful? (This can involve situations in which people have felt unable to carry out specific rituals due to their actions, their current setting, or other circumstances.)

Is there a history in the family of people from different religious or spiritual traditions coming together and what had been the impact of this on the family (e.g., acceptance, cutoffs in the family)?

Are there past spiritual or religious traditions that are influencing how the current situation is being experienced?

Are there any resources within the spiritual tradition (beliefs, practices, community) that might be helpful to you in coping with the current situation? Do people feel that they can avail themselves of these resources or do they feel alienated or unable to do so (for example, Mrs. J. who felt that she could not participate in the ritual of reconciliation)?

Have there been deep wounds that have had an impact on the spiritual or religious life of the family or its members?

Answers to questions addressing these domains can help identify potential spiritual resources, the meaning systems that influence how life events are experienced, as well as potential tensions and burdens created by the spiritual or religious traditions. This information can help guide the counselor in drawing upon whatever sources of resiliency there are within the spiritual or religious realm of the family as well as identifying barriers in this process. This assessment is not predicated on the assumption that spiritual/religious issues are necessarily helpful or harmful for the family members—it is a respectful inquiry process.

Hodge (2005) has also developed the spiritual ecogram for identifying potential strengths and issues both in earlier times and currently. This tool combines aspects of the eco map and the genogram described earlier. Prior to using this tool with families, the social worker needs to inquire if families are interested in learning more about how spirituality and/or religion has played a role in their family in the past as well as their coping with current issues. The clients are the experts and decide whether or not they wish to engage in such a process.

Figure 5 represents a spiritual ecogram that links the family members' past with their current circumstances. As reflected in this ecogram, spiritual issues represent both sources of support and tension. Marilyn and Jacob N. contacted the center because Marilyn is feeling overwhelmed with the care of their five-year-old son. In this situation, she is especially feeling the pain of being cut off from her own parents. Her parents disapproved of her marriage to Jacob because he is Jewish. Jacob and his family have been very closely attached to their Jewish faith and the synagogue. For Marilyn's parents the Baptist Church and all that it represents to them in terms of faith and association is equally important. Marilyn and her husband have also been feeling alienated from her only brother. The family members are active in the synagogue and have close ties to other members. Their daughter Mary is a good student and the family has good relationships with the school in terms of Mary. Their son William is having serious learning disabilities and this has created strain between the family and the educational system. There is also tension with the health care system as it relates to William's care.

In the spiritual ecogram, the current family situation is located within the center of the page. The earlier generations are presented similar to the genogram in which men are represented as squares and women as circles. Lines indicate relationships between people with the strength of the line representing the strength of the relationship. In this version, different religious traditions are represented by italics and bold. Important life events in the spiritual journey can be represented by symbols that are important for the family members. This aspect of the ecogram can reveal family legacies, potential tension, and religious traditions. The second part of the ecogram represents the links between the family and relevant aspects of the current spiritual/religious life. Such aspects can include elements of the faith community, rituals, and relationship with God or other transcendent relationships.

Treatment Process

A treatment process that incorporates spirituality follows the lead of the family in terms of potential needs and resources. This lead can be reflected in terms of the actions initiated by the family or the family response to statements or questions by the counselor. Helmeke and Bischof (2002) have developed guidelines for recognizing and raising spiritual issues based on whether or not the issue is raised by the client or the counselor and if the issue is religious or spiritual in nature.

Spiritual issues raised by the client (Helmeke & Bischof, 2002, p. 201). Clients may raise these issues through talking about matters of purpose or meaning in life or making a comment about spirituality in a specific manner. The counselor can acknowledge with family members that they have made a comment about something related to spirituality and then explore further if this is important to them and ask if they would like to add to these thoughts. If counselors do not make this connection, family members could interpret their silence as lack of interest or unwillingness to discuss these issues. The counselor can further explore whether these issues related to

FIGURE 5. Spiritual Ecogram

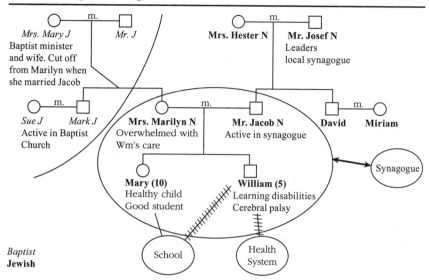

spirituality are associated with the problem they are presenting, either in terms of potential resources or contributing factors. Understanding the client's path to spirituality can suggest other relevant issues. The counselor can also inquire if there are any ways the family members would like spiritual issues to be part of the counseling process. Helmeke and Bischof (2002) further indicate that use of spiritual rather than religious language suggests the type of language that would be meaningful for this family.

Religious issues raised by the client (Helmeke & Bischof, 2002, p. 202). Members of the family can refer to something specifically related to religion. Family members might describe their anger toward God for the death of a child or how their faith made it possible for them to survive the death of a child. It is valuable for the counselor to learn about the family's religious perspective. This might mean learning about the religious tradition that the family is associated with. For example, what is the meaning of death and the deity in the family's religion? If a family is close to their religious leader and feels comfortable with this individual, engaging this individual as a partner can sometimes be helpful. The leader has knowledge and expertise and can offer important support as well as identify other support systems within the faith community. Frequently the religious leader is likely to have an ongoing relationship with family members that can represent a more long-term resource than the family counselor. Referral to a religious leader depends, of course, on the comfort of the family in meeting with such individuals. While this is a resource for some families, others are struggling with such alienation that they would not be receptive to such a step.

The counselor also needs to attend to the language used by the family in order to use appropriate language that facilitates the joining process (Helmeke & Bischof, 2002). Using the language of the family helps to create an effective working relationship.

Counselors also need to be aware of ways in which religion can camouflage other pervasive problems within the family that need to be addressed (Helmeke & Bischof, 2002) or can be symptomatic of more serious illnesses. For some people, religious concerns can become early signs of more serious psychotic problems that require the family to access serious mental health interventions. Other times, religious issues can be manifestations of family issues either presently or in the past. Sue (age 25) sought help because she had committed the "unpardonable sin" and felt that she had no hope. She was a member of a very religious family in which issues like the "unpardonable sin" were important concepts. Gradually an exploration of her family gave some clues as to why she clung so strongly to this fear despite extensive help. Her father was a very religious man and spent his free time listening to religious radio broadcasts and ignored his family members. Her sister became ill with a psychotic illness as a young teenager and has remained very disabled. The mother has been absorbed in the daughter's care. Shortly before Sue's fears and symptoms began, the brother was arrested for a serious crime and imprisoned, to the great distress of the family. The counselor gradually realized that for this young woman, illness of some type—especially related to doing something bad in the religious sense—had begun to represent the only identity possible for her in this family that would receive any recognition. In short, without her fear of the unpardonable sin, she would be nothing. While it was not possible to engage the other family members in the treatment process, an understanding of the family context enabled the counselor to use the counseling sessions to help Sue experience that she had other aspects of her person that could interest and engage others. Conversations regarding recipes and art gradually began to monopolize the session time and the issue of the "unpardonable sin" faded away in her life.

Spiritual issues raised by the counselor (Helmeke & Bischof, 2002, p. 205). The counselor can explore with clients if there may be any relevant spiritual issues in terms of the problem they are facing. The counselor then needs to respect the clients' perspective in terms of whether or not clients view these issues as relevant or useful. As Helmeke and Bischof (2002) caution, "the buried treasure that might be found may be gold to the therapist but merely dross to the client" (p. 205), and the challenge for the counselor is to respect the clients' evaluation. Again, failure to raise these issues when families are facing critical life issues can give a message that the counselor is not interested or that they are not germane to a counseling process. This message could deter families from raising this issue. Issues related to loss and grief, serious illness, or recovery from addictions especially lend themselves to this exploration (Helmeke & Bischof, 2002).

Religious issues raised by the counselor (Helmeke & Bischof, 2002, p. 208). This situation requires the most caution and requires the greatest self-understanding on the part of the counselor. Intake forms that indicate Catholic, Hindu, Muslim, Jehovah's Witness, and so on, for example, might suggest a religious tie that can be explored with the family in terms of whether this is important for them regarding their current situation. A hospital counselor working with the parents of a severely ill child, for example, might explore what meaning, if any, their religion has for them at this time. These questions open doors and let the family decide if this is a relevant dimension for the family. Helmeke and Bischof (2002) warn that counselors from similar religious backgrounds to the family can risk making the assumption that the family members' interpretations and experience are similar to their own, and they stress the importance of exploring these issues with an open mind.

Genograms are appropriate places to ask about religion. Other situations that suggest the value of exploring the relevance of religious issues include clients who have raised other related spiritual or religious issues, are addressing issues related to faith issues (e.g., life after death, interfaith marriage), or are families with strong religious community ties (Helmeke & Bischof, 2002).

Application

The following discussion points out ways in which spirituality and faith issues (beliefs, community, practices) can play a role both as risk and protective factors and can support treatment efforts in different models of family treatment.

Family members need to have their basic physical and interpersonal needs as well as their spiritual issues of meaning and sense of purpose met. The needs of families can be organized around one or more of these aspects of life. Any spiritual assessment of families is embedded within the larger assessment of the risk and protective factors of family members. The following is a brief description of some approaches that draw upon spiritual and faith resources based on the need of families.

Basic needs. Some families are struggling to meet some of their basic needs, for example, housing or income. Survival needs are primary for these families. Counselors can explore if there are potential resources within the current spiritual or faith community of the family or the community at large that can help this family meet these essential needs. Faith communities from a wide range of religious traditions embrace the concept of charity and offer a variety of resources for their members and others in the community, for example, food pantries, help with housing, and job placement. Identifying such resources within the community can be part of a multisystems approach to working with families. Individual congregations also work through other community programs related to their spiritual or religious faith groups and general community organizations. Social workers can connect families with resources as well as educate faith communities about needs within the community and ways that these communities can help in a manner that bestows on the recipients dignity and respect.

Interpersonal family issues. Many faith communities offer support groups for families experiencing a variety of difficult situations (e.g., grief, divorce, single parenting, caregiving). These programs can be resources for family members who are feeling alone with their problem and can benefit from supportive ties. Again, while some of these programs are for members of the group, others reach out to the community at large. Counselors can identify the services available in the community and how comfortable people are with services offered through such auspices. In addition to support, members can also gain new coping skills and encouragement to use these skills from others who are attending the group as well as from the leader. Their participation can support efforts involved in social learning/cognitive and structural approaches that seek to improve important life skills and strengthen leadership structures within families.

Sense of community. Parents' faith and participation in a religious group can represent a framework for meaning, a source of hope, and community. For some parents whose children have serious disabilities, the religious community represented an important place of acceptance for their children; however, for others there was hurt created by lack of such acceptance (Poston & Turnbull, 2004).

Sense of meaning. Resiliency is fostered by belief systems that provide a sense of meaning and hope. Spiritual and religious beliefs can also be helpful in terms of creating a sense of meaning for life events. For parents of children with disabilities, this especially included viewing their child as a gift of God or a blessing rather than a curse (Poston & Turnbull, 2004). For Mexican American parents of chronically ill children, religion and spirituality had important roles. They viewed God as an active partner with the health team and themselves. The themes in this process included (a) God determines the outcome of the child's illness, (b) God and the health team are closely linked, (c) parents take an active role in carrying out God's will, (d) families have an obligation to God, (e) the family and others seek intercession with God, and (f) faith encourages family optimism (Rehm, 1999).

During times of crisis, some individuals feel alienated from their faith or spiritual tradition while others can feel supported through a spiritual connection with what they view as the transcendent in their lives. Others vacillate between these responses. Beliefs that God is punishing them and other punitive beliefs can increase distress (Pargament, 1997; Van Hook & Rivera,

2004). Depending where people stand on these issues can be important in understanding their response to life events and how they view themselves in this process. Alcoholics Anonymous and related self-help organizations have long identified the strength that some people draw from their higher power and have explicitly built this into their program. Pargament and Brandt (1998) suggest that religious coping is effective because it offers a response to the "problems of human insufficiency." When people are pushed beyond the limits of their own resources, they are reminded of their own basic vulnerability. At these times, religion can offer help in terms of spiritual support, answers regarding puzzling and difficult life events, and a sense of control. A longitudinal study of poor young people from a variety of ethnic groups on the island of Kauai, for example, revealed that for people from a wide variety of religious groups—including Buddhism, Catholicism, Mormonism, Jehovah's Witnesses, and others—religion "strengthened these families through times of adversity by providing a sense of purpose, mission, and salvation" (Walsh, 1999, p. 38). Counselors can thus explore with family members if there are any spiritual connections that can be meaningful for the family members involved at this difficult time. It is important to recognize that studies reveal only trends and the importance of learning from individuals their own response.

As indicated previously, resiliency is supported by the ability "to give meaning to a precarious situation, having faith that there is some greater purpose or force at work, and finding solace and strength in these outlooks" (Walsh, 1999, p. 38). Dialogue with families in terms of spirituality and stories of faith can help elicit this sense of purpose. Discussing the family's sense that these events and their lives have a purpose in the counseling session can help support such views. During the devastating 2005 hurricanes in the U.S. Gulf Coast area, some of the resilient survivors described the greater purpose that they felt was taking place as a result of this event.

Family interventions can address issues of meaning, and family stories can draw upon these views of purpose in ways that give meaning and thus help counter some of the negative family stories. Counselors can explore how a sense of meaning or purpose in past life events helped them cope and explore this in addressing the current situation. Without assuming an unrealistically positive stance, counselors can explore what meaning such past events had for families. Sometimes families are able to identify ways in which the family grew and became stronger and thus begin to view the current situation as potentially having a sense of purpose and meaning in their lives. Depending on the family, these interpretations can play important roles in solution and narrative approaches.

As illustrated by the following studies of people from a variety of backgrounds and religious orientations, people can receive affirmation through their spirituality and faith, beliefs, relationship with the deity, and affirming relationships with other members. Women who had been sexually abused reported this important form of healing (Valentine & Feinauer, 1993). Older adults coping with HIV/AIDS were comforted and supported with a sense of belonging, a personal relations with God, reduction of the fear of death, improved self-acceptance, and a sense of meaning through their spiritual and religious beliefs and practices (Siegel & Schrimshaw, 2002). House-bound lonely older adults with a sense of spirituality were less likely to become depressed (Han & Richardson, 2010). African American women struggling with serious health problems reported the strength they gained from their religious faith and spirituality (Clay, Talley, & Young, 2010). African American women who had experienced or witnessed violence as children reported coping by using spirituality/religion through rituals (especially prayer), beliefs, pastoral counseling, and involvement in the church organization (Bryant-Davis, 2005).

A study of African American survivors of Hurricane Katrina, however, reflects the mixed picture in terms of the interplay between life events and spirituality. While some reported that religious or spiritual practices and their relationship with God (who gives strength) were helpful, others reappraised their faith in negative ways—if God really loves us, why did he let people die in this way (MHum, Bell, Pyles, & Runnels, 2012)? Chinese individuals with severe mental illness were supported by their spirituality (Young, 2010). Again, depending on the individual, these findings suggest resources that might emerge in solution-focused and narrative models of treatment.

Early life relationships. People frequently develop a sense of spirituality/religion through early family experiences. Concepts like "God as father" can mean that one's early images of God reflect one's experience with a parent. From a risk perspective, a judgmental parent can translate into an angry and judgmental God. Such object relations within the arena of spirituality can intensify risk factors in the area of spirituality and add to the distress of family members. On the other hand, caring early object relations contribute to the comfort offered by such beliefs. Children who have been traumatized can have difficulty maintaining their religious and spiritual beliefs and lose their sense of trust or feelings of self-worth (Bryant-Davis, Ellis, Burke-Maynard, Moon, Counts, & Anderson, 2012). Explorations drawn from family systems and object relations can potentially help people begin to separate parental and other early relationships from spiritual images and enable people to begin to make adult spiritual journeys in their current family life.

Suffering

Many families seeking help are suffering in profound ways. Wright (1999) describes from her experience that conversations about suffering frequently open the door to a discussion of spirituality if the parties involved are comfortable with this type of dialogue. Suffering prompts questions of meaning.

Again, counselors need to be able to enter into such conversations and permit families a safe haven for their intense feelings at this time. Suffering can evoke feelings of anger that further prompt guilt. Walking through the valley of pain together with family members can contribute to the healing process. At this time, a safe haven for family members can be a very important healing context, especially when people can gain an understanding that their response is not an uncommon one even among people of faith. Based on an attempt to understand why some survivors of the Nazi concentration camps were able to maintain good health and lead a good life despite the suffering they experienced, Antonovski developed the concept of "sense of coherence" described earlier. It is based on three components that reflect a sense of meaning: comprehensibility (life makes sense), meaningfulness (life make sense emotionally), and manageability (ability to use available resources to deal with life events) (Peres, Moreira-Almeida, Nasello, & Koenig, 2007). Spirituality and faith issues and community can help people address issues of meaning and offer emotional and social support.

Shared stories related to suffering can be healing. A pastor colleague of mine lost his son as a result of a tragic accident. He became very angry with God and felt that he had to "have it out with God." As he paced the beach and shouted his rage at God, he experienced silence and God's acceptance of him and his anger. He told this story to a gathering of others, including a devoutly religious man who had recently lost his young son-in-law as a result of another accident. He too had been feeling angry with God and struggling with this guilt. Hearing the pastor's story helped him heal his sense of guilt. As a church leader he was subsequently visiting an elderly widow who had recently lost her son. As he told his story about his son-in-law and his reaction, tears of relief came to her eyes. She shared her sense of guilt for being angry with God and how his story had now given her peace. As each person told their story, they shared the gift of healing.

Rituals

Rituals can be very important for families. Rituals help families deal with loss, welcome new members, mark changes in the life cycle, establish closeness to the transcendent, celebrate group ties, and serve many other purposes. Some community-supported rituals are tied to the spiritual or religious life of the family. Counselors can explore the role of rituals in the life of the family. Are there important rituals tied to the faith or spiritual tradition that can offer comfort and healing to family members facing a current situation or seeking healing from a past life event?

Culture plays a key role in shaping the nature of these rituals. The nature of how the family grieves and honors the person who has died is a critical part of the family cycle. The following two contrasting cultural pre-scriptions indicate how culture and religious traditions shape this transitional ritual during a key life transition—the death of a father.

> Dr. E. was on a faculty exchange in the United States with his family when his father died suddenly in rural Albania. The Muslim tradition is that a person is buried almost immediately after death. Because it would be impossible for Dr. E. to be there for the burial, the family did not inform him of his father's death until after the burial had occurred. Their intention was to protect him from feeling guilty that he was unable to be there. In contrast, my son-in-law who lives in Boston is the oldest son of a Christian Ghanaian family. When his father died suddenly, it was important that he attend the service, but there was no rush to hold the service. Instead he spent weeks working overtime to help support a very lengthy and expensive funeral in which a large number of people would come for several days. It also required time to arrange for a reasonably priced flight from Boston to Accra. After a period of about a month, he was finally able to leave for Ghana and participate in the funeral and burial of his father.

Both of these men shared a love for their fathers, yet the rituals designed to honor the father who had died and maintain important family rituals differed drastically. Family members can be helped to create meaningful rituals or identify ways in which they can restore important ones. These rituals can create ways to remember important family members. Sometimes just being supportive of family members' use of their important rituals to address problems can be important.

A medical social worker shared the following example of the power of drawing on the customs of culture and spirituality. An older woman was hospitalized and suffering from great pain. When she refused pain medication, the social worker was urged by the medical staff to institute the process of involuntary commitment. The social worker, sensitive to possible cultural and spiritual resources within the life space of the client, engaged the family as allies. The extended family came, formed a circle around the patient, and began to sing music from their traditional religion. The effect on the woman was remarkable. The sounds of the music and the healing touch of her family helped the pain to recede. She had come from a poor Caribbean community where access to medication was very limited. People had developed rituals for healing that evoked music and the spiritual power of the community to address issues of pain and illness (Van Hook, 2008).

Social workers can identify ways in which family members are feeling unable to carry out important rituals. This can be particularly difficult for families who have left their homeland and have had difficulty carrying out their traditional spiritual rituals in their new country. Helping family members identify ways in which they might be able to restore these rituals or at least some version of them can potentially be useful. Family tensions can occur if these rituals remain important for one generation and are dismissed as unimportant or irrelevant by the younger generation.

Other people might feel unable to carry out important rituals because of ways in which they feel they have made themselves unworthy in terms of their faith tradition. Helping link people with understanding leaders within their faith tradition can be useful here.

> Mr. Kent sought counseling because of severe anxiety attacks that led him to seek medical help from the emergency room. Exploration revealed that he was feeling guilty because of an affair he had several years ago. At this time, he had long ago given up this relationship and was working hard to improve his marriage. As a result of his past actions, he had not availed himself of the sacrament of Reconciliation of the Catholic Church since that time. During this discussion, Mr. K. began to see the link between his sense of anxiety and his increasing sense of distance from his faith community. He sought out an understanding priest who helped him restore his ties with the church and participate again in the sacrament. His sense of anxiety began to subside dramatically.

In this context, the social worker provided a setting in which Mr. K. was able to explore his situation in ways that incorporated the spiritual dimension and in the process to draw upon the resources present within his spiritual tradition.

Forgiveness

Family relationships can be distorted and hurt by anger and feelings of betrayal within the family circle or in the wider context of relationships. Family members can find it difficult to forgive others as well as themselves. It is certainly not the place of the family counselor to make decisions regarding forgiveness for the family members. Counselors also need to be aware of unrealistic pressure on family members to forgive that are imposed by others. At the same time, forgiveness has been shown to have great healing power (Canda & Furman, 1999, 2009; Friedman's study as cited in Frame, 2003). The mother of one of the teenagers slain in Ohio in a recent school shooting gave a very moving account of her forgiveness of the troubled teenager who had killed her son. She indicated that she could not live with the poison of this hatred and it would also not be an appropriate testimony to the life of her son.

The concepts and obligations of forgiveness have different meanings with diverse religious traditions. The Amish community who experienced the tragedy of their children being shot in the school and who forgave the shooter and embraced his family is a powerful example of a religious culture with a message of forgiveness. It is valuable for the counselor to understand the meanings of forgiveness within the family's tradition. If family members are agreeable and interested, it can be useful for family members to identify some of the barriers to forgiving others and themselves and to recognize the corrosive impact of their ongoing resentments.

As family members are exploring the possibility of forgiveness, they can be helped to understand that forgiveness does not necessarily mean reconciliation because reconciliation typically involves the offending party making some type of amends. Unlike reconciliation, forgiveness can occur regardless of the intentions of the other person. Family members can also be helped to understand that forgiveness does not require people to place themselves in ongoing harm's way. People who have been hurt by others certainly should not continue to put themselves in harm's way either physically or emotionally. If family members decide that they would like to build a bridge toward reconciliation, the counselor needs to help family members recognize that they are unable to control the response of the other person and can truly only be responsible for their own behavior.

The following represents an example in which family reconciliation efforts were initially rebuffed and the importance of support during this process.

> The counselor and the family pastor agreed to help a young woman try to become reconciled with her parents who disapproved of her divorce. Both the counselor and the pastor previously discussed with her the possibility that her parents might not change their minds and asked what would be her response if this occurred. Unfortunately, in the family session with the young woman, her parents, the counselor, and the pastor, her angry mother could not accept her decision and instead indicated that she would rather have her daughter "dead than divorced." These words dashed the daughter's hopes for reconciliation. Her pastor continued to be a strong source of support and she was able to take comfort in the fact that she had made an effort toward reconciliation. A couple of years later, her parents sought to be reconciled with her and she was able to move past these words of hurt and establish a relationship with her parents. It was, however, a reconciliation based on their acceptance of her decision about her divorce.

Forgiveness does not mean glossing over the hurt that has occurred because part of the forgiveness process is recognizing the reality of the hurt that has occurred and the opportunity for expressing these feelings to others and experiencing validation for these feelings. As part of the process of forgiveness, people do need to give up revenge. They are helped to gain empathy for the offending party (Friedman's study as cited in Frame, 2003).

Some families have been powerful examples of the healing power of forgiveness both for the family and the larger community. A family's daughter who had gone to work with very poor people in South Africa was murdered by a member of the community. In the context of their grief, the parents established a program to reach out to these poor and alienated young people as a way of honoring her daughter and her work.

Family members can also feel guilty for their actions toward others in the family and others. Sometimes people can be struggling unrealistically with guilt and counselors need to help them lift these feelings and work on the process of self-forgiveness. There are also situations in which feelings of guilt or remorse are legitimate and the appropriate response is for family members to acknowledge what they have done wrong and to make amends. Counselors can be supportive of the strength involved in taking such steps.

Religious Leaders

Counselors can also help family members access the resources of spiritual and religious leaders in their community. The specific nature of these depends on the needs and interests of the individual family. Such individuals can be helpful in addressing some of the more specific spiritual or religious issues facing family members. As indicated earlier, such referrals are the result of an assessment that families are receptive to and interested in this step. The situation of Mrs. Joseph described at the beginning of this chapter represents the important role that religious leaders can play.

Specific Life Issues

As indicated earlier, suffering is part of the life experience and has a profound impact on people. For some individuals, spirituality and faith become strengthened and serve as important resources, while others become alienated. The following studies regarding parents who have lost children and caretakers of family members with Alzheimer's disease reveal these differences.

Loss of a Child

A variety of studies regarding how parents cope after the death of a child reveal that while many parents eventually turn to their religious belief systems at this time and report a deepening of their faith, for others this is a time of loss or confusion regarding spiritual beliefs. Many parents question God's mercy and are angry with those who seek to place the death of the child within some framework of the spiritual purpose of God (Brotherson & Sonderquist, 2002). For some parents, ongoing experiences of connection with their dead child serve to help parents cope with their loss. The wide variations of spiritual and religious beliefs influence how this difficult life event is experienced.

An exploratory study including qualitative interviews with white parents who had lost their children from accidents or illness revealed some important themes regarding the role of spirituality and religion in coping. These findings identified both sources of support as well as increased pain. Their responses were organized around four key areas: "(1) struggle with or loss of particular beliefs, (2) spiritual beliefs and practices as a coping resource, (3) a sense of spiritual connection with their child, and (4) lack of support for or rejection of these spiritual aspects" (Brotherson & Sonderquist, 2002, pp. 62–63).

Struggles with religious doubts and a breakdown of their belief system either for a short period or on a more lasting basis were reported by some of the parents. One theme related to the fear of parents that they had done something wrong that had caused this death. Others asked how God could let something like this happen (Brotherson & Sonderquist, 2002). On the other hand, some parents reported a deepening of their faith because the solace they found in their faith allowed them to cope with this tragic event. Beliefs that death was tied into some divine plan or that the child was alive in a better place were helpful. Parents also held to beliefs that the dead child remained as part of the family. Parents also coped through specific religious practices that permitted them to express their emotions and receive comfort (Brotherson & Sonderquist, 2002).

Spiritual connections with the child were also important. Parents continued to talk to their children and often created special places where they could feel this connection. Dreams were also ways to feel close to their child. Parents also found comfort in sensing their child as present in some special way (Brotherson & Sonderquist, 2002).

Perceived lack of support from others proved difficult for these parents. Some individuals withdrew from them because they felt uncomfortable dealing with their grief or urged parents to move beyond their grief. Parents reported that others might not validate their sense of the special presence of their children. They found it difficult when their religious leaders could not offer support or could not allow them to express their spiritual struggles. It was particularly difficult if parents felt blamed in some manner (Brotherson & Sonderquist, 2002).

Addressing families struggling with these intense issues requires counselors to be able to enter into intense and potentially painful discussions. The counseling setting can potentially be a haven for the family to reveal their pains, their doubts, their anger, and their hopes in general as well as those related to their spiritual life.

Caregiving for Ill Family Members

Caregiving can be an extremely difficult experience. Several studies have indicated that the use of spiritual and religious coping strategies can be helpful for caregiving related to a variety of health problems.

A recent study conducted with caregivers of families with Alzheimer's disease revealed ways in which spirituality and religion both helped in coping as well as posed burdens (Smith & Harkness, 2002). In terms of social support, respondents described the support they received from the clergy and their church community in mixed terms. While the majority described people as kind, a minority also revealed negative experiences. They used terms like "hypocritical" and "phony" in their descriptions of the response of others who they felt had not visited or otherwise showed an appropriate interest. Caretakers reported finding support from their spiritual life and their relationship to God even though some had gone through times of anger. Creating a sense of meaning for this experience was also important to respondents. Part of this sense of meaning was carrying out the legacy of the family member who was ill (Smith & Harkness, 2002).

SUMMARY

Incorporating spirituality and religion can enrich the counseling experience with families by identifying potential protective and risk factors related to these dimensions of life. Life events can raise issues of meaning and purpose in life. Opening the door to spirituality can enable some family members to discuss issues of profound importance to them and to identify potential resources as well as burdens. Such an approach requires family counselors to have a thorough self-understanding and to recognize that the family members are the experts on this journey. Counselors need to learn about the traditions of the family members in order to understand how life events are experienced. The specific ways in which these elements are incorporated into counseling depend on the family and its views of what is helpful, their religious and spiritual traditions, and the situation facing the family. Partnerships with spiritual and religious leaders can potentially be useful in helping some families. Spirituality also involves a genuine valuing of family members by the counselor.

DISCUSSION QUESTIONS

Discuss why it might be valuable for the counselor to open the door to spiritual issues with family members.

In what ways can spirituality/religion potentially be both a resource and a burden to family members?

How can object relations issues during development influence how people experience religion?

Discuss the role of rituals in spiritual life.

Discuss why it is very important for counselors to have self-understanding in addressing spiritual issues.

What does it mean to walk through the valley of suffering with people?

Discuss the role of healing as it relates to spirituality.

Discuss ways in which religious traditions can shape how people experience some important life transitions.

Part III

Resiliency-Based Practice Framework Applications

14

Families Coping with Difficult Life Circumstances

Families seeking help from social workers are frequently contending with one or more difficult events in the life of the family. A few of the many circumstances include a family member who has lost a job with consequent economic problems for the family or a family struggling with the burden of a chronically ill family member. Other families are referred for problems related to their children—perhaps behavior problems in school or suspicion of child neglect or abuse. Some families are coping with difficult transitions to a new culture and country. For many families, there is a pileup of life events that contributes to major stress.

This chapter addresses these struggles from a resiliency perspective by describing some of the challenges represented by these issues, including the potential risk and protective factors that have been identified in terms of specific life circumstances. Understanding these patterns can help social workers and other family counselors in their search for sources of resiliency as they seek to enhance and support the ability of families to cope. This information can also help in the ongoing process of clinical judgment, especially in terms of identifying useful intervention approaches with a particular family facing a unique set of problems within a current context. While information in this chapter is organized in terms of specific problem areas, it is always essential to assess individual families and their members to identify their unique combination of risk and protective factors and their interpretation of this life event. In addition, many families are facing several problems simultaneously. As a result, while this chapter includes a discussion regarding links between the research and clinical literature of risk and protective factors and treatment models, it is done with the caveat that in practice such information must be set within the context of the characteristics of the individual family in making any treatment decisions. It is also important to expand the perspective to include the wider community and social context. The life events discussed in this chapter naturally only deal with a few of the many difficult ones that family members might have to face and don't do justice to the multiple problems that can be part of their life circumstances. Many of the case illustrations in earlier chapters reflect one or more of these difficult life circumstances.

Illness

The entire family experiences stress when a member becomes ill, especially if the illness is disabling or fatal. As discussed in "Psychoeducational Family Counseling" and other chapters of this book, Lillian's, Bradley's, and the Patel and Rodriguez families' situations illustrate how the illness of a family member ripples throughout the family system. Chronic illness creates an ongoing source of stress for families that presents the family with a number of additive stressors over the years in ways that particularly challenge the coping ability of families. Severe illness can challenge the resources of families and sometimes confronts them with the potential loss of a family member. Family members' ability to cope is strongly influenced by how they interpret the illness, including the cause and consequences of the illness, as well as the skills that the family members possess to deal with the situation and the resources available to family members. As illustrated in my granddaughter who was critically ill with malaria, her family had access to a type of excellent care that is not available for many children who contract this illness. As discussed earlier, family members also can be required to provide extended home care to family members.

Lim and Zebrack's (2004) review of studies conducted with families who were caring for family members with chronic health problems included the following stressors (risk factors): demands on the caregiver, the duration and intensity of care, problematic behavior of the ill person, role changes, and lack of self-efficacy. Protective factors included social support and the following behavior by caretakers: use of logical analysis and problem-solving coping, information seeking, and emotional regulation.

Children with Chronic Illness

As described earlier, families coping with illness seek information about the illness and ways to cope with it along with social support. Social support from extended family was very important for African American mothers of children with sickle cell disease, a disease that makes heavy demands on the caretaker (Hill, 2003). Parents of children with disabilities cited the following as improving their family quality of life: finding a way to enjoy life together, and the ability to do things that are important to them. Spiritual beliefs can also be helpful in terms of creating a sense of meaning for life events, especially viewing their child as a gift of God or a blessing rather than a curse (Poston & Turnbull, 2004). Participation by all the family members in the religious community was helpful if the child was accepted but contributed to distress if the child was excluded. As described in chapter 13, spirituality and religion were important for Mexican American parents of chronically ill children who linked God, the health team, and the parents as active partners in the process (Rehm, 1999).

In addition to support from the health team, family, work, and community, a study of parents of children with cancer revealed the following resiliency factors: the ability to mobilize the family rapidly to address the situation, and appraisals that made the situation more manageable and meaningful (McCubbin, Balling, Possin, Frierdich, & Bryne, 2002). The importance of a supportive health team also emerged as a protective factor with parents of children with sickle cell disorder (and the converse that unsympathetic and incompetent health teams increased family stress) (Atkin & Ahmad, 2008; Hill, 2003).

Children with Autism

The increase in the numbers of individuals diagnosed with autism spectrum disorder means that more families are having to cope with this problem. Fortunately, families are no longer held responsible for causing the problem through problematic parenting as was once the situation. Yet they must struggle to meet the needs of a person with important developmental, cognitive, and interpersonal issues as this individual moves from early childhood to adulthood. A study examining the emotional well-being of mothers of adolescents and adults with autism reveals the importance of a strong social support system in reducing anxiety and depression of the mother. Perhaps reflecting additional life experience, older mothers in general demonstrated greater emotional well-being than did younger mothers in coping with this situation. In time, parental anxiety also decreased as they developed adaptive strategies. Yet an increase in behavioral problems increased both anxiety and depression by parents. As a result, interventions designed to promote the social support network of parents and to help them develop strategies to address behavioral difficulties represent important family interventions to help families cope with this long-term responsibility (Barker, Hartley, Seltzer, Floyd, Greenberg, & Orsmune, 2008).

HIV/AIDS

The AIDS crisis has had a devastating impact on millions of people and their families throughout the world. As discussed in chapter 4, the AIDS epidemic has had an especially harsh impact on African American families living in both the United States and Canada (Canada Aids Statistics by Year and Age, 2012; Centers for Disease Control and Prevention, 2012b; Leading Together, 2005). Rates of HIV/AIDS among African American women in the United States were fifteen times that of white women (Centers for Disease Control and Prevention, 2012b). HIV/AIDS has been a leading cause of death among African American women between 25 and 44 years, a period during which women typically have major responsibilities for the family (Centers for Disease Control and Prevention, 2005a, 2005b, 2011).

Although blacks accounted for only 2.2 percent of the Canadian population, they accounted for 15.2 percent of people with a known ethnicity in 2001 and 9.3 percent in 2009 with AIDS (note—in 56% of AIDS cases ethnicity was not reported). In Canada, members of the Aboriginal people have been especially at a high and increasing risk—in 2001, 3.3 percent of the population and 6.4 percent of the people with AIDS and in 2009, 20.4 percent of the people with AIDS (again, the majority of people did not identify their ethnicity).

The route of transmission among groups varies and has a bearing on the appropriate types of prevention. For example, in Canada intravenous drug use is the major route of transmission in Aboriginal communities, heterosexual contact among black Canadians, and sex between men for white Canadians (Canada AIDS Statistics by Year and Age, 2012). In the United States, the primary route of transmission for men is sex between men, followed by intravenous drug use and heterosexual contact. Women are primarily likely to become infected through heterosexual contact, followed by intravenous drug use (Centers for Disease Control and Prevention, 2012b).

Because African American young women of childbearing age are at high risk for HIV/AIDS, understanding what contributes to their medication adherence is important. A study of young women of childbearing age who are HIV-positive revealed the following risk and protective factors in terms of adherence. Women who reported supportive family members and who had young children were most likely to adhere. Those who perceived stigma, felt unloved and uncared for, were in turbulent relationships, and had husbands who were HIV-positive were least likely to adhere to their medication regime. Women viewed both emotional and instrumental forms of social support as important (Edwards, 2006).

The combination of risk and protective factors for many of these women is compounded by long-term poverty, along with drug addiction, and the accompanying stressors that are frequently part of their lives in addition to their HIV/AIDS (Leading Together, 2005; Centers for Disease Control and Prevention, 2012b). Reflecting this context, African American women who are HIV-positive tend to report the stress of lack of financial resources, lack of support from their community, violence and crime, stigma regarding the illness, and tension within the family circle (Centers for Disease Control and

Prevention, 2005a, 2012b; Greenwood et al., 1996). The association between HIV/AIDS and drug use and homosexuality has created stigma that has reduced the support available in some black churches as well as other religious communities. A recent Canadian report indicates that while stigma has decreased, it is still a major factor that prevents people from diagnosis and treatment (Leading Together, 2005).

Protective factors include family support by members of the immediate, extended, and "fictive kin" as well as reliance upon religion. Recognizing that families with a member suffering from AIDS vary widely in many dimensions, a review of the literature reveals that mothers in general have tended to be the most likely to accept and to provide care for the ill person (Thompson, 1999). A treatment approach (structural ecosystems therapy) is based on a systems approach and has been effective in empowering individuals and their families. Key components include skills to negotiate more effectively with the environment and to improve family interaction and communication (Greenwood et al., 1996). The Centers for Disease Control and Prevention has created two programs to empower African American women to address this issue: Women Involved in Life Learning from Other Women (WILLOW), designed to foster gender pride among HIV-positive women (Centers for Disease Control and Prevention, 2009); and Sister to Sister, which offers culturally appropriate health information (Centers for Disease Control and Prevention, 2012c). The Canadian scene is marked by a large array of services for individuals with HIV/AIDS. A recent effort by Leading Together describes efforts to coordinate prevention and service efforts for all members of Canadian society (Leading Together, 2005).

The AIDS epidemic has further created 80,000 orphaned children and adolescents, with at least 80 percent of these being African Americans or Hispanics in the United States. Grandmothers care for the majority of these children within the African American community (Winston, 2003). A recent qualitative study including African American grandmothers who are caring for their grandchildren who have been orphaned by AIDS revealed the following risk and resiliency factors in dealing with their pain and added responsibilities.

In terms of risk factors, the further loss of children and grandchildren compounds the stress experienced. These grandmothers suffered strong feelings of anxiety, guilt, and loss in the context of the physical suffering of their children as well as the impending and present death. The stigma of AIDS reduced their support systems because they were reluctant to discuss the circumstances of the illness and death with non-family members. Assuming primary care for their grandchildren was also stressful. It meant relinquishing the pleasure of grandparenthood to assume parental roles and often involved major changes in their lives. These included remaining in employment longer or moving away from their communities and support systems. They also experienced a variety of health problems as they assumed these new responsibilities (Winston, 2003). In terms of protective factors, the women found the strength to cope through a variety of sources that reflected supportive relationships and beliefs. Cultural beliefs within the African American community of the primacy of the family with its strong extended kinship structure supported their new roles. The presence of the children helped them turn from loss and death to life. Their spiritual relationship with God was a major source of resiliency. They viewed the death of their child as part of the will of God. While they had initially prayed for healing, they later asked that their child be released from suffering. Their religion also provided a support system through religious services and inspirational reading or programs. They worked to keep the memory of their child alive through pictures, rituals, and conversation. Caring for their grandchildren became part of sustaining the continuity of the family (Winston, 2003).

In a study including white mothers of family members with AIDS, the unpredictable nature of the illness shaped the nature of their successful coping efforts. These included "taking one day at a time" and managing their emotions on a daily basis by addressing issues as they arose. They sought to maintain a sense of normalcy by focusing on daily living and emphasized living in the moment. They remained flexible to meet the various needs that arose which served as an active coping style given the reality of the illness (Thompson, 1999). They sought support in terms of relevant information and emotional support from professionals, other family members, and others who were also facing the illness. Mothers worked closely with the health care system to cope with the medical complexities of AIDS. As a reflection of family cohesion and flexibility, other family members joined forces to offer the mother support in her caring role (Thompson, 1999).

Appraisal strategies were also valuable. Despite the sadness and sense of loss, many mothers were able to see positive aspects in terms of increased connectedness with the ill family member, renewal of strained relationships between the ill family members and others within the family, and personal growth (Thompson, 1999).

Families also used issues related to family organization to help cope. Family members either defined family boundaries to temporarily exclude members who contributed to stress and conflict or expanded boundaries to include others outside the family who offered support. Spirituality and religion emerged as valuable coping strategies. Participants also coped by politicizing the issue through becoming engaged in advocacy and education efforts (Thompson, 1999).

There is a growing problem of HIV/AIDS among older adults that creates a new set of challenges for families. A study with older HIV-infected adults revealed the following ways in which spirituality served as a protective factor for older family members that can reduce the challenge of the illness for the family as a whole: it evoked comforting emotions, offered strength and a sense of control, eased the emotional burden of the illness, gave social support and a sense of belonging, gave spiritual support through a relationship with God, helped provide a sense of meaning and acceptance of the illness, helped maintain health, relieved fear of death, and reduced self blame (Siegel & Schrimshaw, 2002).

Diabetes

Diabetes represents another growing health problem for both children and adults. Based on a series of studies conducted with families living with non-insulin-dependent family members, the following helpful coping skills emerged: family organization and relationship skills and effective family communication and cohesiveness. Control of diabetes requires specific coping skills, including monitoring food intake. Knowledge of the dietary demands was only the first and easiest step. Changes in long-term dietary habits required critical negotiation and problem-solving skills on the part of both partners (Chesla, 1999). Unfortunately African American women are at heightened risk for type 2 diabetes and frequently must contend with a variety of other social/economic stressful life demands with the potential for creating role overload. Active coping strategies that engage support within the family and social world are helpful in reducing stress. Expectations that one can or should be a "superwoman" decrease the ability to seek out this type of help (Murry, Owens, Brody, Black, Willert & Brown, 2003).

A series of recent studies identified family patterns that were associated with improved outcomes for children with type 1 diabetes. One protective factor included a collaborative involvement between parents and their children that gave their children a role in participating in their care (Chisholm, Atkinson, Donaldson, Noyes, Payne, & Keinar, 2011; Wysocki, Nansel, Holmbeck, Chen, Laffel, Anderson, & Weissberg-Benchell, 2008). Maternal close involvement in the management of the diabetes was positive for younger children (10–15) but needed to be adjusted as children (especially girls) grew older (Wiebe, Berg, Korbet, Palmer, Beveridge, Upchurch, Lindsey, Swinyard, & Donaldson, 2005). In terms of parents, mothers' depression as well as general family stress (Hegelson, Becker, Escobor, & Siminero, 2012; Wiebe, Gelfan, Butler, Korbel, Fortenberry, McCabe, & Berry, 2011) were linked with poorer diabetes outcomes.

Mental Illness

Mental illness can represent major responsibilities for family members along with the loss sometimes of family dreams. Such family responsibilities are typically long-term and require different approaches depending on the current state of the illness. Parents worry about who will care for the ill family member when they are no longer able to do so. As discussed in the chapter

"Psychoeduational Family Counseling," Gregg's parents typify family members who are frightened about the impact of this illness on their family members and are confused regarding what to do. In terms of risk factors, regardless of culture, the most difficult sources of strain for families were the level of behavioral problems of the ill family member combined with uncertainty about how to handle them. Contextual issues related to problems in the service delivery system also contributed to this distress (Lefley, 1998). A study of women family caregivers of adults with serious mental illness revealed the importance of positive cognitions in enhancing resourcefulness and sense of coherence as protective factors that helped reduce the burden created by strain, stigma, client dependence, and family disruption (Zauszniewski, Bekhet, & Suresky, 2009).

Cultural backgrounds influence how families cope. Families that belong to cultures that are more collectivist with an emphasis on interdependence are more likely to include family members in the basic healing process and to provide support for the individuals involved (Lefley, 1998). In a study comparing African American and white families, African American families with a member with a psychiatric disability tended to experience this situation as less of a burden than did white families. African American parents were more likely to score higher on the dimensions of mastery and self-esteem, with greater ability to adjust expectation levels appropriate to the disability. White parents found it more difficult to accommodate to lower levels of expectations (Lefley, 1998).

An earlier study including primarily women caretakers who are members of Latino and African American families revealed some sources of strength that echo those of other studies. Family appraisals of the situation, self-efficacy, and social supports emerged as important protective factors. Appraisals influenced both the nature of the illness and the caretaker role. These family members avoided the blame that has sometimes burdened families. African American parents attributed the illness of the family member to hardship in life or traumatic events, for example, the death or abandonment of the father. Latino families blamed external factors or events or the intrinsic weakness of the ill person that prevented the person from dealing with the difficulties of life. They used the concept of *nervios* in contrast to *locura*, which refers to enduring madness. Their concepts of the illness engendered hope. Their religious beliefs in the power of God gave them faith that one could be cured. They viewed mental illness along a continuum of severity. While family members did not necessarily expect a complete cure, they were hopeful that the person might be able to function independently. They were also able to take a strengths-based perspective by identifying the strengths of the ill person and nourishing these strengths. Cultural appraisals of caregiving also helped. Caregiving was viewed as "this is what one does for family or the ill." Those who provided care were able to take a sense of pride in being able to care for an ill family member rather than viewing it as a burden. They also developed important skills that helped them be more effective caregivers. They became knowledgeable about the illness of the person and were able to recognize when the ill person needed additional help. Social support systems were important in terms of other members of the family, church, and the neighborhood. They also sought and received help from the mental health services. Latino caregivers also received help from traditional healers (Parra & Guarnaccia, 1998). While the preceding discussion reflects general patterns, it is always essential for family counselors to assess individual members of any group in terms of their perspectives and coping resources.

Children with Attachment Disorders

As described earlier in chapter 1, the introduction to resiliency theory, and further in chapter 11 on object relations family therapy, the quality of an individual's attachment to—connection with—early caretakers plays an important role in the person's development. Unfortunately, some young children do not have caretakers who provide the valuable protective elements of "acceptance, trust, open communication, encouragement of wider social relationships, and congenial parent relationships" along with "the consistency of family life including regular routines, consistency of parenting, and participation of members in family activities" (Bowlby, 1973, p. 335). The nature of these early attachments can play an important role throughout the life of an individual (Levy & Orlans, 2003). An interpersonal climate that does not promote appropriate attachment can occur as parents are too overwhelmed by external circumstances to meet the needs of a child, are caught up in some type of addiction, or are too damaged from their own earlier life experiences. I remember the hurt in a six-year-old child's eyes when she realized that her mother would not be taking the necessary steps (stop using drugs, find a home) in order to make a home for her. I struggled with how to help this little girl realize that she was a wonderful person and that she was not the reason; instead it was her mother's sickness (addiction). Fortunately, this little girl had loving grandparents to give her a base of security. These issues can emerge within biological parent-child interactions, couples, and foster or adoptive parent-child relationships as well as the potential difficulties facing individuals. Social workers working in the child protective system, with foster parents, and adoptive families are particularly likely to find themselves addressing these situations. The shadow of attenuated or traumatic attachment histories can, however, emerge in a variety of interpersonal relationships. At the same time, young children can be placed in loving homes that provide them with the security they need to create strong attachments. When I consider the wonderful boy who became a member of our family via adoption by my son and his family, I think of the family who sadly could not care for him as a small child and lost the opportunity to be a part of this child's life.

In their excellent discussion of the issue of attachment, Levy and Orlans (2003) draw upon attachment theory and clinical contributions to identify the following parental, family circle, and community contexts that contribute to attachment. The following represent protective factors in the attachment process, while the inability to meet these needs contributes to risk. Children need caretakers who are able to be sensitive and attuned to the individual child's needs and respond accordingly. At the same time, parents and children do not need to be totally in sync as children gain the skills to learn how to cope when they are not in accord. "Children can deal with their parental imperfections if such are balanced by sufficient love and understanding" (p. 169). Children need parents who demonstrate nurturing, compassionate, and loving care. This helps children gain a sense of security, of being wanted, as well as develop the capacity for empathy with others. Children also need parents who set consistent limits and give the message that it is the parents who are in charge. Parents also need to give children appropriate responsibilities. As children carry these out, they develop self-confidence. In this process, children learn the art of give and take. The parent's own attachment history influences the parent's ability to create an atmosphere characterized by secure and loving relationships. Living in a context that builds on a secure interpersonal base enables children to begin to experience an appropriate degree of autonomy and independence. It is the confidence of this secure base that permits the child to explore his or her world. Children need appropriate limits that enable them to live in a world with others and to internalize structure. Children need parents who communicate in a loving manner while encouraging children to use their problem-solving skills. Children and their parents do not live in isolation. Children need teachers and others within their environment that can encourage children to feel that they belong and have something worthwhile to contribute. Family can be supported by their wider social system or undermined and feel further overwhelmed.

Recognizing that many children with attachment problems do not come to the attention of the child welfare system and are not removed from their homes, statistics regarding children in foster care in the United States and Canada indicate that many children are facing severe enough problems that they are removed from their homes on at least a temporary basis. These are children who are potentially at risk for attachment problem issues. The United States Children's Bureau reports that in 2010, 408,425 children had been removed from their homes and were currently placed in some type of foster care (relative or non-relative) or a group facility. Among these, 250,000 entered and left care in a typical year. These included 48 percent white, 24 percent black, 21 percent Hispanic, and 20 percent other groups. The rate of First Nations children in foster care in the United States is about double their population (2% in foster care—although this varies widely from state to state [Adams, 2012]). The average age for a child to be placed was 6.7 years. In Canada, 76,000 children were placed out of their homes. Among these 30–40 percent were Aboriginal people, primarily members of the First Nations (Farris-Manning & Zandstra, 2012) As a result of difficult times and policy issues, many children in some other countries of the world have been placed in orphanages that were inadequate to meet the developmental needs of children. In the corrective attachment therapy program conducted by Levy and Orlans (2003), the majority of families seeking services had adopted children from these foreign orphanages or foster care programs. In response to their earlier life circumstances, these children "tend to have negative core beliefs, antisocial attitudes, and antisocial behaviors" that are reflected in oppositional, controlling, and mistrusting behaviors (Levy & Orlans, 2003).

Children who have developed attachment problems are likely to demonstrate a variety of behaviors that they have learned through earlier experiences or coping strategies arising from their core beliefs. They can be overly compliant and become withdrawn. Children can behave in such a way to prompt rejection that gives them an illusion of control. The ensuing interaction results in a power struggle between the child and the parents. Other children can attempt to cope by triangulating their parents—loving toward one and hostile toward the other parent. Children can be resentful and abusive toward their siblings. This is a recipe for parental conflict, sibling resentment, and family isolation (Levy and Orlans, 2003).

The challenge in addressing attachment issues within the family setting is to find a way to reestablish a sense of trust, to alter the core beliefs that create barriers in relationships, and to change the resulting behavior. Specific therapeutic modalities and approaches have been developed to help children with these needs, parents who were not able to create a climate that facilitated attachment, foster parents who are trying to help children with these problems, and adoptive parents. While it is beyond the scope of this book to describe in detail the many programs, the following is a general description of some of these basic approaches that are designed to provide corrective experiences within the family systemic context to address attachment issues. The role of the therapist is particularly important in these types of therapy. Therapists must be able to understand, to sooth the intense anxiety, and to deal with the desperate emotions experienced by individuals with attachment issues (Whiffen, 2003).

Young families who have been challenged to create an attachment-affirming family context. Steele, Murphy, and Steele (2010) describe a group approach for mothers and their children. These mothers have lacked the parental skills or have been too overwhelmed by other life issues to create these bonds with their children. The young mothers tend to be isolated with a history of adverse life experiences and ongoing poverty and violence in their families or community. These young women bring to parenthood their own attachment issues; for example, 54 percent reported not having confidence that as a child they had someone they could trust to care for them. Many experienced out-of-home placements. The therapists used a group approach to give the young women emotional connections with others and to encourage (and in the process educate and mentor) mothers to interact in such a way to create bonds with their young children. Group sessions with the mothers were used to give the mothers additional support. The environment of respect was a new and therapeutic experience for these young women. As therapists used a supportive and encouraging approach, mothers gradually begin to interact in a more positive manner for longer periods of time as a basis for creating a parent-child attachment.

Foster parents. Levy and Orlans (2003) propose the following strategies and solutions that foster parents can use with children with attachment issues. These are basic approaches that can be used by parents generally who are trying to help children with attachment issues.

- Understand the children's core negative beliefs regarding themselves and others that contribute to problematic behavior. Parents can tune into the child's perceptions and offer praise for specific behavior and resist personalizing the child's negative responses.

- Balance connection and control—love accompanied by appropriate limits.

- Teach reciprocity by encouraging children to ask for help and giving them opportunities to contribute to the family.

- Understand and meet the needs of individual children to look beyond negative behavior to the attachment needs and fears.

- Increase parents' self-awareness of their own attachment history and emotional reactions and encourage them to take care of themselves.

- Help children learn how to manage their emotions by remaining emotionally neutral in the face of negative behaviors and expressing positive emotions to positive behavior. Teach children how to identify and express their emotions in a safe context.

- Understand the nature of attachment styles of their children and respond accordingly:
  - Avoidant response—child keeps his or her distance and projects self-reliance

    Provide support and comfort
  - Ambivalent—child is clingy and hyper-aware of potential rejection

    Set limits and be consistent
  - Disorganized—children have experienced severe trauma and are punitive to others

Seek support for the family to provide safety and additional services

- Increase the sense of belonging by encouraging the child to be part of the family activities.

This can be challenged by frequent moves that destroy a child's sense of belonging.

Couple with attachment issues. Johnson and Best (2003) describe an approach called "emotionally focused therapy" that addresses the emotions and the emotional communication process within the couple. The model operates on the assumption that internal representation models of attachment can be altered and draws upon a series of interventions in the couple therapy. The focus of the therapist is upon two basic tasks: "accessing and reformulating of emotional responses and the shaping of new interaction based on these responses" (Johnson & Best, 2003, p. 176).

Johnson and Best (2003) describe three basic stages and the nine basic steps associated with these stages in treatment. The steps are organized in terms of mutually assessing the reoccurring cycle and attachment issues, changing the interaction patterns, and consolidating change.

STAGE 1. CYCLE DE-ESCALATION

Step 1. Assessment: Creating an alliance and articulating the core conflicts and attachment issues.

Step 2. Identifying the problematic cycle that maintains the attachment insecurity and distress.

Step 3. Accessing the unacknowledged emotions that organize the interactional positions and placing these in an attachment frame.

Step 4. Reframing the problem in terms of the systems cycle and the underlying attachment emotions and needs. . . .

STAGE 2. CHANGING INTERACTIONAL POSITIONS.

Step 5. Promoting identification with disowned attachment needs and aspects of self, and integrating these into relationship patterns.

Step 6. Promoting the other's acceptance of these needs and aspects of self.

Step 7. Facilitating the expression of specific needs and wants, and creating emotional engagement. . . .

STAGE 3. CONSOLIDATING AND INTEGRATION.

Step 8. Facilitating the emergence of new solutions to old problematic relationship issues in an atmosphere of collaboration and safety.

Step 9. Consolidating new positions characterized by accessibility and responsiveness and new cycles of attachment behaviors. (pp. 172–173)

In the first task, the therapist focuses on the emotion that is particularly relevant to the client's experience and attachment issues. The following example describes how fear can be expressed as anger, creating a vicious cycle that intensifies the fear experienced by both and that can destroy the relationship.

> Mark's withdrawal produces the experience of fear in his wife Joan as it reactivates her fear of rejection related to the abandonment of her father when she was three. As Joan expresses her fear as anger, Mark withdraws further. His emotional response is also fear as it evokes his helplessness when he was being verbally abused as a young child by his mother.

The attachment issues of both create responses that in turn create distance and further tension within the couple.

The second task draws upon structural techniques. The therapist reframes the events in terms of cycle interactions that reflect an experience common to both parties in the relationship (for Mark and Joan it is fear related to abandonment and helplessness). The therapist then begins to create new enactments that begin to reshape the interaction pattern in ways that can heal attachment issues within the couple. The goal is to reshape the interaction sequence. Both the husband and wife are encouraged to share the fears that they are feeling rather than respond by angry shouting and withdrawal. As described previously in "Structural Family Therapy," change in this interaction pattern also helps reshape interpretations.

Families with adolescents. Diamond and Stern (2003) describe a family approach with parents and adolescents, especially those who are depressed. This approach recognizes that many of these adolescents have experienced trauma either through physical or sexual abuse or witnessing violence or have experienced emotional abuse that has threatened their sense of security. Attachment-based family therapy (ABFT) in this context is based on the assumption that "family conversations may also serve a reparative function in families where the attachment bond has been compromised" (Diamond & Stern, 2003, p. 192). Adolescents with insecure attachments can lack the confidence to move forward into appropriate independence and instead remain harboring anger and resentment. As in the couple approach described previously, this model also includes an enactment element drawn from structural family therapy. Similar to structural family therapy, the therapist acts as a coach and mentor to facilitate a positive interchange. This version of ABFT includes three phases designed to increase understanding on the part of both the parents and the adolescent and to use this understanding to begin creating healing in the attachment process. The following summary illustration does not do justice to the true intensity and difficulties present in this process.

Phase A—Adolescent disclosure. The adolescent expresses his or her angry and vulnerable feelings and explores his attributions of the past trauma. The parents listen in an empathic mode.

> Bill, age thirteen, expressed his angry feelings toward his mother because she had been emotionally unavailable to him during the last couple of years. His father was dead and thus his mother was his only available parent. He felt that she didn't love him—that he had really lost two parents. Bill's mother doesn't interrupt him but listens in an attentive and empathic manner.

Phase B—Parent disclosure. The parents tell their side of the story. The adolescent begins to deepen his or her understanding of the situation.

> Bill's mother states that she is very sorry that she had not been available to him during this time. She had been in a state of shock with the sudden death of her husband and his father when he died in a car crash. Unfortunately, she handled her grief by turning to drinking. She later realized what she was doing to her son and herself and recently sought treatment that has allowed her to begin a new life. She hopes that Bill will give her a chance to make things better between the two of them.

Phase C—Conversation between the adolescent and the parents. The goal is to enable this conversation to become more mutual and reciprocal (Diamond & Stern, 2003, p. 195).

> Bill and his mother together talk about what they have gone through (their mutual loss of the husband/father and feelings of grief), his feeling of being abandoned by his mother, her feelings of guilt for how she had not been there for him, and her wish to have a better relationship between the two of them. This leads to a conversation about what this relationship can be like and what they can do to repair things. It also includes a discussion of the steps the mother is taking to ensure her sobriety to help reassure Bill that the cycle will not repeat itself.

Contextual issues. While the emphasis in this discussion has been on the parent-child interaction process, it is also important to look at the wider context that either promotes parents' ability to respond to their children's needs or impedes this. Parents who are depressed, who are struggling with their own addictions, or who are worried about survival can find it difficult to respond in a consistent, caring way with their children. As a result, addressing the needs of families requires this wider ecological approach. For Bill and his mother, they might also include concern on the part of the mother about what supports she will need to remain sober at this time.

Implications for treatment. Although the above situations vary in terms of age and life circumstances, there is a common core of beliefs that lead to distrust that people will care for one and that one is worthy of being cared for. Treatment is organized around giving people needed emotional support and experiences that can address these belief systems and give people an experience that helps support the trust needed for attachment. From a resiliency perspective, these approaches address belief systems and try to create experiences that build positive family interactions that in turn help affirm new and more positive belief systems.

Substance Abuse Issues

Although only one person in the family might be abusing legal or illegal substances, in reality, it is a family disease. Problems with substance abuse impact all the members of the family through the inability of parents to provide for the needs of other family members, family conflict, and potential lost income. Children are removed from their homes because mothers or fathers cannot provide the care they need. Unfortunately for children, substance abuse by parents not only increases their children's risk for out-of-home placement into foster care but has been also associated with increased level of reentry into foster care after unification (Brook & McDonald, 2009).

As a Guardian ad Litem volunteer in the court system working with children in the child welfare system, the majority of the children I have worked with have had one or more parents unable to provide care for them due to addiction issues. It can be painful for a child to experience that drugs mean more to her mother or father than she does. Children are pulled into a parental triangle as parents seek to gain allies in their conflict or are pulled into efforts to control the parent's drinking. Children can also begin to assume roles within the family designed to cope with the problems within the family and ultimately to enable the drinking pattern to continue. In addition to the roles identified in families generally (victim, peacemaker, parental role-taking), these include the responsible one, placater, adjuster, hero, scapegoat, lost child, and mascot (Janzen & Harris, 1997). The hero child helps justify the normalcy of the family and thus contributes to the denial of the problem. The scapegoat distracts attention from the problems created by the alcoholic. The lost child helps maintain the denial because the child causes no trouble but her/his own needs are neglected. The mascot relieves tension within the family by minimizing the seriousness of the family problems (Janzen & Harris, 1997). Teenagers die as they experiment from substances and leave behind grieving family members. In addition, a history of substance abuse in the family is one of the risk factors for children having similar problems (Jensen, 2004). Other family members become enablers, people whose behavior ends up protecting the addict's use of substances. Substance abuse issues either currently or in the family history emerge in many of the families or individuals seeking help for a variety of issues.

Jensen (2004) draws upon the research literature to identify the following key risk and protective factors for drug abuse by youth generally. Wagner, Ritt-Olson, Chou, Pokhrel, Duan, Baezconde-Garbanati, Soto, and Unger (2010) further examined risk factors related to family and youth in general with an emphasis on Hispanic youth. Since many substance abuse problems begin in adolescence or young adulthood, understanding these risk factors is especially important. They range from broad community factors to the individual. The more risk factors in the life of the child, the more likely the child will develop problems in this area, although some children with multiple risk factors do not emerge with such problems. There is also an interactive process at work here; for example, substance abuse problems can reduce one's ability to connect with and do well in school, can lead one to associate with peers who are also users, can contribute to depression, and can create conflict within the family. Culture can also influence ways in which parents respond to children differently depending on gender; for example, Hispanic families tend to monitor adolescent girls more than their sons (Wagner et al., 2010).

Risk Factors

Community context. Social norms that promote or tolerate alcohol or illicit use by adolescents are associated with increased abuse of substances. While data are mixed regarding the impact of family poverty per se, living in neighborhoods with high crime and drug use and disorganization can contribute to increased drug use.

Family and peers. Growing up in a family with parents or siblings with serious alcohol or drug use increases the risk of youth having similar behavior. The risk of adolescent substance abuse is also increased by family conflict, lack of or excessively severe discipline, poor parent-child communication, and sexual abuse. Low parental monitoring is associated with higher rates of substance use. Child maltreatment is linked to substance abuse through potentially increasing externalizing behavior that in turn creates externalizing behavioral problems and association with similar peers (Oshri, Burnette, & Cicchetti, 2011). A study of First Nations youth revealed the powerful influence of siblings and cousins who were involved in substance use and persuaded youth to begin to use them (Waller, Okamoto, Miles, & Hurdle, 2003). Family issues (substance abuse by parents, family conflict, involvement with the child welfare system), lack of commitment to a school as marked by school mobility and school dropouts, and deviant peer affiliation in the adolescent years also characterized people who became substance abuses by age twenty-six among African American individuals with low incomes (Arteaga, Chen, & Reynolds, 2010).

Youth who are not attached to the school scene are also at increased risk. Associating with peers who are using drugs emerges as one of the strongest predictors of alcohol or drug abuse.

Individual characteristics. Genetics can play a role in alcoholism. Youth who are sensation seekers, who have attention deficit disorders, hyperactivity, or poor impulse control are at greater risk. These co-occurring disorders are common patterns—substance abuse with depression, paranoia, hostility, and suicidal ideation. Males are more likely to develop substance abuse problems than females.

Protective Factors

Community. Community supports are important for children exposed to multi-risk factors. Community members such as teachers, ministers, and neighbors play protective roles. Community and school activities that offer potential participation by youth are important. Commitment to school is protective. In adults, commitment to a job emerges as a protective factor.

Family and peers. Positive relationships between children and parents and grandparents during early years are protective. These create strong attachments between children and parents. Appropriate levels of monitoring and good parent-youth communication are also protective. Pro-social peers, including those within the extended family circle, also play a positive role. Developing these strong social bonds requires the following conditions:

- Opportunities to be engaged in pro-social activities.
- Possession of the behavioral and cognitive skills to be successful in these activities.
- Recognition for positive behavior.

Individual. Competence in social and problem-solving coping skills is important. Related to this is self-efficacy in these areas. Youth with a general pro-social attitude, a positive temperament, and who share the norms of society are also less likely to have substance abuse problems.

Assessment and interventions. In terms of substance abuse and the family, these can be conceptualized in terms of stages related to change identified by Prochaska, DiClemente, and Norcross (1992) and discussed earlier in chapter 2. The following discussion acknowledges that the family as well as the person with a substance abuse problem go through stages and that family members and the person with an addiction can be at different stages in this process.

Pre-contemplation. Family members as well as the person with the substance abuse problem are not really acknowledging the presence of an abuse problem. Various issues can be involved in this "coverup"—for example, fear of what might happen if they acknowledged the presence of the problem, or the challenge of loyalty issues.

Voicing some of these concerns might begin to open the door for family members to consider them. Counselors can question certain behaviors that might reflect substance abuse-related issues, but one has limited ability to convince family members of the existence of a problem if they do not acknowledge them.

Contemplation. Family members are concerned about the substance abuse but are continuing to protect the person—covering up/enabling. Psychoeducational approaches that educate family members about the nature of substance abuse (for example, what are the signs to look for that a person is having abuse problems, the impact that this can have on the family, and ways that family members can help by stop covering up, and beginning to be their own persons again) can be helpful. It is important to explore what families anticipate and fear might happen if they stop covering up—if he loses his job, if she gets dismissed from school. Support from community programs such as Alanon can be useful. Family members can also nourish relationships during times when substance abuse is not in the picture.

Contemplation/preparation. Family members are willing to acknowledge that there is a problem but the person who is abusing is not. If the family is willing to confront the person, interventions can be designed that involve family and the person with the problem. Family members must agree on consequences that they are willing to require. In terms of the family, members are preparing themselves to approach the family member with the addiction problem and developing a plan of action. The action stage for the family begins when family members share with the person what the impact of the drinking/drug abuse has been on them—not to accuse but to let them know the consequences.

Action. Both family members and the person with the substance abuse problem are willing to acknowledge that there is a problem and are willing to try to change. The person with the addiction is engaged in a program or process that is enabling them to address their addiction. An inpatient program for the person with a substance abuse problem might be required, although many people are able to be helped on a community basis. This initial stage is only the first one and must be followed by a relapse prevention program (maintenance). Involvement of the family in the treatment process has been shown to be very useful in the alcoholic's treatment (Janzen & Harris, 1997). The discussion regarding treatment of substance abuse in chapter 8, "Solution-Focused Family Therapy," represents a possible model of treatment involving the family. Identification of risk (triggers) and protective factors is important in this process and plays a key role in family interventions.

Maintenance. The essential relapse prevention process can be complicated by several issues. At the family level, it can be complicated by barriers in truly letting the individual back into the family. Family members can be hurt, distrustful, and puzzled because not all the problems are gone even though the person is no longer drinking. These tensions can increase the risk for relapse. Some of the past problems were covered up by drinking. Some of the ongoing problems are still present. The potential presence of the person back in the family can create tensions (for example, family roles have been created that did not include this individual). Depending on the assessment, several intervention strategies discussed earlier can be useful. Intervention regarding communication skills can be used to help people begin to reestablish relationships and problem solving. Satir's approach that uses communication to create healing and enhance the positives in a family can be valuable here. Solution approaches can be used to help family members rebuild trust. Family members can identify what small steps would help them gain trust. The person who had been addicted can identify what small steps family members can make that would make him or her feel part of the family circle again. Family members can identify ways that they can assume more normal ways of behaving within the family.

Dementia

Caretakers of family members with various types of dementia must contend with long-term and emotionally and physically draining responsibilities that frequently lead to the distress of caregivers. These responsibilities are replete with the additive stressors identified in the risk and resiliency literature. This distress can contribute to depression and negative health outcomes. In the context of a growing number of individuals providing such care and with recognition of the potential for distress experienced by caregivers, there has also been recent attention to the factors that contribute to resiliency among caregivers.

Several themes have emerged that identify sources of resiliency in the face of these realistically difficult responsibilities. Studies of caretakers revealed the protective role of perceived mastery and self-efficacy and positive coping strategies (Au, Lai, Lau, Pan, Lam, Thompson, & Gallagher-Thompson, 2009; Harmell, Chattilion, Roepke, & Mausbach, 2011). These protective factors also emerged in a study of the role of psychoeducational programs (Coon, Thompson, Steffen, Sorocco, & Gallagher-Thompson, 2003). Self-efficacy in terms of viewing this difficult situation as a challenge rather than a threat was valuable. Identification with the caregiving role also supported the well-being of caretakers (Greene & Cohen, 2005). These themes suggest the need for approaches that can enhance the perceived competence of caregivers.

Social support also plays a protective role. In a study comparing African American and white caregivers differences emerged between members of these groups. African American caregivers displayed fewer depressive symptoms and reported high levels of life satisfaction that are partially explained by their higher levels of satisfactions with their social support (Clay, Roth, Wadley, & Haley, 2008). Moving beyond negative reactions to a sense of personally gaining from the caregiving experience, caretakers in a study set in Singapore reported personal gain from this experience. The most important gains were becoming more patient and understanding, becoming stronger/more resilient, having increased self-awareness and knowledge, an improved relationship with the care recipient and others in the family, and gains in spirituality, relation with God, and a more enlightened perspective on life (Netto, Jenny, & Phillip, 2009).

Assessment and Treatment

Although the specific illnesses and treatments in the preceding discussion vary widely, some important themes regarding risk and protective factors support the value of psychoeducational models in helping families. These programs offer a combination of accurate information about the specific illness and types of treatment and help family members develop more effective coping strategies that in turn enhance their sense of self-efficacy. Such programs further provide information about the impact of the illness on the family to help members address the needs of the family members as a whole. Social workers also need to help family members establish links to key health care providers as well as others within the ongoing support system of family members.

Identifying the meaning of this illness for the families is important. Views that give family members a sense of meaning and purpose as they cope are especially valuable. For some families, spirituality has been valuable in offering this sense of meaning and support. Families may need support to maintain effective leadership in coping with the illness and changes within the family organization. Multisystems models that address both the functioning of the individual family as well as available resources within the larger context in which families operate can be useful for families in which the structure of the family is challenged and the need for external resources becomes especially critical.

Sexual Abuse

Tragically, approximately 16 to 34 percent of girls and 10 to 20 percent of boys are sexually abused in some way during their childhood. These life events can create scars that pose ongoing pain and suffering for those involved (American Psychological Association Task Force on Violence and the Family, 1996). Studies set in a range of countries and drawing upon both clinical and non-clinical groups of participants have identified some of the signs of distress experienced by people who have been sexually abused. In reviewing this list, it is important to remember that individuals vary widely in terms of their behavioral response to this life event, with some evidencing signs of serious distress and others without any such result. Some of the forms that this distress takes include a tendency to ruminate on sadness (Conway, Mendelson, Giannopoulis, Csank, & Holm, 2004), depression and anxiety (Walrath, Ybarra, Holden, Liao, Santiago, & Leaf, 2003), substance abuse (Lynskey & Fergusson, 1997), suicide attempts (Ystgaard, Hestetun, Loeb, & Mehlum, 2004), and dissociation (Dalenberg & Palesh, 2004). Abuse by multiple individuals and longer length of sexual abuse contribute to additional trauma (Steel, Sanna, Hammond, Whipple, & Cross, 2004), as does living in a context of ongoing neglect, parental substance abuse, and other forms of family problems and violence (Dong, Anda, Dube, Giles, & Felittle, 2003; Peleikis, Mykletunm, & Dahl, 2004). While attempts by young people to deal with the pain by withdrawal and avoidance might be adaptive immediately, they are associated with greater long-term distress and severity of symptoms (Bal, Van Oost, De Bourdeaudhuij, & Crombez, 2003; Steel et al., 2004). Internalizing through self-blame also intensified distress (Steel et al., 2004). Women who had been sexually abused described recovery as an ongoing active process accompanied by struggles with substance abuse and a negative view of themselves. New trauma represented an important risk factor (Banyard & Williams, 2007).

Emotional support from parents, caretakers, and friends during childhood and subsequent years was especially important in the path to recovery. This support enhanced self-worth (Banyard & Williams, 2007; Jonzon & Lindblad, 2006; Rosenthal, Feiring, & Taska, 2003; Valentine & Feinauer, 1993). Relationships with their children and spirituality also emerged as important (Banyard & Williams, 2007). Female members of the Church of Jesus Christ of Latter Day Saints who had been sexually abused described the protective role of religion in terms of creating a meaning for the experience that freed them from guilt and blame and gave them a sense of value along with a positive support network. This enabled them to envision a future without abuse and to gain a sense of their power in taking control of their lives (Valentine & Feinauer, 1993).

The larger context of people's lives was important in the resiliency process. People who were abused by those outside of their family, had relatively stable families, and did not experience violence again did relatively well compared with women for whom sexual abuse was part of a larger problematic context that set in motion another series of troubled life events, further compromising their ability to function effectively (Hyman & Williams, 2001).

Assessment and Treatment

The prevalence of sexual abuse means that family counselors in the course of their work with families will encounter individuals who have been sexually abused at some time in their lives. A child might have been abused recently and the child's safety from future abuse is paramount. It may also involve removal of the abusing family member and support for the child and other family members. A multisystems approach could be helpful if the family needed extensive help from the larger system. This can be especially important if the abuse is set within a context of a family overwhelmed by many challenges that in turn can add to the experience of trauma. Protecting the child from other types of related abuse is essential. Addressing the scars of abuse is also important.

In other families, one of the members was abused earlier by someone outside the current family. Women who had been abused earlier reported being helped by life experiences that gave them a sense of their ability to take control of their own lives, to absolve themselves of blame and guilt, and to feel loved and cared for in their current family relationships. This helped women gain trust that while the abuse was part of their past, it did not have to be part of their future. While the literature cited above refers to sexual abuse of women, it is important to remember that boys can also be sexually abused by family members or others with very painful consequences.

Several family models can potentially be useful depending on the unique family situation. Solution-focused therapy specifically places the control of the direction of treatment in the hands of the family members and reinforces this sense of control, which can be very healing for those who experienced lack of control in a very painful manner. The narrative approaches help people distinguish between themselves and the events that have happened to them and to replace problem-saturated stories and identities with more empowering ones. Family members can thus begin the process of editing their story in ways that look at their strengths in terms of survival and the new possibilities in their present context. This was an important step for the James family where the cloud of "damaged goods" hung over the family. Psychoeducational approaches can be useful by educating people about the potential impact that sexual abuse can have on the parties involved. This information can be valuable not only for the individual who was abused but also to help the partner realize that her or his reactions in certain situations are the consequence of previous life experiences. In my counseling experience, this information can be very valuable since the partner can take these reactions personally rather than recognizing their source. Both individuals can be helped to identify ways to help the abused partner recapture a sense of control and to feel loved and cared for in their current relationship in ways that meet the needs of both partners. For individuals who were abused in the past with ongoing shadows in terms of their current relationships, object relations family therapy can be a means of altering the destructive patterns that have been brought from past problematic relationships into the present family life in order to help individuals experience the potential reality of feeling loved and cared for.

Trauma

Refugee Trauma

Millions of families are refugees from political turmoil, war, natural disasters, and political and religious persecution. Almost every day newspapers tell the story of new groups of people fleeing danger. Refugee families have experienced or feared for violence in their homeland and are now trying to establish new lives in a new setting, sometimes in the context of resentment of their presence (Barwick, Beiser, & Edwards, 2002; Mayadas, Elliott, & Ramanathan, 1999; Weine, 2011). As discussed in chapter 1, the Lo family's experience of the traumas of the past can carry over to the present life of the family in ways that can potentially limit their view of realistic options. Many of these families come from cultures that are organized around the family and view both trauma and coping through the lens of the family.

Young people who have been exposed to extensive violence and trauma are more likely to have post-traumatic symptoms, and there are lingering effects twelve to fourteen years afterwards. Refugee families can face social isolation, loss of their traditional support networks, and uncertainty about the well-being of loved ones (who can be still living in potentially dangerous situations). The move can bring with it loss of income, loss of meaningful life roles, and role changes in terms of family members who are able to obtain employment. Language difficulties and discrimination from the wider community can intensify problems. Inability to carry out traditional rituals can be painful. The support of the refugee community can be an important resource for family members (Fong, 2004; Miller & Rasco, 2004).

Weine (2011) describes the value of taking a resiliency approach as an organizing principle for prevention programs for refugee families. In the context of the trauma and uncertainty experienced by these families, this approach is particularly useful because it is built on a recognition of a family's strengths and seeks to strengthen their resources. As a result, it is especially likely to be acceptable to people. It also takes a multidimensional approach that goes beyond the family to the wider community and involves families as partners in this process. This collaboration helps create programs that are culturally appropriate and acceptable to the people involved. Such a program can help family members communicate with each other and with wider community organizations and help parents advocate for their children and family. It also helps parents to invest in their children.

A recent study with refugee Bosnian families currently living in Chicago identified both sources of distress and resiliency. These families had experienced a degree of trauma to the extent that at least one member met the criteria for post-traumatic stress disorder. Weine, Muzurovic, Kulauzovic, Besic, Lezic, and Mujagic (2004) identified issues related to family organization (roles and obligations), communication, social support involving the family and the broader ethnic community, and family belief systems that emerged as sources of pain and resiliency. Families reported negative changes regarding family roles and obligations in several areas: greater dependence on the children by the parents and grandparents, decreased time to spend with the family because of pressures to provide financially for the family, and challenges to traditional patriarchal customs. Men have lost their traditional control over the family as women and teenagers are working (Weine et al., 2004).

Families described the following strategies as promoting resiliency, although some are two-edged swords because they carry both the potential for healing as well as distress. In terms of beliefs and hope, children represent the hope for the future for the family. Seeing their children doing well is restorative for parents. At the same time, it is extremely difficult for parents to see their children having difficulties. Second, families have developed greater flexibility in terms of family roles. Third, family togetherness has become a primary goal of the families as they band together to survive. Fourth, when grandparents are part of the extended family scene, they assume more central roles to meet the family needs left by parents' extensive work demands. This change has kept grandparents from becoming isolated and permits sharing across generational lines (Weine et al., 2004).

Family communication and related memories bring pain as well as help rebuild the life of the family. Memories of the past bring pain to family members. Adults can avoid talking about the past because they are seeking to forget this painful time. The children are overwhelmed by the trauma of the past and also do not want these events to be talked about. Family members are also reluctant to talk about the past out of fear of burdening others. Families reported the following strategies for rebuilding their lives. They sought to share the good memories from the past. Talking with children helps parents look at the positive aspects of life. Unfortunately, some of the problems facing children, especially violence, remind them of past traumas. Despite the pain of communicating about the past, family members also find healing through expressing their emotions about the past and sharing with other family members to create a climate of trust (Weine et al., 2004).

Family relationships with their extended family have frequently experienced major disruptions and loss. Many families left important family members behind with a sense of loss and guilt involved, along with fear about what might be happening to them. Others have had to contend with the scattering of family members who once lived close to them. Some families have members with special physical or mental health needs that need extra care. Women who lost their husbands under traumatic conditions must now care for their families without this support. Families contend with these separations by hoping for a return someday to their old community and by working to reunite their family members. Single mothers seek to rebuild some type of family network. Family members also try to give financial help to their family members who were unable to leave (Weine et al., 2004).

Families also contend with changes in their connections with the extended ethnic community and the supporting culture. These tensions can be increased when families live in communities and have sponsoring families that do not appreciate their religious and ethnic traditions. This can create tensions. Many families feel that they were losing their way of life in a new world. Children who no longer use their original language and are adapted to American culture compound this fear. Families coped with these changes by teaching their children their history and language. They also sought to return to their religious traditions to promote continuity, to retain their culture, and to gain spiritual support. Retaining their culture was an important source of resiliency (Weine et al., 2004).

A review of research of refugee children with an emphasis on Southeast Asian families revealed sources of resiliency as well as risks within children (Barwick, Beiser, & Edwards, 2002; Kinzie & Sack, 2002). Patterns of assimilation influenced the resiliency process. A bicultural orientation (ethnic resilience) that permitted children and family members to retain their language and tradition while also learning the new language and cultural ways was associated with a better adjustment than families that insisted on only maintaining their traditional cultural ways or became totally assimilated (Barwick, Beiser, & Edwards, 2002). The support of parents, members of the extended family, as well as others within the ethnic community is an important source of resiliency. In the absence of members of the ethnic community, supportive friendships with other community members can help reduce loneliness and isolation during the adjustment period. Problems in reuniting families, however, can be a major source of distress for families. Hope for the future was an important protection that enabled refugee families living in poorer areas to report less stress than other residents of the neighborhood (Barwick, Beiser, & Edwards, 2002). A combination of stressful family and community issues, including family distress, hostility from the community, and academic problems in the school represents important risk factors (Barwick, Beiser, & Edwards, 2002).

War and children. Tragically, children throughout the world continue to be victims of the violence of war. A review of studies regarding children who experienced the trauma related to war reveals a range of mental health and health problems reported by the children. Risk factors were especially associated with being a victim or witness of violent acts, losing a loved one or threats to loved ones, experiencing prolonged absence of a parent, and forced displacement. The experience of being a child soldier, being raped, or being forcibly displaced contributed further to long-term emotional distress. Older children and those who had experienced the war recently were more likely to report post-traumatic symptoms. Protective factors that moderated the impact of these traumas experienced included a strong bond between the child and the primary caregiver, the social support of teachers and peers, and a shared sense of values. Helpful interventions included school-based interventions staffed by teachers or local trained paraprofessionals (Werner, 2012).

Assessment and Treatment

Research reveals a wide range of potentially difficult issues facing refugee families in adapting to life in their new world. In addition to adapting to a new culture, many families have experienced major traumas that cast shadows over family members. Supportive ties within the immediate and extended family and hopes for a better future help to sustain families. Interventions for families include community-level efforts to create sustaining connections and to educate concerned community groups about the specific needs and cultural issues pertaining to the group in question so that appropriate services and programs can be designed. Case management interventions to connect families with needed services within the community can be vital for some families. In working with refugee families, it is important to assess cultural prescriptions regarding family roles and the extent to which these have been disrupted by the move. Many refugee families come from cultural settings in which the authority of the parents is important and these cultural prescriptions need to be recognized in work with families. Solution-focused efforts can also be used to help families look at their strengths and ways in which the family members can jointly take steps to create a viable adaptation in this new world. Such interventions can tap the family's hopes for a better life in this new world. Support from spiritual leaders associated with the tradition of the refugee group can be a valuable resource (Gozdziak, 2002).

Natural Disaster Trauma

Natural disasters can also be sources of trauma and create major disruptions for families. Tornados, hurricanes, and floods destroy homes and communities and leave dazed survivors who must find a way to move on with their lives. As families look at scenes of total devastation in which they have lost their homes and all their possessions and sometimes family members and friends, the question is asked, how can people find the resources to pick up their lives and go on? Disasters are described as "'collective traumas' that test assumptions, plus the adaptive responses of individuals, families, and communities beyond their capacities, and lead, at least temporarily, to major disruptions of functioning" (Gordon, 2003, p. 4). As has been tragically evident in several of the recent natural disasters globally, such disasters frequently represent community-wide problems that leave large segments of the community struggling to restore normalcy to family life for a long period of time. Consequently, community resources are also severely reduced and communities are fractured. Families must address issues in the external world as well as their own feelings about this traumatic situation.

Studies have examined what contributes to resiliency in this context. An earlier study of families who were forced to abandon their homes in response to a major flood followed by evidence of serious toxicity levels revealed important themes. The role of social support was a complex one. Mid-levels of support were protective, but higher levels posed burdens of reciprocity that people were unable to meet. Interpretations of events mediated levels of distress. Self-blame increased distress and reduced the help-seeking by people who had suffered the effects of the disaster. Men evidenced more signs of distress than women, probably in response to the disruption of their roles as providers (Solomon & Smith, 1994).

Another study of a Kentucky community that experienced periodic flooding revealed problems in social functioning as well as earlier life experiences that supported resiliency. Risk factors included the experience of personal losses (people and possessions), an increased sense of danger, and reductions in the social fabric due to the high demands placed on many within the community. In line with research regarding protective factors, older adults who had experience in dealing with past floods were more able to cope than middle-aged adults (Norris, Phifer, & Kaniasty, 1994). The prior experience of coping with floods appears to be associated with the self-efficacy described earlier in the resiliency literature, possibly as a result of their longer-term experience in coping with such events and consequent sense of self-efficacy.

Families are embedded within the larger community. As is evident from the contrast between tornados that have torn apart towns in the United States and the continuing aftermath of the earthquake in Haiti, the nature of community resources varies dramatically. The nature of the community resources and prior efforts at coping are important in terms of being able to rebound from a disaster. Unfortunately, even in a country with as many resources as the United States, the situations related to Hurricane Katrina in the Gulf and Hurricane Sandy in the Northeast coast revealed how thousands of people can be left in a terrible gap created by an overwhelmed set of responses.

Landau and Saul (2004) describe the importance of nourishing and enlisting the natural support systems of the community in any efforts to deal with a natural disaster. Involvement of natural systems (for example, community leaders, residents, community groups) supports the strengths present within the community (thus enhancing self-efficacy within the community and its members) and also enlists a support system that will be ongoing in the community. Coming together to address practical concerns helps promote well-being and a sense of normalcy. Outsiders then become collaborators with the locals, not the experts in terms of what the community needs. Overcoming such a disaster can increase the sense of competence and connectedness in the community. These disasters have an impact on the family dynamics in terms of youth needing to grow up quickly and assume responsibilities and a sense of fear and loss within the family. Helping community members to regain daily patterns and rituals is valuable. Landau and Saul (2004) describe community resilience as associated with four themes:

1. Building community through strengthening the already existing support systems and coalitions
2. Validating the trauma experience and response through a community narrative
3. Reestablishing the normal rhythms of life
4. Engaging in collective healing rituals

The nature of the impact of the disaster on the parties involved can depend on the phase in the recovery process. These phases reflect the emotional state of the people involved. While written some time ago, this pattern is still relevant. (1) The honeymoon phase lasts from one to six weeks. During this time, the victims feel a sense of community through their common experience and loss. Buoyed by the hope of help, they begin the task of cleaning up. The response of community groups is very important during this time. (2) The disillusionment phase lasts from two months to two years. If promised help is not forthcoming, people begin to feel disappointed, angry, and resentful. The sense of community of the honeymoon stage diminishes as people focus on rebuilding the lives of their own families. Outside agencies stop providing help. (3) The reconstruction phase occurs in the several years after the disaster. Families recognize that they will need to assume primary responsibility for restoring their lives and either move forward or emotional problems may appear (Smith, 1983).

Perceptions of events are important, especially whether they are viewed as crisis-provoking or challenging. Protective family characteristics include problem-solving skills, family organizational patterns, and extended family resources. The ability to solve problematic life events in general translates into coping with such disasters. The family's ability to work together as a team to solve the problems facing them is valuable. Family leadership is also important, especially in being able to restore family life to normalcy as much as possible. Families need to be attuned to the emotional needs and responses of family members, including supporting the use of outside resources as needed to deal with the emotional trauma involved. Strong extended family ties are another important resource (Smith, 1983). Studies of children experiencing disasters also reveal the importance of supportive resources within the family in reducing distress (Saylor, Belter, & Stokes, 1997).

Assessment and Treatment

Events in the United States and globally reveal the ongoing distress that can be created by natural disasters. Interventions with families must be set within the context of social efforts to restore homes and communities. The initial response with families addresses the crisis needs of the family—helping families meet their basic survival needs through case management and community efforts. The recent storms demonstrated the importance as well as the difficulty of these steps and the need for preparedness as a community and on a broader social scale. Crisis models recognize the need to help persons identify their strengths. Even after these needs are met, the upheaval experienced by families can disrupt old patterns that enabled families to survive or reveal ongoing family patterns that pose difficulties. Strength-based efforts are critical for such families who have become demoralized by the major changes and losses that they have experienced. Family efforts need to be paired with community-level interventions that involve community leaders. Multisystems approaches that address the family's struggles with adapting to change, link the family to potential resources, and work cooperatively to address the resource base within the community can fit with these needs. Case management can be essential in negotiating complex systems. Solution-focused treatment can help families identify realistic goals in their current situation, steps that family members can take to help meet them, and ways in which the family is currently managing to survive despite this realistically difficult time.

Childhood Issues

Delinquency and Conduct Disorders of Youth

Many families are referred to social workers because of behavior problems of their children. Williams, Ayers, Van Dorn, and Arthur (2004) reviewed research regarding risk and protective factors in terms of this critical issue. Community-level risk factors included community violence, poverty, limited access to services, high mobility within neighborhoods, and community disorganization. Family risk factors included family management problems, family conflict, family disruption, and parental modeling of inappropriate and illicit behaviors. In terms of parenting, the strongest predictors of problems were poor parental supervision and lack of parental involvement in the lives of their children. School risk factors, especially for males and white youth, were low academic achievement, lack of commitment to school, and discipline problems. Peer relationships that supported delinquent behavior were additional risk factors.

Four major types of family protective factors emerged from longitudinal studies that echo earlier themes: "(1) supportive parent-child relationships and family environment, (2) positive discipline techniques, (3) monitoring and supervision, and (4) family advocacy (seeking information and support for the benefit of their children)" (Williams, Ayers, Van Dorn, & Arthur, 2004, p. 224). In the absence of supportive relationships with parents, peer support can have negative consequences by making youth more vulnerable to high-risk behaviors, including substance abuse. In terms of African American families in this context, important protective factors include "a strong economic base, a strong orientation to achievement, strong spiritual values, racial pride, extended family bonds, community involvement, and commitment to family" (Williams, Ayers, Van Dorn, & Arthur, 2004, p. 224). The combination of risk and protective factors supports efforts to strengthen family coping efforts and the community as well as interventions targeted to youth alone.

Maltreatment of Children

Many families are referred for social work services, frequently on an involuntary basis, because children in the family have been mistreated. Maltreatment leads to children dying each day in the United States. Maltreatment in the form of neglect and physical or sexual abuse can have profound negative implications for the children in terms of problematic behavior as children and adults, poor academic achievement, and health problems (Anda, Felitti, Bremner, Walker, Whitfield, Perry, Dube, & Giles, 2006; Thomlison, 2004). Chronic maltreatment is especially problematic for children and is associated with more aggressive behavior, behavioral problems in general, and social withdrawal than children who had been mistreated for only a short time (Ethier, Lemelin, & Lacharite, 2004).

While maltreatment can occur at all economic levels, a key risk factor for maltreatment is the contextual issue of poverty and the related social conditions. As Thomlison (2004) describes it, "the poorest of the poor are at highest risk" (p. 93). Differences in child maltreatment rates in various racial/ethnic groups are closely linked with poverty and community violence. In terms of the impact of additive sources of stress, longitudinal studies indicate that "the number of risk factors to which a child is exposed is the most salient predictor of maltreatment and the negative development outcomes" (Thomlison, 2004, p. 98). The combination of risk factors has a greater effect than the sum of effects of each risk factor (Anda et al., 2006; Fatusso, McDermott, & Lutz, 1999).

In terms of family issues, distress of the parent-caregiver is the primary individual risk factor. Parental problems emerged in terms of "parental affective disturbances, such as depression, withdrawal, anger, and aggression, low self-esteem, immaturity, rigid or unrealistic expectations, and undue reliance so that the parent's needs conflict with the child's needs" (Thomlison, 2004, p. 98). In terms of relevant skills, lack of knowledge regarding parenting and the associated skills contribute to poor parenting through inappropriate expectations, poor problem-solving skills, and harsh or inconsistent parenting. Current or past substance abuse by parents is an important risk factor. Parental problems in turn are exacerbated by behavioral characteristics of children (impulsiveness, disruptive temperament) and environmental stresses. A key issue for physical abuse is the parent's own history of maltreatment. A weak social support system for parents substantially increases the risk of neglect (Thomlison, 2004).

Protective factors that protect families from maltreating their children reveal the importance of contextual factors. Such factors include "economic stability and access to health, education, and employment" (Thomlison, 2004, p. 100). External social supports both help protect parents from maltreating their children and serve as sources of resiliency for the children themselves. In contrast to fragmented communities, those that are stable and cohesive offer needed support for families through employment, schools, and community members who are appropriate role models; these all help reduce child maltreatment (Thomlison, 2004).

Life circumstances that protect by reducing distress or inhibiting aggression include the presence "of a supportive spouse, socioeconomic stability, success at work and school, social supports, and positive adult role models" (Thomlison, 2004, p. 100). Parents are also enabled to manage crises more effectively (ability to cope with stress) and to reduce their arousal and aggressive behavior with family members (improved ability to regulate moods and reduce anger) (Thomlison, 2004).

Individual parental factors that protect include high self-esteem and self-efficacy and the ability to operate within normal boundaries and to demonstrate social competence. Easygoing temperaments that help parents show warmth and satisfaction in relationships with others also contribute (Thomlison, 2004).

Assessment and Treatment

As a result of these risk and resiliency patterns, a combination of approaches offers the most promise for families. These include those that help parents gain effective parental skills, enable parents to cope more effectively with stress and anger, and strengthen the support system for families through collaborative relationships with parents, teachers, and others in the community (Thomlison, 2004).

Addressing childhood behavior problems and child maltreatment are frequently linked because children from families who are at greatest risk for maltreatment are also the most likely to demonstrate behavioral problems. A dual approach that addresses the environment as well as the ability of family members to parent more effectively and relate to each other in a less toxic manner is appropriate for many of these families. The multisystems model of family interventions incorporates this dual perspective by helping families develop more effective ways of relating to their members and by improving the social context. As discussed in chapter 10, many specific programs incorporate multisystems models. Recognizing that these families are also demoralized by their many problems, these models take an explicit strengths-based approach.

As discussed further in chapter 8, Berg and Kelly (2000) also describe the value of taking a strength-based solution-focused approach that helps validate the strengths of families and helps parents select and address small steps toward caring for their families

SUMMARY

Families seek help as a result of a variety of life circumstances that create distress for family members. While some of the specific risk and protective factors vary depending on these situations, some key resiliency factors identified in the general research on resiliency continue to emerge as themes. Experiencing caring and validation from a social and spiritual support network is an important resource that appears to decrease distress and increase self-esteem. Such support networks often provide valuable role models. A community context that provides a sense of coherence, access to services, and appropriate economic and other opportunities also supports resiliency.

Appropriate skills to cope with the situation at hand are also important, for example, parenting effectively, caring for ill family members, advocating for services, and dealing with new cultural expectations. Families need appropriate information to guide their coping efforts. Families need to be able to communicate effectively to deal with stressors without resorting to undue conflict and to meet the emotional needs of family members. These resiliency factors are aided by self-perceptions of self-efficacy and views of situations as challenging but not impossible. The process is a cyclical one as demonstrating appropriate skills and effectively solving problems in turn enhances the self-efficacy of family members.

The resiliency framework thus serves as a valuable framework for assessing families and developing and implementing strategies for helping families. It provides a respectful, collaborative model that supports strengths-based and culturally competent social work practice with families.

DISCUSSION QUESTIONS

Discuss what it means to say that addiction is a family illness.

What are some of the resources that help family members cope with illness in the family, and how do these help families cope?

How does understanding the nature of an illness help family members deal with it?

What are some of the belief systems that attachment-based therapies hope to address and what role do they play?

Discuss why it is important to take a community empowerment approach in working with communities and families that have been traumatized.

Discuss how future family relationships can promote healing for individuals who have been sexually abused.

Discuss the role of self-efficacy in helping family members cope with the problems described in this chapter as well as others that they might face.

15

Conclusion

In helping families who are struggling with a myriad of problems, the resiliency framework with the accompanying major themes of risk and resiliency represents a useful way to organize the assessment and design of interventions with families. It provides a framework for analyzing the information about families that highlights the resources both within the family and its context as well as the challenges the family faces. The resiliency perspective can also help guide the counselor in creating a therapeutic relationship that highlights the strengths of families. Such an approach fits well with the social work value stance of respect for persons. The framework of resiliency enables the social worker, family therapist, and family counselor to take a strengths-based approach while at the same time being realistic about the challenges facing the family and its current needs. This dual focus is critical in gaining an accurate understanding of the family and in identifying possible ways to strengthen the resources available to the family and the barriers that families face in meeting the needs of their members.

A resiliency perspective helps the family counselor look beyond the family to incorporate the social, economic, and physical contexts of the family that can be sources of resources as well as challenges. These contexts further influence how events, potential resources, and challenges are viewed by family members and key members of their support system. Such a perspective is thus compatible with a culturally competent way of working with families.

While studies can identify the characteristics that generally challenge and support resiliency, each individual family has its unique set that interact throughout the life span of the family and are embedded within a particular contextual and historical environment. The assessment process must thus move beyond any generalizations to understand the specific set of risk and protective factors at work with this family. It is also important to individualize what these mean in the life of an individual family and its members. Such information paired with research regarding the effectiveness of treatment approaches thus becomes the basis for professional judgment regarding the design of the intervention. Studies regarding resiliency in general can represent a valuable first step but must always be viewed through the lens of specific families and their members. Social constructionist perspectives remind us that the meaning of life events and thus of potential solutions is mediated by life experiences and appraisals of individuals and their families. The hovering behavior by parents that in one context might be viewed as unrealistic overprotection, in another more dangerous setting might be viewed as essential protection.

The outcomes of the family's attempts to deal with the challenges facing them have important current and future implications for the family. Families are strengthened by their successful attempts to deal with adversity but can become demoralized by their inability to do so. Unfortunately, many of the families who seek help from social workers have reached the point that they have become discouraged by their inability to address a problem or have been given the message by others that they have not been able to do so appropriately. As a result, they can become demoralized about their ability to cope as a family. The process becomes a cyclical one as some of their cognitive or behavioral responses further impede their ability to cope effectively and thus increase their sense of demoralization. In response, they can fall into patterns of blaming specific family members or others in the environment or become discouraged by past efforts. They can find it even more difficult to develop realistic coping strategies. The problems facing them can come to be viewed as insurmountable. They can come to expect blame and criticism from counselors and in turn become defensive or guarded.

In this context, the use of a resiliency perspective can be helpful in several ways. During the establishment of the working alliance and the assessment process, the search for strengths within the family (e.g., evidence of success in coping with the past or in other areas of life, concern for family members) and the community can help engender hope and begin to reduce some of these problematic responses. Throughout the counseling process and more specifically toward termination, the social worker can help the family take ownership of their enhanced ability to cope as well as to identify what steps the family has taken that have helped make this difference so they can draw upon these when they face some inevitable future challenges. The goal is to enable families to increase their ability to face the challenges as well as their self-efficacy in being able to do so.

The use of the resiliency framework does not limit the family counselor to the use of a single theoretical model. Rather, it suggests the value of being able to consider a variety of intervention models and strategies based on the assessment of the needs of the family as well as the protective factors that can be capitalized on and strengthened. These resources can be present within the family (beliefs, coping skills, relationships among the members, characteristics of individual family members), the links between the family and other social contexts (extended family, friends, community), and the nature of the community (employment patterns, access to health care, educational systems). On the other side of the equation are the risks created by the combination of the characteristics of family members, the family as a unit, the context, and the developmental stages of the family. Based on the assessment of the situation facing the family and the unique combination of risks and protective factors, the social worker can identify treatment models and accompanying strategies that can draw upon and strengthen these protective factors and seek to make the changes that can reduce the risk factors. For one family the emphasis might be on the need to expand specific community resources, while another family might need to learn new coping skills in dealing with a new cultural setting, or to enhance the leadership of the family, or to replace problem-saturated stories with more empowering ones. The key here is emphasis. An essential part of the assessment process is to identify what factors are the most pressing or amenable to change, and what combination of specific strategies seems most appropriate at this time in the life of the family. The way in which the therapy model is implemented, of course, will depend on the family, the counselor, and the unique settings.

Efforts have been made to identify the aspects of family counseling that enhance effectiveness. These efforts reflect the complex nature of counseling with families with all of the difficulties in identifying what works with what family. Friedlander reviewed a large number of studies to identify the themes related to effectiveness in terms of the actions of the therapist with families. These included studies examining the process of family therapy from a variety of theoretical perspectives. Successful approaches incorporated both intrapersonal and interpersonal aspects. The collaborative nature of the therapist relationship characterized by a resiliency approach emerged as essential. While the specific techniques used by the counselor may vary, effective therapy "needs to be conducted in a warm, non-threatening atmosphere in which there is a sense of mutual respect and collaboration" (Friedlander, 1998, p. 526). Effective family therapists also tended to be active and to take charge of the sessions in ways that involved the emotional, cognitive, and behavioral realms of experience (Friedlander, 1998). Interventions that are positive and non-blaming, that highlight the positive aspects of the family (asking about exceptions, selectively attending to positive statements), and include positive reframing can reduce conflict and negativity within families (Sexton, Robbins, Hollimon, Mease, & Mayorga, 2003). These findings support the themes inherent in a resiliency perspective on social work practice with families.

The resiliency-based approach to working with families recognizes the complex nature of families and the world in which they attempt to meet the needs of their members. It sets the stage for a collaborative working relationship between the family and the social worker. Recognition of the family's struggles as well as their strengths and protective factors helps identify which specific approach can be most effective for this specific family at this time in its life cycle. Together the family members and the social worker continue to evaluate whether the approach selected is the best choice for the family at this stage in their development.

Appendix
Family Preservation Models

The Homebuilders (see Kinney, Haapala, & Booth, 1991). A home-based program in which the entire family receives family-based intervention. It is intensive and brief (about six weeks). Specific treatment goals and activities vary depending on the family. It focuses on parenting skills and anger management.

Parent-Child Education Program for Physically Abusive Parents (see Wolfe, Sandler, & Kaufman, 1981). Includes intensive (two hours a week) home-based parent education on a weekly basis for eight weeks. With the goal of reducing power-assertive discipline methods and child abuse, parents receive skill training that includes modeling in positive parenting strategies.

The Incredible Years Training Service (see Webster-Stratton, 2000; Juvenile Justice Bulletin. Washington, DC: Office of Juvenile Justice and Delinquency Prevention). Program helps parents replace negative parenting techniques with positive, nonviolent discipline methods, and supports parent approaches that promote children's self-confidence, pro-social behavior, and academic success. The program is custom-tailored to parents of children of different ages and is designed to help parents learn positive parenting strategies appropriate for that age.

Multisystemic Family Treatment (MST) (see Henggeler, Schoenwald, Borduin, Rowland, & Cunningham, 1998; Sheidow, Henggeler, & Schoenwald, 2003). Incorporates many of the components described earlier. It provides in-home services that include parent education, information about parent-child expectations, marital therapy, advocacy, coaching, and emotional support. This model has been effectively used in a variety of community settings to address serious child behavior problems. Interventions include reframing, joining, and actions to assist in family restructuring. MST provides for a flexible protocol within the parameters of nine basic treatment principles as described below.

Principle 1. The primary purpose of assessment is to understand the fit between the identified problems and their broader context.

Principle 2. Therapeutic contacts emphasize the positive and use systemic strengths as levers for change.

Principle 3. Interventions are designed to promote responsible behavior and decrease irresponsible behavior among family members.

Principle 4. Interventions are present-focused and action-oriented, targeting specific and well-defined problems.

Principle 5. Interventions target sequences of behavior within and among multiple systems that maintain the identified problems.

Principle 6. Interventions are developmentally appropriate and fit the developmental needs of the youth.

Principle 7. Interventions are designed to require daily or weekly effort by family members.

Principle 8. Intervention effectiveness is evaluated continuously from multiple perspectives, with providers assuming accountability for overcoming barriers to successful outcomes.

Principle 9. Interventions are designed to promote treatment generalization and long-term maintenance of therapeutic change by empowering caregivers to address family members' needs across multiple systemic contexts. (Henggeler et al., 1998, p. 23)

Project 12 Ways (see Lutzker, Bigelow, Doctor, & Kessler, 1998). Focuses on enhancing environments and social support for families in three areas: child health, home safety, and parent-child interactions. Activities include parent education and planned parenting activities. Paraprofessionals or volunteers are used to provide the following as needed: marital counseling, financial planning, and home health. Referrals are made to appropriate community services.

Social Support Network Interventions (see Gaudin, Wodarski, Arkinson, & Avery, 1990–1991). Designed to strengthen the informal support network of families in order to reduce family isolation. It includes social skills training from volunteers or neighbor-to-neighbor connection.

References

Aaredondo, P. (2006). Multicultural competencies and family therapy strategies with Latino families. In R. Smith & R. Montilla (Eds.), *Counseling and family therapy with Latino populations: Strategies that work* (pp. 77–96). New York: Routledge.

Abudabbeh, N. (1996). Arab families. In M. McGoldrick, J. Giordano, & J. Pearce (Eds.), *Ethnicity and family therapy* (2nd ed., pp. 333–346). New York: Guilford.

Adams, B. (2012). American Indian children: Too often in fostercare. *The Salt Lake Tribune*, March 24, 2012.

Aguilar, M. (2002). Catholicism. In M. Van Hook, B. Hugen, & M. Aguilar (Eds.), *Spirituality within religious traditions in social work* (pp. 120–145). Belmont, CA: Brooks/Cole.

Albom, M. (1997). *Tuesdays with Morrie.* New York: Doubleday.

Almeida, R. (1996). Hindu, Christian, and Muslim families. In M. McGoldrick, J. Giordano, & J. Pearce (Eds.), *Ethnicity and family therapy* (2nd ed., pp. 395–426). New York: Guilford.

American Psychological Association Task Force on Violence and the Family. (1996). *Violence and the family.* Washington, DC: American Psychological Association.

Anda, R., Felitti, V., Bremner, J., Walker, J., Whitfield, C., Perry, B., Dube, S., & Giles, W. (2006). *European Archives of Psychiatry and Clinical Neuroscience, 256,* 174–186.

Anderson, B. J., Brackett, J., Ho, J., & Laffel, L. M. (1999). An office-based intervention to maintain parent adolescent teamwork in diabetes management. *Diabetes Care, 22,* 713–721.

Anderson, T. (1991). The context and history of the reflecting team. In T. Anderson (Ed.), *The reflecting team: Dialogues and dialogues about the dialogues* (pp. 1–14). New York: Norton.

Antonovsky, A. (1998). The structure and properties of the Sense of Coherence Scale. In H. I. McCubbin, E. Thompson, A. Thompson, & J. Fromer (Eds.), *Stress, coping, and health in families: Sense of coherence and resiliency* (pp. 21–40). Resiliency in Families series. Thousand Oaks, CA: Sage.

Aponte, H. (1994). *Bread and spirit: Therapy with the new poor.* New York: Norton.

Aponte, H. (2002). Spirituality: The heart of therapy. In T. Carlson & M. Erikson (Eds.), *Spirituality and family therapy* (pp. 13–27). New York: Haworth.

Aponte, H. (2003). Structural family interventions. In A. Kilpatrick & T. Holland (Eds.), *Working with families: An integrative model by level of needs* (pp. 104–115). Boston: Allyn & Bacon.

Ariel, J., & McPherson, D. (2000). Therapy with lesbian gay parents and their children. *Journal of Marital and Family Therapy, 26*(4), 421–432.

Arteaga, E., Chen, C., & Reynolds, A. (2010). Childhood predictors of adult substance abuse. *Children and Youth Services Review, 32*(8), 1108–1120.

Atkin, K., & Ahmad, W. (2008). Family care-giving and chronic illness: How parents cope with a child with a sickle cell disorder or thalassaemia. *Health and Social Care in the Community, 8*(1), 57–69.

Atwood, J., & Genovese, F. (2006) *Therapy with single parents: A social constructionist approach.* New York: Haworth Press.

Au, A., Lai, M., Lau, K., Pan, P., Lam, L., Thompson, L., Gallagher-Thompson, D. (2009). Social support and well-being in dementia family caregivers: The mediating role of self-efficacy. *Aging and Mental Health, 13*(5), 761–768.

Avert. (2012). www.avert.org/canada.aids.htn.

Baez, T. (2000). The effects of stress on emotional well-being and resiliency through mediating mechanism of active coping skills and family hardiness. *Dissertation Abstracts International Section A: Humanities and Social Sciences, 60*(7-A) Jan p., 2382. D

Bagley, C., & Carroll, J. (1998). Healing forces in African American families. In H. I. McCubbin, E. Thompson, A. Thompson, & J. Futrell (Eds.), *Resiliency in African American families* (pp. 117–142). Thousand Oaks, CA: Sage.

Bal, S., Van Oost, P., De Bourdeaudhuij, L., & Crombez, G. (2003). Avoidance as a mediator between self-reported sexual abuse and stress-related symptoms in adolescents. *Child Abuse and Neglect, 27,* 883–897.

Bandura, A. (1977). *Social learning theory.* Englewood Cliffs, NJ: Prentice-Hall.

Bandura, A. (1978). The self-system in reciprocal determinism. *American Psychologist, 33,* 344–358.

Banerjee, M., & Canda, E. (2009). Spirituality as a strength of African American women affected by welfare reform. *Journal of Religion and Spirituality in Social Work and Social Thought, 28*(3), 239–262.

Banyard, V., & Williams, L. (2007). Women's voices on recovery: A multi-method study of the complexity of recovery from child sexual abuse. *Child Abuse and Neglect, 31*(3), 275–290.

Barker, E., Hartley, S., Seltzer, M., Floyd, E., Greenberg, J., & Orsmune, F. (2008). Trajectories of emotional well-being in mothers of adolescents and adults with autism. *Developmental Psychology, 47*(2), 551–561.

Barwick, C., Beiser, M., & Edwards, G. (2002). Refugee children and their families: Exploring mental health risks and protective factors. In F. Azima & N. Grizenko (Eds.), *Immigrant and refugee children and their families: Clinical, research, and training issues* (pp. 37–63). Madison, CT: International Universities Press.

Bateson, G., Jackson, D., Haley, J., & Weakland, J. (1956). Toward a theory of schizophrenia. *Behavioral Sciences, 1,* 251–264.

Beardslee, W. (1989). The role of self-understanding in resilient individuals: The development of a perspective. *American Journal of Orthopsychiatry, 59*(2), 266–278.

Beardslee, W., Salt, P., Porterfield, K., Rothberg, P., Van de Velde, P., & Swatling, S. (1993). Comparison of preventive interventions for families with parental affective disorder. *Journal of American Academy of Child and Adolescent Psychiatry, 32*(2), 254–263.

Beavers, W. (1986). *Successful marriages.* New York: Norton.

Beavers, W., & Hampson, R. (1990). *Successful families: Assessment and interventions.* New York: Norton.

Beck, A. (1976). *Cognitive therapy and the emotional disorders.* New York: International Universities Press.

Bell-Tolliver, L., & Wilkerson, P. (2011) The use of spirituality and kinship as contributors to successful therapy outcomes with African American families. *Journal of Religion and Spirituality in Social Work: Social thought, 30*(1), 48–70.

Benzies, K., & Mychasiuk, R. (2009). Fostering family resiliency: A review of the key protective factors. *Child and Family Social Work 14,* 103–114.

Berg, I. K., & DeJong, P. (2005) Engagement through complimenting. *Journal of Family Psychotherapy, 16*(1–2), 51–56.

Berg, I., & Dolan, Y. (2001). *Tales of solutions: A collection of hope-inspiring stories.* New York: Norton.

Berg, I., & Kelly, S. (2000). *Building solutions in child protective services.* New York: W.W. Norton.

Berg, I., & Miller, S. (1992). *Working with the problem drinker: A solution-focused approach.* New York: Norton.

Bernal, G., & Shapiro, E. (1996). Cuban families. In M. McGoldrick, J. Giordano, & J. Pearce (Eds.), *Ethnicity and family therapy* (pp. 155–168). New York: Guilford.

Bernandon, S., & Pernice-Duca, F. (2010). A family systems perspective to recovery from posttraumatic stress in children. *The Family Journal, 18*(4), 349–359.

Berry, M. (1999). Family preservation practice. In C. Franklin & C. Jordan (Eds.), *Family practice: Brief systems methods for social work* (pp. 199–224). New York: Guilford Press.

Besa, D. (1994). Evaluating narrative family therapy using single-system research designs. *Research on Social Work Practice, 43*(3), 309–325.

Besley, A. (2002). Foucault and the turn to narrative therapy. *British Journal of Guidance and Counseling, 30*(2), 125–143.

Biever, J., Gardner, G., & Bobele, M. (1999). Social construction and narrative family practice. In C. Franklin & C. Jordan (Eds.), *Family practice: Brief systems methods for social work* (pp. 143–174). Pacific Grove, CA: Brooks/Cole.

Bigner, J. (1996). Working with gay fathers: Developmental, post-divorce parenting, and therapeutic issues. In J. Laird & R. Green (Eds.), *Lesbians and gays in couples and families* (pp. 370–403). San Francisco: Jossey-Bass.

Bion, W. (1970). *Attention and interpretation.* London: Heinemann.

Black Demographics. (2011). 2011 Black State Populations. www.blackdemographic. com/population.html#anchor_400.

Blundo, R. (2002). Mental health: A shift in perspective. In R. Greene (Ed.), *Resiliency: An integrated approach to practice, policy, and research* (pp. 133–152). Washington, DC: NASW Press.

Bos, H., Van Balen, F., & Van den Boom, D. (2005). Lesbian families and family functioning: An overview. *Patient Education and Counseling, 59*(3), 263–275.

Bos, H., van Balen, F., van den Boom, D., & Sandfort, T. (2004). Minority stress, experience of parenthood and child adjustment in lesbian families. *Journal of Reproductive and Infant Psychology, 22*(4), 291–304.

Boss, P. (2006). *Loss, trauma, and resilience.* New York: Norton.

Boszormenyi-Nagy, I., & Spark, G. (1973) *Invisible loyalties: Reciprocity in intergenerational family therapy.* New York: Harper and Row.

Bowen, D. (1995). Honoring the elders: Interviews with two Lakota men. *Journal of Sociology and Social Welfare, 32*(1), 125–134.

Bowen, G., & Orthner, D. (1993). Family adaptation of single parents in the United States Army: An empirical analysis of work stressor and adaptive resources. *Family Relations, 42*(3), 293–304.

Bowen, M. (1976). Theory in the practice of psychotherapy. In P. Guerin (Ed.), *Family therapy: Theory and practice* (pp. 42–90). New York: Basic Books.

Bowen, M. (1978). *Family therapy in clinical practice.* New York: Jason Aronson.

Bowen Center for the Study of the Family, 2012. www.thebowencenter.org/pages/concepts.html.

Bowlby, J. (1969). *Attachment.* New York: Basic Books.

Bowlby, J. (1973). *Separation: Anxiety and anger.* New York: Basic Books.

Boyd-Franklin, N. (2003). *Black families in therapy* (2nd ed.). New York: Guilford.

Boyd-Franklin, N., & Bry, H. (2000). *Reaching out in family therapy: Home-based, school, and community interventions.* New York: Guilford.

Boyd-Franklin, N., & Lockwood, T. (1999). Spirituality and religion: Implications for psychotherapy with African American clients and families. In F. Walsh (Ed.), *Spiritual resources in family therapy* (pp. 90–104). New York: Guilford.

Bradley, C. (2011). Women in AA: "Sharing experience, strength and hope": The relational nature of spirituality. *Journal of Religion and Spirituality in Social Work: Social Thought, 30*(2), 89–112.

Brashears, F., & Roberts, M. (2001). The black church as a resource for change. In S. Logan (Ed.), *The black family: Strengths, self-help and positive change* (2nd ed., pp. 181–192). Boulder, CO: Westview Press.

Brennan, J. (1995). A short-term psychoeducational multi-group for bipolar patients and their families. *Social Work, 40*(6), 737–743.

Brice-Baker, J. (1996). Jamaican families. In M. McGoldrick, J. Giordano, & J. Pearce (Eds.), *Ethnicity and family therapy* (2nd ed., pp. 85–96). New York: Guilford Press.

Brock, G., & Barnard, C. (1999) *Procedures in marriage and family therapy* (3rd ed.). Boston: Allyn & Bacon.

Brody, G., Dorsey, S., Forehand, R., & Armistead, L. (2002). Unique and protective contributions of parenting and classroom processes to the adjustment of African American children living in single-parent families. *Child Development, 73*(1), 274–286.

Brody, G., & Flor, D. (1998). Maternal resources, parenting practices, and child competencies in rural single-parent African American families. *Child Development, 69*(3), 803–816.

Brody, G., Flor, D., & Gibson, N. (1999) Linking maternal efficacy beliefs, developmental goals, parenting practice and child competencies in rural single-parent African American families. *Child Development, 70*(5), 1197–1208.

Brody, G., Kim, S., Murry, V., & Brown, A. (2004). Protective longitudinal paths: Linking child competence to behavioral problems among African American siblings. *Child Development, 75*(2), 455–467.

Brody, G., Murry, V., Kim, S., & Brown, A. (2002). Longitudinal pathways to competence and psychological adjustment among African-American children living in rural single-parent households. *Child Development, 73*(5), 1505–1516.

Brody, G., Stoneman, Z., Flor, D., & McCrory, C. (1994). Religions role in organizing family relationships: Family process in rural two-parent African American families. *Journal of Marriage and Family, 56*(4), 878–888.

Bronfenbrenner, U. (1979). *The ecology of human development.* Cambridge, MA: Harvard University Press.

Brook, J., & McDonald, R. (2009). The impact of parental substance abuse in the stability of family reunifications from foster care. *Children and Youth Services Review, 31*(2), 193–196.

Brotherson, S., & Sonderquist, J. (2002). Coping with a child's death: Spiritual issues and therapeutic implications. In T. Carlson & M. Erikson (Eds.), *Spirituality and family therapy* (pp. 53–86). New York: Haworth.

Brown, C. (2008). African American resiliency: Examining racial socialization and social supports as protective factors. *Journal of Black Psychology, 34*(1), 32–48.

Bryant-Davis, T. (2005). Coping strategies of African American adult survivors of childhood violence. *Professional Psychology: Research and Practice, 36*(4), 409–414.

Bryant-Davis, T., Ellis, M., Burke-Maynard, E., Moon, N., Counts, P., & Anderson, G. (2012). Religiosity, spirituality, and trauma recovery in the lives of children and adolescents. *Professional Psychology: Research and Practice, 43*(4), 306–314.

Burt, L., & Paysnick, A. (2012). Resilience in transition to adulthood. *Development and Psychopathology, 24*(2), 493–505.

Bushy, A. (2002). *National Rural Health Association Rural Minority Health Resource Book.* Kansas City: National Rural Health Association.

Butler, W., & Powers, K. (1996). Solution-focused grief therapy. In S. Miller, M. Hubble, & B. Duncan (Eds.), *Handbook of solution-focused brief therapy* (pp. 228–247). San Francisco: Jossey.

Campbell, C., & Demi, A. (2000). Adult children of fathers missing in action (MIA): An examination of emotional distress, grief, and family hardiness. *Family Relations, 49*(3), 267–276.

Canada AIDS Statistics by Year and Age, 2012. www.actoronto.org/home.nsf/pages/hivaidsstatscan.

Canda, E. (1988, Winter) Conceptualizing spirituality for social work: Insights from diverse perspectives. *Social Thought,* 30–46.

Canda, E. (2002). Buddhism. In M. Van Hook, B. Hugen, & M. Aguilar (Eds.), *Spirituality within religious traditions in social work.* Belmont, CA: Brooks/Cole.

Canda, E., & Furman, L. (1999). *Spiritual diversity in social work practice: The heart of healing.* New York: Free Press.

Canda, E., & Furman, L. (2009). *Spirituality in social work practice: The heart of healing* (2nd ed.). New York: Oxford University Press.

Capers, M. (2003). From subsistence to sustainability: Treating drug abuse in Alaska. *Substance Abuse and Mental Health Services News, 11*(4), 1, 8–10.

Carlson, T., & Erikson, M. (Eds.). (2002). *Spirituality and family therapy.* New York: Haworth.

Cash, S., & Berry, M. (2003). The impact of family preservation services on child and family well-being. *Journal of Social Service Research, 29*(3), 1–26.

Caspi, A., Elder, G., Jr., & Berm, D. (1987). Moving against the world: Life course patterns of explosive children. *Developmental Psychology, 23*, 308–313.

Ceballo, R. (2004) From barrios to Yale: The role of parenting strategies in Latino families. *Hispanic Journal of Behavior Sciences, 26*(2), 171–186.

Centers for Disease Control and Prevention. (2005a). *HIV/AIDS among women.* http://www.cdc.gov/hiv/pubs/facts/women.htm.

Centers for Disease Control and Prevention. (2005b). *HIV/AIDS among African Americans.* http://www.cdc.gov/hiv/pubs/Facts/afam.htm.

Centers for Disease Control and Prevention. (2009). *Women Involved in Life Learning from Other Women.* http://www.cdc.gov/hiv/topics/research/prs/resources/fact sheets/W iLLOW.htm.

Centers for Disease Control and Prevention. (2011). *HIV Among African Americans.* www.cdc.gov/hiv.topics/aa/index.htm.

Centers for Disease Control and Prevention. (2012a). *The HIV/AIDS Epidemic in the Latino community.* www.cdc.gov/hiv/resources/reports/slep/epidemic.

Centers for Disease Control and Prevention. (2012b). *Monthly Vital Statistics Report.* http://www/cdc/gov/nchs/products/mvsr/mvsr4392.htm.

Centers for Disease Control and Prevention. (2012c). *Sister to Sister: An HIV Reduction Intervention: "Respect yourself, protect yourself, because you are worth it!"* http://www.cdc.gov/hiv/topics/prev_prog/rep/packages/sisters.htm.

Chandra, A., Sandraluz, L., Jaycox, L., Tanielian, T., Burns, R., Ruder, T., & Han, B. (2010). Children on the home front: The experience of children from military families. *Pediatrics, 125*(1), 16–25.

Chavez, N., & Gonzalez, J. (2000). *Mexican immigrant youth and resiliency: Research and promoting programs.* ERIC U.S. Department of Government Educational Research Center.

Chazin, R., Kaplan, S., & Terio, S. (2000). Introducing a strengths/resiliency model in mental health organizations. In E. Norman (Ed.), *Resiliency enhancement: Putting the strengths perspective into social work practice* (pp. 192–210). New York: Columbia University Press.

Chen, J., & George, R. (2005) Cultivating resiliency in children from divorced families. *The Family Journal: Counseling and Therapy for Couples and Families, 220*(10).

Chesla, C. (1999). Becoming resilient: Skill development in couples living with non-insulin dependent diabetes. In H. I. McCubbin, E. Thompson, A. Thompson, & J. Futrell (Eds.), *The dynamics of resilient families* (pp. 99–133). Resiliency in Families series. Thousand Oaks, CA: Sage.

Chisholm, V., Atkinson, L., Donaldson, C., Noyes, K., Payne, A., & Keinar, C. (2011). Maternal communication style, problem-solving and dietary adherence in young children with type 1 diabetes. *Clinical Child Psychology and Psychiatry, 16*(3), 443–458.

Choi, Y. (2011). Risk factors for problem behaviors and conduct disorders among Asian American children and youth. In F. Leon, L. Juan, D. Qin, & H. Fitzgerald (Eds.), *Asian American and Pacific Islander Children and Mental Health.* Vol. 2, *Prevention and Treatment* (pp. 29–52). Santa Barbara, CA: Praeger.

Clay, K., Talley, C., & Young, K. (2010). Exploring spiritual well-being among survivors of colorectal and lung cancer. *Journal of Religion and Spirituality in Social Work and Social Thought, 29*(1), 14–32.

Clay, O., Roth, D., Wadley, V., & Haley, W. (2008) Changes in social support and their impact on psychosocial outcomes over a 5-year period for African American and white dementia caregivers. *International Journal of Geriatric Psychiatry, 23,* 857–862.

Coles, R. (1964). *Children of crisis: A study of courage and fear.* New York: Dell.

Conger, R., & Elder, G. (1994). *Families in troubled times: Adapting to change in rural America.* New York: Aldine de Gruyter.

Conger, R., Wallace, L., Sun, Y., Simons, R., McLoyd, V., & Brody, G. (2002). Economic pressure in African American families: A replication and extension of the model. *Developmental Psychology, 38*(2), 179–193.

Conner, M. (1998). Level of satisfaction in African-American marriages: A preliminary investigation. In H. I. McCubbin, E. Thompson, A. Thompson, & J. Futrell (Eds.), *Resiliency in African-American families* (pp. 159–178). Thousand Oaks, CA: Sage.

Conway, M., Mendelson, M., Giannopoulos, C., Csank, P., & Holm, S. (2004). Childhood and adult sexual abuse, rumination on sadness and dysphoria. *Child Abuse and Neglect, 28,* 393–410.

Coon, D., Thompson, K., Steffen, A., Sorocco, K., & Gallagher-Thompson, D. (2003). Anger and depression management: Psychoeducational skill training interventions for women caretakers of a relative with dementia. *Gerontologist, 43*(5), 678–689.

Coulehan, R., Friedlander, M., & Heatherington, L. (1998). Transforming narratives: A change event in constructivist family therapy. *Family Process, 37,* 17–33.

Cross, T. (1999). Understanding family resiliency from a relational world view. In H. I. McCubbin, E. Thompson, A. Thompson, & J. Fromer (Eds.), *Resiliency in Native American and immigrant families* (pp. 143–157). Resiliency in Families series. Thousand Oaks, CA: Sage.

Dalenberg, C., & Palesh, O. (2004). Relationship between child abuse history, trauma, and dissociation in Russian college students. *Child Abuse and Neglect, 28,* 461–474.

D'Angelo, E., Lierena-Quinn, R., Shapiro, R., Colon, F., Rodriguez, P., Gallagher, K., & Beardslee, W. (2009). Adaptation of the Prevention Intervention Program for Depression for use with predominantly low-income Latino families. *Family Process, 48*(2), 269–291.

DeJong, P., & Berg, I. (1998). *Interviewing for solutions.* Pacific Grove, CA: Brooks/ Cole.

Delgado, M. (2007). *Social work with Latinos: A cultural assets paradigm.* New York: Oxford University Press.

Department of Justice, Canada. (2012). Selected statistics on Canadian families and family law. 222.justice.gc.ca.

deShazer, S. (1994). *Words were originally magic.* New York: Norton.

Diamond, G., & Stern, R. (2003). Attachment-based family therapy for depressed adolescents: Repairing attachment failures. In S. Johnson & V. Whiffen (Eds.), *Attachment processes in couple and family therapy* (pp. 191–212). New York: Guilford Press.

Dixon, L., McFarlane, W., Lefley, H., Lucksted, A., Cohen, M., & Falloon, I. (2001). Evidenced-based practices for services to families of people with psychiatric disabilities. *Psychiatric Services, 52*(7), 903–910.

Dong, M., Anda, R., Dube, S., Giles, W., & Felittle, V. (2003). The relationship of exposure to childhood sexual abuse to other forms of abuse, neglect, and household dysfunction. *Child Abuse and Neglect, 27*(6), 623–639.

Drummet, A. R., Coleman, M., & Cable, S. (2003). Military families under stress: Implications for family life education. *Family Relations, 52*(3), 279–287.

Edwards, L. (2006). Perceived social support and HIV/AIDS medication adherence among African American women. *Qualitative Health Research, 16*(5), 679–691.

Elder, G. (1974). *Children of the Great Depression.* Chicago: University of Chicago Press.

Elder, G., & Conger, R. (2000). *Children of the land.* Chicago: University of Chicago Press.

Epstein, N., Baldwin, L., & Bishop, D. (1983). The McMaster family assessment device. *Journal of Marital and Family Therapy, 9,* 171–190.

Ethier, L., Lemelin, J., & Lacharite, C. (2004). A longitudinal study of the effects of chronic maltreatment on children's behavioral and emotional problems. *Child Abuse and Neglect, 28,* 1265–1278.

Falicov, C. (1996). Mexican families. In M. McGoldrick, J. Giordano, & J. Pearce (Eds.), *Ethnicity and family therapy* (pp. 169–182). New York: Guilford.

Falicov, C. (1998a). *Latino families in therapy: A guide to multicultural practice.* New York: Guilford.

Falicov, C. (1998b). The cultural meaning of family triangles. In M. McGoldrick (Ed.), *Re-visioning family therapy: Race, culture, and gender in clinical practice* (pp. 37–49). New York: Guilford Press.

Falicov, C. (1999). Religion and spiritual folk traditions in immigrant families: Therapeutic resources for Latinos. In F. Walsh (Ed.), *Spiritual resources in family therapy* (pp. 104–135). New York: Guilford.

Falicov, C. (2006). Family organization: The safety net of close and extended kin. In R. Smith & R. Montilla (Eds.), *Counseling and family therapy with Latino populations: Strategies that work* (pp. 41–62). New York: Routledge.

Farris-Manning, C., & Zandstra, M. (2012). *Children in care in Canada.* Ottawa: Canadian Child Welfare League.

Fatusso, L., McDermott, P., & Lutz, M. (1999). Clinical issues in the assessment of family violence involving children. In R. Ammerman & M. Hersen (Eds.), *Assessment of family violence: A clinical and legal sourcebook* (2nd ed., pp. 10–24). New York: Wiley.

Felitti, V. (2012). Adverse childhood experiences and their relationships to adult well-being and disease: Turning gold into lead. Web seminar sponsored by Kaiser Permanente and the Center for Disease Control. August 27, 2012.

Fellenberg, S. (2004). The contribution of enactments to structural family therapy: A process study. *Dissertation Abstracts International Section B. The Sciences and Engineering, Vol. 64* (11B) 2004, p. 5780.S.

Felsman, J. (1989). Risk and resilience in childhood: The lives of street children. In T. Dugan & R. Coles (Eds.), *The child in our times* (pp. 56–79). New York: Bruner-Mazel.

Fisher, L., & Weihs, K. L. (2000). Can addressing family relationships improve chronic disease? *Journal of Family Practice, 49*(6), 561–566.

Fong, R. (2004). *Culturally competent practice with immigrants and refugee children and families.* New York: Guilford Press.

Fraenkel, P., & Shannon, M. (2009). Narrative and collaborative practices in work with families that are homeless. *Journal of Marital and Family Therapy, 35*(30), 325–342.

Frame, M. (2003). *Integrating religion and spirituality into counseling: A comprehensive approach.* Pacific Grove, CA: Thompson.

Fraser, M., & Galinsky, M. (2004). Risk and resilience in childhood: Toward an evidence-based model of practice. In M. Fraser (Ed.), *Risk and resilience in childhood: An ecological approach* (pp. 385–402). Washington, DC: NASW Press.

Fraser, M., Kirby, L., & Smokowski, P. (2004). Risk and resiliency in childhood. In M. Fraser (Ed.), *Risk and resilience in childhood: An ecological approach* (pp. 13–66). Washington, DC: NASW Press.

Fraser, M., Richman, J., & Galinsky, M. (1999). Risk protection and resiliency: Toward a conceptual framework for social work practice. *Social Work Research, 23,* 131–143.

Freedman, J., & Combs, G. (1996). *Narrative therapy: The social construction of preferred realities.* New York: Norton.

Friedlander, M. (1998). Family therapy research: Science into practice, practice into science. In M. Nichols & R. Schwartz (Eds.), *Family therapy: Concepts and methods* (4th ed., pp. 503–553). Boston: Allyn & Bacon.

Friedman, B. (2002). Judaism. In M. Van Hook, B. Hugen, & M. Aguilar (Eds.), *Spirituality within religious traditions and social work practice* (pp. 98–119). Pacific Grove, CA: Brooks/Cole.

Friedman, E. (1986). Resources for healing and survival in families. In M. Karpel (Ed.), *Family resources: The hidden partner in family therapy* (pp. 65–92). New York: Guilford.

Fristad, M. (2006). Psychoeducational treatment for school-aged children with bipolar disorder. *Development and Psychopathology, 18,* 1289–1306.

Fung, J., Ho, L., Louie, J., Martinez, J., & Lau, A. (2011). Directions in understanding, preventing, and treating disruptions in parenting and child behavior problems in Asian American families. In F. Leon, L. Juan, D. Qin, & H. Fitzgerald (Eds.), *Asian American and Pacific Islander Children and Mental Health.* Vol. 2, *Prevention and Treatment* (pp. 175–200). Santa Barbara, CA: Praeger.

Garcia-Preto, N. (1996a). Puerto Rican families. In M. McGoldrick, J. Giordano, & J. Pearce (Eds.), *Ethnicity and family therapy* (pp. 183–199). New York: Guilford.

Garcia-Preto, N. (1996b). Latino families: An overview. In M. McGoldrick, J. Giordano, & J. Pearce (Eds.), *Ethnicity and family therapy* (2nd ed., pp. 141–154). New York: Guilford.

Garmezy, N. (1985). Stress-resistant children: The search for protective factors. In J. Stevenson (Ed.), Recent research in developmental psychopathology. *Journal of Child Psychology and Psychiatry* (Book Supplement No. 4, 213–233). Oxford: Pergamon.

Garmezy, N. (1993). Children in poverty: Resilience despite risk. *Psychiatry, 56,* 127–136.

Gaudin, J., Wodarski, J., Arkinson, M., & Avery, L. (1990–1991). Remedying child neglect: Effectiveness of social network interventions. *Journal of Applied Social Sciences, 15,* 97–123.

Genero, N. (1998). Culture, resiliency, and mutual psychological development. In H. I. McCubbin, E. Thompson, A. Thompson, & J. Futrell (Eds.), *Resiliency in African-American families* (pp. 31–48). Thousand Oaks, CA: Sage.

Gibbons, F., Gerrard, M., Cleveland, M., Wills, T., & Brody, G. (2004). Perceived discrimination and substance use in African American parents and their children: A panel study. *Journal of Personality and Social Psychology, 86*(4), 517–529.

Gingerich, W., & Eisengart, S. (2000). Solution-focused brief therapy: A review of the outcomes research. *Family Process, 39*(4), 477–498.

Giordano, J., & McGoldrick, M. (1996). Italian families. In M. McGoldrick, J. Giordano, & J. Pearce (Eds.), *Ethnicity and family therapy* (2nd ed., pp. 427–441). New York: Guilford.

Glennie, A., & Chappel, L. (2010). *Jamaica: From diverse beginnings to diaspora in the developed world.* June 2010 Migration Information Source. http://www.migra tioninformation.org/feature/display.cfm?ID = 787.

Golby, B., & Bretherton, I. (1999). Resilience in postdivorce mother-child relationships. In H. I. McCubbin, E. Thompson, A. Thompson, & J. Futrell (Eds.), *The dynamics of resilient families* (pp. 238–269). Resiliency in Families series. Thousand Oaks, CA: Sage.

Goldberg-Arnold, J., Fristad, M., & Gavazzi, S. (1999). Family psychoeducation: Giving caretakers what they want and need. *Family Relations, 48,* 411–417.

Goldenberg, I., & Goldenberg, H. (1998). *Counseling today's families* (3rd ed.). Pacific Grove, CA: Brooks/Cole.

Goldenberg, I., & Goldenberg, H. (2000). *Family therapy: An overview* (5th ed.). Pacific Grove, CA: Brooks/Cole.

Goldstein, E. (1995). *Ego psychology and social work practice* (2nd ed.). New York: Free Press.

Gonzales, J. (2003). *Cesar Chavez: A case study of a resilient child's adaptation to adulthood.* ERIC U.S. Department of Government Educational Research Center.

Gonzales, N., & Kim, L. (1997). Stress and coping in an ethnic minority context: Children's cultural ecologies. In S. Wolchik & I. Sandler (Eds.), *Handbook of children's coping: Integration theory and practice* (pp. 481–511). New York: Plenum.

Gordon, J. (2003). What makes a tragedy public? In M. Lattanzi-Licht & K. Doka (Eds.), *Living with grief: Coping with public tragedy* (pp. 3–13). New York: Brunner-Routledge.

Gordon, K. (1996). Resilient Hispanic youths' self-concept and motivational patterns. *Hispanic Journal of Behavioral Social Sciences, 18*(1), 63–73.

Gordon, W. E., & Song, L. D. (1994). Variations in the experience of resilience. In M. Wang & W. Gordon (Eds.), *Educational resiliency in inner-city America: Challenges and prospects* (pp. 27–40). Hillsdale, NJ: Erlbaum.

Gozdziak, E. (2002). Spiritual emergency room: The role of spirituality and religion in the resettlement of Kosovar Albanians. *Journal of Religious Studies, 15*(2), 136–153.

Grall, T. (2009) *Custodian mothers and fathers and their child support: 2007.* U.S. Census Department, Washington, DC, November 2009.

Grant, D. (1999). Effective therapeutic approaches with ethnic families. In C. Franklin & C. Jordan (Eds.), *Family practice: Brief systems methods for social work* (pp. 259–297). Pacific Grove, CA: Brooks/Cole.

Grant, D. (2002). The African-American Baptist tradition. In M. Van Hook, B. Hugen, & M. Aguilar (Eds.), *Spirituality within religious traditions and social work practice* (pp. 205–227). Pacific Grove, CA: Brooks/Cole.

Granvold, D., & Martin, J. (1999). Family therapy with gay and lesbian clients. In C. Franklin & C. Jordan (Eds.), *Family practice: Brief systems methods for social work* (pp. 299–320). Pacific Grove, CA: Brooks/Cole.

Greeff, A. P., & Fillis, A. (2009) Resiliency in poor single-parent families. *Families in Society, 90*(3), 279–285.

Greeff, A. P., & Ilona, N. (2005) Individual characteristics associated with resiliency in single-parent families. *Psychological Reports, 96*(1), 36–42.

Greeff, A., & van der Merwe, S. (2004). Variables associated with resilience in divorced families. *Social Indicators Research, 68*(1), 59–75.

Greene, R. (2002). *Resiliency: An integrated approach to practice, policy, and research.* Washington, DC: NASW Press.

Greene, R., & Cohen, H. (2005). Social work with older adults and their families: Changing practice paradigms. *Families in Society: The Journal of Contemporary Social Services, 86*(3), 367–373.

Greene, R., & Conrad, A. (2002). Basic assumptions and terms. In R. Greene (Ed.), *Resiliency: An integrated approach to practice, policy, and research* (pp. 29–62). Washington, DC: NASW Press.

Greene, R., & Kropf, N. (2003). A family case management approach for Level I needs. In A. Kilpatrick & T. Holland (Eds.), *Working with families: An integrated model by level of need* (3rd ed., pp. 85–103). Boston: Allyn & Bacon.

Greenwood, D., Szapocznik, J., McIntosh, S., Antoni, M., Ironson, G., Tejeda, M., et al. (1996). African American women, their families, and HIV/AIDS. In R. Resnick & R. Rozensky (Eds.), *Health psychology through the lifespan: Practice and research opportunities* (pp. 349–359). Washington, DC: American Psychological Association.

Grigsby, R. (2003). Interventions to meet basic needs of high-risk families with children. In A. Kilpatrick & T. Holland (Eds.), *Working with families: An integrated model by level of need* (3rd ed., pp. 69–84). Boston: Allyn & Bacon.

Grych, J., & Fincham, F. (1997). Children's adaptation to divorce: From description to explanation. In W. Wolchik & I. Sandler (Eds.), *Handbook of children's coping: Linking theory and intervention* (pp. 159–193). New York: Plenum.

Guarnaccia, P. (1998). Multicultural experiences of family caregiving: A study of African American, European American, and Hispanic American families. In H. Lefley (Ed.), *Family coping with mental illness: The cultural context* (pp. 45–61). San Francisco: Jossey-Bass.

Gunderson, J., Berkowitz, C., & Ruiz-Sancho, A. (1997). Families of borderline patients: A psychoeducational approach. *Bulletin of the Menninger Clinic, 61*(4), 446–458.

Gutheil, I., & Congress, E. (2000). Resiliency in older people: A paradigm for practice. In E. Norman (Ed.), *Resiliency enhancement: Putting the strengths perspective into practice* (pp. 40–52). New York: Columbia University Press.

Han, J., & Richardson, V. (2010). The relationship between depression and loneliness among homebound older persons: Does spirituality moderate this relationship? *Journal of Religion and Spirituality in Social Work and Social Thought, 28*(3), 218–236.

Harmell, A., Chattilion, E., Roepke, S., & Mausbach, B. (2011). A review of psychobiology of dementia caregiving: A focus on resilience factors. *Current Psychiatric Reports, 13*(2), 219–224.

Hartman, A. (1999). The long road to equality: Lesbians and social policy. In J. Laird (Ed.), *Lesbians and lesbian families: Reflections on theory and practice* (pp. 91–122). New York: Columbia University Press.

Hartman, A., & Laird, J. (1983). *Family centered social work practice*. New York: Free Press.

Haynes, D. (2002). Mormonism. In M. Van Hook, B. Hugen, & M. Aguilar (Eds.), *Spirituality within religious traditions in social work practice* (pp. 251–272). Pacific Grove, CA: Brooks/Cole.

Helgeson, V., Becker, D., Escobar, O., & Siminero, L. (2012). Families with children with diabetes: Implications of parent stress for parent and child health. *Journal of Pediatric Psychology, 29*(2), 153–159.

Helmeke, K., & Bischof, G. (2002). Recognizing and raising spiritual and religious issues in therapy: Guidelines for the timid. In T. Carlson & M. Erikson (Eds.), *Spirituality and family therapy* (pp. 195–214). New York: Haworth.

Henggeler, S., Schoenwald, S., Borduin, C., Rowland, M., & Cunningham, P. (1998). *Multisystemic treatment of antisocial behavior of children and adolescents*. New York: Guilford.

Hess, C., Dapus, M., & Black, M. (2002). Resilience among African American adolescent mothers: Predictors of positive parenting in early infancy. *Pediatric Psychiatry, 27*(7), 619–629.

Hetherington, E. M. (1989). Coping with family transitions: Winners, losers, and survivors. *Child Development, 60,* 1–14.

Hetherington, E. M., & Elmore, A. (2003). Risk and resilience: Children coping with their parents' divorce and remarriage. In S. Luthor (Ed.), *Resiliency, vulnerability, adaptation in the context of childhood adversity* (pp. 182–212). New York: Cambridge University Press.

Hill, R. (1949). *Families under stress*. New York: Harper & Row.

Hill, R. (1999). *The strengths of African American families: Twenty-five years later.* New York: University Press of America.

Hill, S. (2003). *Managing sickle cell disease in low-income families*. Philadelphia: Temple University Press.

Hines, P., & Boyd-Franklin, N. (1996). African American families. In M. McGoldrick, J. Giordano, & J. Pearce (Eds.), *Ethnicity and family therapy* (2nd ed.). New York: Guilford Press.

Hodge, D. (2003). *Spiritual assessment: Handbook for helping professionals*. Botsford, CT: North American Association for Christians in Social Work.

Hodge, D. (2005). Spiritual ecograms: A new assessment instrument for identifying clients' strengths in space and across time. *Families in Society, 86*(2), 287–296.

Hoffman, L. (1993). *Exchanging voices: A collaborative approach to family therapy*. London: Karnac Books.

Holland, T., & Kilpatrick, A. (2003). An ecological systems-social constructionism approach to family practice. In A. Kilpatrick & T. Holland (Eds.), *Working with families: An integrative model by level of need* (3rd ed., pp. 14–32). Boston: Allyn & Bacon.

Homrich, A., & Horne, A. (2000). Brief family therapy. In A. M. Horne (Ed.), *Family counseling and therapy* (3rd ed., pp. 243–270). Itasca, IL: Peacock.

Horne, A., & Sayger, T. (2000). Behavioral approaches to couple and family therapy. In A. Horne (Ed.), *Family counseling and therapy* (3rd ed., pp. 454–488). Itasca, IL: Peacock.

Horne, A., & Sayger, T. (2003). Social learning family interventions. In A. Kilpatrick & T. Holland (Eds.), *Working with families: An integrative model by level of need* (116–130). New York: Allyn & Bacon.

Hudson, W., & McMurtry, S. (1997). Comprehensive assessment in social work practice: The Multi-Problem Screening Inventory. *Research on Social Work Practice, 7,* 79–98.

Huebner, A., & Mancini, J. (June 2005). *Adjustments among adolescents in military families when a parent is deployed: Final report to the Military Family Research Institute and Department of Defense Quality of Life Office.* Falls Church, VA.

Huebner, A., Mancini, J., Bowen, G., & Orthner, D. (2009). Shadowed by war: Building community capacity to support military families. *Family Relations: Interdisciplinary Journal of Applied Family Studies, 58*(2), 216–228.

Hugen, B. (2002). Spirituality and religion in social work practice: A conceptual model. In M. Van Hook, B. Hugen, & M. Aguilar (Eds.), *Spirituality within religious traditions in social work practice* (pp. 9–17). Pacific Grove, CA: Brooks/Cole.

Hyman, B., & Williams, L. (2001). Resiliency among women survivors of child sexual abuse. *Affilia, 16*(2), 198–219.

Imber-Black, E. (1988). *Families and larger systems.* New York: Guilford.

James, B. (1994). *Handbook for treatment of attachment-trauma problems in children.* New York: Lexington Books/Free Press.

Janzen, C., & Harris, O. (1997). *Family treatment in social work practice* (3rd ed.). Itasca, IL: F.E. Peacock.

Jensen, J. (2004) Risk and protective factors for alcohol and other drug use in childhood and adolescence. In M. Fraser (Ed.), *Risk and resilience in childhood: An ecological approach* (2nd ed., pp. 183–208). Washington DC: NASW Press.

Johnson, S., & Best, M. (2003) A systematic approach to restructuring adult attachment: The EFT model of couples therapy. In P. Erdman & T. Caffery (Eds.), *Attachment and family systems: Conceptual, empirical, and therapeutic relatedness* (pp. 165–189). New York: Brunner-Routledge.

Jones, D., Forehand, R., Brody, G., & Armistead, L. (2002). Psychosocial adjustment of African American children in single-mother families: A test of three risk models. *Journal of Marriage and Family, 64*(1).

Jonzon, E., & Lindblad, F. (2006). Risk factors and protective factors in relation to subjective health among adult female victims of child sexual abuse. *Child Abuse and Neglect, 30*(2), 127–143.

Jordan, C., Cobb, N. H., & Franklin, C. (1999). Behavioral and cognitive-behavior family therapy. In C. Franklin & C. Jordan (Eds.), *Family practice: Brief systems methods for social work* (pp. 73–103). Pacific Grove, CA: Brooks/Cole.

Jordan, C., & Franklin, C. (1999). Structural family therapy. In C. Franklin & C. Jordan (Eds.), *Family practice: Brief systems methods for social work* (pp. 23–44). Pacific Grove, CA: Brooks/Cole.

Jordan, C., Lewellen, A., & Vandiver, V. (1995). Psychoeducation for minority families: A social work perspective. *International Journal of Mental Health, 23*(4), 27–43.

Kantor, D., & Kupferman, W. (1985). The client's interview of the therapist. *Journal of Marital and Family Therapy, 11*(3), 225–244.

Karpel, M. A. (1986). Testing, promoting, and preserving family resources: Beyond pathology and power. In M. Karpel (Ed.), *Family resources: The hidden partner in family therapy* (pp. 175–232). New York: Guilford.

Kerr, M., & Bowen, M. (1988). *Family evaluations.* New York: Norton.

Kilpatrick, A. (2003). Levels of family need. In A. Kilpatrick & T. Holland (Eds.), *Working with families: An integrative model by levels of need* (3rd ed., pp. 1–13). Boston: Allyn & Bacon.

Kilpatrick, A., Becvar, D., & Holland, T. (2003). Ethically informed and spiritually sensitive practice. In A. Kilpatrick & T. Holland (Eds.), *Working with families: An integrative model by level of need* (pp. 49–67). Boston: Allyn & Bacon.

Kilpatrick, A., Kilpatrick, Jr., E., & Callaway, J. (2000). Object relations family therapy. In A. Horne (Ed.), *Family counseling and therapy* (3rd ed., pp. 300–329). Itasca, IL: Peacock.

Kim, J. (2008). Examining the effectiveness of solution-focused brief therapy: A meta-analysis. *Research on Social Work Practice, 18*(2), 107–116.

Kinney, J., Haapala, D., & Booth, C. (1991). *Keeping families together: The homebuilders model.* New York: Aldine de Gruyter.

Kinzie, J., & Sack, W. (2002). The psychiatric disorders among Canadian adolescents: The effects of severe trauma. In F. Azima & N. Grizenko (Eds.), *Immigrant and refugee children and their families: Clinical, research, and training issues* (pp. 95–112). Madison, CT: International Universities Press.

Kirmayer, L., Brass, G., Holton, T., Paul, K., Simpson, C., & Tait, C. (2006). *Suicide among Aboriginal people in Canada: The Aboriginal Healing Foundation.* Research Series. Ottawa, Canada.

Kjellstrand, E., & Harper, M. (2012). Yes, she can: An examination of resiliency factors in middle and upper income single mothers. *Journal of Divorce & Remarriage, 53*(4), 311–327.

Koenig, H. (1999). *The healing power of faith: Science explores medicine's last great frontier.* New York: Simon & Schuster.

Koob, J. (2003). Solution-focused family interventions. In A. Kilpatrick & T. Holland (Eds.), *Working with families: An integrative model by level of functioning* (3rd ed., pp. 131–150). Boston: Allyn & Bacon.

Krasner, B. (1986). Trustworthiness: The primary family resource. In M. Karpel (Ed.), *Family resources: The hidden partner in family therapy* (pp. 116–147). New York: Guilford.

Kurtines, W., & Szapocznik, J. (1996). Family interaction patterns: Structural family therapy within context of cultural diversity. In E. Hibbs & P. Jensen (Eds.), *Psychosocial treatments for child and adolescent disorders: Empirically based strategies for clinical practice* (pp. 671–697). Washington, DC: American Psychological Association.

Kwak, K. (2003). Adolescents and their parents: A review of intergenerational family resources for immigrant and nonimmigrant families. *Human Development, 40,* 115–136.

LaFramboise, T., Hoyt, D., Oliver, L., & Whitbeck, L. (2006). Family, community, and school influences on resiliency among American Indian adolescents in the upper Midwest. *Journal of Community Psychology, 34*(2), 193–209.

LaFranbroise, R., & Howard-Pitney, B. (1995). Zuni Life Skills/Development Curriculum: Design and evaluation of a prevention program. *Journal of Consulting Psychology, 42*(4), 479–486.

Laird, J. (2000). Culture and narratives as metaphors for clinical practice with families. In D. Demo, K. Allen, & M. Fine (Eds.), *Handbook of family diversity* (pp. 338–358). New York: Oxford University Press.

Landau, J., & Saul, J. (2004). Facilitating family and community resilience in response to natural disaster. In F. Walsh & M. McGoldrick (Eds.), *Living beyond loss: Death in the family* (2nd ed., pp. 285–310). New York: W.W. Norton.

Leading Together: Canada takes action on HIV/AIDS 2005–2010. (2005). Canadian Public Health Association. http:www.leadingtogether.ca.

Lee, E. (1996). Asian American families: An overview. In M. McGoldrick, J. Giordano, & J. Pearce (Eds.), *Ethnicity and family therapy* (2nd ed., pp. 227–248). New York: Guilford.

Lefley, H. P. (1998). *Families coping with mental illness: The cultural context.* San Francisco: Jossey-Bass.

Leon, F., Oka, E., & Lannert, B. (2011). Asian American youth's depression and anxiety in cultural context. In F. Leon, L. Juan, D. Qin, & H. Fitzgerald (Eds.), *Asian American and Pacific Islander Children and Mental Health.* Vol. 2, *Prevention and Treatment* (pp. 1–27). Santa Barbara, CA: Praeger.

Levy, T., & Orlans, M. (2003). Creating and repairing attachments in biological, foster, and adoptive parents. In S. Johnson & V. Whiffen (Eds.), *Attachment process in couple and family therapy* (pp. 165–190). New York: Guilford Press.

Lietz, C. (2007). Uncovering stories of family resilience: A mixed method study of resilient families, part 2. *Families in Society: The Journal of Contemporary Social Services, 88*(1), 147–155.

Lietz, C., & Strength, M. (2011) Stories of successful reunification: A narrative study of family resilience in child welfare. *Families in Society: The Journal of Contemporary Social Services, 92*(1), 203–210.

Lim, J., & Zebrack, B. (2004). Caring for family members with chronic physical illness: A critical review of caregiver literature. *Health and Quality of Life Outcomes, 2*(50).

Lindblad-Goldberg, M. (2006). Successful African American single parent families. In L. Combrinck-Graham (Ed.), *Children in family contexts: Perspective on treatment* (2nd ed., pp. 142–162). New York: Guilford Press.

Lott-Whitehead, L., & Tully, C. (1999). The family lives of lesbian mothers. In J. Laird (Ed.), *Lesbians and lesbian families: Reflections on theory and practice* (pp. 243–260). New York: Columbia University Press.

Lutzker, J., Bigelow, K., Doctor, R., & Kessler, M. (1998). Safety, health care, and bonding within an ecobehavioral approach to treating and preventing child abuse and neglect. *Journal of Family Violence, 2*, 283–290.

Lynskey, M., & Fergusson, D. (1997). Factors protecting against the development of adjustment difficulties in young adults exposed to childhood sexual abuse. *Child Abuse and Neglect, 21*(12), 1177–1190.

Madsen, W. (2007). *Collaborative therapy with multi-stressed families* (2nd ed.). New York: Guilford Press.

Magana, S., & Ybarra, M. (2010). Family and community as strengths in the Latino community. In R. Furman & N. Negi (Eds.), *Social work practice with Latinos: Key issues and emerging themes* (pp. 69–84). Chicago: Lyceum Books.

Manley, R., & Leichner, P. (2003). Anguish and despair in adolescents with eating disorders: Healing management of suicidal ideation and impulses. *Journal of Crisis Intervention and Suicide Prevention, 24*(1), 32–36.

Martin, E., & Martin, J. (2002). *Spirituality and the black helping tradition in social work.* Washington, DC: NASW Press.

Masten, W. (2007). *Collaborative therapy with multi-stressed families: From old problems to new futures.* New York: Guilford.

Masten, A., Best, K., & Garmezy, N. (1990). Resilience and development: Contributions from the study of children who overcome adversity. *Development and Psychopathology, 2*(4), 425–444.

Masten, A., & Coatsworth, J. (1998). The development of competence in favorable and unfavorable environments: Lessons from research of successful children. *American Psychologist, 53*(2), 205–220.

Masten, A., & Garmezy, N. (1983). Risk, vulnerability, and protective factors in developmental psychopathology. In B. Lahey & A. Kazdin (Eds.), *Advances in clinical child psychology* (vol. 8, pp. 1–51). New York: Plenum.

Masten, A., & Tellegen, D. (2012). Resiliency in developmental psychopathology: Contributions of the Project Competence Longitudinal Study. *Development and Psychopathology, 24*(2), 345–361.

Mayadas, N., Elliott, D., & Ramanathan, S. (1999). A global model of ethnic diversity conflict: Implications for social work with populations at risk. In S. Ramanathan & R. Link (Eds.), *All our futures: Principles and resources for social work practice in a global era* (pp. 138–155). Belmont, CA: Brooks/Cole.

McAdoo, H. (1998). African-American families: Strengths and realities. In H. I. McCubbin, E. Thompson, A. Thompson, & J. Futrell (Eds.), *Resiliency in African-American families* (pp. 17–30). Thousand Oaks, CA: Sage.

McCubbin, H. I., Dahl, B., & Hunter, E. (1976). *Families in the military system.* Thousand Oaks, CA: Sage.

McCubbin, H. I., Futrell, J., Thompson, E., & Thompson, A. (1998). Resilient families in an ethnic and cultural context. In H. McCubbin, E. Thompson, A. Thompson, & J. Futrell (Eds.), *Resiliency in African American families* (pp. 329–353). Thousand Oaks, CA: Sage.

McCubbin, H. I., McCubbin, M., Thompson, A., & Thompson, E. (1999). Resiliency in ethnic families. In H. I. McCubbin, E. Thompson, A. Thompson, & J. Fromer (Eds.), *Resiliency in Native American and immigrant families* (pp. 3–48). Thousand Oaks, CA: Sage.

McCubbin, H. I., & Patterson, J. (1983). Family transitions: Adaptation to stress. In H. I. McCubbin & C. Figley (Eds.), *Stress and the family: Coping with normative transitions.* New York: Bruner-Mazel.

McCubbin, H. I., Thompson, A., & McCubbin, M. (1996). *Family assessment: Resiliency, coping, and adaptation: Inventories for research and practice.* Madison: University of Wisconsin Press.

McCubbin, H. I., Thompson, E., Thompson, A., Elver, K., & McCubbin, M. (1998). Ethnicity, schema, and coherence: Appraisal processes for families in crisis. In H. I. McCubbin, A. Thompson, E. Thompson, & J. Fromer (Eds.), *Stress, coping, and health in families: Sense of coherence and resiliency* (pp. 41–67). Resiliency in Families series. Thousand Oaks, CA: Sage.

McCubbin, H. I., Thompson, E., Thompson, A., & Fromer, J. (1998). Preface. In H. I. McCubbin, E. Thompson, A. Thompson, & J. Fromer (Eds.), *Resiliency in Native American and immigrant families* (pp. xvi–xvii). Thousand Oaks, CA: Sage.

McCubbin, H., Thompson, E., Thompson, A., & Futrell, J. (1999). *The dynamics of resilient families.* Thousand Oaks, CA: Sage.

McCubbin, M., Balling, K., Possin, P., Frierdich, S., & Bryne, B. (2002). Family resiliency in childhood cancer. *Family Relations, 51,* 103–111.

McCubbin, M., & McCubbin, H. (1996). Resiliency in families: A conceptual model of family adjustment and adaptation in response to stress and crisis. In H. I. McCubbin, A. Thompson, & M. McCubbin (Eds.), *Family assessment: Resiliency, coping, and adaptation: Inventories for research and practice* (pp. 1–64). Madison: University of Wisconsin Press.

McGoldrick, M. (Ed.) (1999). *Re-visioning family therapy: Race, culture, and gender in clinical practice.* New York: Guilford Press.

McGoldrick, M., & Carter, B. (1982). The family life cycle. In F. Walsh (Ed.), *Normal family processes* (pp. 167–195). New York: Guilford Press.

McGoldrick, M., & Gerson, R. (1985). *Genograms in family assessment.* New York: Norton.

McGoldrick, M., & Giordano, J. (1986). Overview: Ethnicity and family therapy. In M. McGoldrick, J. Giordano, & J. Pearce (Eds.), *Ethnicity and family therapy* (2nd ed., pp. 1–27). New York: Guilford.

McQuaide, S. (2000). Women's resiliency at midlife: What is it? How do you mobilize it? In E. Norman (Ed.), *Resiliency enhancement: Putting the strengths perspective into social work practice* (pp. 70–82). New York: Columbia University Press.

McWhirter, J., & Ryan, C. (1991). Counseling the Navajo: Cultural understanding. *Journal of Multicultural Counseling and Development, 19*(2).

Mendenhall, A., & Mount, K. (2011). Parents of children with mental illness: Exploring the caregiver experience and caregiver-focused interventions. *Families in Society, 92*(2), 183–190.

Mendenhall, T., Berge, J., Harker, P., GreenCrow, B., LittleWalker, N., WhiteEagle, S., & BrownOwl, S. (2010). The Family Education Diabetes Series (FEDS): Community-based participatory research with a Midwestern American Indian community. *Nursing Inquiry, 17*(4), 359–372.

MHum, T., Bell, H., Pyles, L., & Runnels, R. (2012). Five years later: Resiliency among older adult survivors of Hurricane Katrina. *Journal of Gerontological Social Work 55.*

Miklowitz, D., George, E., Axelson, D., Kim. E., Birmaher, B., Schneck, C., & Brent, D. (2004). Family focused treatment for adolescents with bipolar disorder. *Journal of Affective Disorders, 82*(1), 113–128.

Miller, D., & Macintosh, R. (1999). Promoting resilience in urban African American adolescence: Racial socialization and identity as protective factors. *Social Work Research, 23.*

Miller, J., Kabacoff, R., Bishop, D., Epstein, N., & Keitner, G. (1994). The development of the McMaster Clinical Rating Scale. *Family Process, 33,* 53–69.

Miller, J., Ryan, C. Keitner, G., Bishop, D., & Epstein, N. (1999). The McMaster approach to families: Theory, assessment, treatment, and research. *Journal of Family Therapy, 22,* 169–189.

Miller, K., & Rasco, L. (2004). *The mental health of refugees: Ecological approach to healing and adaptation.* Mahwah, NJ: Lawrence Erlbaum Associates.

Minuchin, S. (1974). *Families and family therapy.* Cambridge, MA: Harvard University Press.

Minuchin, S., & Fishman, H. (1981). *Family therapy techniques.* Cambridge, MA: Harvard University Press.

Minuchin, S., & Nichols, M. (1991). *Family healing: Strategies for hope and understanding.* New York: Simon & Schuster.

Minuchin, S., Rosman, B., & Baker, L. (1978). *Psychosomatic families.* Cambridge, MA: Harvard University Press.

Mittelman, M., Ferris, S., Shulman, E., Steinberg, G., & Levin, B. (1996). A family intervention to delay nursing home placement of patients with Alzheimer disease: Randomized control trial. *Journal of the American Medical Association, 276*(21), 1725–1731.

Morales, E. (2000). A contextual understanding of the process of educational resilience: High-achieving Dominican American students and the "Resilience Cycle." *Innovative Higher Education, 25*(1), 7–22.

Moskowitz, S. (1983). *Love despite hate.* New York: Schocken.

Murry, V., Bynum, M., Brody, G., Willert, A., & Stephens, D. (2001). African American single mothers and children in context: A review of studies on risk and resilience. *Clinical Child and Family Psychology Review, 4*(2), 133–154.

Murry, V., Owens, M., Brody, G., Black, A., Willert, A., & Brown, A. (2003). Factors and processes associated with physical and psychological health of African-American mothers with Type 2 Diabetes: A heuristic model. *Diabetes Spectrum, 16*(3), 166–171.

Muzio, C. (1999). Lesbian co-parenting: On being/being with the invisible (M)other. In J. Laird (Ed.), *Lesbians and lesbian families: Reflections on theory and practice* (pp. 197–212). New York: Columbia University Press.

Nadir, A., & Dziegielewski, S. (2002). Islam. In M. Van Hook, B. Hugen, & M. Aguilar (Eds.), *Spirituality within religious traditions and social work practice* (pp. 146–166). Pacific Grove, CA: Brooks/Cole.

National Family Preservation Network. (2012). *Engaging reluctant families: The first visit.* www.nfpn.org/news/notes/20120234-engaging-reluctant-families.html.

Netto, N., Jenny, G., & Phillip, Y. (2009). Growing and gaining through caring for a loved one with dementia. *Dementia, 8*(2), 245–261.

Nichols, M., & Fellenberg, S. (2000). The effective use of enactments in family therapy: A discovery-oriented process study. *Journal of Marital and Family Therapy, 26*(2), 143–152.

Nichols, M., & Schwartz, R. (1998). *Family therapy: Concepts and methods* (4th ed.). Boston: Allyn & Bacon.

Nichols, M., & Schwartz, R. (2001). *Family therapy: Concepts and methods* (5th ed.). New York: Allyn & Bacon.

Nichols, M., & Schwartz, R. (2005). *The essentials of family therapy.* New York: Allyn & Bacon.

Norman, E. (2000). Introduction: The strengths perspective and resiliency enhancement—a natural partnership. In E. Norman (Ed.), *Resiliency enhancement: Putting the strengths perspective into social work practice* (pp. 1–16). New York: Columbia University Press.

Norris, F., Phifer, J., & Kaniasty, K. (1994). Individual and community reactions to the Kentucky floods: Findings from a longitudinal study of older adults. In R. Ursano, B. McCughey, & C. Fullerton (Eds.), *Individual and community responses to trauma and disaster: The structure of human chaos* (pp. 378–400). Cambridge, UK: Cambridge University Press.

Nunavut. http://www.Nunavut.com.

O'Connell, B. (1998). *Solution-focused therapy.* Thousand Oaks, CA: Sage.

O'Connor, T., Davis, A., Meakes, E., Pickering, R., & Schuman, M. (2004). Narrative therapy using a reflecting team: An ethnographic study of therapists' experiences. *Contemporary Family Therapy: An International Journal, 26*(1), 23–39.

O'Connor, T., Meakes, E., Pickering, R., & Schuman, M. (1997). On the right track: Clients' experience of narrative therapy. *Contemporary Family Therapy, 19,* 479–496.

O'Hanlon, W., & Weiner-Davis, M. (1989). *In search of solutions: A new direction in psychotherapy.* New York: Norton.

Olson, D. (1993). Circumplex model of marital and family systems. In F. Walsh (Ed.), *Normal family processes* (2nd ed.). New York: Guilford.

Orthner, D., Jones-Sanpei, H., & Williamson, S. (2004). The resilience and strengths of low-income families. *Family Relations, 53,* 159–167.

Ortiz, P. (2010). Si, se puede! Revisite: Latina/o workers in the United States. In R. Furman & N. Negi (Eds.), *Social work practice with Latinos: Key issues and emerging themes* (pp. 45–66). Chicago: Lyceum Books.

Oshri, A., Burnette, F., & Cicchetti, D. (2011) Development pathways to adolescent cannabis abuse and dependence: Childhood treatment, emerging personality, and internalizing versus externalizing psychopathology. *Psychology of Addictive Behavior, 25*(4), 634–644.

Palmer, C. (2008). A theory of risk and resilience factors in military families. *Military Psychology, 20*(3), 205–217.

Pang, E., Jordan-Marsh, M., Silverstein, M., & Cody, M. (2003). Health-seeking behaviors of elderly Chinese Americans: Shifts in expectations. *Gerontologist, 43*(6), 864–874.

Papalos, D. (2002). *The family psychoeducational approach.* http://www.pendlum .org.articles/articles_bipolar.psychoed.html.

Papero, D. (2000). The Bowen theory. In Arthur M. Horne (Ed.), *Family counseling and therapy* (3rd ed., pp. 272–299). Itasca, IL: Peacock Press.

Pargament, K. (1997). *The psychology of religion and coping: Theory, research, and practice.* New York: Guilford.

Pargament, K., & Brandt, C. (1998). Religion in coping. In H. Koenig (Ed.), *Handbook of religion and mental health* (pp. 111–128). New York: Academic.

Park, N. (2011). Military children and families: Strengths and challenges during peace and war. *American Psychologist, 66*(1), 65–72.

Parra, P., & Guarnaccia, P. (1998). Ethnicity, culture, and resiliency in caregivers of a seriously mentally ill family member. In H. I. McCubbin, E. Thompson, A. Thompson, & J. Futrell (Eds.), *The dynamics of resilient families* (pp. 431–450). Resilience in Families series. Thousand Oaks, CA: Sage.

Peleikis, D., Mykletunm, A., & Dahl, A. (2004). The relative influence of childhood sexual abuse and other family background risk factors on adult adversities in female outpatients treated for anxiety disorders and depression. *Child Abuse and Neglect, 28*(1), 61–76.

Peres, J., Moreira-Almeida, A., Nasello, A., & Koenig, H. (2007). Spirituality and resilience in trauma victims. *Journal of Religion and Health, 46,* 343–350.

Perez-Koenig, R. (2000). The Unitas extended family circle: Developing resiliency in Hispanic youngsters. In E. Norman (Ed.), *Resiliency enhancement: Putting the strengths perspective into social work practice* (pp. 143–153). New York: Columbia University Press.

Pittman, J., Kerpelman, J., & McFadyen, J. (2004). Internal and external adaptation in army families: Lessons from Operation Desert Shield and Desert Storm. *Family Relations, 53*(3), 249–260.

Poston, D., & Turnbull, A. (2004). Role of spirituality and religion in family quality of life for families of children with disabilities. *Education and Training in Developmental Disabilities, 39*(2), 95–108.

Prado, G., Pantin, H., & Tapia, M. (2010) Substance abuse prevention and Latino youth. In R. Furman & N. Negi (Eds.), *Social work practice with Latinos: Key issues and emerging themes* (pp. 215–232). Chicago: Lyceum Books.

Prochaska, J., DiClemente, C., & Norcross, J. (1992). In search of how people change: Applications to addictive behaviors. *American Psychologist, 47*(9), 1102–1114.

Pryce, J., Pryce, D., & Shackelford, K. (2012). *The costs of courage: Combat stress, warriors, and family survival.* Chicago: Lyceum Books.

Quinless, J. (2010). The socio-economic conditions of Aboriginal lone parents: Families in Canada understanding diverse realities. Presented at the 2010 Polar Statistic Conference: Yukon Bureau of Statistics, October 2010.

Ramos, B., & Wright, G. (2010). Social work practice with older Latino adults. In R. Furman & N. Negi (Eds.), *Social work practice with Latinos: Key issues and emerging themes* (pp. 223–246). Chicago: Lyceum Books.

Real Warriors. (2012). www.realwarriors.net/family/change/ family resilience/php.

Rehm, R. (1999). Religious faith in Mexican-American families dealing with chronic childhood illness. *Journal of Nursing Scholarship, 31*(1), 33–38.

Reiss, D. (1981). *The family's construction of reality.* Cambridge, MA: Harvard University Press.

Riley, A., Valdez, C., Barrueco, S., Mills, C., Beardsless, W., Sandler, I., & Rawal, P. (2008). Development of a family-based program to reduce risk and promote resilience among families affected by maternal depression: Theoretical basis and program description. *Clinical Child and Family Psychology Review, 11*(1–2), 12–29.

Rivera, C. (1988, Spring). Culturally sensitive aftercare services for chronically mentally ill Hispanics: The case of the psychoeducational treatment model. *Research Bulletin, Hispanic Research Center, 11*(1). New York: Fordham University Press.

Robinson, H. (2000). Enhancing couple resiliency. In E. Norman (Ed.), *Resiliency enhancement: Putting the strength perspective into social work practice* (pp. 102–127). New York: Columbia University Press.

Romeo, I. (2000). A multisystematic look at Mexican American gangs: Adolescents at risk. In M. Flores & G. Carey (Eds.), *Family therapy with Hispanics: Toward appreciating diversity* (pp. 265–280). Boston: Allyn & Bacon.

Rosenthal, S., Feiring, C., & Taska, L. (2003). Emotional support and adjustment over a year's time following sexual abuse discovery. *Child Abuse and Neglect, 27,* 641–661.

Rutter, M. (1984). Resilient children. *Psychology Today, March,* 57–65.

Rutter, M. (2012). Resiliency as a dynamic concept. *Development and Psychopathology, 24*(2), 335–344.

Sadeh, R., & Bahrami, M. (2008). The effect of narrative couple therapy on couples' family functioning in Isfahan. *Journal of Family Research, 4*(2), 179–191.

Saleebey, D. (2000). *The strengths perspective in social work practice* (2nd ed.). New York: Longman.

Saltzburg, S. (2007). Narrative therapy pathways for re-authoring with parents of adolescents coming-out as lesbians, gay, and bisexual. *Contemporary Family Therapy: An International Journal, 29*(1–2), 57–69.

Saltzman, W., Lester, P., Beardslee, W., Layne, C., Woodward, K., & Nash, W. (2011). Mechanisms of risk and resilience in military families: Theoretical and empirical basis of a Family-Focused Enhancement Program. *Clinical Child and Family Psychology Review, 14*(3), 213–230.

Sanchez, T., & Jones, S. (2010). The diversity and commonalities of Latinos in the United States. In R. Furman & N. Negi (Eds.), *Social work practice with Latinos: Key issues and emerging themes* (pp. 31–44). Chicago: Lyceum Books.

Sandler, I., Wolchik, S., MacKinnon, D., Ayers, T., & Roosa, M. (1997). Developing linkages between theory and intervention in stress and coping. In S. Wolchik & I. Sandler (Eds.), *Handbook of children's coping* (pp. 3–40). New York: Plenum.

Sanford, M., Boyle, M., McCleary, L., Miller, J., Steele, M., Duku, E., & Offord, D. (2006). A pilot study of adjunctive family psychoeducation in adolescent major depression: Feasibility and treatment effect. *Journal of the American Academy of Child and Adolescent Psychiatry, 45,* 386–395.

San Miguel, K., Morrison, G., & Weissglass, T. (1998). The relationship of sources of support and service needs. In H. I. McCubbin, E. Thompson, A. Thompson, & J. Fromer (Eds.), *Resiliency in Native American and immigrant families* (pp. 385–400). Thousand Oaks, CA: Sage.

Satir, V. (1967). *Conjoint family therapy.* Palo Alto, CA: Science and Behavior Books.

Satir, V. (1972). *Peoplemaking.* Palo Alto, CA: Science and Behavior Books.

Saylor, C., Belter, R., & Stokes, S. (1997). Children and families coping with disaster. In S. Wolchik & I. Sandler (Eds.), *Handbook of children's coping: Linking theory and intervention* (pp. 361–383). New York: Plenum.

Scharff, D. (2006). Models of the mind for couple and family therapy. In J. Scharff & D. Scharff (Eds.), *New paradigms for treating relationships* (pp. 7–17). New York: Aronson.

Scharff, D., & Scharff, J. (1987). *Object relations family therapy.* Northvale, NJ: Aronson.

Scharff, J., & Scharff, D. (2003). Object-relations and psychodynamic approaches to couple and family therapy. In T. Sexton, G. Weeks, & M. Robbins (Eds.), *Handbook of family therapy* (pp. 59–81). New York: Brunner-Routledge.

Scharff, J., & Scharff, D. (2006). New paradigms for treating relationships. In J. Scharff & D. Scharff (Eds.), *New paradigms for treating relationships* (pp. 19–32). New York: Aronson.

Sexton, T., Robbins, M., Hollimon, A., Mease, A., & Mayorga, C. (2003). Efficacy, effectiveness, and change mechanisms in couple and family therapy. In T. Sexton, G. Weeks, & M. Robbins (Eds.), *Handbook of family therapy* (pp. 229–261). New York: Brunner-Routledge.

Shalay, N., & Brownlee, K. (2007). Narrative family therapy with blended families. *Journal of Family Psychology, 18*(1), 17–39.

Shapiro, J. (2000). Cognitive neuroscience, neurobiology and affect regulation: Implications for clinical social work. *Clinical Social Work Journal, 28*(1), 9–21.

Sheidow, A., Henggeler, S., & Schoenwald, S. (2003). Multisystemic therapy. In T. Sexton, G. Weeks, & M. Robbins (Eds.), *Handbook for family therapy* (pp. 229–261). New York: Brunner Routledge.

Sherwood, D. (2002). Ethical integration of faith and social work practice: Evangelism. *Social Work and Christianity, 29*(1), 1–12.

Shiner, R., & Masten, A. (2012). Childhood personality as a harbinger of competence and resilience in adulthood. *Development and Psychopathology, 24*(2), 507–528.

Shobe, M., & Coffman, M. (2010). Barriers to health care utilization among Latinos in the United States: Recommendations for social workers. In R. Furman & N. Negi (Eds.), *Social work practice with Latinos: Key issues and emerging themes* (pp. 69–84). Chicago: Lyceum Books.

Shonkoff, C., & Philllips, D. (2000). *From neurons to neighborhoods: The science of early childhood development*. Washington, DC: National Academy Press.

Shonkoff, J. (2005, April). The science of early childhood development: Closing the gap between what we know and what we do. Paper presented at the 15th National Conference on Child Abuse and Neglect, Boston, MA.

Shorkey, C., Garcia, E., & Windsor, L. (2010). Spirituality as a strength in the Latino community. In R. Furman & N. Negi (Eds.), *Social work practice with Latinos: Key issues and emerging themes* (pp. 85–101). Chicago: Lyceum Books.

Siegel, K., & Schrimshaw, E. (2002). The perceived benefits of religious and spiritual coping among older adults living with HIV/AIDS. *Journal for the Scientific Study of Religion, 41*(1), 81–102.

Simmons, T., Franks, J., Peters, C., & Burham, V. (2003). Development of a culturally grounded system of care for Alaska Native children. Paper presented at the National Association for Rural Mental Health, Orlando, FL.

Simon, C., McNeil, J., Franklin, C., & Cooperman, A. (1991). The family and schizophrenia: Toward a psychoeducational approach. *Families in Society, 72*(6), 323–333.

Simons, L., Simons, R., Conger, R., & Brody, G. (2004). Collective socialization and child conduct problems: A multilevel analysis with an African American sample. *Youth & Society, 35*(3), 267–292.

Singh, R. (2002). Hinduism. In M. Van Hook, B. Hugen, & M. Aguilar (Eds.), *Spirituality within religious traditions and social work practice* (pp. 34–52). Pacific Grove, CA: Brooks/Cole.

Sirin, S., & Rogers-Sirin, L. (2004). Exploring school engagement of middle-class African-American adolescents. *Youth & Society, 35*(3), 323–340.

Skinner, B. (1953). *Science and human behavior.* New York: Macmillan.

Smith, A., & Harkness, J. (2002). Spirituality and meaning: A qualitative inquiry with caregivers of Alzheimer's disease. In T. Carlson & M. Erikson (Eds.), *Spirituality and family therapy* (pp. 87–108). New York: Haworth.

Smith, R., Bakir, N., & Montilla, R. (2006). Counseling and therapy with Latino families. In R. Smith & R. Montilla (Eds.), *Counseling and family therapy with Latino populations: Strategies that work* (pp. 3–27). New York: Routledge.

Smith, S. (1983). Disaster: Family disruption in the wake of natural disaster. In C. Figley & H. McCubbin (Eds.), *Stress and the family, Vol II: Coping with disasters* (pp. 120–147). New York: Bruner-Mazel.

Solomon, P. (1996). Moving from psychoeducation to family education for families of adults with serious mental illness. *Psychiatric Services, 47*(12), 1364–1370.

Solomon, P. (1998). The cultural context of interventions for family members with a seriously mental ill relative. In H. Lefley (Ed.), *Families coping with mental illness: The cultural context* (pp. 5–16). San Francisco: Jossey-Bass.

Solomon, S., & Smith, E. (1994). Social support and perceived control as moderators of responses to dioxin and flood exposure. In R. Ursano, B. McCughey, & C. Fullerton (Eds.), *Individual and community responses to trauma and disaster: The structure of human chaos* (pp. 179–200). Cambridge, UK: Cambridge University Press.

Southern, S. (2006). Counseling and family therapy with Latino adolescents. In R. Smith & R. Montilla (Eds.), *Counseling and therapy with Latino populations: Strategies that work* (pp. 117–130). New York: Routledge.

Stadter, M., & Scharff, D. (2006). Brief therapy with couples and individuals. In J. Scharff & D. Scharff (Eds.), *New paradigms for treating relationships* (pp. 419–446). Lanham, MD: Aronson.

Statistics Canada. (2007). Population by selected ethnic origins. (2006 census). www .statcan.gc.ca.

Steel, J., Sanna, L., Hammond, B., Whipple, J., & Cross, H. (2004). Psychological sequelae of childhood sexual abuse: Abuse-related characteristics, coping strategies, and attributional style. *Child Abuse and Neglect, 28,* 785–801.

Steele, M., Murphy, A., & Steel, H. (2010). Identifying therapeutic action in an attachment-centered intervention with high-risk families. *Clinical Social Work Journal, 38*(1), 675–687.

Stern, D. (1985). *The interpersonal world of the infant: A view from psychoanalysis and developmental psychology.* New York: Basic Books.

Stewart, M., Reid, G., & Mangham, C. (1997). Fostering children's resilience. *Journal of Pediatric Nursing, 12,* 21–31.

Strumpf, N., Glicksman, A., Goldberg-Glen, R., Fox, R., & Logue, E. (2001). Care-giver and elder experiences of Cambodian, Vietnamese, Soviet Jewish, and Ukrainian refugees. *International Journal of Aging and Human Development, 53*(3), 233–252.

Stuart, R. (1969). An operant-interpersonal treatment for marital discord. *Journal of Consulting and Clinical Psychology, 33,* 675–682.

Sutton, C., & Broken Nose, M. (1996). American Indian families: An overview. In M. McGoldrick, J. Giordano, & J. Pearce (Eds.), *Ethnicity and family therapy* (2nd ed., pp. 31–44). New York: Guilford.

Taylor, P., Lopez, M., Velasco, G., & Motel, S. (2012). *Hispanics say they have the worst of a bad economy.* Pew Hispanic Center, Pew Research Center. Washington D.C. www.pewhispanic.org.

The Jamaican Community in Canada. (2007). Number 12, Statistics Canada. www.statcan.gc.ca.

Thomlison, B. (2004). Child maltreatment: A risk and protective factor perspective. In M. Fraser (Ed.), *Risk and resilience in childhood: An ecological perspective* (pp. 89–132). Washington, DC: NASW Press.

Thompson, E. (1999). Resiliency in family members facing AIDS. In H. I. McCubbin, E. Thompson, A. Thompson, & J. Futrell (Eds.), *The dynamics of resilient families* (pp. 135–164). Thousand Oaks, CA: Sage.

Tighe, A., Pistrang, N., Casdagli, L., Baruch, G., & Butler, S. (2012). Multisystemic therapy for young offenders: Families' experiences of therapeutic processes and outcomes. *Journal of Family Psychology, 26*(2), 187–197.

Tsai, K., & Yeh, N. (2011). Mental health services for Asian American youth. In T. Leong, L. Juang, D. Qin, & H. Fitzgerald (Eds.), *Asian American and Pacific Islander children and mental health*. Vol. 2, *Prevention and treatment* (pp. 201–224). Santa Barbara, CA: Praeger.

Valdez, C., Mills, C., Barrueco, S., Leis, J., & Riley, A. (2011). A pilot study of a family-focused intervention for children and families affected by maternal depression. *Journal of Family Therapy, 33,* 2–19.

Valentine, L., & Feinauer, L. (1993). Resilience factors associated with female survivors of childhood sexual abuse. *American Journal of Family Therapy, 21*(3), 216–224.

Vandiver, V., & Keopraseuth, K. (1998). Family wisdom and clinical support: Culturally relevant practice strategies for working with Indochinese families who care for a relative with mental illness. In H. Lefley (Ed.), *Families coping with mental illness: The cultural context* (pp. 75–88). San Francisco: Jossey-Bass.

Van Hook, M. (1990a). The Iowa farm crisis: Perceptions, interpretations, and family patterns. In V. McLyold & C. Flannagan (Eds.), *New Directions for Child Development, 46,* 71–86.

Van Hook, M. (1990b). Family response to the farm crisis: A study in coping. *Social Work, 35*(5), 425–431.

Van Hook, M. (2002). Protestantism: An overview. In M. Van Hook, B. Hugen, & M. Aguilar (Eds.), *Spirituality within religious traditions in social work practice* (pp. 273–289). Pacific Grove, CA: Thompson.

Van Hook, M. (2008). Spirituality. In A. Strozier & J. Carpenter (Eds.), *An introduction to alternative and complementary therapies* (pp. 31–63). New York: Haworth.

Van Hook, M., & Aguilar, M. (2002). Health, religion and spirituality. In M. Van Hook, B. Hugen, & M. Aguilar (Eds.), *Spirituality within religious traditions in social work practice* (pp. 273–289). Pacific Grove, CA: Thompson.

Van Hook, M., Hugen, B., & Aguilar, M. (2002). *Spirituality within religious traditions and social work practice.* Pacific Grove, CA: Brooks/Cole.

Van Hook, M., & Rivera, O. (2004). Coping with difficult life transitions by older adults: The role of religion. *Christianity and Social Work, 31*(3), 233–253.

Vega, W. (1995). The study of Latino families: A point of departure. In R. Zambrana (Ed.), *Understanding Latino families: Scholarship, policy, and practice* (pp. 1–17). Thousand Oaks, CA: Sage.

Wagner, K., Ritt-Olson, A., Chou, C., Pokhrel, P., Duan, L., Baezconde-Garbanati, L., Soto, D., & Unger, J. (2010). Association between family structure, family functioning, and substance use among Hispanic/Latino adolescents. *Psychology of Addictive Behaviors, 24*(1), 98–108.

Waller, M., Okamoto, S., Miles, B., & Hurdle, D. (2003). Resiliency factors related to substance use/resistance: Perceptions of native adolescents of the South West. *Journal of Sociology and Social Welfare, 30A*(4), 79–94.

Walrath, C., Ybarra, M., Holden, E., Liao, Q., Santiago, R., & Leaf, P. (2003). Children with reported histories of sexual abuse: Utilizing multiple perspectives to understand clinical and psychosocial profiles. *Child Abuse and Neglect, 27,* 509–524.

Walsh, F. (1999). Opening family therapy to spirituality. In F. Walsh (Ed.), *Spiritual resources in family therapy* (pp. 28–58). New York: Guilford.

Walsh, F. (1998). *Strengthening family resilience.* New York: Guilford Press.

Walsh, F. (2006). *Strengthening family resilience* (2nd ed.). New York: Guilford Press.

Walsh, J. (2003). Family systems interventions. In A. C. Kilpatrick & T. Holland (Eds.), *Working with families: An integrated model by level of need* (3rd ed., pp. 151–173). Boston: Allyn & Bacon.

Walsh, J., & Harrigan, M. (2003). The termination stage in Bowen's family systems theory. *Clinical Social Work Journal, 31*(4), 383–394.

Walt, C., Proctor, B., & Smith, J. (2011). *Income, poverty, and health insurance coverage in the United States: 2010 current population reports.* U.S. Census Bureau, Department of Commerce. Washington, DC: Government Printing Office.

Walter, J., & Peller, J. (1996). Rethinking our assumptions: Assuming anew in a postmodern world. In S. Miller, M. Hubble, & B. Duncan (Eds.), *Handbook of solution-focused brief therapy.* San Francisco: Jossey-Bass.

Weber, E., & Weber, D. (2005). Geographic relocation, frequency, resilience and military adolescent behavior. *Military Magazine, 170*(7), 638–642.

Webster-Stratton, C. (2000). *The incredible years training series.* Juvenile Justice Bulletin. Washington, DC: Office of Juvenile Justice and Delinquency Prevention.

Weine, S. (2011). Developing preventive mental health intervention for refugee families in resettlement. *Family Process, 50*(3), 410–430.

Weine, S., Muzurovic, N., Kulauzovic, Y., Besic, S., Lezic, A., Mujagic, A., et al. (2004). Family consequences of refugee trauma. *Family Process, 43*(2), 147–160.

Werner, E. (2012). Children and war: Risk, resilience, and recovery. *Development and Psychopathology, 24*(2), 553–558.

Werner, E., & Smith, R. (1992). *Overcoming the odds: High risk children from birth to adulthood.* Ithaca, NY: Cornell University Press.

Whiffen, V. (2003). What attachment theory can offer marital and family therapists. In S. M. Johnson & V. Whiffen (Eds.), *Attachment processes in couple and family therapy* (pp. 389–398). New York: Guilford Press.

Whitaker, C. (1989). Family therapy. Paper presented at the Iowa National Association for Social Workers Conference, Des Moines, IA.

White, M. (2007). *Maps of narrative practice.* New York: W.W. Norton.

White, M., & Epston, D. (1990). *Narrative means to therapeutic ends.* New York: Norton.

Wiebe, D., Berg, C., Korbet, C., Palmer, D., Beveridge, R., Upchurch, R., Lindsey, R., Swinyard, M., & Donaldson, D.(2005). Children's appraisals of maternal involvement in coping with diabetes: Enhancing our understanding of adherence, metabolic control, and quality of life across adolescence. *Journal of Pediatric Psychology, 30*(2), 167–178.

Wiebe, D., Gelfan, D., Butler, J., Korbel, C., Fortenberry, K., McCabe, J., & Berry, C. (2011). Longitudinal associations of maternal depressive symptoms, maternal involvement, and diabetes management across adolescence. *Journal of Pediatric Psychology, 36*(7), 837–846.

Williams, J., Ayers, C., Van Dorn, R., & Arthur, M. (2004). Risk and protective factors in the development of delinquency and conduct disorder. In M. W. Fraser (Ed.), *Risk and resiliency in childhood* (pp. 209–250). Washington, DC: NASW Press.

Williams, N., & Kurtz, P. (2003). Narrative family interventions. In A. Kilpatrick & T. Holland (Eds.), *Working with families: An integrative model by level of need* (3rd ed., pp. 174–195). Boston: Allyn & Bacon.

Winkelman, M. (2001) *Ethnic sensitivity in social work practice.* Peosta, IA: Eddie Bowers Publishing.

Winston, C. (2003). African American grandmothers parenting AIDS orphans: Concomitant grief and loss. *American Journal of Orthopsychiatry, 73*(1), 91–100.

Wolfe, D., Sandler, J., & Kaufman, K. (1981). A competency-based parent training program for child abusers. *Journal of Consulting and Clinical Psychology Review, 49,* 6333–6340.

Worden, M. (2003). *Family therapy basics* (3rd ed.). Pacific Grove, CA: Brooks/Cole.

Wright, L. (1999). Spirituality, suffering, and beliefs: The soul of healing with families. In F. Walsh (Ed.), *Spiritual resources in family therapy* (pp. 61–75). New York: Guilford.

Wynne, L., Rychoff, I., Day, J., & Hirsh, S. (1958). Pseudo-mutuality in the family relationships of schizophrenics. *Psychiatry, 24,* 205–220.

Wysocki, T., Nansel, T., Holmbeck, G., Chen, R., Laffel, L., Anderson, B., & Weissberg-Benchell, J. (2008). Collaborative involvement of primary and secondary caregivers: Associations with youths' diabetes outcomes. *Journal of Pediatric Psychology, 34*(6), 869–881.

Yeh, C., Borrero, N., & Kwong, A. (2011). Stress and coping among Asian American Pacific Islander and Native Hawaiian children and youth: An asset approach. In F. Leon, L. Juan, D. Qin, & H. Fitzgerald (Eds.), *Asian American and Pacific Islander Children and Mental Health.* Vol. 2, *Prevention and Treatment.* (pp. 101–124). Santa Barbara, CA: Praeger.

Yellow Bird, M. (2001) Critical values and First Nations People. In R. Fong & S. Furuto (Eds.), *Culturally competent practice: Skills, interventions, and evaluations* (pp. 61–74). Boston: Allyn & Bacon.

Yellow Horse Brave Heart, M. (2001). Culturally and historically congruent clinical social work assessment with native clients. In R. Fong & S. Furuto (Eds.), *Culturally competent practice: Skills, interventions, and evaluations* (pp. 163–177). Boston: Allyn & Bacon.

Yellow-Horse Brave Heart, M. (2002). Lakota-Native People's spirituality. In M. Van Hook, B. Hugen, & M. Aguilar (Eds.), *Spirituality within religious traditions and social work* (pp. 18–33). Pacific Grove, CA: Brooks/Cole.

Young, K., (2010). Spirituality and quality of life for Chinese people with severe mental illness. *Journal of Religion and Spirituality in Social Work and Social Thought, 29*(1), 1–13.

Ystgaard, M., Hestetun, I., Loeb, M., & Mehlum, L. (2004). Is there a specific relationship between childhood sexual and physical abuse and repeated suicidal behavior? *Child Abuse and Neglect, 28,* 863–875.

Zauszniewski, J., Bekhet, A., & Suresky, M. (2009). Effects on resilience of women family caregivers of adults with serious mental illness: The role of positive cognitions. *Archives of Psychiatric Nursing, 23*(6), 412–422.

Zimmerman, J., & Dickerson, V. (1994). Using a narrative metaphor: Implications for theory and clinical practice. *Family Process, 33*, 233–245.

Zimmerman, J., & Dickerson, V. (1996). *If problems talked: Adventures in narrative therapy.* New York: Guilford.

Zimmerman, M., Ramirez, J., Washienko, K., Walter, B., & Dyer, S. (1998). Enculturation hypothesis: Exploring direct and protective effects among Native American youth. In H. I. McCubbin, E. Thompson, A. Thompson, & J. Fromer (Eds.), *Resiliency in Native American and immigrant families* (pp. 199–220). Resiliency in Families series. Thousand Oaks, CA: Sage.

Zuniga, M. (2001). Latinos: Cultural competence and ethics. In R. Fong & S. Furuto (Eds.), *Culturally competent practice: Skills, interventions, and evaluations* (pp. 47–60). Boston: Allyn & Bacon.

Index

About the Author

Mary Patricia Van Hook (PhD, Rutgers University; MS, Columbia University) is professor emeritus of social work at the University of Central Florida where she served as the director of the School of Social Work. She has written extensively in the areas of families, rural mental health, spirituality, and women's issues in the United States and abroad. In 2000 she received the Howery Award from the National Association for Rural Mental Health for outstanding contributions to rural mental health and, in 2008, the Distinguished Service to Social Work Award by the North American Association of Christians in Social Work. In addition to clinical and administrative responsibilities in mental health and children's services, she has been a social work faculty member at the University of Central Florida, University of Michigan, Grand Valley State University, and Northwestern College.